York St John
Library and Information Services
Normal Loan

Please see self service receipt for return date.
If recalled the loan is reduced to 10 days

P   gy

The Hampton Press Communication Series
MEDIA ECOLOGY
Lance Strate, supervisory editor

Mediating the Muse: A Communications Approach to Music, Media, and Cultural Change
Robert Albrecht

Online Connections: Internet Interpersonal Relationships
Susan B. Barnes

Bookends: The Changing Media Environment of the American Classroom
Margaret Cassidy

Walter Ong's Contribution to Cultural Studies: The Phenomenology of the Word and I-Thous Communication
Thomas J. Farrell

The Power of Metaphor in the Age of Electronic Media
Raymond Gozzi, Jr.

Perspectives on Culture, Technology and Communication: The Media Ecology Tradition
Casey Man Kong Lum

An Ong Reader
Walter Ong, Thomas J. Farrell, and *Paul A. Soukup (eds.)*

No Safety in Numbers: How the computer Quantified Everything and Made People Risk Aversive
Henry J. Perkinson

The Legacy of McLuhan
Lance Strate and *Edward Wachtel (eds.)*

The Media Symplex: At the Edge of Meaning in the Age of Chaos
Frank Zingrone

forthcoming

Biotech Time—Bomb: How Genetic Engineering Could Irreversibly Change Our World
Scott Eastham

Transforming McLuhan: Critical, cultural and Postmodern Perspectives
Paul Grosswiler

ScreenAgers: Lessons in Chaos from Digital Kids
Douglas Rushkoff

Cybermedia and the Ecology of Digital Media
Lance Strate and *Susan B. Barnes (eds.)*

Perspectives on Culture, Technology and Communication

The Media Ecology Tradition

edited by

Casey Man Kong Lum

William Paterson University

HAMPTON PRESS, INC.
CRESSKILL, NJ 07626

Library of Congress Cataloging-in-Publication Data

Lum, Casey Man Kong.
 Perspectives on culture, technology and communication : the media ecology tradition / edited by Casey Man Kong Lum.
    p. cm. -- (Hampton Press communication series. Media ecology)
 Includes bibliographic references and indexes.
 ISBN 1-57273-622-4 (cl.) -- ISBN 1-57273-623-2 (pbk.)
 1. Mass media--Social aspects. 2. Communication--Social aspects. 3. Mass media--Research--History. 4. Mass media and culture--Research--History. 5. Communication and culture--Research--History. I. Title. II. Series

HM1206.L86 2006
302.23--dc22

                                                                    2005044881

Hampton Press, Inc.
23 Broadway
Cresskill, NJ 07626

This book is dedicated to Neil Postman (1931-2003),
a beloved teacher and mentor and
a truly brilliant idea

Contents

LIST OF FIGURES

Acknowledgments

The idea for this book began to germinate when I was a doctoral student in the Media Ecology Program at New York University during which time I was developing an interest in the intellectual history of the communication discipline, as well as the sociology of knowledge and the history of ideas. I was extremely fortunate to have been under the intellectual guidance of several mentors, Professors Neil Postman, Terence Moran, Christine Nystrom, and Henry Perkinson, who have taught me, among many things, the humanistic approach to teaching and learning and how good scholarship ought to begin with good questions instead of, say, research instruments.

In particular, Neil, that grand story teller, has told many of us, graduate students and colleagues alike, a great deal of fascinating tales about how he came to know the work and person of the like of Marshall McLuhan and Lewis Mumford when he held court in the department's main office at NYU's Shimkin Hall or over regular lunches with us at Bobst Library's faculty dining room—sometimes as often as twice to three times a week. These tales fascinated me not only because they crystalized for me some of the most profound media ecological theories, but also because they vividly made clear to me the contexts in which these ideas came into being to begin with. Moreover, the fact that we also got to meet many of the admiring scholars from across the country and around the world who came to visit him has helped me put faces (and their personae) on some of the theories I was studying; seeing these scholars' interaction also helped me visualize an invisible college of media ecologists that has mostly been unknown in the mainstream communication discipline. In short, for all those wonderful stories and, more generally, the good education that Dr. Postman gave me through the years, I pay tribute to him with my deepest respect and love. The greatest regret I have about this book is the fact that I could not get it done in time so he could see it, feel it, smell its fresh ink. But then again, Neil *knows* all the stories well.

Peter Haratonik, my teacher and mentor since my days as an MA student in media studies at the New School for Social Research (now the New

School), himself a student of Postman's, is responsible for introducing me to the world of media ecology. He too has told me many interesting stories over the years about how media education and media ecology evolved in the US. He encouraged and supported my first-ever conference attendance whereby I began to see first-hand how communication scholarship is first and foremost a human enterprise. He continues to be one of my most trusted and endearing mentors to date.

This book is the result of collaborative contributions from many people. Lance Strate (Fordham University), supervising editor of Hampton's Media Ecology series, has been patient and supportive throughout this book's development. My sincere appreciation is due to Barbara Bernstein, president of Hampton Press, for the generous support and resources that she put behind this project.

Every chapter in this book has gone through a formal blind review and revision process before its acceptance for publication. I am extremely thankful to the following colleagues for their insightful review and helpful editorial suggestions: Mary Alexander (Marist College), Joe Ashcroft (East Straudsburg University), George Back (Rowan University), James W. Carey (Columbia University), Clifford Christians (University of Illinois, Urbana-Champaign), Ronald Deibert (University of Toronto), Tom Farrell (University of Minnesota-Duluth), Thom F. Gencarelli (Montclair State University), Ray Gozzi, Jr. (Ithaca College), Paul Grosswiler (University of Maine), Peter L. Haratonik (The New School), Paul Heyer (Wilfrid Laurier University, Canada), Joli Jensen (University of Tulsa), Judith Yaross Lee (Ohio University), Wendy Leeds-Hurwitz (University of Wisconsin-Parkside), Paul Lippert (East Straudsburg University), Hugh McCarney (Western Connecticut State University), Eric McLuhan (University of Toronto), James C. Morrison (Emerson College), Christine L. Nystrom (New York University), Tony J. Palmeri (University of Wisconsin-Oshkosh), John Pauly (St. Louis University), William Petkanas (Western Connecticut State University), Neil Postman (New York University), Paul Soukup (Santa Clara University), Paul Thaler (Adelphi University), and Donald Theall (Trent University, Canada). While these referees provided their comments and suggestions during the review process, all final editorial decisions are mine and therefore I am solely responsible for any editorial misjudgement or error that may exist in the book.

I would like to thank all the authors in this volume for their professionalism and, on another level, patience and trust in me because the process of putting this book together has been longer than I have initially anticipated. Working with these colleagues has been a positive learning experience to me.

A special mention goes to Paul Thaler (Adelphi University) for his many thoughtful comments and unfailing encouragement during the past few years especially when I was struggling to clarify what I had in mind for the book.

Wendy Leeds-Hurwitz (University of Wisconsin, Parkside), whom I came to know when she was co-editing my first book, has since become a wonderful colleague and informal mentor. In particular, I have been greatly inspired by her work in the intellectual history of intercultural communication which has helped me construct part of the conceptual framework for this book.

My work for this project has been supported in part by a Spring 2003 sabbatical, as well as various Assigned Research Time and Career Development grants at William Paterson University, to which I am greatly appreciative.

I am profoundly grateful to Mrs. Shelley Postman for her permission to reprint in Chapter Two Dr. Postman's speech at the Media Ecology Association's inaugural annual convention in 2000, "The Humanism of Media Ecology." I thank Robert Blechman (St. George's University) for his permission to use his unpublished poem, "Very Model Of A Media Ecologist," in its entirety in Chapter One. Appreciation is also due to *The New Jersey Journal of Communication* (currently *The Atlantic Journal of Communication*) and its editor Gary Radford (Fairleigh Dickinson University) for their reprint permission of Lance Strate and my article on "Lewis Mumford and the Ecology of Technics" and Christine Nystrom's "Symbols, Thought, and 'Reality': The Contributions of Benjamin Lee Whorf and Susanne K. Langer to Media Ecology" in Chapter Three and Chapter 10, respectively; these two articles were originally published in the Spring 2000 special issue of the journal on the "Intellectual Roots of Media Ecology" that I guest-edited. I offer my gratitude to Rowan and Littlefield for its permission of Paul Heyer's adoption of materials from his book on Harold Innis (2003) in the composition of the current book's Chapter Four. On the other hand, Gabriel W. Carras and David Zapotocky at NYU's Steinhardt School of Education have graciously granted me access to the school's archive for my research on the programmatic development of media ecology during its formative years at the school.

I am greatly in debt to my wife, Jenny Chia Chen Liu, for her love, devotion, and companionship; she has always been a source of inspiration and courage. Our two children, Xuanmin Lum and Haumin Lum, have never ceased to endear me with their intelligence, energy, and wit. My wife and our children have sacrificed a great deal of the quality family times that we could have shared together if I were not working on this book so single-mindedly during the past few years. Similarly, I thank my mother Siu Ling Lau for her life-long commitment to my well-being; she will forever be my moral guidepost as a parent. Last, but not least, this book is in loving memory of Chi Kau Wong, my father, whose absence in my life since his premature death when I was too young to really get to know him has been a source of never-ending curiosity as to what my life would have been like if he has been around.

About the Authors

Joe Ashcroft received his PhD in media ecology from New York University in 1990. He has been a professor at East Stroudsburg University in Pennsylvania for 29 years, achieving the rank of Full Professor in 1992. He was named a Distinguished Professor at the University in 2001. Dr. Ashcroft has published numerous articles and over 20 book reviews. He has presented papers at many national and regional conferences in his academic career. Dr. Ashcroft has an eclectic background of study, having received his BA in Philosophy and his MA in Political Science. This background is reflected in the work he has done, which includes papers and articles dealing with media and politics and how media affect thought.

Clifford Christians is a Research Professor of Communications and Professor of Media Studies in the Institute of Communications Research at the University of Illinois at Urbana-Champaign. He is the author or co-author of six books, among them *Media Ethics: Cases and Moral Reasoning* (with Mark Fackler, Kim Rotzoll, and Kathy McKee, 7th ed. 2004), *Good News: Social Ethics and the Press* (with John Ferre and Mark Fackler, 1993), *Communication Ethics and Universal Values* (with Michael Traber), *Moral Engagement in Public Life: Theorists for Contemporary Ethics* (with Sharon Bracci, 2002). He is also the Editor of *The Ellul Forum*. He has a PhD from the University of Illinois at Urbana-Champaign. His teaching and research interests include the philosophy of technology, dialogic communication theory, and professional ethics.

Thomas F. Gencarelli is an Associate Professor in the Department of Broadcasting at Montclair State University, where he teaches both media theory/criticism and production courses. He is the author of numerous articles, book chapters, and conference papers on the subjects of media education, popular culture, and popular music, including an article on the work and thought of Neil Postman published in special issue of the *New Jersey*

Journal of Communication (Spring 2000). Holding his PhD in media ecology from New York University, he is the Treasurer of the Media Ecology Association, Review Editor of the Association's official journal *Explorations in Media Ecology*, and a Past President of both the New York State Communication Association and the New Jersey Communication Association.

Bruce E. Gronbeck is the A. Craig Baird Distinguished Professor of Public Address and Director of the Center for Media Studies and Political Culture at the University of Iowa. He holds his PhD from the University of Iowa and honorary doctorates from Concordia College (MN), Uppsala University (Sweden), and Jyväskylä University (Finland). He is author or editor of 10 books in media theory and criticism, presidential campaigning, rhetorical criticism, argumentation, and public speaking, as well as dozens of articles and book chapters on such subjects. His work focuses on the intersection of rhetoric, politics, and media in the modern and contemporary eras. His principal contribution to media ecology is a book edited with Thomas Farrell and Paul Soukup, *Media, Consciousness, and Culture: Explorations of Walter Ong's Thought* (Sage, 1991).

Paul Heyer did a BA in geography at Concordia University in Montreal, and followed with graduate work in anthropology, earning an MA from the New School and a PhD from Rutgers. He is currently professor of communication studies at Wilfrid Laurier University, Waterloo, Ontario, Canada, and the author of *Communications and History: Theories of Media Knowledge, and Civilization*, *TITANIC Legacy: Disaster as Media Event and Myth*, *Harold Innis*, and co-editor (with David Crowley) of the introductory textbook, *Communication in History: Technology, Culture, Society*. Primarily working in the field of media history, he is completing a project on the radio legacy of Orson Welles and the influence that Welles' use of sound in radio exerted on his motion pictures. A future research project will examine the influence and representation of jazz in American motion pictures. Professor Heyer has taught at Rutgers, McGill, and Simon Fraser Universities, and the University of Western Sydney.

Randolph Kluver is Associate Professor in the School of Communication and Information, Nanyang Technological University in Singapore. He has a PhD from the University of Southern California. His current research interests include Asian political communication, globalization, and cultural and social change in Asia. Dr. Kluver is the author of *Legitimating the Chinese Economic Reforms: A Rhetoric of Myth and Orthodoxy* (1996), and co-editor of two books, *Civic Discourse, Civil Society and Chinese Communities* (1999), and *Asia.com: Asia Encounters the Internet* (2003).

Casey Man Kong Lum is Associate Professor of Communication and Media Studies at William Paterson University. He is the author of *In Search of a Voice: Karaoke and the Construction of Identity in Chinese America* (1996), an ethnographic study of the symbiosis between new media forms and immigrant cultures. He has also published in numerous journals, among them *Critical Studies in Media Communication, Journal of Radio Studies,* and *Mass Communication Research* (in Chinese), as well as books such as *From Generation to Generation: Maintaining Cultural Identity Over Time* (2006), *Our Voices: Essays in Culture, Ethnicity, and Communication* (2004), and *Karaoke Around the World: Global Technology, Local Singing* (1998). He earned his PhD in media ecology from New York University. His research interests include media ecology, the intellectual history of communication research, global media studies, media and education, and Asian and Asian American media and culture. One of the five founders of the Media Ecology Association, Dr. Lum is also the editor of this volume.

James C. Morrison (MA, Columbia; MPA, Harvard) is a Scholar-in-Residence in the Department of Organizational and Political Communication at Emerson College in Boston. He teaches Survey of Publishing: From Text to Hypertext at Harvard Extension School. He has also taught Culture and Communication: Introduction to Media Theory in the Experimental College of Tufts University. An elected member on the Board of Directors of the Media Ecology Association and its Web Editor and Online Archivist, he is on the Editorial Board of *Counterblast: The e-journal of Culture & Communication* and has published articles in *Explorations in Media Ecology, Proceedings of the Media Ecology Association, New Dimensions in Communication, Counterblast,* and *Technology and Culture.*

Christine L. Nystrom worked with Neil Postman and Terence P. Moran to found the doctoral program in media ecology at New York University, joining the full-time faculty after completing her doctoral studies in 1973. From 1980 until her retirement in 2001, she served as Associate Professor and Director of Graduate Studies in Media Ecology, working with Postman and Moran to found NYU's undergraduate program in Communication Studies and create the present Department of Culture and Communication. She is primarily known to media ecologists for her architectural work in the design of the graduate and undergraduate programs in media ecology at NYU, her teaching and shepherding of doctoral dissertations, and her dozens of extensive classroom handouts explicating and elaborating on information theory, general systems theory, the work of Benjamin Lee Whorf, Susanne K. Langer, George Herbert Mead, and the philosophical foundations and principles of media ecology.

Neil Postman was born in 1931 in New York City. He was the Paulette Goddard Professor of Media Ecology and a University Professor at New York University at his untimely passing on October 5, 2003. He was the author of more than 20 books including *Language in America, Teaching as a Subversive Activity* (with Charles Weingartner), *The Disappearance of Childhood, Conscientious Objections,* and *Amusing Ourselves to Death.* His articles, of which over 200 have been published, have appeared in *The New York Times Magazine, The Atlantic, Harper's, Time Magazine, The Saturday Review, The Harvard Education Review, The Washington Post, The L.A. Times, Stern,* and *Le Monde.* He was on the Editorial Board of *The Nation* magazine. He had lectured all over the world and, in 1985, gave the keynote address at the Frankfurt Book Fair. In 1986, Dr. Postman was given the George Orwell Award for Clarity in Language by the National Council of Teachers of English. For 10 years, he was the editor of *Et Cetera,* the journal of General Semantics. In 1988, he was given the Distinguished Professor Award by New York University, where he had taught for 38 years. In the Spring of 1991, he was the Lawrence Lombard Visiting Professor of The Press and Public Policy at Harvard University's John F. Kennedy School of Government. In 1995, the Italian edition of his book on *The End of Education* won the equivalent of the U.S.'s National Book Award. In 1999, his *Building a Bridge to the 18th Century* was published. In 2000, Dr. Postman was awarded an Honorary Doctorate from Brigham Young University and a year later received an Honorary Doctorate from the University of Athens.

John Powers is an Associate Professor of Communication Studies at Hong Kong Baptist University, where he has been since 1992. Prior to his current position, he taught at Texas A&M University for 16 years. He earned his PhD in Speech Communication from the University of Denver in 1977. His research interests include paradigm building in the communication discipline, theory and criticism of public discourse, and the role of language in routine communication practices. He is editor, with Randy Kluver of *Civic Discourse, Civil Society, and Chinese Communities* (1999) and author of *Public Speaking: The Lively Art* (1994). Dr. Powers is currently working on a book on Suzanne Langer's philosophy of mind.

Lance Strate is Associate Professor of Communication and Media Studies at Fordham University, and President of the Media Ecology Association (MEA). He earned his BS at Cornell University, his MA at Queens College (CUNY), and his PhD at New York University. He is the co-editor of several anthologies, including *Communication and Cyberspace* (with Ron Jacobson, and Stephanie Gibson), *The Legacy of McLuhan* (with Edward Wachtel), and *Critical Studies in Media Commercialism* (with Robin

Andersen). He is the editor of *Explorations in Media Ecology* (MEA's official journal) and supervising editor of Hampton Press's media ecology book series. He has also published numerous book chapters and articles in academic journals such as *ETC.: A Review of General Semantics*, *Speech Communication Annual*, and *Western Journal of Communication*. Dr. Strate is currently completing a book on *Understanding Media Ecology*.

Frederick Wasser's book *Veni, Vidi, Video: The Hollywood Empire and the VCR* (2001) won the 2003 Marshall McLuhan award by the Media Ecology Association. Before becoming a professor, he worked for many years in New York and Hollywood post-production on shows ranging from the pilot for *Law and Order* to movies such as *Missing in Action* and *Nightmare on Elm Street Part IV*. He also translated and published a Norwegian drama entitled *The Bird Lovers*, written by Jens Bjoerneboe. Wasser received a PhD from the Institute for Communications Research at the University of Illinois. He was a post-doctoral fellow in the School of Journalism at Columbia University. He has published articles in *Critical Studies in Mass Communication*, *Journal of Communication*, *Cinema Journal* and others. He is currently teaching in the Department of Television and Radio at Brooklyn College-CUNY.

1

Notes Toward an Intellectual History of Media Ecology

Casey Man Kong Lum
William Paterson University

I am the very model of a Media Ecologist.
I also sense the difference 'tween me and a theologist.
I've read a bit of Mumford and a little of McLuhan.
I also have a fair idea of Watzlawick is doing.
Of Levi-Strauss and Jacques Ellul I seem to have a smattering
The work of Ames and Cantril I am very often flattering.
I'm versed on systems theory and on models mathematical
Which I'll dispute with you until the start of my sabbatical.

Chorus:
I know how Shannon-Weaver strove to overcome their channel noise.
I'm well aware that Hayakawa hangs out with the Senate boys.
Although it would better to have been an anthropologist,
I am the very model of a Media Ecologist.

I can recite the history of radio and telephone
As well as why it is Korzybski's ghost is never left alone.
I've studied silent language and the biases of media,
Of structuralistic notions I'm a real encyclopedia.

I've learned proxemics, kinesics, linguistic styles polemical,
I know why Greeks were oral and why monks were academical.
Then I'll recite five verses from a Bible made by Gutenberg
And guess the probability you know the work of Heisenberg.

Chorus:
Early TV is immediate, massaging your right hemisphere.
While functioning discursively is bound to someday disappear.
Although it would be better to have been an ichthyologist,
I am the very model of a Media Ecologist.

When I can tell the difference 'tween a "dub" and "dupe" and "master tape;"
When I can tell a hot film splicer from a waffle plate;
When showing film or video no longer gets the best of me;
When I can show a knowledge of the workings of 'lectricity;
When laser beams and holograms no longer seem so magical;
When my attempts to splice & tape does not turn out so tragical;
In short, when I've a smattering of modern-day technology,
Then I'll feel better saying I know Media Ecology.

Chorus:
For my modern hardware training, though I'm plucky and adventuring,
Has only been brought down to the beginning of the century.
Although it would be better to have been a gynecologist,
I am the very model of a Media Ecologist.

—From *"Very Model of a Media Ecologist"*
by Robert Blechman (1976)[1]

I was enchanted upon my first encounter with the above poem. Robert Blechman was a graduate student in New York when he wrote it, a takeoff on Gilbert and Sullivan's Modern Major General. At the time, he was studying for his doctorate in a new program at New York University with a focus on media ecology. The poem served as the lyrics for a 3-minute video in which he would lip-sync to the camera offering his interpretation of media ecology. The doctoral program had been founded by Neil M. Postman only several years earlier, in 1970, when he was an English education professor. No academic degree program before it ever bore the phrase. In fact, it was so new and esoteric-sounding to even academics then that, according to legend, the phrase was occasionally used as some sort of an ice-breaker or pick-up line at social gatherings. The term's very ambiguity invariably fueled comment and discussion from outsiders, bringing into the circle people who thought they knew something about communication but were stuck—and intrigued—on just what was this thing called media ecology.

But even after three decades of evolution since the coinage of the phrase late in the 1960s, media ecology still draws polite curiosity at communication conferences whereby, for better or for worse, it still works pretty well as an ice-breaker at the bar. On one level, media ecology as a field of study remains as it has throughout much of the last three decades of the 20th century on the fringe of communication research. For example, *Journal of Communication* (*JOC*), considered a premier mainstream refereed journal, published a special issue by the title *Ferment in the Field* (1983) in which 35 scholars from 10 countries offered their assessments of the state of communication research. If this now-fabled *JOC* special issue was any gauge in helping define or legitimize communication scholarship, then media ecology was a nonentity in "the field." The journal has left the distinct impression that communication research was preoccupied mostly by an ongoing debate between the administrative (or empirical) school of communication and the critical school of communication (Rogers, 1982) or, methodologically, between quantitative and qualitative research, respectively. Ten years after, *JOC* reassessed communication scholarship's state of affairs in two other special issues, *The Future of the Field I* (1993a) and *The Future of the Field II* (1993b). Again, media ecology failed to warrant a word of recognition. Similar omissions are seen in numerous other publications that concerned themselves with the intellectual history of communication scholarship at large (e.g., Delia, 1987; Dennis & Wartella, 1996; Dervin, Grossberg, O'Keefe, & Wartella, 1989).

This is not to say, however, that the major thinkers whose scholarships had contributed to the rise of media ecology were ignored entirely. The most notable example was Herbert Marshall McLuhan, who has been among the most visible of all foundational thinkers of media ecology. In the late 1960s and throughout much of the 1970s, McLuhan had been hailed as a media guru whose media theories, probes, and aphorisms attracted widespread attention in both academic and popular venues (e.g., Finkelstein, 1968; J. Miller, 1971; Molinaro, McLuhan, & Toye, 1987; "Playboy interview . . . ," 1969; Stearn, 1967; Theall, 1971). Shortly after his death in 1980, *JOC* published a symposium, entitled *The Living McLuhan* (1981) in which eight scholars[2] wrote on various aspects of his media scholarship. There has also been a renewed interest in McLuhan since late in the 1980s (e.g., Levinson, 1999; Marchand, 1989; E. McLuhan & Zingrone, 1995; Molinaro et al., 1987; Sanderson & Macdonald, 1989; Strate & Wachtel, 2005; Theall, 2001).

Otherwise, the scholarly works of other media ecology paradigm thinkers have also received varying degrees of attention, such as the theories by Jacques Ellul (Christians & Van Hook, 1981; Gozzi, 2000),[3] Harold A. Innis (Acland & Buxton, 1995; Carey, 1988b; Heyer, 2003; Stamps, 1995), Lewis Mumford (Carey, 1981; D. Miller, 1989; Strate & Lum, 2000), Walter J. Ong (Farrell, 2000; Farrell & Soukup, 2002; Gronbeck, Farrell, & Soukup 1992; Soukup, 2004), and Postman (Gencarelli, 2000; Jensen, 1990; Strate, 1994, 2003b). A recent review essay by Lance Strate (2004) also provides an excellent introduction to the scholarship of various media ecology foundational thinkers and some of media ecology's key themes.

Nevertheless, as this book suggests, media ecology is more than just McLuhan studies or, for that matter, Ellul studies, Innis studies, Mumford studies, Ong studies, Postman studies, and the like. Indeed, this book is an historiographic story about media ecology as an intellectual tradition that encompasses a coherent body of theoretical literature and perspectives on understanding culture, technology, and communication. It seeks to shed light on how the media ecology intellectual tradition has evolved into being through an interlocking network of what Diana Crane (1972) and Belver C. Griffith and Nicholas C. Mullins (1972) called "invisible colleges" or closely knit and yet informal groups of like-minded thinkers from multiple scholarly interests, such as media and culture (McLuhan, 1951, 1962, 1964), history and technology (Mumford, 1934, 1967, 1970) and urban studies (Mumford, 1938, 1961), behavioral sciences (Watzlawick, Bavelas, & Jackson, 1967; see also Watzlawick, 1976), structural anthropology (Levi-Strauss, 1966), sociology of technological culture (Ellul, 1964) and propaganda (Ellul, 1965), perceptual psychology (Cantril, 1960), information and systems theories[4] (Shannon & Weaver, 1949; see also Wiener, 1948, 1950), general semantics (Hayakawa, 1964; Korzybski, 1933), cultural anthropology (e.g., Hall, 1959), history of communications (e.g., Innis, n.d.), temporal and spatial analyses of media (Innis, 1951, 1952), nonverbal communication (e.g., Birdwhistell, 1952, 1970), classics (e.g., Havelock, 1963, 1976), history of typography (e.g., Eisenstein, 1979), and physics and philosophy (Heisenberg, 1962), to cite only those whose names are mentioned or hinted in Blechman's poetic musing above. As such, this story is composed of various historical, theoretical, as well as interpretive accounts about the intellectual origins of media ecology. More specifically, it seeks to explain some of media ecology's defining ideas, theories, or themes about culture, technology, and communication; the thinkers behind these ideas; the social, political, and intellectual contexts in which these ideas came into being; as well as how and the extent to which we may use these ideas in our times.

But media ecology is not an easy story to tell due simply to the complexity and multiplicity of issues, perspectives, and interpretations. I choose the word "Notes"[5] in this chapter's title precisely because I do not know the whole story; so all I can claim is a humble contribution to an initial, if somewhat sketchy, historiographic framework for understanding media ecology. This is also why 12 other scholars have been invited to contribute their interpretations in the telling of various aspects of this story. The word "interpretations," as it is used in the book's title, has two levels of meaning. On one level, it refers to the various interpretations of the interrelationship among culture, technology, and communication that are reflected in the scholarships of the major thinkers being featured in this volume, such as Elizabeth Eisenstein, Jacques Ellul, James W. Carey, Eric Havelock, Harold A. Innis, Susanne K. Langer, McLuhan, Lewis Mumford, Walter J. Ong, Postman, and Benjamin L. Whorf. On another level, it refers to the chapter authors' interpretations of these thinkers' interpretations — meta-interpretations, if you will. In the end, it is hoped that their collective wisdom will help us better understand the many facets of media ecology.

This chapter is meant to give the readers a framework to understand media ecology's development in the North American context beginning at the turn of the 20th century. Its last section provides an overview of the ensuing chapters, which will provide a much more detailed description, synthesis, and analysis of the various aspects of the intellectual origins and theoretical approaches of media ecology.

A NOTE ON THE HISTORIOGRAPHY OF MEDIA ECOLOGY

James W. Carey (1996) begins his insightful historiographic account of "The Chicago School and Mass Communication Research" with an argument that there is no history of communication research. He later suggests, seemingly with a hint of self-mocking irony in part because he himself has been one of the most captivating story tellers and intellectual historians of American media and cultural studies, that,

> the history of mass communication research is a recent literary genre, albeit a minor one: It is a self-conscious creation (and now an endless recreation) that sifts, sorts, and rearranges the accumulated literary debris into a coherent narrative. The narrative that emerges serves ultimately a variety of purposes: principally to focus, justify, and legitimate a 20th-century invention, the mass media, and to give direction and intellectual status of professional teaching and research concerning these same institutions. But it is hardly an innocent history, for it was invented for political reasons: to cast loyalties, resolve disputes, guide public policy, confuse opposition, and legitimate institutions; in short, the history that emerged was a minor episode in the social-political and ideological struggles of the 20th century. (Carey, 1996, pp. 21-22)

But despite the fact that Carey's remarks may seem to have focused on North American mass communication research, it is suggested that they are applicable to just about any other genres of academic research, including the media ecology story that this book is telling, on two levels.

First, as suggested earlier, media ecology as an intellectual tradition has been in the main muted in the genealogy of North American communication research. This book is therefore a conscious effort in giving media ecology a voice in the intellectual history and, to a certain extent, sociology of communication scholarship. As such, the ideas behind this book are inspired not only by the media ecologists before me but in particular by William Kuhns' (1971) pioneering historiographic account in *The Post-Industrial Prophets: Interpretations of Technology* of some of the major theorists in the media ecology tradition, a special issue of the *New Jersey Journal of Communication* on "The Intellectual Roots of Media Ecology" (Lum, 2000a), as well as the 2002 inauguration of the Media Ecology Association's refereed journal *Explorations in Media Ecology*. And, in no small part, homage is also paid to the ongoing, fascinating stories that Carey has told about the intellectual roots of media ecology. Carey does not use the term media ecology in most of his writings on Innis, McLuhan, and Mumford (e.g., Carey, 1968, 1981, 1988b), although the terms seems to have made some inroads into his scholarship's vocabulary in recent years (e.g., Carey, 1997, 2003a, 2003b).

On the second level, no claim is made here that the telling or re/construction of media ecology's intellectual history is an "innocent history" or, if one prefers, a "natural history." After all, doing scholarship is by and large a human enterprise that is always situated in concrete social contexts, as the sociology of knowledge of various disciplines would remind us (e.g., Kuhn, 1962; Mannheim, 1946; Stark, 1958). And as Gertrude J. Robinson (1996) said in her argument for an historiographic approach to understanding the intellectual history of communication research, "The development of a field must therefore be viewed as a social process in which various groups of researchers compete for the ascendancy of their scholarly interpretations" (p. 158).

In short, therefore, this book is an historiographic story of media ecology as part of the North American communication and cultural studies tradition—the type of story or narrative that is framed within what Postman calls the "non-fiction division" in the social sciences (Postman, 1988, p. 3). For this purpose, we begin by conceptualizing media ecology as a theory group.[6]

Media Ecology as a Theory Group

There is always an argument in every story, at least in the kind that academics tell. The story this book is telling begins with an argument, in that media ecology has an intellectual tradition, as the book's subtitle suggests. Of course, claiming that there has been a "media ecology tradition" is a risky business particularly because one of the book's primary objectives is to shed light on what media ecology is or does to begin with. So for the time being, I rely on the reader's good faith in accepting three interrelated assumptions in order that the argument can be made. First, it is assumed that media ecology has an identifiable intellectual history to the extent that the scholars and their works in question can be documented to have shared such a history. Second, it is assumed that the reconstruction of this intellectual history can be framed within the larger social, economic, political, as well as cultural contexts of a period of time that began in the late 19th century. Third, by extension, it is assumed that the works of these scholars can be said to share a set of similar theoretical underpinnings, perspectives, or questions for understanding culture, technology, and communication that form what can be considered as media ecology's paradigm content—the type of theoretical issues and methods of inquiry that define the substance and character of a field of study.

To help examine these assumptions and conceptualize media ecology as an intellectual tradition, I borrow the concept of "theory groups" that has its roots in the sociology of science (e.g., Fleck, 1979; Kuhn, 1962). An earlier variant of this theory was proposed by Griffith and Mullins (1972) using the term invisible colleges (see also Crane, 1972), which was subsequently tested and formalized by Stephen O. Murray (1994, 1998) in his social history of theory groups and the study of language in North America. Theory groups as a concept are used to explain the formation of distinct groups led by theorists whose scholarly works help define the paradigm content of their respective topics of scientific inquiry. The concept also helps us understand why some theory groups fail to persist after their initial formation or why others never succeed in forming distinguishable theory groups at all (Murray, 1994).

Typically, a theory group consists of a closely knitted community of scholars who share a more or less coherent set of ideas or theoretical perspectives; their ongoing work in research and teaching helps facilitate theoretical, as well as methodological advancements within the existing paradigm of their field or "normal science" (Kuhn, 1962). In certain, much less common instances, the ideas, theories, and or methods of inquiry championed by a theory group over time help facilitate a paradigmatic shift in an entire discipline—a foundational change in how the discipline in question conceptualizes the nature of what it studies (its epistemology) as in the case of the shift from Newtonian physics to quantum physics. The latter instance is called "revolutionary science."

In his studies, Murray (1994, 1998) formulated two models for understanding theory groups, the functionalist model and the model of rhetoric of revolution/continuity (or the "conflict model"). The functionalist model posits that three prerequisites must be met for any coherent theory group to form, namely, good ideas, intellectual leadership, and organizational leadership. Good ideas, according to Murray (1994), "are ideas judged by scientists to solve existing puzzles or to open new areas of inquiry" (p. 22). But because these "good ideas" often begin with claims from the researchers who think of them (as "good"), how and the extent to which these ideas would be accepted in the discipline at large, where competing "good ideas" abound, depends on how well these ideas are articulated and propagated.

This is why intellectual leadership is also needed in theory group formation. In Murray's (1994) conception:

> Intellectual leadership consists of (1) laying a conceptual foundation for a line of research, (2) explaining the research implications of the "good ideas," (3) approving and validating the work of others as competent, relevant and/or within the framework. Usually, intellectual leaders also (4) produce a program statement, specifying what research should be done and how such research fits into basic theory, and/or (5) produce exemplary research, showing how research should be done. More than one scientist may perform these 'tasks' at a particular juncture. There also may be a succession of leaders in the history of a particular group. (p. 22)

But various administrative tasks must be performed for intellectual leadership to be effective so good ideas can be effectively formulated, validated, propagated, used, and perpetuated over time.

Therefore, organizational leadership is similarly essential in theory group formation. Organizational tasks, in this regard, may include such matters as funding acquisition, research and instructional program administration, publication management, conference planning, and so on. A single leading scholar may perform the dual roles of intellectual leader and organizational leader but a theory group can also have "more than one leader of both kinds" (Murray, 1994, p. 23). In short, good ideas, intellectual leadership, and organizational leadership are all necessary in the formation of distinct theory groups, but do not necessarily co-exist in one scholar.

On the other hand, the model of rhetoric of revolution/continuity (or the "conflict model") seeks to conceptualize the relative, intellectual positioning among theory groups. Revolutionary rhetoric, according to Murray (1994), "refers to claims (by group members) to major discontinuities, not to claims of persecution/rejection at the hands of an establishment" (p. 23). Simply put, the conflict model points to the existence of conflicting claims among theory groups about how and the extent to which their respective paradigm content may provide a breakthrough or major advance in normal science ("rhetoric of continuity") or represent a paradigm shift ("rhetoric of revolution"; see also Kuhn, 1962).

So from the functionalist perspective, we would ask: How did media ecology come into being as a theory group? What are the "good ideas" about culture, technology, and communication that have been the theoretical foundations or paradigm content of media ecology? How did these ideas come about and why have they been deemed "good" by those who thought of them? Moreover, who provided the intellectual leadership behind media ecology's theoretical formulation and how has this intellectual leadership expressed itself? Who provided the necessary organizational leadership for the development of media ecology as a coherent theory group? From the conflict model perspective, we would ask: Has there been any claim of paradigmatic breakthrough in communication studies made by media ecology as a theory group?

To address these questions, we begin our story with a discussion of some of the preparadigmatic currents within the larger social and historical contexts of the first half of the 20th century when North American communication research as we know it today began to emerge.

A PRE-HISTORY OF MEDIA ECOLOGY

The story of media ecology as a theory group did not formally begin until the phrase's coinage sometime in the 1960s. In a personal communication (March 1999), Postman credited McLuhan as the first person to use the term supposedly around the time of the publication of McLuhan's two influential books, *The Gutenberg Galaxy* (1962) and *Understanding Media* (1964). As he later suggested in his 2000 keynote speech to the inaugural convention of the Media Ecology Association, "The only time I know of that McLuhan used the phrase 'media ecology' is in a letter he wrote to Clare Booth Luce in which he remarked that it may be necessary for a culture to limit its use of some medium in the interests of promoting a balance in the media ecology" (Postman, 2000, p. 6).[7]

But it seems unlikely that McLuhan first used the phrase in this context because he did not begin corresponding with Luce (1903-1987), a playwright and widow of the famed magazine publisher Henry Luce (1898-1967), until after their first meeting in Honolulu in 1972 (Molinaro et al., 1987, p. 474). So if McLuhan indeed coined the term, he would have had done so in another context before 1968, when Postman was the person to first use it publicly. In fact, by all accounts thus far (Nystrom, 1973; Strate, 2002), it was Postman who himself was responsible for coining the term, which in turn served as a guiding metaphor, as Thomas F. Gencarelli (2000) observes, for generating or mining "ideas that he was working on and to divine a coherence across his somewhat eclectic readings of scholars he thought important and whose ideas influenced him" (pp. 91-92).

In the Beginning

Postman was a graduate student at Columbia University's Teachers' College (TC) in the 1950s when he first met McLuhan, then a professor of literature and literary history at the University of Toronto, as the latter gave one of his annual guest lectures at the invitation of Louis Forsdale,[8] one of Postman's professors at TC (Culkin, 1989). Postman and McLuhan began a long-standing friendship because in part they shared a unique ecological perspective on understanding media and culture. This perspective held that media's impact on culture is formal and environmental while people's modes of thinking and social organization are shaped by the dominant modes of communication they internalize—a central theme of media ecology's paradigm content. "I distinctively remember having that point of view that the school was just one medium through which a culture communicated some of its important ideas and I understood that there were other media in the culture to do it," recalled Postman in a personal communication (March 1999). He began to have this idea since his days as an undergraduate student at the State University of New York at Fredonia, where he earned his baccalaureate degree in education in 1953. Such an ecological perspective manifests itself in a highly influential book that he had just co-authored with Charles Weingartner called *Teaching as a Subversive Activity* (Postman & Weingartner, 1969).

It was during *Subversive Activity*'s final publication preparation—10 years after he earned his EdD from Columbia and at a time he was establishing a voice in the United States as an authority in the school curriculum reform and teacher education debate[9] at the height of the raging 1960s—when Postman first publicly introduced the phrase media ecology in his address to the 1968 annual meeting of the National Council of Teachers of English that was later published under the title of "The Reformed English Curriculum" (Postman, 1970 cited in Strate, 2002). In it, he defined media ecology as "the study of media as environments" (p. 161), one of the key ideas that will be explained in greater details in the "Studying Media as Environments" section. As should be clear, Postman's intellectual agenda at the time did not focus on communication media alone. Instead, he was concerned with how culture and education have been impacted upon by the rapid changes in the larger social environments whereas such changes seemed to have been facilitated by the shift from print to electronic technologies, a theme that has been a defining feature of Postman's scholarship (e.g., Postman, 1979, 1982, 1985, 1999).

Nonetheless, a somewhat subtle and yet important point should be emphasized here. The term media ecology has been used by people as a metaphor (as in the environments created or defined by communication media), including McLuhan after its coinage. It is a poetic wordplay that has helped many to see media and culture from a new vantage point. Therefore, by giving the term a formal definition as "the study of" media environments, Postman semantically transformed the metaphor into a proper noun—one that was now larger or more encompassing than the metaphor itself—in naming an entirely new field of media studies. It is with this understanding that the formal naming of media ecology as an academic field of inquiry and as a theory group is dated in 1968.

But what were the "good ideas" or paradigm-defining issues that led to media ecology's emergence in the 20th century? What were the founding thinkers of media ecology concerned with? Why the ecological perspectives? Why did media ecology come on the scene as a theory group within the North American contexts during the 1960s?

Technology and Change in the 20th Century: Pre-Paradigmatic Currents

The genesis of media ecology should be understood within the larger context of the rise of North American communication and cultural studies, which in turn has been the result of diverging intellectual responses to the major social, economic, political, and cultural currents that helped shape the 20th century as a century of change. From the point of view of Robinson (1996), for example, "the origin and parentage of U.S. communication studies must be sought in the work done by sociologists and social psychologists who grappled with problems of industrialization and social change at the turn of the century" (p. 159), which became a signature feature of the progressive scholarship of the Chicago School of Sociology (e.g., Cooley, 1909; Dewey, 1916; Mead, 1934; Park, 1922; see also Carey, 1996). Industrialization and modernization not only redefined the mode of production and livelihood as people in the old, agrarian economy knew it, but also drastically changed the ways in which they had related among themselves, if not to the world around them (Berger, Berger, & Kellner, 1973); it helped quicken the pace of urbanization, which in turn helped accelerate the transformation of communities and communal life across the United States (Stein, 1960). Large-scale global migration of people, such as immigration from the European continent early in the 20th century to urban areas in the United States had sparked intense sociocommunicative studies of the formation of new communities (Carey, 1996; Czitrom, 1982) and, in particular, the role of the press in the lives of new immigrants (e.g., Park, 1920, 1922, 1925). The rise of modern advertising and public relations, themselves responses to the need for helping promote and support industrial production and commercial interests of Corporate America, have been major impetuses for an ever-increasing interest in behavioralistic studies of media consumption in the service of advertising and marketing research not only in the professional fields but also in the academy (Bernays, 1965; Ewen, 1976, 1996; Marchand, 1985; Pope, 1983). Scholars from diverse political and academic backgrounds were also concerned with the role and impact of propaganda during various global military conflicts such as the two world wars (e.g., Ellul, 1965; Fraser, 1957; Lasswell, 1927; A. Lee & Lee, 1939; E. Lee & Lee, 1979; Lerner, 1951; Lippmann, 1922).

At the same time, the rapid succession of innovations in transports and electronic communications that began in the latter part of the 19th century, such as the telegraph, the telephone, phonograph, rotary press, motion pictures, automobile, airplane, the radio, sound movies, and television, had also been powerful agents of changes in society and facilitated much incentive for various kinds of media studies. What came with these new transports and media technologies were not only new ways in human mobility or information transmission but also unforeseen social, economic, and political issues and challenges. What the telegraph hath wrought, as its inventor Samuel Morse might have suspected but did not seem to have foretold (Frommer, 1987), were not only a speedier way to send messages over long distance but also new industries and business practices, new social relations, and new ways of conducting international diplomacy or warfare (Standage, 1999); similarly, it engendered new sociopolitical geographies, new definitions of news if not information itself, and, metaphysically, new concepts of time and space in human imagination (Carey, 1988b). On another level, the rise of modern mass media also facilitated an ongoing debate over their cultural impact on the so-called mass society (e.g., Rosenberg & White, 1957, 1971).

The immediate post-World War II decades also saw the surge of research in developmental communication (e.g., Lerner, 1958; Schramm, 1964) and other related areas of inquiry such as diffusion of innovation studies (e.g., Rogers, 1995) when the United States was exporting its technology, a well as technical and managerial know-how to the newly decolonized, developing nations around the world. What is known as intercultural communication as a field of study also had its beginning during this period as more and more overseas-bound U.S. government servicemen and women, corporate managers, and technicians from the industries were in need of better communication skills when interacting with their foreign counterparts (Leeds-Hurwitz, 1990). There was also a heightened awareness in critical communication studies when, for example, some scholars saw as the increasing dominance of American communications around the world (e.g., Schiller, 1976, 1969/1992; A. Smith, 1980; Tunstall, 1977). In short, these and many other issues that came with the telegraph and its new sibling media technologies in the electronic revolution—including the Internet— have also been the catalysts for ongoing media and communication research to date.

But as a young academic field with roots in multiple disciplines, North American communication research has always been marked by theoretical contests due in part to its lack of theoretical cohesion (Merton, 1967, paraphrased in Robinson, 1996), so much so that Robert T. Craig (1999) has argued that "communication theory is not yet a coherent field of study" (p. 120).10 Many of the theoretical contests have been the results of disagreements among competing perspectives on understanding the source of media's influence, as well as diverging methodological orientations, as the "conflict model" of theory group suggests (Murray, 1994). The theoretical disagreements between the Administrative School of Communication and the Critical School of Communication that has been made evident by *Ferment in the Field* (1983), for example, is symptomatic of such disagreements.

The Administrative or Empirical School is mainly associated with what are generally known as media effects studies that are typically characterized by "quantitative empiricism, functionalism, and positivism" (Rogers, 1982, p. 125). Such media effects studies have generally been concerned with empirically verifiable short-term behavioral impact of media content on its users or consumers (Bryant & Thompson, 2002). Some of the earlier media effects research have been hailed as "milestones" in mainstream communication research in the United States (Lowery & DeFleur, 1995). Some of these research included the Payne Fund Studies on the effects of movies on children in the 1920s; sociopsychological studies of the seeming mass hysteria surrounding Orson Welles' 1938 Mercury Theatre radio play broadcast of The War of the Worlds; the daytime radio serials uses and gratification research in the late 1930s to the 1940s; propaganda analyses during World War II; political campaign studies from the 1940s onward; studies on television in children's lives late in the 1950s, and examinations of television violence in the 1960s.

From within the mainstream mass media content effects research, or what critical media theorist and social commentator Todd Gitlin (1978) calls "the dominant paradigm," there has also been an ongoing debate over how mass media content may exalt power over or impact on the audience, namely, from the so-called "magic bullet theory," that suggests that the mass media can impact on a passive and defenseless audience; to theories about the mediating power of the so-called opinion leaders in between the mass media and the audience members (Katz, 1957; Katz & Lazarsfeld, 1955); and onto theories about how receiving public has all that is necessary to defend themselves by selecting what they want to see or hear or what would only reinforce their existing beliefs and such (Klapper, 1960).

On the other hand, the 1960s also saw the revival of Marxist or Marxian scholarship in the midst of political unrest in the United States (e.g., Marcuse, 1965) that would later be related to the rise of critical communication scholarship. As the Critical School has also been concerned with mass media content's impact on society, it maintains a politico-ideological, as well as theoretical perspective that is somewhat diametrically opposed to that of the dominant paradigm of the Administrative School (*Ferment in the Field*, 1983; Rogers, 1982). Originating in part from the Frankfurt School and what would later be known as neo-Marxism[11] (Lum, 1992), Critical School scholarship focuses more broadly on the political economy of the mass media with particular concerns in media ownership, as well as how political and corporate control over the media may play an essential role in media content production, distribution, and access (e.g., Adorno & Horkheimer, 1977; Enzensberger, 1974; Schiller, 1976). One of their concerns has been on how and the extent to which concentrated ownership can create an informational environment, which includes media content, that is limited in its social and cultural sensitivity, as well as political and ideological diversity—an informational monopoly that only serves the interests of the political, industrial, and corporate elites (e.g., McChesney, 2000; Schiller, 1991).

Emerging Media Ecological Perspectives

But although the field of communication research in the United States may have been dominated by mass media content effect studies, as well as competition from the critical school studies in the political economy of media, ecological approaches to understanding media and technology's formal and foundational impact on culture and society had already sprouted in diverse academic fields or, more generally, in the world of ideas beginning earlier on in the 20th century. In what can be considered a ground-breaking work in the intellectual history and historiography of media ecology, *The Post-Industrial Prophets: Interpretations of Technology*, William Kuhns (1971) provides a brilliant synthesis of the interdisciplinary scholarship of seven major thinkers whose writings have helped lay down part of media ecology's theoretical underpinnings, Mumford (1934, 1967, 1970), Siegfried Giedion (1948, 1967), Norbert Wiener (1948, 1950), Innis (1950, 1951), McLuhan (1951, 1962, 1964), Ellul (1964, 1965), and R. Buckminster Fuller (1963, 1969a, 1969b).[12] Kuhns was by no means the first intellectual biographer or historian in this regard because others before him had already begun their respective expositions (e.g., Carey, 1968). But it was *The Post-Industrial Prophets* that was the first conscious effort to bring together in a group intellectual biography this many major ecological thinkers who share a common interest in the formal and foundational impact of technology on culture even as they may differ in their interpretations.

Kuhns did not use the phrase media ecology per se nor did he identify these thinkers as media ecologists. His book did not demonstrate an awareness of the fact that Postman was founding a graduate degree program at NYU that required its students to read these same seven scholars, among others.[13] But the conception behind Kuhns' synthesis is clearly media ecological. In one of his 12 postulates toward the end of *The Post-Industrial Prophets*, for example, he suggests that "communication is environmental" while paraphrasing Innis, McLuhan, and their forebears; he also raises such questions as "Is television essentially a medium of communication or an environmental phenomenon?" (Kuhns, 1971, p. 257).

What is equally remarkable is the fact that, regardless of their diverging interpretations, the seven "post-industrial prophets" in Kuhns' discourse (or media ecologists in the current narrative) have been similarly concerned with how technology may have large-scale or environmental and formal, structural impact on society and culture. In the first half of the 20th century, the academe by and large saw what Christine L. Nystrom (1973) characterized as an epochal change in the status, organization, and application of knowledge in a movement away from compartmentalized academic studies and toward cross-, multi-, or meta-disciplinary inquiries. Increasing integration was seen between the physical and the social sciences with the rise of multi- and interdisciplinary studies.

The rise of multi- and interdisciplinary studies coincided with the rise of critical consciousness on the world's ecology. Put slightly differently, one may consider the rising ecological consciousness during the first half of the 20th century as a socio-scientific catalyst for the emergence of multi- and interdisciplinary thinking in the academy, in the political sphere, and in the court of public intellectuals. Through their writings, Kuhns' postindustrial prophets from multidisciplinary orientations—and their like-minded counterparts in the world at large—engaged in some sort of a public discussion on the challenges and opportunities that had been engendered by the rapid succession of technological innovations and diffusion in society. As the maddening pace of technological innovations and diffusion quickened, the 20th century also bore witness to a host of fundamental, if not traumatic, changes.

But although change was inevitable, it was nonetheless not without its price. There has been an increasing deterioration of the world's environments: Natural resources are being depleted at a faster rate; many once pristine waterways are now poisoned with chemical toxins from industries; forests and wetlands are being destroyed. City streets are clogged by ever-worsening traffic as more and more highways are being built; the air in urban centers is filled with pollutants from automotive and industrial emissions. Human costs also escalate. The United States alone, for example, accounts for tens of thousands of annual automobile-related deaths. These fatalities of progress do not include the many thousands more that are attributable to other technological casualties, such as industry-related deaths, injuries, as well as social and psychological disorder of all kinds. And the list goes on.

What is significant to note has been the fact that the environmental consequences brought forth by rapid technological advances in the early part of
the 20th century has fostered an ecological paradigm or way of thinking
about the interconnectedness of things in people's lives. As Father Walter J.
Ong (2002) put it eloquently:

> given our now intensive and detailed knowledge of the total intercon-
> nected universe and its evolutionary history, we do live in what can well
> be styled the ecological age. Interconnectedness is the mark of our age,
> at least as apprehended by the human sensibility, and his interconnect-
> edness is seemingly destined to grow more and more massively and cir-
> cumstantially in and with all succeeding ages, which will likewise more
> and more massively interconnect in human consciousness with one
> another. (p. 11)

It is within this larger intellectual context at the dawning of the "ecological
age" that we see the significance of the convergence of interests from among
diverse academic orientations in understanding the foundational and ecological impact of technology, a defining issue of media ecology's paradigm content, as such a convergence of intellectual energies is chronicled in *The Post-
Industrial Prophets*.

But not all of the postindustrial prophets were critical or pessimistic in
their forecast. Buckminster Fuller, for example, while being fully aware of
the enormous large-scale ecological change that new technologies could
bring, nevertheless saw them as opportunities for human progress or the
betterment of the human condition. Hence, according to Kuhns' synthesis,
one can discern from among their techno-ecological scholarship at least
three prevalent positions or "schools" (p. 259): "Encroachment of the
Machine" (e.g., Mumford, Giedion, Ellul, and Wiener); "Media Dictates
Culture" (e.g., Innis and McLuhan); and "Technology Breeds Utopia" (e.g.,
Fuller).

Meanwhile, the inclusion of Ellul, Innis, McLuhan, and Giedion among
the seven postindustrial prophets indicates that the emergence of what
would later be called the media ecological perspective on culture and technology was not confined to the United States alone. By 1950, for instance,
there arose north of Niagra Falls a succession of thinkers from diverse disciplines who congregated around their common interests and work at the
University of Toronto (UT). Four of the most notable scholars in this regard
included Innis, who began teaching at the University of Toronto upon completing his doctoral studies in political economy at the University of
Chicago until his untimely passing in 1952 (Heyer, 2003), and Eric
Havelock, an associate professor of classics at UT's Victoria College
between 1929 and 1947.[14] McLuhan, whose work had been profoundly

inspired by Innis, became a member on the faculty of UT's St. Michael's College in 1946 after having taught at the University of Wisconsin in 1936–1937, at St. Louis University in 1937–1944, and at Assumption University in Windsor in 1944–1946 (Kuhns, 1971, p. 171). There also was a young anthropologist and archeologist in their midst, Edmund (Ted) Carpenter, whose shared editorial leadership with McLuhan at the academic journal *Explorations in Communication* (e.g., Carpenter & McLuhan, 1960) and book on *Oh, What a Blow That Phantom Gave Me!* (Carpenter, 1972) had provided original ethnographic data and anthropological insights into technological diffusion and human adaptation of technology in primitive cultures.[15]

What is interesting to note here is the way in which Carpenter positioned, almost literally, how he and his contemporaries approached their observations and analyses while commenting that "from Toronto, you could see it happening. It was like living on an island, studying the mainland. You saw the whole show. Its main event was the electronic revolution"[16] (cited in Theall, 2001, p. 251). An important subplot of this "show" was how the seat of global power was shifting from the European theater to the rising American empire in the midst of the electronic communications revolution. As Carpenter and his colleagues in Toronto were watching the show from the outside, so to speak, their contemporaries south of the Falls were literally living in and looking at the show from within.

"What's Going On?"[17]

At this point, we should notice the timing of the emergence of media ecology as a theory group. Such timing is noteworthy because the 1960s was by many measures a traumatic decade in the history of the United States. Somehow, all the social and political, as well as media-technological changes—in addition to the excitement, tensions, and confusion that came with them—seemed to have converged in that American decade. The rapid succession of advancements in and diffusion of media technology and telecommunications, from the transistor and videotape recorder (VTR) to the satellite, has facilitated much change to the media industries. What Daniel Boorstin (1961/1987) calls the Graphic Revolution and, more particularly, the rise of imaged-based electronic media such as television, began to challenge the dominance of literacy and print. In part because of the rising dominance of graphic communications in the larger social and media environments, predominantly print-based educators such as Postman and his contemporaries began to see subtle and yet profound changes in their classrooms or, better, in how their students learn or otherwise come to understand the world; the school reform debate and movement can in fact be viewed as a communal cry on the part of the educators as they were wondering out loud as to what was going on to print-based literacy and education as they knew it.

Politically, the United States was increasingly divided over the worsening war in Vietnam, for instance, not long after the first combat troops were sent in March 1965 (Karnow, 1983). Antiwar protests intensified and voices of dissent echoed across the land: from the streets of San Francisco to Woodstock in upstate New York; on college campuses, from UC Berkeley on the west coast, Kent State in the midwest, to Columbia in the east. Radiating from the segregated South, the Civil Rights Movement was in full swing, challenging the country's discriminatory racial policy at the systemic level and otherwise rampant racism in America society; and along with it came scores of other anti-establishment movements: the Women Liberation Movement, Black Power, the American Indian Movement, the Gay and Lesbian Movement, the Asian American Movement, the New Left Movement (Gitlin, 1980), just to name a few. No less important, the deterioration of the natural ecology prompted the rise of the environmental movement, which in no small part entailed the protest over the development and use of nuclear power (Mumford had been one of nuclear power's earliest and most vocal critics). These and many other similarly tumultuous events seemed to have picked up a momentum so fast and furious toward the end of the 1960s that Gitlin (1987) recalls the years from 1967 to 1970 in United States history as "a cyclone in a wind tunnel" (p. 242).

So even as the answer might have simply been blowin' in the wind to some, the timing of the rise of the media ecology movement during this period was significant precisely because it was a period of time during which scores of media ecological thinkers from diverse disciplinary backgrounds were posing new and important questions about what they saw as foundational change in the world around them. Through their writings, such as those by Kuhn's postindustrial prophets, these thinkers engaged in some sort of a public discussion on the challenges and opportunities that had been engendered by the rapid succession of media technological innovations and diffusion in society.

In short, the emergence of media ecology as a theory group and a theoretical perspective late in the 1960s can be seen as a result of the coming together of an interlocking network of invisible colleges of like-minded thinkers who shared similar concerns over media technology and change within larger social, economic, political, and intellectual contexts that began at the turn of the 20th century. On a more specific academic disciplinary level, or from the perspective of the conflict model in theory groups, it was a response to the dominance of mainstream (mass media content) effects tradition in much the same way as the Critical School was rising up against the dominant paradigm in North American communication research.

INITIAL INSTITUTIONALIZATION OF MEDIA ECOLOGY

The two decades between 1970 and 1992 were crucial in media ecology's formation as a theory group because it was during this period of time when it had its first formal institutional home. According to Murray's (1994, 1998) functionalist model, although having good ideas or paradigm content that embodies significant and useful questions for the advancement of knowledge is a necessary condition, strong and persistent co-existence of both intellectual leadership and organizational leadership is critical for the formation and perpetuation of theory groups. Note also that such intellectual leadership and organizational leadership can be provided by more than one individual. In this regard, our discussion in this section focuses on how and why the formation of media ecology as a theory group would have taken place in New York in the late 1960s. More specifically, we examine closely the intellectual and organizational leadership role of Neil Postman and his colleagues at New York University in the rise of media ecology.

Neil Postman and the Founding of the Media Ecology Program

At the time of his public definition of media ecology as a new field of media studies in 1968, Postman was just promoted to full professor in English education at NYU's School of Education.[18] Coincidentally, McLuhan was in New York in 1967–1968 as an Albert Schweitzer Chair in the Humanities at Fordham University that had been arranged by John Culkin (1989).[19] Postman (2000) credited McLuhan with having provided much encouragement to him in establishing a formal course of study in media and culture at NYU from the ecological perspective. This course of study would later evolve into the Media Ecology Program, the first institutional base of media ecology as a theory group.

Up until the end of the 1966–1967 academic year, Postman was listed under the English Education Department heading as the instructor of six graduate courses, three each in the course grouping of Linguistic Foundations of Oral and Written Communication (The Study of Language; Language and Human Behavior; Language and Culture), as well as in the course group of Communications in Education (The Mass Mind; Culture in America and the Communications Revolution; The Language of Communications), respectively (*New York University Bulletin: School of Education*, 1966).[20] A look at the bulletin's description of some of these courses provides a sense of an emerging media ecological perspective in Postman's work in this stage.[21] For example, one section of The Study of Language is described as an "inquiry into the language of contemporary media and modes of communication" whose attention "is given to the work of Wiener, Seldes, Hayakawa, McLuhan, and Richards" (*NYU Bulletin*, 1966, p. 145). Similarly, the course in language and culture examines the "relationships among language, perception, and culture" while giving particular emphasis "to the works of Whorf, Lee, Sapir, Carpenter, and McLuhan" (p. 145). One section of The Language of Communications entails the study of "major manifestations of man's primal urge to transmit his ideas, emotions, and artistic feelings to others, from the tribal narrative and cave drawing to the radio, newspaper, cinema, and televison of the modern era. Aesthetic, as well as sociopsychological, factors in communication are examined" (p. 123). Interestingly, the description of this latter course already embeds in it traces of what would later emerge as what can be called an "epochal historiography of media" (see a later section by this title) not only in Postman's degree program curriculum but also as one of media ecology scholarship's defining theoretical underpinnings.

There was a noticeable turn toward a more overtly communication-centered curriculum in Postman's program building within the curricular paradigm of English education between the academic years of 1967 and 1970, during which time the three courses under the grouping of Communications in Education (The Mass Mind; The Language of Communications; The Communications Revolution and Culture in America, slightly revised from its former title) were now moved to a new program grouping called Communications. In the meantime, new communication-based courses were also introduced into the curriculum during this period, such as Linguistic Environments, as well as Language and Persuasion. The course Language and Persuasion, for example, would later be expanded into two separate courses: Communication and Persuasion: Sociological Propaganda, and Communication and Political Propaganda, respectively.

Of notable significance of Postman's communication-centered curriculum at this stage were two important developments in the 1970–1971 school year. First, and foremost, the doctoral-level Program Seminar in Communications (six credits in two semesters) was first introduced, thus signaling the actual beginning of Postman's doctoral program in media ecology even though the phrase media ecology was not formally adopted until a year later, making its first appearance in the 1971–1972 edition of the *NYU Bulletin* (1971).[22] This is why later the school catalogue description identifies 1970 as the founding year of the Media Ecology Program. Once the degree program was officially named into existence, media ecology as a body of knowledge about culture and technology began to take shape at the same time Media Ecology as an academic program was being institutionalized over the ensuing two decades.

The second important development was the fact that Postman was listed as the program's director, thus documenting his leadership role in media ecology's early institutionalization. In this important regard, Postman was a primary driving force behind this process.

The Triad at NYU: The Leader, the Organizer, and the Theoretician/Codifier

If Postman was the intellectual leader and public spokesperson of media ecology in the United States in its first decades, then Terence P. Moran and Christine L. Nystrom would have been the two most important behind-the-scene builders of the degree program at NYU. Over the course of three decades since the degree program's 1970 founding, the three formed the pillars on which it was built for the first generation of media ecologists. Both Moran and Nystrom were themselves Postman's graduate students in English education in the 1960s, earning their doctorates with a focus in language and communication under his mentorship in 1971 and 1973, respectively. But although it is difficult, if at all possible, to quantify the extent of their respective contributions to the degree program's building, it would be fair to suggest that they contributed to this process in their equally unique ways.

Just one year after earning his PhD, Moran was appointed director of the program (for both the MA and PhD degrees) in the 1972–1973 school year as an assistant professor of English education; he would serve in this capacity until 1992.[23] Moran spearheaded the organizational leadership for the initial institutionalization of media ecology as a field of study at NYU. He rendered the day-to-day administrative supports, such as curricular design and implementation, budgeting or fund allocation, as well as class staffing and scheduling, the kind of supports that were needed for the programmatic development and curricular execution of the overall intellectual vision engendered by Postman (Moran, personal communication, May 6, 2003). A passing and yet endearing comment that Postman made in the mid-1970s before a group of incoming graduate students should serve to indicate Moran's organizational leadership and prominence very early on: "We can talk about how [Richard] Nixon is part of a technological empire, over which he may have less control than, say, Terry Moran has over this Department" (Postman, 1975, p. 5). An effective teacher and doctoral dissertation advisor,[24] and with a profound interest in the scholarly works by Ellul (e.g., 1964, 1962, 1965, 1980, 1981, 1985, 1990), he has been the key instructor in the media and propaganda component of the degree program's curriculum.[25] Together with Postman and Nystrom, he also spearheaded the founding of a baccalaureate degree program in communication studies, in 1986; this ever-expanding undergraduate program would later prove to be an important income source for helping to support the graduate Media Ecology Program.

Equally effective as a teacher and dissertation advisor, Nystrom was what can be called the theoretician-codifier in the degree program. Indeed, her 1973 doctoral dissertation, *Towards a Science of Media Ecology: The Formulation of Integrated Conceptual Paradigms for the Study of Human Communication Systems*, was the first major treatise on media ecology as an emerging field of media studies. With a profound interest in the works by such scholars as Sapir, Whorf, and Langer, Nystrom had been a key instructor in the language and culture component of the degree program's curriculum. She served as the director of graduate degree program from 1980 until her retirement in 2001. No less important, she has also been responsible for explicating the underlying theoretical propositions of media ecology while having created dozens of extensive classroom handouts explicating and elaborating on information theory, general systems theory, the work of Whorf, Langer, George Herbert Mead, and the philosophical foundations and principles of media ecology (a list of such theoretical propositions are introduced later). Nystrom's role as the theoretician-codifier throughout the years has helped lay down the intellectual architecture of the degree program while helping Postman to crystalize his own thinking about media ecology's paradigm content in his numerous publications over the years.[26] In short, together, Postman, Moran, and Nystrom formed an intellectual triad in media ecology's early theoretical formulation and programmatic institutionalization at NYU.

Inventing Media Ecology

[If] you were a member of our faculty, and you were trying to invent media ecology, what would you include in it? (Postman, 1975, p. 3)

In hindsight, Postman was not being entirely rhetorical when he challenged a group of incoming doctoral students in 1975 that part of their education was to help *invent* a new field of media studies. Although it is being argued that media ecology has an intellectual tradition with a more or less coherent body of theoretical literature, the said intellectual foundation, much less tradition, was still in its genesis early in the 1970s—at least as far as having a systematized program of study was concerned. A case in point, no formal program description was published until the 1976–1977 edition of the *NYU Bulletin* (1976). As Postman recalled more than 20 years later in a personal communication (March 1999), the degree program's early years were mainly a period of explorations and experimentation through which media ecology's intellectual character was shaped.

Under Postman's intellectual leadership, and given the institutional mandate of program building, the degree program's slowly expanding core and adjunct faculty developed and introduced courses of study, pulling together like-minded ideas and theories from disparate academic disciplines under one roof. Postman's earlier classes in English education were carried over to communications-centered classes between 1967 and 1970 that were subsequently revised or incorporated in classes developed for the new degree program. As early as in 1970, there already existed an unpublished reading list by the title "A Preliminary Bibliography in Communications" that was credited to Don Hausdorff (1970) that was distributed to incoming doctoral students. This reading list, which has been periodically revised since, identifies many of the authors, such as those included in Kuhns (1971) and in Blechman's poem, whose works were pulled together and would eventually be consolidated to form among the most important intellectual resources in the education of the first generations of media ecologists. It is similarly important to note that other faculty members and some doctoral students also contributed to building the media ecology curriculum by bringing in readings that were deemed relevant. For example, Robert Young, one of the program's assistant professors during its first several formative years, was credited to have introduced to the media ecology curriculum the writings by Paul Watzlawick and his associates at the Palo Alto Group (Watzlawick et al., 1967; see also, Watzawick, 1976).[27] During these formative years, courses often overlapped with similar ideas and readings (Postman, personal communication, March 1999). Yet, emerging out of this time was a coherent program and a consistent vision of what media ecology is or can be in understanding the interrelationship among culture, technology, and communication.

In addition to the degree program's content development and institutionalization, two other important theory group-building venues should also receive their due attention in this discussion. The first was the Media Ecology Conference. Until some time very late in the 1980s, the conference was held twice annually (fall and spring) at a small resort hotel in the Catskill region in upstate New York. It was meant as an informal intellectual retreat for faculty members, graduate students, and, equally important, invited speakers. Over the years, an impressive roster of scholars have been invited to speak at the conference, such as David J. Bolter (1984), Jerome S. Bruner (1962, 1983, 1986), Carey (1988a; see also Munson & Warren, 1997), Elizabeth Eisenstein (1979, 1983), Havelock (1963, 1976, 1982, 1986), Julian Jaynes (1976), Sherry Turkle (1985, 1995), Mumford (1934, 1967, 1970), and Joseph Weizenbaum (1976). The conference was a vibrant meeting ground—a coming together of important theorists who shared related intellectual ideas but were typically isolated from the each other. It also gave graduate students, themselves budding media ecologists, an invaluable opportunity to be acquainted with academic networking. It was assumed that invited speakers would leave the conference with a more enriched understanding, if not appreciation, of media ecology as a theoretical perspective and perhaps bring it back to their respective disciplines. In this important regard, the conference served as a conduit for people in the degree program to reach out to the disciplines while at the same time enhancing the visibility of media ecology as a new field of studies outside of NYU's institutional confines.

Another of the venues that also played an important role in media ecology's formative years at NYU was the journal *ETC.: A Review of General Semantics* of which Postman was the editor between 1977 and 1986. Academic journals are among the most important of channels not only for sharing and propagating but also for defining and legitimizing scholarship in any given academic field of study (Fleck, 1979; Kuhn, 1962; Murray, 1994). In this regard, Postman's editorship of *ETC.* opened up an important forum for scholarly exchange and for establishing the legitimacy of the media ecological approach.

As Postman has always liked to tell his graduate students over the years that one of the degree program's founding missions has been to explore McLuhan's famous aphorism, "the medium is the message," made famous since its first uttering in the latter's book *Understanding Media* (McLuhan, 1964). The theoretical essence and spirit of this aphorism subsequently found its partial expression in the Media Ecology Program's first published program description, in the 1976-1977 edition of the *NYU Bulletin* (1976):

> Media ecology is the study of transactions among people, their messages, and their message systems. More particularly, media ecology studies how media of communication affect human perception, feeling, understanding, and value. Media ecology attempts to specify our assumptions about media, to discover the roles various media force us to play, to explicate how media structure what we see and what we do. (p. 114)

Subsequently, some 11 years after he publicly introduced the phrase media ecology and an outline of its paradigm content, Postman (1979) would publish his first major program statement of media ecology as a field of study in *Teaching as a Conserving Activity* (see also Gencarelli, 2000; chapter 8, this volume). Note that "program statement" in this context does not mean narrowly a statement about what Postman's NYU degree program is about or does; instead, it refers to Postman's general defining statement about what he believes to be the paradigm content of media ecology. In the ensuing years, he elaborated on the various aspects of his more refined interpretations of media ecology's paradigm content in a succession of books (e.g., Postman, 1982, 1985, 1992, 1999).

Media Ecology Reaching Out

I have suggested previously that media ecology was a virtually unknown theoretical perspective in communication up until the latter part of the

1980s. One reason for media ecology's obscurity at the time was that it still was an emerging, young theory group. In addition, as one of media ecology's paradigm founders and the theory group's principal intellectual leader and spokesperson, Neil Postman came from an English education background and his work was not immediately known in the communication discipline. What established him as a public intellectual and a national figure in the academy between the 1960s and the 1980s was his pioneering and provocative work in the school reform movement. Postman typically attended annual conventions of the National Council of Teachers of English and other similar education-related professional events. But with the establishment of his doctoral degree program at NYU, Postman founded his own conference that catered to the unique interest of aspiring media ecologists. Reaching out to the mainstream communication research community was not a primary concern during the early formative years of media ecology. After all, the emergence of the media ecological perspective was, in a real sense, a revolt against what Gitlin (1978) called the dominant paradigm in communication at the time.

The 1985 publication of *Amusing Ourselves to Death* was a turning point for Postman's national standing and, by extension, his NYU program. Even as Postman's media ecology was becoming more and more pronounced in his writings in language and education since the 1970s, it was *Amusing Ourselves to Death*—an eloquent, yet forceful media ecological critique of American television culture—that brought him widespread attention outside of the education discipline. Not only was the book a success in the United States as both an academic volume and a mass market popular seller, *Amusing* achieved critical acclaim outside of North America, most notably in Germany where it was on a bestseller list for weeks and where Postman himself was received warmly during his lecture tours.[28] On one level, therefore, the success of *Amusing Ourselves to Death* was a vehicle that has helped facilitate media ecology's foray into the communication discipline or, at the least, was a step into North American mainstream communication research.

Another book instrumental in bringing the communication field's attention to media ecology was *No Sense of Place* by Joshua Meyrowitz (1985). Meyrowitz was among the early NYU-educated media ecologists with Postman as one of his doctoral sponsors. Based on his doctoral dissertation, the book synthesizes McLuhan's (1964) media theories and Erving Goffman's (1959) dramaturgical analysis of social interaction in an insightful examination of how electronic media (particularly television) redefine the various regions of human interaction and behavior. And as the book has brought Meyrowitz critical acclaim[29] and propelled him to a successful career in the academy, at the same time it helped promote media ecology scholarship.

Perhaps not coincidentally, it was shortly before *Amusing Ourselves to Death's* formal release when Postman and his NYU colleagues participated in the 1984 annual conference of the International Communication Association in San Francisco; this being among their first appearances at a major mainstream communication convention. The panel on which Postman, Christine Nystrom, and Terence Moran would speak on issues relating to language, media, and education was proposed by Peter L. Haratonik, the director of the MA in media Studies Program at the New School for Social Research at the time. Himself a student of Postman's, Haratonik was among the first-generation media ecology scholars who sought to reach out to the mainstream communication research community.

There was some degree of irony in that as increasing numbers of NYU graduates began taking full-time teaching positions at universities nationwide in the 1990s, in effect, promoting media ecology scholarship to a wider constituency, a gradual but fundamental shift in the academic focus of the PhD degree program began to take root. The recruitment of Herbert I. Schiller and Todd Gitlin in the mid- and late-1990s,[30] respectively, was an indication of this change in the then newly renamed Department of Culture and Communication. Schiller and Gitlin's presence in Postman's department might have easily intrigued some observers because they have long been associated with the Critical School, which offered some of the harshest criticism of McLuhan's writings as being apolitical. Subsequent faculty appointments seemed to confirm an increasing interest within the department in media sociology and cultural studies.

Nonetheless, the diversification of academic interest in the NYU degree program should not have come as a surprise to students of theory groups. "Since universities seek diversity of specialists," as Murray (1998) reminds us, "it is practically impossible to maintain very many scientists doing the same kind of research at one university for very long" (p. 251). With the program's gravitational pull away from its original orbit, its first cohorts of media ecologists established themselves in various academic settings as either faculty members or administrators.

But the dispersion of these media ecologists from their birthplace at NYU can be a mixed blessing. On the one hand, through their own research, teaching, and professional outreach, these scholars have helped to propagate media ecology's theoretical perspective and canonical literature to their respective institutions and, more generally, to a wider constituency in the communication discipline at large (see the epilogue). On the other hand, however, their dispersion can also hinder the perpetuation or even survival of media ecology as a coherent theory group. In Murray's (1998) words, "Although geographical dispersion is not necessarily fatal to cluster formation, disciplinary dispersion may be. Interdisciplinary status makes cluster formation difficult, because advancement and prestige are determined intradisciplinarily, and because education and professional socialization are primarily intra-disciplinary" (p. 252).

Indeed, on one level, Postman's degree program managed to maintain a very high degree of disciplinary coherence precisely because of its tight and persistent clustering of the core faculty—the triad of Postman, Moran, and Nystrom—for some 30 years and its almost single-minded media ecological focus. But with Nystrom's retirement in 2002 and Postman's untimely passing in October 2003, and coupled with the fact that many NYU-educated media ecologists have dispersed outside of the New York metropolitan area, the concern exists whether media ecology as a theory group can maintain its intellectual coherence.

The Rise of Media Ecology: In Short

At this point, we should be mindful that this section of our discussion is not meant to privilege, promote, or otherwise mythologize particular institutions and their research centers and academic programs (such as NYU's Media Ecology Program or the UT's McLuhan Center for Culture and Technology) or individuals (such as Postman and McLuhan). Instead, our goal is to help explicate media ecology's formation not only as a theoretical endeavor but also as a social process. Such is not a "natural" process of evolution but one that involves the (sometime intuitive) works of interlocking networks of individuals in some fluid intellectual and institutional contexts. It is not an "innocent" process either, because imbedded in it is a conscious intellectual agenda for addressing various social, economic, political, cultural, as well as ideological issues.

Equally important, such an intellectual endeavor inevitably involves and engages the contributions from many like-minded individuals over time. Therefore, as Postman is clearly a leading figure in this aspect of our story, it is just as essential that we acknowledge the work of his network of professional colleagues (both in and outside of NYU), thinkers, and graduate students who have also played various important roles in media ecology's emergence as a theory group. Media ecology is the cumulation of the collective wisdom of many thinkers from many disciplines. Put slightly differently, media ecology cannot (and probably ought not) be equated to Postman studies, McLuhan studies, Mumford studies, Ellul studies, Ong studies, Langer studies, and so on. The intellectual whole of media ecology is greater than the sum of its theoretical parts.

To summarize, and referring back to Murray's (1994) conception and characterization of theory groups, Postman—as a scholar, educator, and public intellectual—provided the necessary intellectual leadership in the envisioning and initial constitution of media ecology as a theory group. He and his colleagues at NYU, most notably Moran and Nystrom, rendered the equally vital organizational leadership for building up a doctoral degree program in which the study of media ecology was formalized. It is the first such academic program that grants the PhD degree with a focus on studying media ecology and its fundamental significance is therefore twofold. First, through graduate course works, dissertation research, and the conferring of degrees, the program institutionalizes the legitimacy of media ecology as an academic subject. Second, it is within this formal academic-institutional structure that the first generations of media ecologists were produced; they in turn would perpetuate and develop media ecology scholarship beyond the confines of any single institution over time.[31]

Studying Media as Environments

When Postman (1970) publicly introduced and defined media ecology in 1968 as the study of media as environments, he referred to media as complex message systems and media ecology as an attempt to unveil their implicit, intrinsic structures and impact on human perception, understanding, and feeling. The concept of how environments may impact people, in this regard, can be traced back to ecological thinkers at the turn of the 20th century at the latest. Patrick Geddes (1904, 1915), for instance, pioneered the study of the interrelationships between natural and built environment, and human culture. Mumford, Geddes' most celebrated disciple and one of media ecology's earliest foundational thinkers, wrote extensively on the impact of human-made environments, such as the city on people and human civilization (e.g., Mumford, 1938, 1961). On another level, scholars in language and culture such as Langer (1942) and Whorf (1956) also explored how the form and structure of symbolic systems we inherit or internalize may shape the ways in which we interact with the world around us. McLuhan (1962) similarly pointed out the fundamental symbolic change that occurs when there is a change in a society's dominant medium for communication such as the shift from the oral to the chirographic and print; he also emphasized that such change entails a fundamental shift in the human sensorium when people engage in mediated communication. In this regard, we may understand this aspect of media ecology as the study of environments on at least two levels.

Media as Sensorial Environments

On the physiological-perceptual level, we can conceptualize every communication medium as a sensorial environment. In the main, we perceive our immediate surroundings by using more or less all of our senses. How and the extent to which we sense our surrounding on the physiological level depends in part on the sensory apparatus we inherit. People with differing sensory apparatuses perceive their surroundings differently partly because their senses give them correspondingly dissimilar sense data from and about the world around them. The visually impaired, for example, typically develop heightened auditory, tactile, olfactory, and gustatory senses as a compensation of their lack of sight. This is one reason why physiology is considered one of three main factors that form the basis of our perception, with the other two factors being our need and past experience (e.g., Cantril, 1960).

From this perspective, communication media are our (sensory) extensions, as McLuhan (1964) rightfully pointed out. Every medium embodies a set of sensory characteristics. The use of each communication medium entails the employment the user's senses in a way that is generally defined by these characteristics: The act of reading extends or emphasizes our visual sense; the act of listening to the radio extends our auditory sense; playing video games extends a combination of our visual, tactile, and auditory senses; and so on. Put differently, the "reality" we sense or re/construct through a medium— something that we put "in between" our surroundings and ourselves, as it were—is a version of "reality" that has been filtered by that medium's sensorial characteristics. Of course, this says nothing about our attempt in compensating the altered senses in this regard (such as we try to "visualize" a baseball game on the radio). Nonetheless, the act of our using any given medium reconfigures our (biologically defined) sensorium. This is the very fundamental perceptual level at which McLuhan (1964) observed that "the medium is the message" in that he referred to how a change in the media reconfigures our sensorium and how such a sensory change alters the ways in which we receive sensory data with which we comprehend and re/construct the world around us. On this level, studying media as environments suggests the examination of the sensorial environments into which we enter when we use our media for understanding the world or, more specifically, a world that is to be constructed for our comprehension by the sensory data that our media are (or a given medium is) designed to encode and decode.

Media as Symbolic Environments

On the second, symbolic level, we can conceptualize every communication medium as a symbolic environment that is systemically constituted by a unique set of codes and syntax. To make use of standard written English as a medium for communication, for example, we must master its vocabulary (i.e., its symbols and their assigned meanings) and grammar (such as the syntactical rules or regulations that govern the construction of meanings). To be "fluent" as a filmmaker, we would need to master the elements of sight and sound in the cinematic vocabulary and grammar. But as we master these media, or any medium, we are also acculturated into the symbolic environment that is the medium itself. Although we feel or otherwise sense the physical world around us through our sight, sound, smell, touch, and taste, we think, perceive, and talk about or represent it from within the intrinsic symbolic universe of the medium. The limit of our language is the limit of our world, to paraphrase Wittgenstein, because our language's internal symbolic structure or logic is the parameter within which we come to conceptualize or ideate about what we, in turn, believe to be the world around us, the world that we "think" we "know."

From the above perspective, to a writer the world "reads" like a book; to a filmmaker it "looks" like a series and juxtaposition of images and sounds; and so on. On this microscopic-symbolic level of understanding "media as environments," we do not stand outside of a communication medium when we are "using" it; instead, we are in the middle of it. In this regard, media ecology is interested in understanding the role that a communication medium's intrinsic symbolic structure plays in human perception, human consciousness, or the human minding process, such as how a particular writing system structures or defines the ways in which its users conceptualize and describe their experience.

It must be noted that, in real life, people do not always consciously separate the sensorial from the symbolic when they use the media either for gathering information or communicating with others. On this level, therefore, our study would of course become more complicated because it expects us to understand media not as two sets of environments (the sensorial and symbolic) but how the two interact in people's construction of their surroundings.

Single-Medium or Multiple-Media Environments

The study of media as environments can get even more complicated. On one level, we may examine the intrinsic characteristics of the sensorial-symbolic environment of a single communication medium (e.g., Meyrowitz, 1994). But on another, realistic level, we live in a multimedia society in the sense that we use a combination of a number of media or symbol systems at our disposal for communication purposes. To varying degrees, people use or otherwise are exposed to engage in more than just one medium in their everyday life for news and information, entertainment, and communication. As can be imagined, this multimedia sensorial-symbolic environment is a great deal more complex in nature and difficult to study than the single-medium sensorial-symbolic environment that has been described previously. On this level, our theoretical concern is not only about the inherent sensorial-symbolic structure or characteristics of each of the many media people use in their everyday life. Instead, our task is to examine the dynamics among the co-existing media and how their interactions may result in or constitute to a sensorial-symbolic environment whose whole is qualitatively different from the sum of its (multimedia) sensorial-symbolic parts. For example, what would happen in or to the psychodynamics of people who are primarily oral as literacy is being introduced and diffused in their midst? Similarly, we cannot conceptualize the Internet as an entity that is one part writing, one part (still and moving) image, one part sound, one part computer, one part telephone, and so on; instead, it is a unique symbolic environment whose complex new languages, as Carpenter (1960) would have suggested, has yet to be deciphered.

Understanding Environments as Media

Equally important, it is at the multimedia society level of understanding "media as environments" where we may conceptualize "environments as media." Traditionally, when communication scholars talk about media, they tend to refer to informational devices such as the radio, newspaper, television, movies, sound records, the computer, and so on. But while media ecology no doubt considers these as its focus of attention, it nonetheless also looks at how the symbolic structure of environments—such as social environments—may define human interaction or the production of culture; on this level, environments can in theory be regarded as media. The institution of school, to paraphrase Postman, is a complex, multimedia symbolic environment with a unique set of vocabulary and rules that define what its inhabitants do and how they conduct their business, how they relate among themselves, and how they interact with everything else outside of the confines of this environment. Here, we can see a clear lineage of the sociological thinking of Erving Goffman (1959, 1963, 1974) to this aspect of the media ecological approach. His dramaturgical studies, for example, have much to contribute to our understanding of how the symbolic structure of social settings define the parameter for human behavior and interaction (Goffman, 1959). From this angle, we may conceptualize such social-symbolic environments as movie theaters, places of worship, social clubs, or bedrooms as media for communication.

Inherent in this discussion are two conceptions of the relationship between people and their media. The first conception, according to the "normal science" in communication scholarship, refers communication media mainly to informational devices such as the radio, TV, newspaper, CD player, and so on. From this conception, we are standing outside of our communication media, so to speak, as we are using them for communicating with others. The second conception, on the other hand, is the media ecological notion of understanding media as environments or environments as media. From this conception, we are situated within the symbolic structures of media, that is, we are "engaging in" the media for our communication purposes.

MEDIA ECOLOGY'S UNDERLYING THEORETICAL PROPOSITIONS

Embedded in the concept of "media as environments" (or "environments as media") are three interlocking theoretical propositions.

Theoretical Proposition 1

To begin with, media ecology posits that communication media are not neutral, transparent, or value-free conduits for carrying data or information from one place to another. Instead, media's intrinsic physical structure and symbolic form plays a defining role in shaping what and how information is to be encoded and transmitted and therefore how it is to be decoded. On this level of theorizing, a medium's symbolic form entails the characteristics of the code in which the medium presents information (e.g., analogic vs. digital symbols) and the structures in which symbols are put together (e.g., propositional vs. presentational structures). Similarly, a medium's physical structure refers to the characteristics of the technology that carries the code and the physical requirements for encoding, transmitting, storing, retrieving, decoding, and distributing information.

This is an important theoretical proposition because it defines an important aspect of media ecology's paradigm content, arguing that it is the structure of a medium (or media) that defines the nature of information. For example, it is not uncommon that some readers are unhappy about how their favorite novels have been mis/adapted in movies. Of course, one may complain or argue that the unsatisfactory adaptation has been the result of the incompetence on the part of the movie's screenplay writer, director, producer, the actors, and so on. Although this may be a reasonable explanation, the first theoretical proposition of media ecology would suggest that it is pointless to view what is "contained" in the two media, the novel and the movie, as the same information. Instead, it suggests that the novel and the movie embody two very different sets of symbolic and physical structures or forms and therefore what they deliver to their audience, readers and viewers, respectively, are two different set of information or "realities" even as they may have been based on the same source (the "story" contained in the novel).

Theoretical Proposition 2

As a logical extension of the first proposition, media ecology also posits that each medium's unique set of physical, as well as symbolic characteristics carry with them a set of biases. For our understanding, we may consult a set of theoretical generalizations that Nystrom devised:

- Because of the different symbolic forms in which they encode information, different media have different intellectual and emotional biases.
- Because of the different physical forms in which they encode, store, and transmit information, different media have different temporal, spatial, and sensory biases.
- Because of the accessibility of the symbolic forms in which they encode information, different media have different political biases.
- Because their physical form dictates differences in conditions of attendance, different media have different social biases.
- Because of the ways in which they organize time and space, different media have different metaphysical biases.
- Because of their differences in physical and symbolic form, different media have different content biases.
- Because of their differences in physical and symbolic form, and the resulting differences in their intellectual, emotional, temporal, spatial, political, social, metaphysical, and content biases, different media have different epistemological biases. (cited in Lum, 2000b, p. 2)

In short, the different physical and symbolic forms inherent in different communication media presuppose correspondingly different biases.

It is important to delineate this theoretical proposition a bit further by placing it in a larger context partly because no communication medium originates or exists in a vacuum and partly because we need to pinpoint where and when a communication medium's physical and symbolic forms are constituted and, no less, why. In essence, embodied in every communication technology are some human ideas for addressing some pre-existing, real or perceived communication issue; that is, there are always some human reasons or intentions behind the conception and development of any communication technology. On this level, it is these human reasons or intentions that help to decide the physical and symbolic forms of the communication technology in question.

Theoretical Proposition 3

As a logical extension of the second proposition, media ecology further posits that communication media facilitate various psychic or perceptual, social, economic, political, and cultural consequences that are relative to the media's intrinsic biases. This theoretical proposition speaks directly to one of the key theoretical issues of media ecology's paradigm content, namely, the relationship between technology and culture (or vice versa), particularly how communication technology may impact upon culture.

Along a Theoretical Continuum: Soft Determinism, Technology/Culture Symbiosis, Hard Determinism

It is imperative that we view this theoretical proposition as a continuum, and capping the two ends of this continuum are two different interpretive perspectives. At one end of this continuum is what has been called "soft determinism," which posits that although media make events possible, to paraphrase Levinson (1997), the shape and impact "are the result of factors other than the information technology at hand" (p. 3); in other words, human agency plays a determinant role in the consequences of media's development, diffusion, and use. At the other end of the continuum is "hard determinism" which, at its extreme, maintains that technology is the prime determinant of unavoidable social change or, more broadly, history (e.g., M. Smith, 1994).

In addition, located somewhere in the middle of this theoretical continuum is what I would call "culture/technology symbiosis," a perspective on looking at human culture as the result of the ongoing, interdependent and therefore mutually influential interaction between people and their technologies or media (e.g., Lum, 1996). By nature, the concept of "culture/technology symbiosis," when it is placed in the conceptual middle point of this theoretical continuum, does not privilege or bias against either media/technology or human agency in understanding their symbiotic relationship.

In short, all these perspectives acknowledge the defining role of communication technology in culture or human communication, but they differ in their interpretations of how human agency may play a role in social change in the face of technological diffusion or media change. It is also important to point out that these perspectives are meant only as our conceptual aids in understanding this aspect of media ecology's theoretical underpinnings and, by implication, they are not meant as rigid, compartmentalized categories in black or white terms. How any of these theoretical propositions or "deterministic" interpretative perspectives can be put to use most appropriately or effectively would depend on the specific questions being addressed and the specific social and historical contexts the issues are located.

AN EPOCHAL HISTORIOGRAPHY OF MEDIA

Based on the three general theoretical propositions briefly explained here, we should begin to see one of the central, defining features of media ecology's paradigm content: the study of how changes in communication media can facilitate fundamental, large-scale, or ecological changes in culture. In part influenced by the epochal historiography of technology that has been introduced by Mumford (1934; see also Innis, n.d.; Strate & Lum, 2000), media ecology has a unique way of analyzing the evolution of history, or what can be called an "epochal historiography of media." It conceptualizes human history according to the four major communication epoches: orality (as in oral cultures), literacy (as in literate or chirographic cultures), typography (as in typographic cultures), and electronic media (as in cultures dominated by electronic communication technologies).

First Communication Epoch: Orality

What has been known as "orality-literacy studies" has contributed much to media ecology's inquiry into the epochal-historical significance of orality and literacy in history or human development. It is a branch of study in media ecology that draws its inspirations from the works by scholars from many academic fields of study, such as archaeology, classics, folklore, general semantics, linguistics, linguistic anthropology, and media studies. They include Jack Goody (1968, 1977), Havelock (1963, 1976, 1982, 1986), S. I. Hayakawa (1964), Robert K. Logan (1986/2003), Ong (1967, 1982), Postman (1982), Denise Schmandt-Besserat (1996), Edward Sapir (1921), and Whorf (1956). It examines the various psychological, social, economic, political, cultural, and epistemological characteristics of oral cultures. The study of oral cultures in this context focuses mainly on what is known as primary oral cultures. Primary oral cultures are societies that have no writing; equally important, people in primary oral cultures do not even know writing ever exist; that is, all the words they speak do not have a visual or written component to them.

In other words, the major means for communication that primary oral people have are oral speech and other nonwritten aids—such as picture drawings, body language such as facial expression and hand gesture, object arrangements, and so on—for encoding, recording, transferring or transporting, retrieving, and decoding information. As such, some of the fundamental media ecology questions would be: How do primary oral people think and conceptualize the world (or "reality") around them? (They certainly do not "see" any word in their mind when they speak because all their spoken words are pure sound, as we literate people would or could see in our mind the written components of our spoken words as we are sounding them out.) What kind of social, economic, political, and cultural systems do primarily oral people maintain (that, for example, may be significantly different from their counterparts in cultures where formal writing systems exist, if not widespread)? And, equally important, how do we know these characteristics of primary oral cultures since they do not have any written records for our studies?

Second Communication Epoch: Literacy

Similar questions are also posed when media ecologists study cultures with varying degrees of literacy diffusion. For example, how would the introduction of literacy in a society redefine that society's power structure and why? How would primary oral people's thinking processes, or what Ong (1982) calls their psychodynamics, be changed by their exposure to writing (such as when they begin to learn how to write) and how would this shift change how they understand the world around them (or "reality")? Who in a predominately oral society would tend to benefit the most from the introduction of literacy and why? How would the introduction of formal writing systems refine people's concept of "information" and why? Conversely, why do some cultures take longer time in adopting literacy than others; that is, why isn't literacy's diffusion uniform across cultures? And, again, how can we find out about literacy's impact on oral cultures? These are only some of the many questions that media ecologists attempt to address when they examine the role of media change in the transformation of culture.

We may use one example to illustrate this aspect of the media ecology approach to understanding the role of media in cultural change. From the media-epochal historiographic perspective, the elders have tended to be the social elites in primary or predominantly oral cultures because they are these cultures' most important information media: they have accumulated more knowledge and skills through more years of experiencing life. In this regard, the elders are the most cherished reference sources for information, knowledge, and wisdom, as well as practical skills in oral cultures. This is one major reason why, for example, "Having an elder at home is like having a treasure around" has been a time-honored idiom in the predominantly oral culture of China of yesteryear.

But the introduction of literacy gradually takes away the elders' privileged roles in society because they no longer enjoy the kind of control over information in a literate culture as they did in an oral culture. In literate cultures, people learn more and at faster rate even at a young age for as long as they learn to read and write and have access to adequate reading materials. Using a current "college age" standard as a gauge, a person in a literate society can develop a reasonable degree of expertise in a profession by the age of 21, a feat that would have taken someone in an oral culture a substantially longer period of time, if not many lifetimes, to accomplish. Hence, such a media shift has a profound social impact from oral cultures in that an entire social class (the elders as treasures in oral cultures) is displaced or, in Innis' conception, the seat of "the monopoly of knowledge" is shifted from one class to another, from one communication media epoch to another.

Third Communication Epoch: Typography

The third communication epoch in media ecology's media historiography is typography or typographic culture. The development and diffusion of printing technology is by many measures a significant technological improvement in human communication because, with it, people can reproduce a massive quantity of identical information from only one original. The diffusion of Gutenberg metal movable type printing technology in early modern Europe exalted a great deal of short-range, or more immediate changes in societies (Eisenstein, 1983): the creation of new vocations (e.g., type makers, typesetters, printers, etc.), new professions (e.g., writers, editors, book sellers, etc.), and even new industries (e.g., printing machine makers, ink producers, type casters, etc.).

The diffusion of printing technology can also facilitate other more far-reaching social, economic, political, and cultural consequences. For example, how does the diffusion of printing refine society's notion of the nature of information? Here, one may argue that inherited in printing technology is a means for democratizing information that was once held by the social, religious, or political elites in societies with limited means (and little inclination) to reproduce information for mass consumption. If this argument proves to be correct, then what can such a democratization of information do to redefine a culture's existing social, economic, and political order or system? One of the most important scholars whose works have contributed to this part of media ecology's media historiography is Elizabeth Eisenstein (1979, 1983), an historian at the University of Michigan before her retirement. In her detailed historical study of the Gutenberg printing press, Eisenstein (1979) argues that printing technology helped to exalt profoundly far-reaching changes in early modern Europe. Specifically, she suggested that Gutenberg's printing press was instrumental in creating fundamental social, political, cultural, as well as epistemological changes in Europe as seen in the Reformation, the rise of modern science, and the Renaissance. But many other scholars have also contributed a great deal to this particular aspect of media ecology, including Innis (1950, 1951), McLuhan (1962), Postman (1982), as well as some of the writings by Havelock and Ong.

Fourth Communication Epoch: Electronic Media

The fourth communication epoch in media ecology's media-epochal historiography commenced with the rise of electronic media, beginning with electric telegraphy early in the 19th century. Put into a larger historical perspective, rapid technological changes seem to have defined this electronic communication epoch, particularly considering the fact that it took humans millions of years to develop oral speech, thousands of years to develop writing systems, much less to develop printing. Then, within just a little more than a brief century, scores of new media technologies are introduced: the telegraph, the telephone, phonograph, rotary press, motion pictures, automobile, airplane, the radio, sound movies, the transistor, television, the computer, the satellite, laser, video disc, VTRs and VCRs, video games, the Internet, the World Wide Web, wireless personal communications, and so on.[32] Human history seemed to have been suddenly thrust into an electronic communication epoch in which changes were commonplace but, perhaps more importantly, the rate and nature of change itself had also been changed.

Regardless of one's media ecological orientation, it seems reasonable to suggest that what electronic communication technologies have introduced is an entirely new way of knowing and perceiving because they have a set of temporal and spatial, as well as symbolic and physical structural biases that are unlike the previous three communication epochs. This is McLuhan's (1964) brilliance as evoked in his famous aphorism, "the medium is the message"—the change that electronic media have facilitated is not the "content" of what people talk about but the ways in which people come to know and talk about their world. Electronic media completely obliterate our traditional notion of time and space in human communication and culture. The linear, rationalistic way of thinking, one of the defining characteristic of literate and typographic cultures, is now being challenged by the multidirectional, intuitive way of thinking, seeing, and knowing that is symptomatic of postmodern cultures where all sorts of electronic media, such as television, the Internet, and multimedia, reign.

But how and the extent to which electronic media may impact culture is still a hotly debated subject among scholars from diverse academic fields and along the theoretical continuum described earlier. Some sources are listed herein (by years of publication) for an initial understanding of the various media ecological approaches in this regard: Wiener (1948), Innis (1951), McLuhan (1964), Daniel Boorstin (1961/1987), Tong Schwartz (1973), Weizenbaum (1976), R. Murray Schafer (1980), Bolter (1984), Meyrowitz (1985), Postman (1985), Beniger (1986), Gary Gumpert (1987), Carey (1988a), McLuhan and McLuhan (1988), Perkinson (1991), Paul Thaler (1994, 1997), Lum (1996), Deibert (1997), Bolter and Richard Grusin (1999), Ray Gozzi, Jr. (1999), Levinson (1999), Strate, Ron Jacobson, and Stephanie Gibson (1996), Susan Barnes (2001), and Strate (in press).

ORGANIZATION OF THE BOOK

This book was conceived to give the readers a general historiographic framework for understanding some of the issues, theories, or themes, as well as some of the major thinkers behind them that define the paradigm content of media ecology as a theory group and an intellectual tradition. Our interest is not entirely vested in the theories alone. By also knowing the historical and intellectual background behind them presents a more grounded understanding of the theories' relative strengths and weaknesses and application to explain media and culture in our times.

Editorial Principles

To achieve this general goal, Chapters 2 through 13 focus on a short list of media ecology's foundational thinkers and some of the key theoretical issues they share. Two sets of themes are evident among these thinkers to varying degrees: the relationship between technology and culture, as well as the relationship between language and culture.

The book's ensuing discussion begins with Postman's essay on "The Humanism of Media Ecology" (Chapter 2) in which Postman who, as the founding intellectual leader of media ecology as a theory group, gives us a glimpse at the early conception and the humanistic underpinnings of media ecology. Chapters 3 through 13 synthesize and analyze the scholarly works of a short list of media ecology paradigm thinkers such as Eisenstein, Ellul, Havelock, Innis, Langer, McLuhan, Mumford, Ong, Postman, and Whorf, as well as that of Carey's, whose intellectual-historical writings about the like of Innis, McLuhan, and Mumford have been an inspiration to many aspiring media ecologists. Of special mention is the fact that, due to its limited space, this volume regrettably cannot feature other media ecology paradigm thinkers, such as Patrick Geddes, Alfred Korzybski, and Norbert Weiner, to name just a few, whose scholarship has contributed to the rise of media ecology as a theoretical perspective. The epilogue is a brief discussion on some recent developments, particularly in the area of institutional development, in media ecology.

There is a secondary organizing principle in the ordering of these chapters. Although all the chapters have an interest in technology and culture, Chapters 10 through Chapter 13 have a distinct focus on language and culture. Chapters 10 and 11, on Whorf/Langer and Langer, respectively, serve as a general theoretical orientation to some basic concepts in language, thought, and culture, as well as the philosophy of symbols. Chapters 12 and 13 address three specific key themes in media ecology that are arranged more or less in accordance to media ecology's epochal historiography of media: orality and literacy (Chapter 12, on the work of Havelock, Ong, Perry, etc.) and typography (Chapter 13, on the work of Eisenstein, McLuhan, Postman, etc.). Although many of the featured paradigm thinkers of media ecology have addressed issues relating to electronic media, the reader may specifically consult Morrison's Chapter 7 on McLuhan and

Gencarelli's Chapter 8 on Postman for two ecological perspectives on understanding the impact of electronic media.

Another editorial principle has also been applied in order to facilitate subject focus and format coherence among the various chapters. Although every effort has been made to retain each chapter author's distinct voice and creativity, all authors were given a set of general guidelines for their chapters' overall development and formatting. The reader should expect to see that a brief intellectual biography is integrated in the introduction and discussion of featured media ecologists; such a biography is meant to highlight how and the extent to which their education, as well as their immediate social and political surroundings may have played a role in the development of their ideas. Typically, each chapter is organized according to the major themes or theories that are associated with the media ecologist(s) being featured. Wherever appropriate, each chapter also provides a comparative analysis of works among some of foundational media ecologists that are featured in the volume, as well as an assessment of the strengths and weaknesses of the theories being examined.

Prologue to the Chapters

The followings are brief overviews of the ensuing 12 chapters with contributions from the authors' chapter abstracts.

Chapter 2. Neil Postman's chapter on "The Humanism of Media Ecology" comes from his keynote speech at the inaugural annual convention of the Media Ecology Association in 2000. In this slightly edited version from the convention electronic Proceedings, he gives us a glimpse at his conception of media ecology and its initial institutionalization as a degree program at New York University. But the significance of this chapter lies in his articulation of the humanistic dimensions of media ecology. To Postman (1988), media ecology is a branch of moral theology and therefore studying media without a moral or ethnical context is pointless. He asks media ecologists to take a humanistic position when examining media's impact on culture. To this end, Postman offers four guiding questions: To what extent does a medium contribute to the uses and development of rational thought? To what extent does a medium contribute to the development of democratic processes? To what extent do new media give greater access to meaningful information? To what extent do new media enhance or diminish our moral sense, our capacity for goodness? Postman's humanism or moralist concerns form the basis of his thinking and writings not only as an innovative scholar and educationist but also as an effective social critic and public intellectual.

Chapter 3. In "Lewis Mumford and the Ecology of Technics," Lance Strate and I suggest that although Mumford's scholarship does not focus specifically on communication media per se, his profound understanding of technology's ecological and foundational impact on the development of human civilization has contributed much to the theoretical underpinnings of media ecology. Our study also highlights how the work of Mumford's mentor, Geddes, a founder of the ecological movement at the turn of the 20th century who coined the term human ecology, had deeply influenced his thinking. Mumford is presented here as one of media ecology's earliest foundational thinkers. After a biographical sketch with an emphasis on the larger cultural and historical contexts in which his scholarship is located, the chapter focuses its analysis on three aspects of Mumford's voluminous works: his epochal historiography of technology, the techno-organicism in his thinking about technology and human development, and his critique of the megamachine. Suggestions are also made that some of Mumford's ideas have predated some of McLuhan's. The chapter concludes with a discussion of the humanism and ecological ethics inherent in Mumford's work, his life, and the activism embedded in his media ecology.

Jacques Ellul the sociologist is often regarded by many as a hardcore technological determinist in his interpretation of technology and the human conditions (e.g., M. Smith, 1994). But it is argued that such a conception of Ellul's thinking while ignoring his theological inquiry into spiritual freedom and redemption from the confines imposed by technology can only undermine our understanding of the complexity of his scholarship. To more fully examine his dialectical thinking, two chapters on Ellul are included in this volume not only to give the readers a better understanding of him as both a sociologist and a theologian but also an opportunity to see how he attempted to understand human conditions from two seemingly diametrically-opposed lenses, as well as an often-overlooked spiritual dimension of media ecology (see also Gozzi, 2000).

Chapter 4. In "Jacques Ellul: Technique, Propaganda and Modern Media," Randy Kluver acknowledges Ellul as a major social theorist for his insightful and intriguing analyses of the sociological and political systems of the modern world but one whose deep concern with issues of human communication is almost unknown among writers within that discipline. He further explores Ellul's sociological insight into the nature of the technological order, particularly in reference to the mass media and modern society—one that should be a welcome challenge to the presumptions that underlie media consumption. This study examines the major concepts that form the basis of two of Ellul's most profound and influential sociological theories, *la technique* and propaganda, and demonstrates how they have contributed to a defining aspect of media ecology's theoretical underpinnings. This chapter serves as an overview of Ellul's sociological thought for understanding contemporary society and the role of media in society; it also illustrates how his scholarship relates to that of other major thinkers in the media ecology tradition.

Chapter 5. Whereas Kluver was asked to focus his analysis on Ellul's sociological writings, Clifford Christian was charged with the task of illuminating Ellul's scholarship dialectically, that is, assessing his body of scholarly works within a larger context of both his sociological as well as theological theories. In "Ellul as Theologian in Counterpoint," Christian begins his analysis with an historiographic account of Ellul's early intellectual upbringing, noting Marxism's profound impact on his perspective on the political, economic, and social problems of his time. He also points out the importance of Ellul's conversion to Christianity, which took place after reading Epistle to the Roman. From then, Ellul would embark upon a lifelong quest for the spiritual understanding of the technological society and the human condition of modernity. This essay suggests that Ellul, influenced by Barth's dialectical theology as a method of inquiry, would provide theological counterpoints to his major sociological theories. Ellul's dialectical scholarship, as Christian notes, was not so much an attempt to reconcile between the sociological and the theological as much as it was Ellul's way of wanting to understand the seeming contradiction between the two in his quest for genuine human restoration from the tyranny of *la technique*. Christian concludes with a brief assessment of Ellul's scholarship as it relates to that of Mumford, McLuhan, and Postman's, as well as a critique of some of the inadequacies of Ellul's scholarship.

Chapter 6. Paul Heyer's chapter on "Harold Innis' Legacy in the Media Ecology Tradition" is an intellectual-biographical examination of the life and work of Harold Innis and how his scholarship has played a role in the rise of the media ecology theoretical perspective. It provides an assessment of Innis' early work in political economy, both on its own terms and with respect to how it provided him with a conceptual starting point for exploring the role of communication media in history. Innis's historiography is viewed as the programmatic foundation for an innovative approach to studying the relationship between communication and culture. An effort is also made to explain some of the key concepts he developed in working through this project—time bias, space bias, the oral tradition, monopolies of knowledge, and the mechanization of culture. Finally, Innis's influence on the tradition of communication studies/media ecology is considered by a brief analysis of how his work has been utilized by scholars such as James Carey, Daniel Czitrom, Joshua Meyrowitz, and Neil Postman.

Chapter 7. In "Marshall McLuhan: The Modern Janus," James C. Morrison examines the work of Marshall McLuhan, one of media ecology's most visible and influential public figures. McLuhan was among the most important intellectual founders of media ecology and the ways in which his original and at times prophetic ideas about media and culture have formed a cornerstone of media ecology scholarship. But McLuhan's scholarship has also been controversial, the author contends, partly because it is original and perhaps even threatening to the academically entrenched at the time of his writings. Nonetheless, McLuhan's unconventional thinking, and eclectic presentation of his ideas, often frustrated many of his supporters and critics alike. For this reason, Morrison sets out to help dispel some of the common misconceptions of McLuhan's work for seasoned scholars who may still be struggling with its challenges and for novices who are just beginning to engage it. He provides a careful analysis of McLuhan's seeming nonmoralistic stance, his intellectual roots in Modernism, post-Newtonian science, as well as ancient and medieval rhetoric and how they are expressed in his media scholarship. Equally important, this chapter highlights the relevance of McLuhan's ideas to our understanding of today's electronic communication environments.

Chapter 8. In "Neil Postman and the Rise of Media Ecology," Thomas F. Gencarelli provides an insightful analysis of an important chapter in the intellectual history of media ecology's rise as a theory group. This chapter addresses two interrelated questions. First, how does Postman's thinking and writing embody both a theory of media ecology? In addressing the first question, he also places and examines Postman's scholarship in the larger context of the media ecology canon. In the chapter's first part, Gencarelli chronicles the evolution of Postman's thought through an examination of 17 of his 20-plus major works and what each of them has contributed to the whole of his media ecological theory. The chapter's second part delineates the recurring themes running through these works, including some of Postman's signature ideas embedded in these themes. It is these themes and ideas, according to Gencarelli, that comprise the fundamental paradigm content of what we today refer to as media ecology.

Although James W. Carey is more often identified with American cultural studies and journalism than with media ecology, many of his writings over more than four decades have been embraced by the media ecologically minded, so much so that at the 2003 annual convention of the Media Ecology Association he was given a Louis Forsdale Award for Outstanding Educator in the Field of Media Ecology.[33] Considered by many the dean of American cultural studies, Carey has been one of the most insightful interpreters of the scholarly works of several major media ecological thinkers, such as Mumford, Innis, and McLuhan, as well as the Chicago School scholars whose pioneering research has contributed much to the foundations of North American communication studies. Carey himself is among the most original thinkers in the communication discipline and his scholarship has inspired and helped facilitate a cultural turn in a field that had otherwise been preoccupied with empiricist research on short-term behavioral impact of media (e.g., Carey, 1975, 1988a). On another level, in his scathing critique of what he considers as a profound lack of political sensitivity in McLuhan's media scholarship (Carey, 1997), as well as his discontent over the inadequacy of Mumford's humanism and the absence of hope in Ellul, Carey argues for an ethics and morals of democracy as the underpinning of media ecology in the building of a more humane and participatory society.

Chapter 9. It is within the above context that the relevance of Fredrick Wasser's chapter on "James Carey: The Search for Cultural Balance" can be more fully understood. In his study, Wasser provides an analytical survey of Casey's scholarly works along three concurrent and interweaving lines of thinking: Carey's elaboration of the ritual functions of communication; his insistence on the mutually determining relations of technology and communication and his use of communications history to explore the tensions between economics and culture; and his abiding and influential examination of the uses of journalism education. A former student of Carey's, Wasser also highlights Carey's persuasive power in citing rich intellectual histories of such thinkers as DeTocqueville, Dewey, Innis, Mumford, and McLuhan as part of his methodology.

Chapter 10. As has been briefly suggested above, one of media ecology's major theoretical concerns has been the interrelationship among language, thought, and culture. In "Symbols, Thought, and Reality: The Contributions of Benjamin Lee Whorf and Susanne K. Langer to Media Ecology," Christine Nystrom suggests that media ecology may be defined as the study of how our symbol systems and media technologies shape how we construct "reality" and its implications on our social institutions, cultural practices, and values. This chapter begins with a discussion of the works by Albert Einstein and Werner Heisenberg in physics early in the 20th century with a particular focus on the origins of the idea that our technologies and systems of symbolic representation play any role in "reality" construction. The discussion then proceeds to an examination of how this idea has become prominent in the studies of language, culture, and communication through the ground-breaking work of linguistic anthropologists such as Whorf and symbolic philosophers such as Langer. This essay is set out to highlight and explicate some of the key ideas that Whorf and Langer set forth in their work that have been part of media ecology's theoretical underpinnings and intellectual foundations.

Chapter 11. Whereas Nystrom's chapter illuminates some of Langer's key ideas and how they relate to media ecology's paradigm content, John Powers' chapter on "Susanne Langer's Philosophy of Mind: Some Implications for Media Ecology" is an attempt to explain Langer's symbolic philosophy as a whole and to provide something of a general reference for media ecologists who would like to try to extract from her work the concepts and theories that can contribute to the larger goal of constructing a coherent and comprehensive media ecology paradigm. This chapter introduces the readers to the larger body of Langer's work, including nine of her major works that spanned more than five decades beginning with *The Practice of Philosophy* (1930) and culminating in the three volumes of *Mind: An Essay on Human Feeling* (1967, 1972, 1982). Some of the issues examined include Langer's sense of what philosophy is, how she approached problems of media and symbolism, how a coherent taxonomy of media forms might be developed from those theories, how Langer's philosophy can be used to draw segregated theories into closer and more mutually supporting alignments than now exist, and how it can be used to provide a set of criteria for critiquing and evaluating competing theories.

Chapter 12. In "The Orality-Literacy Theorems and Media Ecology," Bruce Gronbeck provides an analytical introduction to one of media ecology most important theoretical canons in that changes in communication media would result in changes in the operations of human consciousness and human culture. In it, he examines the scholarly works by classicist Eric Havelock and the literateurs McLuhan and Ong, as well as those by anthropologists Ernst Mayr, Claude Lévi-Strauss, Jack Goody and Ian Watt in their formulation of what he calls the orality-literacy theorems, on both the macro and the micro levels. On the macro level, the orality-literacy theorems address issues relating to the roles played by dominant media in societies in general, such as questions about media determinism or pragmatism in oral, literate, typographic, and electronic societies. On the micro level, the theorems in question are concerned more with the theories of cognitive processes with specific attention to how the mind processes messages especially through acoustic, literate, and visual channels. In his synthesis, Gronbeck also provides an assessment of the various strengths and weaknesses of these theorems, as well as how the reader may use these theorems productively in understanding issues relating to orality and literacy in today's multimedia environment. Orality and literacy embodies the first two major eras in the epochal historiography of media.

Chapter 13. Typography is at the third stage in media ecology's epochal historiography of media. Joseph Ashcroft's chapter on "Typography and Its Influence on Culture and Communication: Some Media Ecological

Interpretations" is a summary of some of the media ecological theories of how print may have impacted upon culture, primarily in the Western world, in the centuries that followed the introduction of the Gutenberg (metal moveable type) printing press. By synthesizing the scholarship of Eisenstein, Havelock, McLuhan, Ong, Postman, Lucien Febvre and Henri-Jean Martin (1976), and others, the author discusses the various long-term impact of the diffusion of typography as it related to the Protestant Reformation, the rise of nationalism, the rise and transformation of modern science, and the emergence of individualism and democracy. The chapter also considers how print may have transformed people's conception of their relationship to what they read, to others, and to the world around them, as well as how the concept of childhood may have been a consequence of print. In concluding his synthesis and analysis of the media ecological study of print, the author suggests that media ecologists are interested in the broad cultural effects of media, rather than individual effects. Moreover, media ecology's methodology is mostly qualitative, that is, theory-building rather than theory-testing. How individuals are influenced by media is studied primarily within the context of the cultural environment within which the individual lives.

Epilogue. At the end of the book, I tie some of the loose ends together with a brief discussion of some of the recent developments in the field, including the founding of the Media Ecology Association and how it may signal and symbolize the beginning of a new chapter in the intellectual history of media ecology as a theory group.

In Summary

This book is designed to provide a general historiographic framework for understanding the development of media ecology that has a multidisciplinary intellectual tradition with a more or less coherent set of theoretical underpinnings. The 13 chapters (and the epilogue) seek to highlight, synthesize, and analyze some of media ecology's defining ideas, theories, or themes about the formal, foundational, and ecological impact of media technology on culture and human communication; the thinkers behind these ideas; the intellectual contexts in which these ideas came into being; as well as how and the extent to which we may use these ideas in our times. There exists among these chapters a degree of theoretical and thematic overlap. But such overlap is both inevitable and essential, for two reasons. First, it helps create and maintain a narrative coherence among the chapters even as the authors retain their distinct voices and in some cases hold diverging interpretations. Second, the overlap is inevitable and essential because, as has been suggested above, media ecology as a theory group and an intellectual tradition is manifested in part by a coherent body of multidisciplinary literature and theoretical perspectives.

Taken together, it is hoped that the chapters in this book can give the reader a solid foundation for an initial understanding of the media ecology tradition that has been a missing chapter in the intellectual history and historiography of North American communication scholarship. In short, this book seeks to synthesize the various theoretical threads that link the media ecology tradition, while narrating an intriguing history of men and women, whose collective wisdom has presented us with a vital world view of the relationship among culture, technology, and communication and, essentially, our place in our modern technological society.

ENDNOTES

1. "Very Model Of A Media Ecologist" is copyrighted by Robert Blechman (1976), a member of the class of 1977 of NYU's Media Ecology Program. It is reproduced in its entirety in this chapter with the expressed consent of the author whose generosity is gratefully acknowledged herein. Blechman suggested to his classmates to prepare a 3-minute talk on the topic "My Metaphor for Media Ecology" that he would videotape for presentation at the 1977 Media Ecology Conference so "Not only would each of us get three minutes of fame, but this would also allow those who couldn't attend the conference to be present 'in spirit.' This multi-part address was very much in keeping with the 'do your own thing' atmosphere of the times. As it turns out, we also created a mini time capsule of who we were and what we thought about way back when" (Robert Blechman, personal communication, June 27, 2003). Blechman sang his poem in his 3-minute video presentation at the conference.
2. The *Journal of Communication* symposium on *The Living McLuhan* also carries a co-authored essay by McLuhan and Powers (1981).
3. See also the International Jacques Ellul Society (http://www.ellul.org/).
4. See also Jeremy Campbell (1982) for an excellent journalistic synthesis of the rise of information sciences, particularly cybernetics and information theory.
5. The use of the word "Notes" in this manner has been inspired by Wendy Leeds-Hurwitz's (1990) ground-breaking essay on the intellectual history of intercultural communication.
6. Strate (2003a) suggested, somewhat playfully, that media ecology could be considered a "genre" of media studies.
7. This quote comes from a personal copy of the keynote speech that Postman gave me for inclusion in the volume. The keynote has later been included in the online Proceedings of the 2000 inaugural annual convention of the Media Ecology Association (http://www.mediaecology.org) and is retrievable at http://www.mediaecology.org/publications/proceedings/v1/humanism_of_media_ecology.html.
8. While a professor in education, Forsdale has long had a profound interest in communication (e.g., Forsdale, 1981).

9. *Teaching as a Subversive Activity* (Postman & Weingartner, 1969) and *Teaching as a Conserving Activity* (Postman, 1979) are cited in Postman's entry in a "Who's Who in the Great Debate" list when the United States was engaged in yet another school reform debate in the 1980s (Gross & Gross, 1985). See also *The School Book: For People Who Want to Know What All the Hollering is About* for another statement by Postman and Weingartner (1973) about their position on the school debate during that period of time.

10. In the same research, Craig (1999) later suggested how communication theory can and should be a field of study.

11. It should be noted that not all critical scholars are Marxists.

12. For a more comprehensive overview of Fuller's thinking, Zung (2001) provides a very useful anthology of select chapters from Fuller's 20-plus books.

13. Select publications by the seven "postindustrial prophets" in Kuhns (1971) are included in a six-page "Preliminary Bibliography in Communication" that is attributed to Don Hausdorff (1970), one of the early faculty members in NYU's Media Ecology Program.

14. Before joining the classics faculty at the University of Toronto (UT; 1929-1947), Havelock taught at Acadia University in Nova Scotia in 1926-1929. He subsequently left UT for Harvard University (1947-1963) and later for Yale University (1963-1971). See Farrell (2000, n. 1, pp. 198-199) for a more detailed chronology of Havelock's academic appointments.

15. Donald Theall (1988) has suggested that the gathering and works of these and other like-minded scholars—including Dorothy Lee (1954, 1959), who had contributed to *Explorations*—at UT formed the basis of what he called the Toronto School of Communication.

16. The "electronic revolution" coincided with what Thomas L. McPhail (2002), who has taught with Marshall McLuhan in Canada, calls "electronic colonialism" that began in the 1950s. Electronic colonialism, according to McPhail, "represents the dependent relationship in LDCs [less developed countries] on the West established by the importation of communication hardware and foreign-produced software, along with engineers, technicians, and related information protocols, that establish a set of foreign norms, values, and expectations that, to varying degrees, alter domestic cultures, habits, values, and the socialization process itself" (p. 14).

17. Lyrics from Marvin Gaye's 1971 popular song "Mercy, Mercy Me (The Ecology)."

18. For full disclosure—borrowing a term in standard journalistic practice—I studied under Neil Postman, Terence Moran, Christine Nystrom, and Henry Perkinson between 1985-1989 and earned my PhD degree in media ecology from NYU in 1989. It is important to emphasize that a discussion of the development of the graduate degree program at NYU is included in this chapter because it is an important chapter in the initial institutionalization of media ecology as a theory group. Therefore, the discussion herein should not be construed as institutional promotion.

19. A Jesuit priest and media educator, Culkin left Fordham sometime after McLuhan returned to Toronto in 1968 and founded a nonprofit organization by the name Center for Understanding Media. In 1975, he founded the Graduate

Media Studies Program at the New School for Social Research, currently the New School, that he characterized as having "based entirely on McLuhan's ideas" (Culkin, 1989, p. 109). Unfortunately, Culkin's work as a media educator and activist in the media ecological tradition has been grossly under-acknowledged in the literature.

20. For Postman's program or curricular development at NYU, I have consulted all the editions of *New York University Bulletin: School of Education* between the academic years 1966 and 2003; but only several editions are actually cited in the current study. Note also that George N. Gordon, who was on the faculty until the mid-1960s and a mentor of Terence Moran, had played an important role in curriculum development and teaching in the department. The focus of some of the courses is reflected in his scholarly publications (e.g., Gordon, 1965, 1969, 1971, 1975, 1977). Gordon would later retire as a professor in communication at Fordham University.

21. The reader would find it useful to cross-reference this discussion on Postman's curricular activities at NYU with the discussion on his four phases of writings in Gencarelli's chapter on Postman's scholarship in this volume.

22. The doctoral program was entitled "Communications" in the 1970-1971 edition of the *NYU Bulletin* (1970, p. 169). The title was formally changed to Media Ecology the year thereafter.

23. Moran ceased to be the director of the MA program in media ecology at NYU as of the end of Summer 2005.

24. My assessment of Moran's effectiveness as a teacher and dissertation director has been based on my observation between 1985 and 1989, during which time I was a doctoral candidate and fellow in the Program and my personal experience with him as my dissertation committee director.

25. By Moran's acknowledgment, Gordon (e.g., 1971), one of his former professors in the department, had had an important influence on his interest in propaganda studies.

26. Nystrom retired from full-time teaching at NYU at the end of the 2001-2002 school year.

27. Young's introduction of Watzlawick's scholarship in the Media Ecology Program's curriculum has been collaborated independently between one of the program's first doctoral degree holders from the class of 1974, Hugh McCarney (personal communication, April 8, 2003), and Moran (personal communication, May 6, 2003).

28. Over various occasions late in the 1980s, Postman told his doctoral students how young German readers of *Amusing Ourselves to Death* waited for his autograph in front of his hotel in Germany where he was invited as a guest speaker.

29. Meyrowitz's (1985) *No Sense of Place* received a "Best Book On Electronic Media" award in 1986 from the National Association of Broadcasters and Broadcast Education Association.

30. After his retirement as a professor emeritus at the University of California in San Diego 1990, Schiller taught as an adjunct professor in the Department of Culture and Communication for several Spring semesters in the 1990s (*New York University Bulletin*, 1994). He passed away on January 29, 2000 (for an intellectual biography of Schiller see Maxwell, 2003). Gitlin was recruited from the

University of California in Berkeley later in the 1990s (*New York University Bulletin*, 1997). He had joint appointments in a number of academic units at NYU, including the Department of Culture and Communication in the School of Education and in the Department of Journalism and Mass Communication at the Graduate School of Arts and Sciences. He subsequently left NYU for Columbia University's Graduate School of Journalism in 2002.

31. As discussed in the epilogue of this book, it was a small group of PhD graduates from the NYU program who would later founded the Media Ecology Association, which can be considered as the second institutional base of media ecology as a theory group.

32. The observation of the rapid-change nature of the electronic media epoch was made and noted in one of the doctoral seminars I attended with Postman and Nystrom in the late 1980s.

33. Carey has also been invited to make special appearances (including a few keynote speeches) at NYU's Media Ecology Conference and the annual convention of the Media Ecology Association (which is independent of NYU) since the mid-1990s (e.g., Carey, 2003a). Flayhan (2001) also notes the relationship between Carey's cultural studies and media ecology.

REFERENCES

Acland, C. R., & Buxton, W. J. (Eds.). (1995). *Harold Innis in the new century: Reflections and refractions.* Montreal, Canada: McGill-Queen's University Press.

Adorno, T., & Horkheimer, M. (1977). The culture industry: Enlightenment as mass deception (abridged). In J. Curran, M. Gurevitch, & J. Woollacott (Eds.), *Mass communication and society* (pp. 349-383). London: Edward Arnold (Publishers) Ltd. & The Open University Press.

Barnes, S. (2001). *Online connections: Internet interpersonal relationships.* Cresskill, NJ: Hampton Press.

Beniger, J. R. (1986). *The control revolution: Technological and economic origins of the information society.* Cambridge, MA & London: Harvard University Press.

Berger, P., Berger, B., & Kellner, H. (1973). *The homeless mind.* New York: Random House.

Bernays, E. (1965). *Biography of an idea: Memoirs of public relations counsel Edward L. Bernays.* New York: Simon & Schuster.

Birdwhistell, R. L. (1952). *Introduction to kinesics.* Louisville, KY: University of Louisville Press.

Birdwhistell, R. L. (1970). *Kinesics and context: Essays on body motion communication.* Philadelphia: University of Pennsylvania Press.

Blechman, R. (1976). *Very model of a media ecologist.* Unpublished poem.

Bolter, J. D. (1984). *Turing's man: Western culture in the computer age.* Chapel Hill: University of North Carolina Press.

Bolter, J. D., & Grusin, R. (1999). *Remediation: Understanding new media.* Cambridge, MA: MIT Press.

Boorstin, D. J. (1987). The image: A guide to pseudo-events in America (25th anniversary edition). New York: Atheneum. (Original work published 1961 as *The image: What happened to the American dream*)

Bruner, J. S. (1962). *On knowing: Essays for the left hand*. Cambridge, MA: Belknap Press of Harvard University Press.

Bruner, J. S. (1983). *Child's talk: Learning to use language*. New York: W.W. Norton.

Bruner, J. S. (1986). *Actual minds, possible worlds*. Cambridge, MA: Harvard University Press.

Bryant, J., & Thompson, S. (2002). *Fundamentals of media effects*. New York: McGraw-Hill.

Campbell, J. (1982). *Grammatical man*. New York: Touchstone.

Cantril, H. (Ed.). (1960). *The morning notes of Adelbert Ames, Jr.* New Brunswick, NJ: Rutgers University Press.

Carey, J. W. (1968). Harold Adams Innis and Marshall McLuhan. In R. B. Rosenthal (Ed.), *McLuhan: Pro and con* (pp. 270-308). New York: Funk & Wagnalls.

Carey, J. W. (1975). Communication and culture. *Communication Research, 2*, 176-197.

Carey, J. W. (1981). McLuhan and Mumford: The roots of modern media analysis. *Journal of Communication, 31*(3), 162-178.

Carey, J. W. (1988a). *Communication as culture: Essays on media and society*. Boston: Unwin Hyman.

Carey, J. W. (1988b). Space, time, and communications: A tribute to Harold Innis. In J.W. Carey (Ed.), *Communication as culture: Essays on media and society* (pp. 142-172). Boston: Unwin Hyman.

Carey, J. W. (1996). The Chicago School and mass communication research. In E.E. Dennis & E. Wartella (Eds.), *American communication research: The remembered history* (pp. 21-38). Mahwah, NJ: Erlbaum.

Carey, J. W. (1997). Harold Innis and the origins of media ecology. Unpublished keynote speech to the Media Ecology Conference, Rosendale, NY.

Carey, J. W. (2003a). At the scene of creation: Toronto, 1948. Unpublished keynote speech given at the fourth annual convention of the Media Ecology Association, Hempstead, NY.

Carey, J. W. (2003b). The democratic dimensions of media ecology. Remarks made on a panel on "The philosophical dimensions of media ecology" at the annual convention of the National Communication Association.

Carpenter, E. (1960). The new languages. In E. Carpenter & H. M. McLuhan (Eds.), *Explorations in communication: An anthology* (pp. 162-179). Boston: Beacon.

Carpenter, E. (1972). *Oh, what a blow that phantom gave me!* Toronto, Canada: Bantam Books.

Carpenter, E., & McLuhan, H.M. (Eds.). (1960). *Explorations in communication: An anthology*. Boston: Beacon.

Christians, C. G., & Van Hook, J.M. (Eds.). (1981). *Jacques Ellul: Interpretive essays*. Urbana: University of Illinois Press.

Cooley, C. H. (1909). *Social organization: A study of the larger mind*. New York: Scribner's.

Craig, R. T. (1999). Communication theory as a field. *Communication Theory, 9*, 119-161.

Crane, D. (1972). *Invisible colleges*. Chicago: University of Chicago Press.

Culkin, J. (1989). Marshall's New York adventure: Reflections on McLuhan's year at Fordham University. In G. Sanderson & F. Macdonald (Eds.), *Marshall McLuhan: The man and his message* (pp. 99-110). Golden, CO: Fulcrum.

Czitrom, D. J. (1982). *Media and the American mind: From Morse to McLuhan.* Chapel Hill, University of North Carolina Press.

Deibert, R. (1997). *Parchment, printing, and hypermedia: Communication and world order transformation.* New York: Columbia University Press.

Delia, J. G. (1987). Communication research: A history. In C. Berger & S. Chaffee (Eds.), *Handbook of communication science* (pp. 20-98). Newbury Park, CA: Sage.

Dennis, E. E., & Wartella, E. (Eds.). (1996). *American communication research: The remembered history.* Mahwah, NJ: Erlbaum.

Dervin, B., Grossberg, L., O'Keefe, B.J., & Wartella, E. (Eds.). (1989). *Rethinking communication* (Vols. 1-2). Beverly Hills, CA: Sage.

Dewey, J. (1916). *Democracy and education.* New York: Macmillan.

Eisenstein, E. L. (1979). *The printing press as an agent of change: Communications and cultural transformations in early modern Europe.* Cambridge, England: Cambridge University Press.

Eisenstein, E. L. (1983). *The printing revolution in early modern Europe.* Cambridge, England: Press Syndicate of the University of Cambridge.

Ellul, J. (1964). *The technological society* (J. Wilkinson, Trans.). New York: Vintage Book. (Original work published, 1954 as *La Technique, ou l'enjeu du siècle.* Paris: Armand Colin)

Ellul, J. (1965). *Propaganda: The formation of man's attitude* (K. Kellen, Trans.). New York: Knopf. (Original work published 1962 as *Propagandes.* Paris: Armand Colin)

Ellul, J. (1980). *The technological system* (J. Neugroschel, Trans.). New York: Continuum.

Ellul J. (1981). *Perspectives on our age* (J. Neugroschel, Trans.). New York: The Seabury Press.

Ellul, J. (1985). *The humiliation of the word* (J. Hanks, Trans.). Grand Rapids, MI: Eerdmans.

Ellul, J. (1990). *The technological bluff* (G. Bromiley, Trans.). Grand Rapids, MI: Eerdmans.

Enzensberger, H. M. (1974). *The consciousness industry.* New York: Seabury Press.

Ewen, S. (1976). *Captains of consciousness: Advertising and the social roots of the consumer culture.* New York: McGraw-Hill.

Ewen, S. (1996). *PR! A social history of spin.* New York: BasicBooks.

Farrell, T. J. (2000). *Walter Ong's contributions to cultural studies.* Cresskill, NJ: Hampton.

Farrell, T. J., & Soukup, P. (Eds.). (2002). *An Ong reader: Further challenges for inquiry.* Cresskill, NJ: Hampton Press.

Febvre, L., & Martin, H. (1976). *The coming of the book: The impact of printing 1450–1800* (D. Gerard, Trans.). London: Humanities Press.

Ferment in the field [Special issue]. (1983). *Journal of Communication, 33*(3), 1-368.

Finkelstein, S. (1968). *Sense & nonsense of McLuhan.* New York: International Publishers.

Flayhan, D. (2001). Cultural studies and media ecology: Meyrowitz's medium theory and Carey's cultural studies. *The New Jersey Journal of Communication, 9*(1), 21-44.

Fleck, L. (1979). Genesis and development of a scientific fact. Translated by F. Bradley and T. J. Trenn. Chicago: University of Chicago Press. (Original work published 1935 as *Entstehung und Entwicklung einer wissenschaftlichen Tatsache: Einfuhrung in die Lehre vom Denkstil und Denkkollektiv*. Basel, Switzerland: Benno Schwabe)

Forsdale, L. (1981). *Perspectives on communication*. New York: Random House.

Fraser, L. (1957). *Propaganda*. London: Oxford University Press.

Frommer, M. (1987). *How well do inventors understand the cultural consequences of their inventions? A study of: Samuel Finley Breese Morse and the telegraph, Thomas Alva Edison and the phonograph, and Alexander Graham Bell and the Telephone*. Unpublished doctoral dissertation, New York University.

Fuller, R. B. (1963). *Ideas and integrities, a spontaneous autobiographical disclosure*. Edited by R. W. Marks, Ed.). Englewood Cliffs, NJ: Prentice-Hall.

Fuller, R. B. (1969a). *Operating manual for spaceship earth*. Carbondale: Southern Illinois University Press.

Fuller, R. B. (1969b). *Utopia or oblivion: The prospects of humanity*. New York: Bantam Books.

The future of the field I [Special issue]. (1993a). *Journal of Communication, 43*(3), 1-238.

The future of the field II [Special issue]. (1993b). *Journal of Communication, 43*(4), 1-190.

Geddes, P. (1904). *City development: A study of parks, gardens and culture institutes: A report to the Carnegie Dunfermline Trust*. Edinburgh, Scotland: Geddes and Colleagues.

Geddes, P. (1915). *Cities in evolution: An introduction to the town planning movement and to the study of civics*. London: Williams & Norgate.

Gencarelli, T. F. (2000). The intellectual roots of media ecology in the work and thought of Neil Postman. *The New Jersey Journal of Communication, 8*(1), 91-103.

Giedion, S. (1948). *Mechanization takes command*. New York: Oxford University Press.

Giedion, S. (1967). *Space, time and architecture* (Rev. ed.). Cambridge, MA: Harvard University Press.

Gitlin, T. (1978). Media sociology: The dominant paradigm. *Theory and Society, 6*, 205-253.

Gitlin, T. (1980). *The whole world is watching*. Berkeley: University of California Press.

Gitlin, T. (1987). *The Sixties: Years of hope, days of rage*. New York: Bantam.

Goffman, E. (1959). *The presentation of self in everyday life*. New York: Doubleday.

Goffman, E. (1963). *Behavior in public places: Notes on the social organization of gatherings*. New York: The Free Press.

Goffman, E. (1974). *Frame analysis*. New York: Harper Colophon Books.

Goody, J. (1968). *Literacy in traditional societies*. London: Cambridge University Press.

Goody, J. (1977). The domestication of the savage mind. Cambridge, England & New York: Cambridge University Press.

Gordon, G. N. (1965). *Educational television.* New York: Center for Applied Research in Education.

Gordon, G. N. (1969). *The languages of communication: A logical and psychological examination.* New York: Hastings House.

Gordon, G. N. (1971). Persuasion: The theory and practice of manipulative communication. New York: Hastings House.

Gordon, G. N. (1975). *Communications and media: Constructing a cross-discipline.* New York: Hastings House.

Gordon, G. N. (1977). *The communications revolution: A history of mass media in the United States.* New York: Hastings House.

Gozzi, R., Jr. (1999). *The power of metaphor in the age of electronic media.* Cresskill, NJ: Hampton Press.

Gozzi, R., Jr. (2000). Jacques Ellul on technique, media, and the spirit. *New Jersey Journal of Communication, 8*(1), 79-90.

Griffith, B.C., & Mullins, N.C. (1972). Invisible colleges: Small, coherent groups may be the same throughout science. *Science, 177,* 959-964.

Gronbeck, B. E., Farrell, T. J., & Soukup, P. A. (Eds.). (1992). *Media, consciousness, and culture: Explorations of Walter Ong's thought.* Newbury Park, CA: Sage.

Gross, B., & Gross, R. (Eds.). (1985). *The great school debate: Which way for American education?* New York: Simon & Schuster/Touchstone.

Gumpert, G. (1987). *Talking tombstones & other tales of the media age.* New York: Oxford University Press.

Hall, E. T. (1959). *The silent language.* New York: Doubleday.

Hausdorff, D. (1970). A preliminary bibliography in communications. Unpublished reading list for doctoral students in the Media Ecology Program, New York University.

Havelock, E. A. (1963). *Preface to Plato.* Cambridge, MA & London: Belknap Press of the Harvard University Press.

Havelock, E. A. (1976). *Origins of western literacy.* Toronto, Canada: The Ontario Institute for Studies in Education.

Havelock, E. A. (1982). *The literate revolution in Greece and its cultural consequences.* Princeton, NJ: Princeton University Press.

Havelock, E. A. (1986). *The muse learns to write: Reflections on orality and literacy from antiquity to the present.* New Haven, CT: Yale University Press.

Hayakawa, S. I. (1964). *Language in thought and action.* (4th ed.). New York: Harcourt Brace Jovanovich. (Original work published 1939)

Heisenberg, W. (1962). *Physics and philosophy.* New York: Harper & Row.

Heyer, P. (2003). *Harold Innis.* Boulder, CO: Rowman & Littlefield

Innis, H. A. (1950). *Empire and communication.* New York: Oxford University Press. [Rev. ed. published 1972 by University of Toronto Press.]

Innis, H. A. (1951). *The bias of communication.* Toronto, Canada: University of Toronto Press.

Innis, H. A. (1952). *Changing concepts of time.* (Reprinted in 2003 with a Foreword by J. W. Carey.) Boulder, CO: Rowman & Littlefield.

Innis, H. A. (n.d.). A history of communications: An incomplete and unrevised manuscript. Montreal, Canada: McGill University's McLennan Library.

Jaynes, J. (1976). *The origins of consciousness in the breakdown of the bicameral mind*. Boston: Houghton Mifflin.

Jensen, J. (1990). *Redeeming modernity: Contradiction in media criticism*. Newbury Park, CA: Sage.

Karnow, S. (1983). *Vietnam: A history*. New York: Viking.

Katz, E., (1957). The two-step flow of communication: An up-to-date report on an hypothesis. *Public Opinion Quarterly, XXI*, 61-78.

Katz, E., & Lazarsfeld, P. (1955). *Personal influence: The part played by people in the flow of mass communications*. Glencoe, IL: The Free Press.

Klapper, J. T. (1960). *The effects of mass communication*. Glencoe, IL: The Free Press.

Korzybski, A. (1933). *Science and sanity*. Lancaster, PA: Science Press Printing Co.

Kuhn, T. S. (1962). *The structure of scientific revolution*. Chicago: University of Chicago Press.

Kuhns, W. (1971). *The post-industrial prophets*. New York: Weybright & Talley.

Langer, S. K. (1930). *The practice of philosophy*. New York: Henry Holt.

Langer, S. K. (1942). *Philosophy in a new key: A study in the symbolism of reason, rite, and art*. Cambridge, MA: Harvard University Press.

Langer, S. K. (1967). *Mind: An essay on human feeling*, (Vol. I, Parts 1-3). Baltimore: Johns Hopkins University Press.

Langer, S. K. (1972). *Mind: An essay on human feeling*, (Vol. II, Part 4). Baltimore: Johns Hopkins University Press.

Langer, S. K. (1982). *Mind: An essay on human feeling*, (Vol. III, Parts 5 & 6). Baltimore: Johns Hopkins University Press.

Lasswell, H. (1927). *Propaganda techniques in the world war*. New York: Knopf.

Lee, A. M., & Lee, E. B. (1939). *The fine art of propaganda*. New York: Harcourt, Brace.

Lee, D. (1954). The self among the Wintu. *Explorations, 3*, 89-95.

Lee, D. (1959). *Freedom and culture*. Englewood Cliffs, NJ: Prentice-Hall.

Lee, E. B., & Lee, A. M. (1979). The fine art of propaganda analysis—then and now. *ETC.: A Review of General Semantics, 36*(2), 117-127.

Leeds-Hurwitz, W. (1990). Notes in the history of intercultural communication: The Foreign Service Institute and the mandate for intercultural training. *Quarterly Journal of Speech, 76*, 262-281.

Lerner, D. (Ed.). (1951). *Propaganda in war and crisis*. New York: George W. Stewart. (Reprinted in 1972 by Arno Press, New York)

Lerner, D. (1958). *The passing of traditional society*. Glencoe, IL: The Free Press.

Levinson, P. (1997). *The soft edge: A natural history and future of the information revolution*. London & New York: Routledge.

Levinson, P. (1999). *Digital McLuhan: A guide to the information millennium*. New York: Routledge.

Levi-Strauss, C. (1966). *The savage mind*. Chicago: University of Chicago Press.

Lippmann, W. (1922). *Public opinion*. New York: Macmillan.

The living McLuhan [Symposium]. (1981). *Journal of Communication, 31*(3), 116-199.

Logan, R. K. (1986). *The alphabet effect: The impact of the phonetic alphabet on the development of western civilization.* New York: Avon. (Later edition published in 2003 as *Alphabet effect: A media ecology understanding of the making of Western civilization* by Hampton Press, Cresskill, NJ)

Lowery, S. A. & DeFleur, M. L. (1995). *Milestones in mass communication research: Media effects* (3rd ed.). White Plains, NY: Longman.

Lum, C. M. K. (1992). Captains and corporals: The debate between the neo-Marxist and the reflective perspectives on advertising. *The Speech Communication Annual, 6* (50th Anniversary Edition), 31-44.

Lum, C. M. K. (1996). *In search of a voice: Karaoke and the construction of identity in Chinese America.* Mahwah, NJ: Erlbaum.

Lum, C. M. K. (Guest Ed.). (2000a). The intellectual roots of media ecology [special issue]. *The New Jersey Journal of Communication, 8*(1).

Lum, C. M. K. (2000b). Introduction: Intellectual roots of media ecology. *The New Jersey Journal of Communication, 8*(1), 1-7.

Mannheim, K. (1945). American sociology. In G. Gurvitch & W. Moore (Eds.), *Twentieth century sociology* (pp. 507-537). New York: Philosophical Library.

Marchand, P. (1989). *Marshall McLuhan: The medium and the messenger.* New York: Ticknor & Fields.

Marchand, R. (1985). *Advertising the American dream: Making way for modernity, 1920-1940.* Berkeley: University of California Press.

Marcuse, H. (1965). *One dimensional man.* Boston: Beacon Press.

Maxwell, R. (2003). *Herbert Schiller.* Lanham, MD: Rowman & Littlefield.

McChesney, R. W. (2000). *Rich media, poor democracy: Communication politics in dubious times.* New York: The New Press.

McLuhan, E., & Zingrone, F. (Eds.). (1995). *Essential McLuhan.* New York: Basic Books.

McLuhan, H. M. (1951). *The mechanical bride: Folklore of industrial man.* Boston: Beacon Press.

McLuhan, H. M. (1962). *The Gutenberg galaxy.* Toronto, Canada: University of Toronto Press.

McLuhan, H. M. (1964). *Understanding media: The extensions of man.* New York: McGraw-Hill.

McLuhan, H. M., & McLuhan, E. (1988). *Laws of media: The new science.* Toronto, Canada: University of Toronto Press.

McLuhan, H. M., & Powers, B. (1981). Ma Bell minus the Natucket gam: Or the impact of high-speed data transmission. *Journal of Communication, 31*(3), 191-199.

McPhail, T. L. (2002). *Global communication: Theories, stakeholders, and trends.* Boston: Allyn & Bacon.

Mead, G. H. (1934). *Mind, self, & society from the standpoint of a social behaviorist.* Chicago: University of Chicago Press.

Merton, R. K. (1967). On the history and systematics of sociological theory. In R. K. Marton (Ed.), *On theoretical sociology* (pp. 1-37). New York: The Free Press.

Meyrowitz, J. (1985). *No sense of place: The impact of electronic media on social behavior.* New York: Oxford University Press.

Meyrowitz, J. (1994). Medium theory. In D. Crowley & D. Mitchell (Eds.), *Communication theory today.* Stanford, CA: Stanford University Press.

Miller, D. L. (1989). *Lewis Mumford: A life*. New York: Weidenfeld & Nicolson.

Miller, J. (1971). *McLuhan*. London: Fontana.

Molinaro, M., McLuhan, C., & Toye, W. (Eds.). (1987). *Letters of Marshall McLuhan*. Toronto, Canada: Oxford University Press.

Mumford, L. (1934). *Technics and civilization*. New York: Harcourt Brace.

Mumford, L. (1938). *The culture of cities*. New York: Harcourt, Brace.

Mumford, L. (1961). *The city in history: Its origins, its transformations, and its prospects*. New York: Harcourt Brace & World.

Mumford, L. (1967). *The myth of the machine: I. Technics and human development*. New York: Harcourt Brace & World.

Mumford, L. (1970). *The myth of the machine: II. The pentagon of power*. New York: Harcourt Brace Jovanovich.

Munson, E. S., & Warren, C. A. (Eds.). (1997). *James Carey: A critical reader*. Minneapolis: University of Minnesota Press.

Murray, S. O. (1994). *Theory groups and the study of language in North America*. Amsterdam: John Benjamins.

Murray, S. O. (1998). *American sociolinguistics: Theorists and theory groups*. Amsterdam: John Benjamins.

New York University Bulletin: School of Education, 1966-1967. (1966). New York: New York University.

New York University Bulletin: School of Education, 1970-1971. (1970). New York: New York University.

New York University Bulletin: School of Education, 1971-1972. (1971). New York: New York University.

New York University Bulletin: School of Education, 1976-1977. (1976). New York: New York University.

New York University Bulletin: School of Education, 1997-1999. (1997). New York: New York University.

Nystrom, C. L. (1973). *Towards a science of media ecology: The formulation of integrated conceptual paradigms for the study of human communication systems*. Unpublished doctoral dissertation, New York University.

Ong, W. J. (1967). *The presence of the word: Some prolegomena for cultural and religious history*. New Haven, CT: Yale University Press.

Ong, W. J. (1982). *Orality and literacy*. London: Methuen.

Ong, W. J. (2002). Ecology and some of its future. *EME: Explorations in Media Ecology, 1*(1), 5-11.

Park, R. (1920). Foreign language press and social progress. *Proceedings of the National Conference of Social Work*, 493-500.

Park, R. (1922). *The immigrant press and its control*. New York: Harper & Brothers.

Park, R. (1925). Immigrant community and immigrant press. *American Review, 3*, 143-152.

Perkinson, H. (1991). *Getting better: Television and moral progress*. New Brunswick, NJ: Transaction.

Playboy interview: Marshall McLuhan. (1969, March). *Playboy*, pp. 26-27, 45, 55-56, 61, 63.

Pope, D. (1983). *The making of modern advertising*. New York: Basic Books.

Postman, N. (1970). The reformed English curriculum. In A.C. Eurich (Ed.), *High school 1980: The shape of the future in American secondary education* (pp. 160-168). New York: Pitman.

Postman, N. (1975). Unpublished remarks to new graduate students at New York University, New York.

Postman, N. (1979). *Teaching as a conserving activity.* New York: Delta.

Postman, N. (1982). *The disappearance of childhood.* New York: Delacorte Press.

Postman, N. (1985). *Amusing Ourselves to Death.* New York: Viking Penguin.

Postman, N. (1988). *Conscientious objections: Stirring up trouble about language, technology, and education.* New York: Alfred A. Knopf.

Postman, N. (1992). *Technopoly: The surrender of culture to technology.* New York: Vintage Books.

Postman, N. (1999). *Building a bridge to the 18th century.* New York: Vintage Books.

Postman, N. (2000). The humanism of media ecology. Keynote speech at the first annual convention of the Media Ecology Association, New York.

Postman, N., & Weingartner, C. (1969). *Teaching as a subversive activity.* New York: Delacorte Press.

Postman, N., & Weingartner, C. (1973). *The school book: For people who want to know what all the hollering is about.* New York: Delacorte Press.

Robinson, G. J. (1996). Constructing a historiography for North American communication studies. In E. E. Dennis & E. Wartella (Eds.), *American communication research: The remembered history* (pp. 157-168). Mahwah, NJ: Erlbaum.

Rogers, E. (1982). The empirical and critical schools of communication research. In M. Burgoon (Ed.), *Communication yearbook* (pp. 125-144). New Brunswick, NJ: Transaction.

Rogers, E. (1995). *Diffusion of innovations* (4th ed.). New York: The Free Press.

Rosenberg, B., & White, D. M. (Eds.). (1957). *Mass culture: The popular arts in America.* New York: The Free Press.

Rosenberg, B., & White, D. M. (Eds.). (1971). *Mass culture revisited.* New York: Van Nostran Reinhold Co.

Sanderson, G., & Macdonald, F. (Eds.). (1989). *Marshall McLuhan: The man and his message.* Golden, CO: Fulcrum.

Sapir, E. (1921). *Language.* New York: Harcourt, Brace.

Schafer, R. M. (1980). *The tuning of the world.* Philadelphia: University of Pennsylvania Press.

Schiller, H. I. (1976). *Communication and cultural domination.* White Plains, NY: International Arts & Sciences Press.

Schiller, H. I. (1991). *Culture, Inc.: The corporate takeover of public expression.* New York: Oxford University Press.

Schiller, H. I. (1992). *Mass communication and American empire* (2nd ed.). Boulder, CO: Westview. (Original work published 1969 by Augustus M. Kelley Publishers)

Schmandt-Besserat, D. (1996). *How writing came about.* Austin: University of Texas Press.

Schramm, W. (1964). *Mass media and national development: The role of information in the developing countries.* Stanford, CA: Stanford University Press.

Schwartz, T. (1973). *The responsive chord*. New York: Doubleday.

Shannon, C. E., & Weaver, W. (1949). *The mathematical theory of communication*. Urbana: University of Illinois Press.

Smith, A. (1980). *The geopolitics of information: How western culture dominates the world*. New York: Oxford University Press.

Smith, M. R. (1994). Technological determinism in American culture. In M. R. Smith & L. Marx (Eds.), *Does technology drive history?* (pp. 1-35). Cambridge, MA: MIT Press.

Soukup, P. A. (2004). Walter J. Ong, S. J.: A retrospective. *Communication Research Trends, 23*(1), 3-23.

Stamps, J. (1995). *Unthinking modernity: Innis, McLuhan and the Frankfurt School*. Montreal - Kingston, Canada: McGill-Queen's University Press.

Standage, T. (1999). *The Victorian internet: The remarkable story of the telegraph and the 19th century's on-line pioneers*. New York: Berkley Books.

Stark, W. (1958). *The sociology of knowledge*. Glencoe, IL: The Free Press.

Stearn, G. E. (Ed.). (1967). *McLuhan hot & cool: A critical symposium*. New York: The Dial Press.

Stein, M. R. (1960). *The eclipse of community*. Princeton, NJ: Princeton University Press. (Harper Torchbooks edition, 1964)

Strate, L. (1994). Post(modern)man, or Neil Postman as postmodernist. *ETC.: A Review of General Semantics, 51*(2), 159-170.

Strate, L. (2002). Media ecology as a scholarly activity. Unpublished President's Address to the third annual convention of the Media Ecology Association, New York.

Strate, L. (2003a). From archetype to cliche. Unpublished President's Address to the fourth annual convention of the Media Ecology Association, Hempstead, New York.

Strate, L. (2003b). Neil Postman, defender of the word. *ETC.: A Review of General Semantics, 60*(4), 341-350.

Strate, L. (2004). A media ecology review. *Communication Research Trends, 23*(2), 3-48.

Strate, L. (in press). *Understanding media ecology*. Cresskill, NJ: Hampton Press.

Strate, L., Jacobson, R., & Gibson, S. (Eds.). (1996). *Communication and cyberspace*. Cresskill, NJ: Hampton Press.

Strate, L., & Lum, C. M. K. (2000). Lewis Mumford and the ecology of technics. *The New Jersey Journal of Communication, 8*(1), 56-78.

Strate, L., & Wachtel, E. A. (Eds.). (2005). *The legacy of McLuhan*. Cresskill, NJ: Hampton Press.

Thaler, P. (1994). *The watchful eye: American justice in the age of the television trial*. Westport, CT: Praeger.

Thaler, P. (1997). *The spectacle: Media and the making of the O. J. Simpson story*. Westport, CT: Praeger.

Theall, D. F. (1971). *The medium is the rear view mirror: Understanding McLuhan*. Montreal, Canada: McGill-Queen's University Press.

Theall, D. F. (1988). McLuhan, telematics, and the Toronto School of Communication. *Canadian Journal of Political and Social Theory, 10*(1-2), 79-88.

Theall, D. F. (2001). *The virtual Marshall McLuhan*. Montreal, Canada: McGill-Queens University Press.

Tunstall, J. (1977). *The media are American*. London: Constable.

Turkle, S. (1985). *The second self: Computers and the human spirit*. New York: Touchstone.

Turkle, S. (1995). *Life on the screen*. New York: Simon & Schuster.

Watzlawick, P. (1976). *How real is real? Confusion, disinformation, communication: An anecdotal introduction to communication theory*. New York: Random House.

Watzlawick, P., Bavelas, J. B., & Jackson, D. D. (1967). *Pragmatics of human communication: A study of interactional patterns, pathologies, and paradoxes*. New York: W. W. Norton.

Weizenbaum, J. (1976). *Computer power and human reason*. San Francisco: W.H. Freeman.

Whorf, B. L. (1956). *Language, thought and reality: Selected writings of Benjamin Lee Whorf*. Cambridge, MA: MIT Press.

Wiener, N. (1948). *Cybernetics, or control and communication in the animal and the machine*. Cambridge, MA: MIT Press.

Wiener, N. (1950). *The human use of human being: Cybernetics and society*. New York: Avon.

Zung, T. T. K. (Ed.). (2001). *Buckminster Fuller: An anthology for a new millennium*. New York: St. Martin's Press.

2

The Humanism
of Media Ecology

Neil Postman
New York University

As indicated in the text presented here, this speech was given by Neil M. Postman at the first convention of the Media Ecology Association. In it, he tried to explain the origins of the program in media ecology at New York University (NYU), as well as the name media ecology. Primarily, he tried to express the point of view from which the study of media is most useful.[1]

I am, of course, honored to have been asked to give the keynote address at the first convention of the Media Ecology Association. I must assume I have been judged an appropriate person to do this, not merely an available one, and I thank the organizers for that. But what is appropriate is not always the best. Jacques Ellul would have been much better, but he is dead, and even worse, spoke French. McLuhan is dead. So are Eric Havelock and Susanne Langer. I don't mean to compare myself to these great scholars. They are, after all, the Abraham, Moses, David, and Esther of media ecology, which is not to say that they were Jewish, but to say that their work gave form to the fundamental questions of media ecology. I know they are here in spirit but if any one of them could have stayed long enough to be here this evening, it would have been the best possible start for the association. I should add here, on the question of who would be best to give this address, that there are a half dozen or more young people, some of whom are graduates of the Media Ecology Program at NYU and some of whom are not, who have taken the idea of media ecology further than I have and who, without much argument, could do a better job than I.

Nonetheless, I am not a bad choice because along with Christine Nystrom and Terence Moran, I helped to organize the first graduate program on the planet that chose the phrase "media ecology" to signify a university course of study. And so I should like to begin by saying what we meant by using that term and I do this without the intention of imposing our meaning on you.

You may be surprised to know that our first thinking about the subject was guided by a biological metaphor. You will remember from the time when you first became acquainted with a petri dish, that a medium was defined as a substance within which a culture grows. If you replace the word *substance* with the word *technology*, the definition would stand as a fundamental principle of media ecology: A medium is a technology within which a culture grows; that is to say, it gives form to a culture's politics, social organization, and habitual ways of thinking. Beginning with that idea, we invoked still another biological metaphor, that of ecology. In its origin, the word had a considerably different meaning from how we use it today. As found in Aristotle, it meant "household." Aristotle spoke of the importance to our intellectual equanimity of keeping our household in order. Its first use in its modern meaning is attributed to Ernst Haeckel, a German zoologist, in the late 19th century. He used the word as we do now, to refer to the interactions among the elements of our natural environment, with a special emphasis on how such interactions lead to a balanced and healthful environment. We put the word *media* in the front of the word *ecology* to suggest that we were not simply interested in media, but in the ways in which the interaction between media and human beings give a culture its character; and one might say, help a culture to maintain symbolic balance. If we wish to connect the ancient meaning with the modern, we might say that the word suggests that we need to keep our planetary household in order.

In the early days of our department, we were subjected to a good deal of derision, some gentle and some nasty, about our use of the phrase *media ecology*. I think the objection was the term was too trendy but more than that, the term was more comfortable in biology than in social studies and should remain there. But from our point of view, we had chosen the right phrase because we wanted to make people more conscious of the fact that human beings live in two different kinds of environments. One is the natural environment, and consists of things like air, trees, rivers, and caterpillars. The other is the media environment, which consists of language, numbers, images, holograms, and all of the other symbols, techniques, and machinery that make us what we are.

From the beginning, we were a group of moralists. It was our idea to have an academic department that would focus its attention on the media environment, with a particular interest in understanding how and if our media ecology was making us better or worse. Not everyone thought that this was a good idea; Marshall McLuhan for one. Although McLuhan had suggested that we start such a department at NYU, he did not have in mind that we should interest ourselves in whether or not new media, especially electronic media, would make us better or worse. He reminded me several times of the lines in Steven Vincent Binet's long poem *John Brown's Body*. At the end of the poem, Binet makes reference to the Industrial Revolution, and finishes with these lines:

> Say neither, it is blessed nor cursed.
> Say only "It is here."

No room for moralists there. McLuhan claimed that we should take the same point of view in thinking about modern media: that they are neither blessed nor cursed, only that they are here. He thought that this moral neutrality would give the best opportunity to learn exactly how new media do their stuff. If one spent too much time on the question of whether or not that stuff was good, one be distracted from truly understanding media. As a consequence, although I believe McLuhan liked me, I feel sure he would not have much liked my books, which he would have thought too moralistic, rabbinical or, if not that, certainly too judgmental.

I think there is considerable merit in McLuhan's point of view about avoiding questions of good and bad when thinking about media. But that view has never been mine. To be quite honest about it, I don't see any point in studying media unless one does so within a moral or ethical context. I am not alone in believing this. Some of the most important media scholars, Lewis Mumford and Jacques Ellul, for example, could scarcely write a word about technology without conveying a sense of either its humanistic or anti-humanistic consequences. And it is that issue that I address here.

In thinking about media from a humanistic point of view, one must take into account the obvious fact that people will have different ideas about what is good for them and bad for them. This year [2000], we are celebrating the 600th anniversary of the birth of Johannas Gutenberg. I suppose we can all agree, in the year 2000, that his printing press with movable type was, all things considered, a good thing, that is to say, a humane advance in the history of communication. But people did not agree about that in the early days of its invention, especially because of the role it played in the breakup of the Holy Roman Church. The press put Word of God on every Christian's kitchen table. That being the case, who needs popes and priests to interpret it? Which is why Martin Luther said of the printing press that it was "God's highest grace by which the gospel is driven forward." It would have been difficult to find, in the 16th century, any devoted member of the Church to agree with that judgment. We might say that it took 200 years before the quarrel between Catholics and Protestants—quarrel incited by print—subsided.

Which leads to another point: In assessing the humanistic consequences of a new medium, one must take into account the factor of time. I think some of you know that among the severely negative consequences of television— at least as I see them—is its role in making the institution of childhood obsolete. I would call that a moral decline. Of course, there are some people, especially merchants, who think that the disappearance of childhood is a good idea. But even those, like me, who think it is a catastrophe, have to keep in mind that 100 years from now, it may not seem so. In fact, people might believe that the idea of childhood was no great advantage, at anytime, either to the young or to the old, and the sooner television wrecked it the better.

And so we must keep in mind, first, that people differ about what is good for them and what isn't, and, second, that changes over time will make us see things differently from the way they might have first appeared. In keeping these factors in mind, is one taking the position of a moral relativist? Not necessarily. It is possible, for example, to say that when people have differed over the moral implications of a new medium, one group was wrong. And I think it also possible to say that although time may change the way people judge the effects of a new medium, time can be wrong. I mean, let us say, that the negative effects of a medium might still be a problem, and remain one despite the passage of time. In other words, time does not always erase the disadvantages of a medium. Neither does it necessarily weaken the advantages. A good example of this is to be found in the prophecies made by Socrates about the written word. I think most of you know that in the Phaedrus, Socrates spoke against writing on the grounds that it would weaken our memories, make public those things that are best left private, and would change the practice of education. Writing, he said, forces a student to follow an argument rather than to participate in it. I should say that the passage of 2,500 years has not changed those negative consequences. I should add that the positive consequences that Plato saw are also still perfectly evident.

I might offer, as another example, an even more ancient prophecy concerning media. I remind you of the implied prophecy in the Second Commandment of the Decalogue. It is the commandment that forbids Israelites to make graven images or any likenesses of anything in the world. I take it that the author of that prohibition believed that the making of concrete, visual images would weaken the capacity of people to conceive of abstract ideas, specifically a God that has no material existence but exists only in the Word and through the Word. That idea about a medium's effect on human psychology is as certain today as it was 3,000 years ago.

What I am leading up to is that although we must keep in mind that not all people agree on what is an advantage or a disadvantage, and that time might alter our judgment of the effects of a medium, one can still take a definite view about whether or not a medium contributes to or undermines humane concepts. Which leads me to say something about what one might mean by a humane concept. Let us start with McLuhan and Harold Innis. As most of you know, both McLuhan, who often denied it, and Harold Innis, who never denied it, had a definite idea about what was good for people in relation to media. McLuhan thought that it was better for people if the media they used promoted a balance in their sensorium. Innis believed that it was better for people if their media promoted a balance in people's conceptions of time and space. The only time I know of that McLuhan used the phrase media ecology is in a letter he wrote to Clare Booth Luce in which he remarked that it may be necessary for a culture to limit its use of some medium in the interests of promoting a balance in the media ecology.[2] For his part, Innis worried that a medium that emphasizes space over time is likely to make a culture obsessed with military conquest. In other words, there is in fact a moral dimension to the way in which both of them assessed media and media change.

What, then, do I think are the humanistic issues one should consider in trying to understand media? I should like to offer some in the form of a series of questions, and when I am done you will have, I hope, an idea of what I regard as humane progress.

The first question is this: To what extent does a medium contribute to the uses and development of rational thought?

This question suggests that I believe that rational thinking is one of humanity's greatest gifts, and that, therefore, any medium that encourages it, such as writing or print, is to be praised and highly valued. And any medium, such as television, that does not, is to be feared. This is not to say that writing or print do not have disadvantages, and television, advantages; only that in this important sphere of humanity's development we have a clear case of one medium that assists it and of another that undermines it. I am prepared to go quite far on this matter. For example, I would remind you that all the people who helped to create the electric world—from telegraphy to the Internet—were themselves educated almost exclusively by the written and printed word—that is, by pen, paper, and books. How did they get so smart? Well, you know my answer: Their intellectual powers were developed by a medium that fostered abstract thought. If you want any elaboration of this view, I suggest you begin by reading about the 18th century. It was then that most of the humane ideas we have carried forward were conceived: religious freedom, free speech, inductive science, women's rights, childhood, an abomination of slavery, the right of the governed to choose their governors, even the idea of progress, and, you might be surprised to know, the idea of happiness. We owe these ideas to rationalism—a way of thinking fostered by print. David Riesman once said that print is the gunpowder of the mind. We need have no fear that we are in danger of having too much of it.

Here is a second question: To what extent does a medium contribute to the development of democratic processes?

There is no question that the printed word was a key factor in the emergence of democracy, not least because it undermined the oral tradition and placed great emphasis on individuality. In *Democracy in America*, Toqueville worried that the printed word would lead Americans away from a sense of community and toward what he called egotism. Toqueville could not know of radio, television, or the Internet, but if he could, I'm sure he would ask of them: 'Do they help maintain a balance between a sense of social cohesion and individuality, both of which are necessary to a humane democracy?' I do not think he would be impressed by media whose formats encourage isolation. After all, we can listen to music alone, watch television alone, watch videos alone. And now with the aid of computers, we can shop at home, we will be voting at home, and going to college at home—that is to say, alone. Of course, we also read alone, which in fact was, as I mentioned, an important element in the development of individualism, but the imbalance fostered by new media creates a problem that will have an important effect on our understanding and practice of democracy.

In 1995, Lawrence Grossman wrote a book called *The Electronic Republic* in which he enthusiastically predicted that in the future, representative democracy would be replaced by what he called participatory democracy. He meant by this that digital technologies would make it possible for plebiscites to be conducted every week; that is to say, citizens would be able to vote on whether or not troops should be sent to Bosnia, the President should be impeached, or the Social Security system should be changed. The Senate and Congress would become largely unnecessary. In other words, we become faceless citizens voting alone on issues we do not have the time or place to discuss. My only comment on this possibility is that Madison, Jefferson, and Washington would have left the country if such a system were employed.

A third question—related to the previous two—is: To what extent do new media give greater access to meaningful information?

In the 19th century, we clearly suffered from the problem of information scarcity. In the 1830s, information could travel only as fast as a human being, which was about 35 miles per hour on a fast train. And so, we addressed the question of how to get more information, to more people, faster, and in diverse forms. We started to solve this problem with the invention of telegraphy and photography in the late 1830s and early 1840s. Not everyone was enthusiastic about the early attempts to solve that problem. Henry David Thoreau remarked in Walden,

> We are in great haste to construct a magnetic telegraph from Maine to Texas; but Maine and Texas, it may be, have nothing important to communicate. . . . We are eager to tunnel under the Atlantic and bring the old world some weeks nearer to the new; but perchance, the first news that will leak through into the broad flapping American ear will be that Princess Adelaide has the whopping cough.

Nonetheless, the issue of what is significant or useful information was not much discussed, and for 170 years we have been obsessed with machinery that would give access, and give it fast, to a Niagara of information.

Obviously, the Internet does that and we must give all due praise for its efficiency. But it does not help us, neither does television or any other 19th- or 20th-century medium (except perhaps the telephone), to solve the problem of what is significant information. As far as I can tell, the new media have made us into a nation of information junkies; that is to say, our 170-year efforts have turned information into a form of garbage. My own answer to the question concerning access to information is that, at least for now, the speed, volume, and variety of available information serves as a distraction and a moral deficit; we are deluded into thinking that the serious social problems of our time would be solved if only we had more information, and still more information. But I hope I need not tell you that if children are starving in the world, and many are, it is not because we have insufficient information. If crime is rampant in the streets, it is not because we have insufficient information. If children are abused and women are battered, that too, has nothing to do with insufficient information. The solutions to those problems lie elsewhere and Bill Gates and Nicholas Negroponte have not yet noticed that and it is not likely that they will.

Here is a final question: To what extent do new media enhance or diminish our moral sense, our capacity for goodness?

I know that this question will strike some as strange, or perhaps unanswerable. It is, in any case, not the sort of question that is of interest to technologically oriented people, or even the professors of technologically oriented people. And yet, it is a version of the question asked by Jean Jacques Rousseau in an essay he published in 1749. The essay made him famous, and even better, opened the way to the point of view we now call Romanticism. Rousseau asked if scientific progress contributed to the corruption or purification of morality? I retrieve the question because it was asked at a moment, not unlike ours, when there were great scientific and technological advances, when there was great enthusiasm for invention of all kinds, when there existed, prominently, the belief that technological innovation was the same thing as humane progress. In his essay, Rousseau ridiculed the so-called advances of civilization, claiming that such advances lead to materialism and atheism, which he thought demeaning to the human spirit. Rousseau placed himself on the side of religion and spirituality, as did so many of the great Romantic poets who followed in his path. Wordsworth, Keats, Blake, Coleridge, Byron, Heine, Beaudelaire, and most of all, Percy Shelley, who argued that because science and technology proceed without a moral basis, they do not make the mind receptive to moral decency. He thought, of course, that poetry did. "The great instrument of moral good," he wrote, "is the imagination, and poetry administers to the effect by acting on the cause."

I don't say that I see as clearly as Shelley what are the instruments of moral good, or the instruments of moral evil or even moral indifference. But it seems to me that those of us who are interested in media ecology should give more time than we do in addressing the role media play in, as Rousseau put it, corrupting or purifying our morality. After all, no one can dispute that in the 20th century more advances were made in technology than in all the previous centuries put together. How, then, can we account for the fact that more people were slaughtered in the 20th century, including as many as 10 million children, by wars and mayhem that in all the previous centuries? How can we account for the fact that the three most influential ideologies of the 20th century were Nazism, Fascism, and Communism, each of which reduced the significance of the human spirit so that people fled from them whenever they could? Is it not possible that behind the noon-day brightness of technological ingenuity, there lurks something dark and sinister, something that casts a terrible shadow over the better angels of our nature?

Esther Dyson, who is one of the more prominent cheerleaders for technological growth, remarks in her recent book that those who worry too much about the electronic world can rest easy in the assurance that human nature will remain the same. Not surprisingly, she misses the point. Human nature may stay the same. But it is part of human nature to hate and kill, and it is part of human nature to love and protect. The question is, what part will be released and nurtured? What part will be suppressed and shriveled? And, of course, is there any connection between our obsession with our technology and our capacity for moral growth? This last question is what Rousseau, Shelley, Blake, Carlyle and Huxley thought and wrote about. Do we?

It seems to me that there is something shallow, brittle and even profoundly irrelevant about departments of communication that ignore these questions, that are concerned to produce technological cheerleaders, and even neutralists that offer little historical or philosophical moral perspectives. What I mean to say, I suppose, is that media ecology is properly a branch of the humanities.

Well, there are, of course, many other questions to ask on the general subject of media and humanistic advance. You will notice I have said nothing about the question of the contribution of media to the growth of artistic expression, and not very much about whether or not media enhance or diminish the quality of human interactions; neither did I say anything about the extent to which new media encourage or discourage an interest in historical experience. These are important questions, and I hope there are those among you who are interested to ask them and to try to answer them.

Let me conclude, then, by saying that as I understand the whole point of media ecology, it exists to further our insights into how we stand as human beings, how we are doing morally in the journey we are taking. There may be some of you who think of yourselves as media ecologists who disagree with what I have just said. If that is the case, you are wrong.

ENDNOTES

1. Before his untimely passing late in 2003, Professor Neil Postman provided this abstract in his initial permission for publishing his speech in this book. Subsequent permission to reprint the essay in this volume has been granted by Shelley Postman.
2. Editor's note: It would seem impossible for McLuhan to have coined or first used the phrase *media ecology* in a letter to Clare Booth Luce, a playwright and widow of the publisher Henry Luce, because they began corresponding only after their first meeting in Honolulu in 1972; for reference see Molinaro et al., 1987, p. 474). The term's coinage must have had taken place before its public debut in Postman's keynote speech to the 1968 annual meeting of the National Council of Teachers of English.

REFERENCE

Molinaro, M., McLuhan, C., & Toye, W. (Eds.). (1987). *Letters of Marshall McLuhan*. Toronto, Canada: Oxford University Press.

3

Lewis Mumford and
The Ecology of Technics

Lance Strate
Fordham University

Casey Man Kong Lum
William Paterson University

In the first major treatise on media ecology as an emerging discipline, *Towards a Science of Media Ecology: The Formulation of Integrated Conceptual Paradigms for the Study of Human Communication Systems*, Nystrom (1973) identifies Lewis Mumford's (1934) *Technics and Civilization* as the field's founding work. Similarly, Kuhns (1971) situates Mumford as the first of the postindustrial prophets in his survey of major media ecology scholars.[1] Given that his work extends to the study and criticism of architecture, there is indeed an aptness in positioning Mumford as the foundation of the house of media ecology. In the course of construction, foundations generally become obscured by the buildings they support, however, and likewise, Mumford's role in laying the groundwork for media ecology often goes unacknowledged.

A house can be understood both structurally and genealogically, both in terms of building up from a foundation and descending from a founder. Even more so in this respect, Mumford is more often than not unsung and overshadowed by Neil Postman, who formally introduced the term *media ecology*, as well as institutionalizing it as a graduate program at New York University (Nystrom, 1973; Postman 1970; Postman & Weingartner, 1971);

by McLuhan, who introduced environmental and ecological metaphors in his discussions of media (e.g., McLuhan, 1964), and otherwise popularized the perspective; and by Harold Innis (1950, 1951), who McLuhan acknowledged as the first to study the impact of communication technologies. Innis is also recognized as the first of the Toronto School, a group of media ecologists associated at one time or another with the University of Toronto, including McLuhan, Eric Havelock, and Edmund Carpenter. It is therefore not unheard of to equate media ecology with the Toronto School.

Although there is no denying the central role that the Toronto School played in the early development of media ecology theory, and there is no doubt that Innis would serve as an exemplary founder of the media ecology tradition, he is, in fact, preceded by Mumford, who in turn can be seen as the first of the New York School (Strate, 1996). In this instance, the New York School refers not to a single university (e.g., NYU), but to the city itself. Early members of the New York School included Louis Forsdale from Columbia University, John Culkin from Fordham University and the New School for Social Research, Gary Gumpert and Charles Weingartner from Queens College, Neil Postman and Christine Nystrom from NYU, and Manhattan-based media producer Tony Schwartz. The point here is not to substitute one locale or lineage for another, however, but rather to understand the house of media ecology in terms of a complex, cosmopolitan network of intellectual kinship relations.

If Mumford's position as progenitor is all too often forgotten, it no doubt has something to do with changes to the family name. He did not encounter the term *media ecology* until late in life, after he had written his major works. Indeed, he rarely foregrounded either media or communication, although he did discuss them along with art and culture, particularly in relation to his two major themes: technology and the city. In regard to the city, it is easy to forget today how strong was the connection between mass-mediated communication and urban centers for most of the 19th and 20th centuries. Mass communication and urbanization were two of the main components of mass society. As for technology, it was through the Toronto School that a definition of media limited to the material and technical (as opposed to the institutional and organizational), but broadened to include all manner of artifacts (as opposed to only the media of communication) was introduced. In this way, Mumford's work on technics was incorporated under the heading of media theory.

Mumford may have come to the study of media through the back door, but his connection to ecology was quite forward-looking. Whereas many other media ecologists at best use ecology as a metaphor, Mumford is concerned in concrete and practical ways with both the biological and technological habitats of the human species. At the age of 22, Mumford wrote a proposal for his first book on the ecology of urban development:

> Mumford proposed a book different from anything that had yet been written on the American city. The civic renascence in America, which had been going forward since the Chicago Exposition in 1893, had created a growing body of literature about cities—civic surveys, city histories, and city guidebooks—that reported city problems from every conceivable angle, focusing on rents and taxes, budgets and charters, education and housing. But Mumford found one aspect "strangely neglected." No one had yet attempted "to describe concretely the problem of cities in relation to their environments," and to the environments of the regions of which they were a part (what Mumford called *ecological history*) (Miller, 1989, p. 84, italics added)

Although it would be another two decades before he actually wrote his first major study of the city (Mumford, 1938), his notion of ecological history would also evolve into an ecology of technics. This chapter discusses some of the salient features of Mumford's media ecology that appear in his voluminous writings: his epochal historiography of technology, his techno-organicism, his critique of the megamachine, and finally his ecological ethics. First, however, Mumford's own personal and intellectual ecology are considered.

MUMFORD'S WORKS AND DAYS

Lewis Mumford was a native New Yorker, born in 1895 in Flushing, Queens. His mother, Elvina, came from a working-class German Protestant immigrant family. Twelve years before Lewis' birth, she was briefly married to an Englishman named John Mumford, and she kept his name even though the marriage was annulled. Lewis' father was Lewis Mack, who came from an affluent German Jewish family. Elvina was working as a servant for his uncle, Jacob Mack, and her affair with Lewis was as brief as her previous marriage. It was Jacob, and not Lewis Mack, who became one of Lewis Mumford's legal guardians, and tried to fill the role of father during Mumford's early childhood. But more than anything else, Lewis Mumford was a son of Manhattan. As he put it, "New York exerted a greater and more constant influence on me than did my family" (Mumford, 1982, p. 25). He spent much of his formative years as a young boy and, later, an aspiring writer witnessing the rapid and often traumatic changes facing the city and the world at large. He was growing up at a time when new forms of architecture, transportation, and communications were forcibly transforming not only the face of his city but also the vary fabric of its culture. The year he was born, Marconi invented radio telegraphy and the Lumiere brothers invented a motion picture camera. In 1903, when Mumford was 8, the Wright brothers took humankind's first successful powered flight. A year later, the New York City subway system made its debut, and Arthur Korn transmitted the first photographs telegraphically, from Munich to Nuremberg.

From childhood, when he spent a great deal of time walking through the streets of New York with his grandfather, Mumford took delight in studying the neighborhoods in New York as the city experienced tremendous physical and demographic transformations. In the early decades of the 20th century, neighborhood upon neighborhood was torn down to make way for skyscrapers, new development projects, and highway construction. Just as dramatically, new neighborhoods sprung into life, such as those in the Lower East Side of Manhattan, due to the influx of immigrants. As Miller's (1989) authoritative biography amply illustrates, Mumford's experiences and observations in these formative years seemed to have instilled in him a profound interest in the city, architecture, and technology as subjects of ongoing inquiry.

A graduate of Stuyvesant High School, Mumford enrolled in the evening session of the City College of New York in 1912. He briefly flirted with the idea of pursuing a PhD, but eventually dropped out before completing his baccalaureate, not wanting to be confined by a formal curriculum. Although he later took courses at the New School for Social Research (currently the New School), Columbia University, and NYU, he preferred exploring the world of ideas on his own. Mumford spent a great deal of time in the libraries of New York City, which he viewed as a secular church, and reading widely in diverse fields of study. This partly explains the interdisciplinary nature and encyclopedic breadth of Mumford's thinking and scholarship. By the same token, it may account for the fact that he did not develop a single line of argument or body of theory.

If Mumford's mother city became his classroom, his need for a father figure to serve as schoolmaster was satisfied sometime between 1915 and 1916, when he first read about city planning in the writings of Patrick Geddes. A Scottish biologist, Geddes' work ranged from botany, ecology, and paleontology to sociology, demographics, economics, anthropology, religious studies, and urban studies. Born in 1854, Geddes published several works, including *City Development* (Geddes, 1904) and *Cities in Evolution* (Geddes, 1915). Geddes' greatest influence, however, was achieved interpersonally:

> Like Socrates, Geddes was primarily an oral teacher, an incessant talker, barely audible sometimes, his rapid-fire soliloquies muffled by his thick red beard and mustache. And he was hopelessly disorganized, leaving behind hundreds of unfinished projects and tasks. Ideas flew off him like sparks from a fireball. Many of his most original ideas were picked up and carried further by others, for Geddes had neither the patience nor the discipline to fully develop them. (Miller, 1989, p. 52)

Geddes' ideas took root in American soil, where he was admired by and inspired some of the leading intellectuals of the early 20th century:

In the United States, he conferred with such associates as John Dewey, Jane Addams, and Thorstein Veblen. Lewis Mumford became Geddes's major disciple, and Geddes's programs were embodied in the newly formed Regional Planning Association of America, whose charter members included Gifford Pinchot, Henry Wright, and Stuart Chase. In these circles Geddes sparked a movement around the goals of public electric power and community planning. (Carey, 1989, p. 129)

For Mumford, the power of Geddes' ideas stemmed from his biological, evolutionary, and ecological perspective:

Geddes' demonstration of how certain biological principles could inform the study of human culture ultimately had a . . . critical, far-reaching influence on Mumford's thought and writing. Trained as a biologist in the laboratory of Thomas Huxley, Geddes became interested in relationships existing throughout the natural environment—plant, animal, and human. Geddes' notion of a "human ecology" was important in shaping both Mumford's method of historical analysis and the scope of his interests. In fact, Mumford claims that Geddes went further than any other philosopher "in laying the ground for a systematic ecology of human culture." (Novak, 1995, p. 25)

Human ecology was one of those ideas of Geddes' that was picked up by others, notably members of the Chicago School. The term is strongly associated with The University of Chicago sociologists Robert E. Park, Earnest W. Burgess, and Roderick D. McKenzie, whereas Geddes' own contribution is often overlooked (see, e.g., Hawley, 1986). This similarity makes for a fascinating parallel between Geddes, as the father of human ecology, and Mumford as the founder of media ecology. Geddes is also a missing link between the New York and Toronto schools, having had a major influence on the work of Harold Innis directly, and indirectly through the Chicago School (Carey, 1989). Geddes' human ecology included technological history, and he was one of the first to argue for the revolutionary potential of electric technology, what Carey (1989) calls "the myth of the electronic sublime" (p. 139). This theme was incorporated into Mumford's early work (Mumford, 1934) and became a major motif for McLuhan in *Understanding Media* (McLuhan, 1964). Mumford attributed to Geddes the introduction of "the future, as so to speak, a legally bounded terrain in social thought" (cited in Carey, 1989, p. 185). In other words, Geddes was the first futurist. Innis found in Geddes someone who "identified the oral tradition, with its emphasis on dialogue and dialectic, values and philosophical speculation, as the countervailing culture to the technological culture of sensation and mobility" (Carey, 1989, p. 135). Geddes' thought ranged from orality to electricity, and it certainly would be possible to argue that it was Geddes rather than Mumford or Innis who was the true founder of media ecology.[2]

As for Geddes' impact on Mumford, Novak (1995) sums it up by pointing to three factors. First, there was Geddes' ecological perspective. Second, there was Geddes' interdisciplinary and generalist approach to thinking and scholarship, as well as to his work in urban planning. Third was Geddes' view of the intellectual as activist: He believed scholars should put what they studied into practice in order to improve urban life. This idea helps explain Mumford's active promotion of ecological regionalism, as one of the founders of the Regional Planning Association of America (Luccarelli, 1995). It also accounts for Mumford's ongoing public debate with Robert Moses, New York City's construction czar for almost half a century, whose highways, public parks, and numerous other housing and construction projects have changed the face of much of New York (Caro, 1975).

Geddes was not Mumford's only influence by any means. Another scholar who had a major impact on Mumford's intellectual development was Thorstein Veblen, the University of Chicago economist.[3] According to Mumford's biographer, Miller (1989), "Mumford had read with enthusiasm all of his books, finding him much like Geddes in his refusal 'to recognize the no-trespass signs that smaller minds erected around their chosen fields of specialization.' Veblen was at once a linguist, sociologist, ethnologist, anthropologist, historian, philosopher, folklorist, and economist" (p. 109). Mumford was influenced by *The Theory of the Leisure Class* (Veblen, 1899), which he had read at City College, and by Veblen's later, lesser known works. Veblen's critique of capitalism, and search for socialist alternatives represented an alternative to Marxism that appealed to Mumford and was reflected in his work (see Mumford 1934, 1967, 1970). Mumford took a course taught by Veblen at the New School for Social Research and later worked together with him, as well as John Dewey, when he joined the staff of *The Dial*, a literary review, in 1919.

Before obtaining this job, Mumford spent a year in the Navy during which he was assigned to the Radio Training School at Cambridge, Massachusetts. After a year at *The Dial*, he briefly served as editor of the *Sociological Review*. During the 1920s, Mumford exploded onto the American intellectual scene, publishing four books: *The Story of Utopias* (Mumford, 1922), *Sticks and Stones* (Mumford, 1924), which was his first book on architecture, *The Golden Day* (Mumford, 1926), and *Herman Melville* (Mumford, 1929). During this period, he also founded the Regional Planning Association of America and through them took part in the planning of Sunnyside Gardens in Queens, and Radburn in Fair Lawn, New Jersey. By the end of the decade, he had accepted a visiting professorship at

Dartmouth College and joined the staff of the *New Yorker* magazine, as well as publishing *The Brown Decades* in 1931. The year 1934 is noteworthy because Mumford was appointed to the New York City Board of Education, in addition to publishing the first book in his optimistic Renewal of Life series, *Technics and Civilization*. The second, *The Culture of Cities*, was published in 1938. In the years leading up to the United States entry into World War II, Mumford was a strong activist advocating American involvement, to the extent that it cost him a number of friendships, including that of the isolationist Frank Lloyd Wright. The war itself cost him the life of his only son, Geddes, who was killed in combat in Italy in 1944. Not surprisingly, Mumford's criticism of military power intensified in the years that followed. During the World War II period he published *Men Must Act* (Mumford, 1939), *Faith for Living* (Mumford, 1940), *The South in Architecture* (Mumford, 1941), the third in the series Renewal of Life entitled *The Condition of'Man* (Mumford, 1944), and *City Development* (Mumford, 1945). He also joined the faculty at Stanford University as head of the School of the Humanities for a brief time.

The post-war period was a turbulent time for Mumford as he became involved in the movement against the development of atomic weapons and engaged in an ongoing dispute with Robert Moses that was "one of the most important urban policy debates of the twentieth century" (Miller, 1989, p. 477; see Caro, 1975). In 1951, he became a visiting professor at The University of Pennsylvania, and in 1957 at The Massachusetts Institute of Technology. He continued to publish: *Values for Survival* (Mumford, 1946); a biography of his son entitled *Green Memories* (Mumford, 1947); the final volume of the Renewal of Life series, *The Conduct of Life* (Mumford, 1951); *Art and Technics*, based on a Columbia University lecture series (Mumford, 1952); *In the Name of Sanity* (Mumford, 1954); *From the Ground Up* (Mumford, 1956a); *The Transformations of Man* (Mumford, 1956b); *The City in History* (Mumford, 1961), for which he won the National Book Award; and *The Highway and the City* (Mumford, 1963).

During the 1960s, he became involved in the antiwar movement, while he was also awarded the Presidential Medal of Freedom. By the end of the decade, he had completed his two-volume history of technology and culture, *The Myth of the Machine I: Technics and Human Development* (Mumford, 1967), and *The Myth of the Machine II: The Pentagon of Power* (Mumford, 1970), in many ways his crowning achievement, but for some overly polemical in its critique of technology. Between the two volumes, he published his last major work on the city, *The Urban Prospect* (Mumford, 1968). His final works consist of one collection, *Interpretations and Forecasts* (Mumford, 1972), and three autobiographical books, *Findings and Keepings* (Mumford, 1975), *My Works and Days* (Mumford, 1979), and *Sketches from Life* (Mumford, 1982). His last two decades were also full of

celebrations, honors, and awards, including the National Medal for
Literature received in 1972, and the National Medal of Arts, received in
1986. Lewis Mumford died in 1990 at the age of 94, having lived a truly
remarkable life.

MUMFORD'S EPOCHAL HISTORIOGRAPHY
OF TECHNOLOGY

The idea of dividing the past into distinct periods or epochs is not a new one,
but Mumford is noteworthy for dividing human history into a set of epochs
based not on reigns or dynasties, wars or wanderings, or ideas and Zeitgeists,
but on technological developments. In *Technics and Civilization*, Mumford
(1934) offers his readers more than simply a history of invention, but rather
he offers an entire historiography based on the machine, or as he puts it, "the
entire technological complex" (p. 12). Here, too, Mumford follows his master's lead. Using paleontology as a model, specifically the notion of early and
late paleolithic periods, Geddes gave names to the early industrial era, with
its reliance on steam power, he gave the name paleotechnic, and to the late
industrial era, characterized by electric power, he gave the name neotechnic.
To this, Mumford added a third period, as well as a degree of complexity,
and shifted the emphasis from industrialization to mechanization. He
divides the development of the machine and machine civilization into "three
successive but *over-lapping and interpenetrating phases*" (Mumford, 1934, p.
109): the eotechnic phase (about AD 1000 to 1750), the paleotechnic phase
(after 1750), and the neotechnic phase (beginning in the 20th century). Each
of these phases, according to Mumford:

> has its origin in certain definite regions and tends to employ certain spe-
> cial resources and raw materials. Each phase has its specific means of uti-
> lizing and generating energy, and its special forms of production.
> Finally, each phase brings into existence particular types of workers,
> trains them in particular ways, develops certain aptitudes and discour-
> ages others, and draws upon and further develops certain aspects of the
> social heritage. (Mumford, 1934, pp. 109-110)

Emphasizing both energy and matter, Mumford calls the eotechnic phase a
water-and-wood complex, the paleotechnic phase a coal-and-iron complex,
and the neotechnic phase an electricity-and-alloy complex (Mumford, 1934,
p. 110). One of the ways in which these three phases differ is the extent to
which their respective energy sources, materials, and modes of production
alter the natural environment (and therefore the human ecology). Water,
wind, and wood, which characterized the eotechnic phase, are renewable

natural resources. During this period, economic activities were often concentrated wherever water and wind could be most conveniently and profitably exploited, such as along waterways or wherever canals could be constructed. As a result, human settlements formed in these regions. On the other hand, coal and iron in the paleotechnic phase are depletable resources and their extraction (e.g., strip mining) has caused much ecological damage. Heavy industries in this period tended to stay close to the mines, which Mumford describes as the most inhuman of environments, and in regions where cheap transportation could be had, such as along canals or rivers. In *Technics and Civilization,* Mumford (1934) was cautiously optimistic about the potential of the neotechnic era, and especially electricity, to represent a reversal of paleotechnics. The neotechnic phase differs from the paleotechnic phase, as he puts it, "almost as white differs from black" (p. 212). As a relatively cheap and clean energy source, and one that decentralizes activities, Mumford believed that electricity could allow for a restoration of ecological balance, if it were shielded from capitalistic exploitation. This is a view he would later reverse, as he came to see that the new technics still supported and even extended centralized power, and that the fossil fuels and atomic generators that supplied electrical power posed significant threats to the environment (see Mumford, 1967, 1970).

Another way in which the three phases differ is in their impact on human life and culture. With the flexibility of wood as a material and tools that were relatively primitive, craftsmen in the eotechnic period were able to experiment freely with their materials, thereby developing skills that were both sophisticated and idiosyncratic. Comparatively, they also enjoyed a much higher degree of creativity, versatility, and autonomy in the production process than their counterparts who worked with machineries in the factory system of later times. In contrast, the paleotechnic phase was characterized by quantification, mechanization, and, ultimately, industrialization. The newer form of energy, coal and steam, caused the shifting of the industrial center of gravity, from the artisan and craftsmen's shops to the factories of heavy industries, thus creating new classes of social and economic, as well as power elites. Meanwhile, wage workers in the factories were transformed into interchangeable human parts of the machine. Life was patterned on the machine in the paleotechnic phase. In the neotechnic phase, Mumford (1934) saw the possibility of a reversal from the mechanical, inorganic, and dehumanizing nature of the paleotechnic phase. He writes of the organic nature of electricity as a form of energy and, with it, the possibility that the machine can be patterned on life, to serve human beings rather than be served by them. In this instance as well, Mumford's early optimism dissolved following World War II.

The specifics of Mumford's epochal historiography of technology are much more familiar today than they were in 1934, but the significance of his

achievement is in outlining a perspective on human history in which technology plays the leading role. As Kuhns (1971) notes, like other media ecologists who come after him, Mumford defines the machine not in terms of its
internal structure, but rather based on its effects. Thus, various phases of civilization are the effects, various forms of technics are the causes. His work
sets the stage for later studies of technology such as Giedion's (1948)
Mechanization Takes Command, Ellul's (1964) *Technological Society,*
Bolter's (1984) *Turing's Man,* Beniger's (1986) *The Control Revolution,* and
Postman's (1992) *Technopoly.* In the latter work, Postman posits three technological epochs, tool-using, technocracy, and technopoly, that more or less
correspond to Mumford's eotechnic, paleotechnic, and neotechnic phases.

Innis was also influenced by Geddes and Mumford, but identified significantly different "defining technologies," to use Bolter's (1984) phrase, in
constructing his own epochal history. Innis emphasized communication
media, rather than energy and materials, in *Empire and Communication*
(Innis, 1950) and *The Bias of Communication* (Innis, 1951). It is through
both Innis and Mumford, however, that the notion of a media environment
is derived, implicitly or explicitly, in the work of McLuhan (1951, 1962,
1964; McLuhan & McLuhan, 1988; McLuhan & Parker, 1969), Havelock
(1963, 1976, 1978, 1986), Ong (1967, 1977, 1982), Goody (1977, 1986, 1987),
Postman (1979, 1982, 1985), Eisenstein (1980), Meyrowitz (1985), Levinson
(1988, 1997), and others.

Mumford's failure to single out communication media or indeed to isolate any single defining technology ultimately leaves him lost in the particulars, unable to develop a coherent theory of technological change. It also
makes his work somewhat less compelling, at least less exciting than that of
other media ecologists, who emphasize the revolutionary impact of specific
innovations. On the other hand, highlighting media and technological revolutions often goes hand in hand with a degree of overstatement and hyperbole and a tendency toward technological determinism. Although he is
sometimes mistakenly associated with technological determinism (e.g.,
Smith, 1994), which itself is something of a straw man, Mumford is decidedly nondeterministic, arguing that if technics is out of control it is only
because its has been allowed to be. He emphasizes ecological homeostasis
and gradual evolution, as Kuhns (1971) points out: "Mumford considers
technics as a principle of modification within a larger persisting framework.
. . . His three "phases" of technical growth . . . serve less to emphasize the
importance of change that to underscore the primacy of persistence" (p. 29).
What is it that persists? Humanity itself, as Kuhns (1971) explains:

> The humanistic perspective is at once Mumford's genius and his pitfall.
> By stressing persistence over change, he has shown the panoply of tech-
> nical innovations somewhat as shifts in geological strata over a vast ter-
> rain. But the terrain, however much its topography has been altered,

remains the same place, resting on the same rock. Mumford has made man the unchanging principle against the flux of environmental change. But in doing so he has inadvertently set man against the machine. Implicit in this perspective, however, is a basic attitude toward man and his technologies: that no matter how much environments change, man remains essentially the same. Mumford refuses to allow that the threshold of change, the degree to which technologies can indeed change man, can reach and affect man as a species. The idea of some sort of technological or cultural evolution *of the species* thus remains alien to Mumford. (p. 58)

Is this a defect in Mumford's approach? According to Kuhns (1971) it is, but from Carey's (1997) point of view, this makes Mumford a better scholar and a more significant cultural theorist than McLuhan.

MUMFORD'S TECHNO-ORGANICISM

The melding of the technological and the biological as both a scientific and an aesthetic principle has been identified with postmodern culture (Bukatman, 1993; Gray, 1995; Haraway, 1991), and although the specific term techno-organic was not used by Mumford, the concept manifests itself in a number of ways in his thought. For Mumford, it is the separation between the technological and the biological that is artificial, a result of mechanization and industrialization. In *Art and Technics,* Mumford (1952) notes the close relationship between technology and biology: "Man's technical contrivances have their parallel in organic activities exhibited by other living creatures: bees build hives on engineering principles, the electric eel can produce electric shocks at high voltage, the bat developed its own radar for night flight long before man" (p. 17). Here he presents technics and organics as parallel, but in *Technics and Human Development* (Mumford, 1967), he takes the point even further, arguing that technics is a part of organics:

> In any adequate definition of technics, it should be plain that many insects, birds, and mammals had made far more radical innovations in the fabrication of containers, with their intricate nests and bowers, their geometric bee hives, their urbanoid anthills and termitaries, their beaver lodges, than man's ancestors had achieved in the making of tools until the emergence of *Homo sapiens.* In short, if technical proficiency alone were sufficient to identify and foster intelligence, man was for long a laggard, compared with many other species. The consequences of this perception should be plain: namely, that there was nothing uniquely human in tool-making until it was modified by linguistic symbols,

esthetic designs, and socially transmitted knowledge. At that point, the human brain, not just the hand, was what made a profound difference; and that brain could not possibly have been just a hand-made product, since it was already well developed in four-footed creatures like rats, which have no free-fingered hands. (p. 5)

Invoking such authorities as Mead, Cassirer, Langer, and Huizinga, Mumford (1952, 1967) argues that what makes the human species unique is not tools, industry, or labor, but rather language, art, and play. Even the opposition between art and technics is artificial:

technics has never till our own age dissociated itself from the larger cultural whole in which man, as man, has always functioned. The classic Greek term *"tekhne"* characteristically makes no distinction between industrial production and "fine" or symbolic art; and for the greater pan of human history these aspects were inseparable . . . technics, at the beginning, was broadly life-centered, not work-centered or power-centered. As in any other ecological complex, varied human interests and purposes, different organic needs, restrained the overgrowth of any single component. (Mumford, 1967, p. 9)

Mumford describes a situation in which a balance existed between the organic, the aesthetic, and the technical, one that would become unbalanced due to overemphasis on the latter with the advent of automatic machinery and steam power. Like Geddes before him, Mumford (1934) at first was tempted by what Carey (1989) calls the myth of the electronic sublime, suggesting that neotechnics could reverse the biases of paleotechnics and allow for a renewal of life:

The reawakening of the vital and the organic in every department undermines the authority of the purely mechanical. Life, which has always paid the fiddler, now begins to call the tune . . . the clue to modern technology was the displacement of the organic and the living by the artificial and the mechanical. Within technology itself this process, in many departments, is being reversed: we are returning to the organic: at all events, we no longer regard the mechanical as all-embracing and all-sufficient. (Mumford, 1934, pp. 371-372)

The theme of technological reversal is one McLuhan (1964) would pick up on, but Mumford (1934) took it where McLuhan did not, into the realm of politics, suggesting that an organic ideology was replacing a mechanical one. Mumford's own proposal for a democratic socialism was rooted in a techno-organicism, as were other socialist programs of that time, including the Soviet Union's Marxist-Leninism, which was also known as scientific socialism, as well as Germany's National Socialism. Mumford's humanistic socialism was as opposed to such totalitarian systems as it was to the excesses of capitalism, but it is interesting to note the prevalence of organic metaphors during the early 20th century.

Carey (1997) discusses the many ways that the early Mumford (1934) anticipates McLuhan's (1964) own techno-organicism, including the idea that technologies are extensions of the biological, that communication media are extensions of the sense organs, and that they can alter perceptions, that the content of a medium is another medium, that the printing press played a key role in the mechanization of the west (although Mumford argued that it played a secondary role, amplifying the effects of the mechanical clock), and that electricity was restoring organic unity and ecological balance. Much as McLuhan and other media ecologists refer to media as an invisible environment, Mumford (1961), in *The City in History,* argued that systems of communication constitute an "invisible city" (pp. 563-567). McLuhan drew heavily on Mumford's work and celebrated the electronic revolution, albeit from a political position to the right of Mumford's. Mumford (1967, 1970), in turn, came to reject the reality of neotechnics, seeing in it a continuation of the "myth of the machine."[4] Not surprisingly, his critique of contemporary technics also included a sharp critique of McLuhan (see Mumford, 1970).

Mumford's techno-organicism anticipated systems theory (Nystrom, 1973) in its overall ecological perspective as well as many of its particulars. From Geddes, he derived a holistic outlook on technics, culture, and the city: "Long before Jan Smuts coined the term, Geddes practiced what we now call holism, arguing that no living organism could be understood except in terms of the total environment in which it functioned. This is one of the most important ideas he passed on to Lewis Mumford, who became, in time, America's leading proponent of holistic thinking" (Miller, 1989, p.54). Similarly, just as systems theory maintains that the whole is greater than the sum of its parts, that phenomena emerge out of the interaction or synergy of the parts, Mumford (1934) discusses the idea of "technical syncretism" (p. 107). Whereas cybernetics focuses on the science of control through communication and feedback, Mumford (1934) writes about the clock as a mechanism for controlling and coordinating human activity. Whereas systems theory includes the concept of a boundary separating the system from its environment, Mumford (1961, 1967) emphasized the container as a technology. Unlike tools and weapons, which truly were extensions of man, container technologies are an often overlooked form of technics that according to Mumford (1961) were extensions of the feminine:

> in woman the soft internal organs are the center of her life: her arms and
> legs serve less significantly for movement than for holding and enclos-

ing, whether it be a lover or a child; and it is in the orifices and sacs, in mouth, vulva, vagina, breast, womb, that her sexually individualized activities take place. Under woman's dominance, the neolithic period is pre-eminently one of containers: it is an age of stone and pottery utensils, of vases, jars, vats, cisterns, bins, barns, granaries, houses, not least great collective containers like irrigation ditches and villages. The uniqueness and significance of this contribution has too often been overlooked by modem scholars who gauge all technical advances in terms of the machine. (pp. 15-16)

Tool, weapon, and machine are culturally coded as masculine, whereas organisms and biological reproduction are coded as feminine, as are containers, architecture, and cities. Mumford (1961) refers to the city as the "maternal enclosure" (p. 15), and "a container of containers" (p. 16), or metacontainer (Strate, 1996). His emphasis on container technology links Mumford's work on technics to his urban studies. Moreover, in contrast to the medium as extension, technology as container is more closely related to the notion of a media environment or technological system (see also Eastham, 1990).

Mumford's Critique of the Megamachine

As noted earlier, in *Technics and Civilization* Mumford (1934) sets up a polar opposition between the ideology of the machine and organic ideology. More than a half century later, Postman (1992) writes: "embedded in every tool is an ideological bias, a predisposition to construct the world as one thing rather than another, to value one thing over another, to amplify one sense or skill or attitude more loudly than another" (p. 13). In other words, neither are technologies neutral, nor are they reducible to the material. Associated with every technology is an idea, an approach, an organizing principle. This is true of individual technologies, as Postman points out, but it also applies to "the machine," to "the entire technological complex" (Mumford, 1934, p. 12). The ideology of the machine is based on order, control, efficiency, and power (Mumford, 1934, 1967, 1970). In contrast, organic ideology is rooted in life, survival, and reproduction. The irony is that machine ideology is in fact an extension of organic ideology, an extension that ultimately amputates what it is extending, or reverses into its opposite, to use McLuhan's (1964) pet phrases. As Mumford puts it:

Machines have developed out of a complex of non-organic agents for converting energy, for performing work, for enlarging the mechanical or sensory capacities of the human body, or for reducing to a measurable order and regularity the processes of life. The automaton is the last step in a process that began with the use of one part or another of the human body as a tool. In back of the development of tools and machines lies the

attempt to modify the environment in such a way as to fortify and sustain the human organism: the effort is either to extend the powers of the
otherwise unarmed organism, or to manufacture outside of the body a
set of conditions more favorable toward maintaining equilibrium and
ensuring its survival. (Mumford, 1934, pp. 9-10)

At what point does the extension of organic ideology flip into the ideology of the machine, that is, when does the techno-organic become the
techno-mechanic? At first, Mumford (1934) traces its origins back to the
middle ages, but later, moves it further back to the ancient and prehistoric
world. In *The City in History* (Mumford, 1961), the origin of mechanical
ideology is connected to the origin of civilization and of the city:

the gigantic forces of nature were brought under conscious human
direction: tens of thousands of men moved into action as one machine
under centralized command, building irrigation ditches, canals, urban
mounds, ziggurats, temples, palaces, pyramids, on a scale hitherto
inconceivable. As an immediate outcome of the new power mythology,
the machine itself had been invented: long invisible to archaeologists
because the substance of which it was composed—human bodies—had
been dismantled and decomposed. (p. 34)

Mumford's remarkable insight into the origins of the machine is based
on the fact that he defines the machine in terms of effects rather than form
(Kuhns, 1971), and in terms of inherent ideology rather than necessary
materials. The first machine is a human machine, its invention made possible by a new human ecology. Mumford (1967, 1970) further elaborated on
this idea in his two-volume *Myth of the Machine* series. In it, as Miller (1986)
summarizes:

Mumford unfolds his complex, radically speculative theory of human
origins and technological advance, concluding with what is perhaps his
most controversial thesis: that the modern power state is merely an
updated and vastly magnified version of an ancient bureaucratic-mili-
tary system he calls the megamachine, a labor machine composed entirely of human parts, assembled by the Egyptian Pharaohs to build the
great pyramids. (p. 301)

To build the pyramids required thousands upon thousands of human laborers on any given day and decades of ongoing coordination and control of
these laborers. As Mumford (1967) points out:

The difficulty was to turn a random collection of human beings,
detached from their family and community and their familiar occupa-

tions, each with a will or at least a memory of his own, into a mechanized group that could be manipulated at command. The secret of mechanical control was to have a single mind with a well-defined aim at the head of the organization, and a method of passing messages through a series of intermediate functionaries until they reached the smallest unit. Exact reproduction of the message and absolute compliance were both essential. (pp. 191-192)

Compliance required some measure of coercive force, at least in the form of a threat. Thus, organized military power not only constituted one form of the human machine, the "military machine" (Mumford, 1967, p. 188), but also was responsible for setting up and maintaining other "labor machines" (p. 188). Machine ideology also required a machine language, a system of communication that would allow the human parts of military and labor machines, separated in space and time, to function as a single unit. That is why the origins of the machine, the city, and civilization are strongly associated with systems of notation:

If one single invention was necessary to make this larger mechanism operative for constructive tasks as well as for coercion, it was probably the invention of writing. This method of translating speech into graphic record not merely made it possible to transmit impulses and messages throughout the system, but to fix accountability when written orders were not carried out. Accountability and the written word both went along historically with the control of large numbers; and it is no accident that the earliest uses of writing were not to convey ideas, religious or otherwise, but to keep temple records of grain, cattle, pottery, fabricated goods, stored and disbursed. (Mumford, 1967, p. 192)

In this sense, writing was also a container technology, one that stored not materials but information and ideas. These, in turn, would be processed by the container of containers, the city, which functioned as the first, human computer (see Strate, 1996). The human machine also demanded such inventions of the mind as "mathematics and astronomical observation, writing and the written record, and finally, the religious idea of a universal order derived from observation of the heavens, an idea that gave divine authority to the king" (Miller, 1989, p. 522), who would carry out the heavenly mandate. It was through the introduction of the institution of royalty that monopolies of power and knowledge were formed within the walls of citadels (Mumford, 1961). As centers of divine command and control, the citadel was the source of order and power, of royal edict and law, of military coercion and bureaucratic organization, through which human beings were made into servomechanisms of the machine. As every machine has an inventor, so Mumford (1967) identifies the divine king as the inventor of the human machine:

> In doing justice to the immense power and scope of Divine Kingship both as myth and active institution I have so far left one important aspect for closer examination, its greatest and most durable contribution—the invention of the archetypical machine. This extraordinary invention proved in fact to be the earliest working model for all later complex machines, though the emphasis slowly shifted from the human operatives to the more reliable mechanical parts. The unique act of kingship was to assemble the manpower and to discipline the organization that made possible the performance of work on a scale never attempted before. (p. 188)

The human or archetypal machine is also referred to by Mumford (1967) as the "invisible machine" (p. 188) and, "when all the components, political and economic, military, bureaucratic and royal, must be included . . . the 'megamachine': in plain words, the Big Machine" (pp. 188-189). Insofar as the megamachine served as the archetype and model of all other machines, it might also be referred to as the metamachine.

In *Technics and Civilization,* Mumford (1934) had suggested that the machine originated with the invention of the clock in the Bendictine monasteries of the 12th and 13th centuries, and within the expanded perspective of the megamachine, one can see this as an important turning point in the diffusion of the ideology of the machine. In Mumford's analysis, the invention of the mechanical clock was driven in part by the desire to maintain regularity in the routine of the monasteries and, on another level, to impose order on human conduct. According to Mumford (1934), "Benedict added a seventh period to the devotions of the day, and in the seventh century, by a bull of Pope Sabinianus, it was decreed that the bells of the monastery be rung seven times in the twenty-four hours. These punctuation marks in the day were known as the canonical hours, and some means of keeping count of them and ensuring their regular repetition became necessary" (p. 13).

The mechanical clock was conceived as a means to keep track of or signal the canonical hours; ultimately, it became the regulator of human actions within the monastic walls. The desire and necessity for maintaining regularity, order, and regimentation was the inherent agenda of the mechanical clock. This invention of the monasteries, Mumford (1934) observed, "helped to give human enterprise the regular collective beat and rhythm of the machine; for the clock is not merely a means of keeping track of the hours, but of synchronizing the actions of men" (pp. 13-14). The concept of time that was once associated with organic ideology, that of a sequence of subjective human experiences that may not have any definitive shape or boundary, and that of a stable and nurturing environment (all things in their own good time) was retooled to fit the ideology of the machine; the clock, with its discrete hours, minutes, and seconds "dissociated time from human events and

helped create the belief in an independent world of mathematically measurable sequences: the special world of science" (Mumford, 1934, p. 15).

As the clock echoed outside the walls of the monastery and its ideology
diffused throughout secular society, "the regular striking of the bells
brought a new regularity into the life of the workman and the merchant. The
bells of the clock tower almost defined urban existence. Time-keeping
passed into time-serving and time-accounting and time-rationing"
(Mumford, 1934, p. 14). Contrary to the popular view that the invention of
the steam engine circa 1760 initiated the age of the capitalism and the views
of media ecologists such as Innis (1950, 1951), McLuhan (1962, 1964), and
Eisenstein (1980) that the advent of the printing press in the 1450s had laid
the foundation for mass production and consumption, Mumford (1934) suggested that capitalism was the offspring of the mechanical clock, which he
described as:

> a new kind of power-machine, in which the source of power and the
> transmission were of such a nature as to ensure the even flow of energy
> throughout the works and to make possible regular production and a
> standardized product. In its relationship to determinable quantities of
> energy, to standardization, to automatic action, and finally to its own
> special product, accurate timing, the clock has been the foremost
> machine in modem technics: and at each period it has remained in the
> lead: it marks a perfection toward which other machines aspire. (pp. 14-
> 15)

The clock was the "defining technology" (Bolter, 1984) of the mechanical,
industrial, capitalist era, that is, the paleotechnic epoch. It was during this
period that the ideology of the machine became widely diffused and adopted, displacing that of the organic. As Miller (1986) observes: Subjectivity,
intuition, and feeling had no place in a framework of ideas emphasizing
organization, regularity, standardization, and control. This denial of the
organic, in Mumford's view, allowed the West to surrender to the machine, to
turn inventions and mechanical contrivances that other cultures, such as the
Chinese, possessed in abundance into what he called "the machine." (p. 300)

As Mumford moved away from his early optimism concerning the possibility of a return to organic ideology expressed in *Technics and
Civilization* (Mumford, 1934), he came to the conclusion that electricity and
other 20th-century technologies had in fact extended and intensified the ideology of the machine, and retrieved the ancient megamachine in new guise:

> The first intimation that a new megamachine was in fact being assem-
> bled came only after the First World War, with the rise of the totalitari-
> an states, beginning with Soviet Russia and Italy. . . . The new form of
> the fascist or communist dictatorships was that of a single party organ-

ization, based on a self-appointed revolutionary junta, and headed by a flesh-and-blood incarnation of the old-time "king by divine right," one no longer anointed by God, but, like Napoleon, self-crowned: a ruthless dictator (Lenin), a demonic Fuhrer (Hitler), a bloody tyrant (Stalin), proclaiming the lawfulness of unqualified power, unlawfully seized. (Mumford, 1970, p. 244)

Similar to its predecessor in the Pyramid Age, the modern megamachine also emphasized order, control, efficiency, and power. Combining human and artificial parts, the modem megamachine also depends on communication technology to function effectively:

Though the ancient megamachine would hardly have been conceivable without the invention of writing, earlier totalitarian regimes fell down repeatedly because of slowness in communication; indeed one of the chief concerns of older megamachines was the improvement of road and water communication, with relays of runners and horses, or with galleys pulled in machinelike unison by slaves. Once the telegraph was invented, followed by telephone and radio, these limitations on effecting long-distance control were abolished. Theoretically, any spot on earth can now be in instant oral communication with every other spot, and instant visual transactions anywhere are only a short distance behind. An almost equal acceleration in speed has taken place in transporting the human body. . . . Power, speed, and control have been the chief marks of absolute monarchs in all ages: the doing away with previous natural limitations in these areas is the common theme that unites the ancient and modem megamachine. (Mumford, 1970, pp. 258-259)

In this passage can be seen the extent to which Mumford eventually incorporated the insights of Innis, McLuhan, and Ellul into his own ecology of technics. Again, Mumford also points to the role of military coercion, so much so that he gives the second volume of *The Myth of the Machine* the title *The Pentagon of Power* (Mumford, 1970). Of particular concern for him was military technics, especially nuclear weapons. World War II and the Cold War had led to the formation of a military-industrial megamachine in the United States, in the service of capitalism, and serviced by the organization man. Mumford (1970) even saw a parallel between the building of the pyramids and the space program, noting the similarity between the mummy in his tomb and the astronaut in his space capsule; in both instances, the purpose was to send a select few to what was conceived of as the heavens. In this way, a parallel to Divine Kingship was resurrected. But the most important common feature shared by the ancient and modern megamachine is that, as Mumford (1970) puts it, "The ideology that underlies and unites the ancient and the modem megamachine is one that ignores the needs and purposes of life in order to fortify the power complex and extend its dominion" (p. 260).

Mumford opposed this ideology with the entirety of his being, for the entirety of his life.

MUMFORD'S ECOLOGICAL ETHICS

By way of conclusion, the ecological ethics inherent in Mumford's work and his life should be considered. Mumford ultimately affirmed human agency and personal responsibility, even in the face of the megamachine or, perhaps, especially under such conditions. If technology has gone out of control, like a runaway locomotive, the solution was to regain control, get back in the driver's seat. Ethics means engagement with the world, and Mumford was never one to remain hidden in the ivory tower, locked away in an academic citadel. Rather, he was a public intellectual and activist who would not stand quietly by while the megamachine went about its business, but instead would take a stand, and organize opposition.

Mumford was a champion of rationality and planning. This might be seen today as quaintly modern, instead of cynically postmodern. No doubt, rational, logical approaches to the world had much to do with the diffusion of modem technics and the ideology of the machine, but Mumford saw an irrational drive to power (and profit) at its core. The irrationality of power has been pushing people in the direction of alienation, dehumanization, and annihilation through war and environmental destruction, and the only solution for Mumford is the conscious application of rational thought and guidance. From Geddes, he learned about the possibility of planning, of using logic to devise more stable, sustainable, and equitable living arrangements. This makes Mumford a champion of Enlightenment ethics, a position Postman would later adopt (Postman, 1985, 1992, 1999; see also Strate, 1994).

Rationality alone would not be enough, however. In terms of urban development, Mumford championed planning with regionalism in mind. This meant resisting the drive to megalopolis, restricting the size of urban communities, and insisting on their harmonious coexistence with their regional environment. Ecological ethics implies harmony, balance, and a sense of proportion. Moreover, Mumford's plea for reviving the organic ideology implies an ethics in which what takes precedence is life and its drives, that is, survival, reproduction, and, yes, pleasure. The sensual and the sensuous, art and love, are part of this ideology. From the point of view of Mumford's ethics, conventional morality is unnecessarily repressive.

In the end, Mumford remained open to the possibility of salvation through the organic, even in the face of the megamachine and its megatechnics:

> In so far as an organic model pervades all human activities . . . it has
> saved mechanization from many embarrassments, just as humane village

customs and traditions and even older animal loyalties have often modified harsh legal codes that left no merciful loopholes. . . . If we are to
prevent megatechnies from further controlling and deforming every
aspect of human culture, we shall be able to do so only with the aid of a
radically different model derived directly . . . from living organisms and
living complexes (ecosystems). . . . This new model will in time replace
megatechnics with biotechnics; and that is the first step toward passing
from power to plenitude. Once an organic world picture is ascendant,
the working aim of an economy of plenitude will be, not to feed more
human functions into the machine, but to develop further man's incal-
culable potentialities for self-actualization and self-transcendence.
(Mumford, 1970, p. 395)

Mumford's hope and vision for a techno-organic future is one in which
the machine does not disappear but is brought back under human control
and into organic harmony and ecological balance. It is one in which progress
does not come to an end, but rather is directed toward the human condition
instead of technological expansion. It is one in which a house can be constructed in which all can live, an ecology in which all can thrive, a whole in
which people will never be reduced to machine parts.

ENDNOTES

1. Kuhns (1971) does not use the specific term media ecology, but does refer to
   media environments and information ecologies.
2. It is important to acknowledge at this point that the need to identify a founder is
   often based on a cultural if not mythical imperative, rather than a logical necessity (see Kirk, 1983). Intellectual history is an exercise in intertextuality that is
   not without its relevance, but by its very nature defies closure. Thus, for example, Geddes was, in turn, influenced by the work of the Russian prince, Petr
   Kropotkin.
3. Veblen also was influential in the education of Harold Innis (Stamps, 1995), making him another intellectual connection between the Toronto and New York
   schools.
4. Carey (1997) notes that Mumford's reversal of position on electric technology
   runs counter to McLuhan's own reversal between *The Mechanical Bride*
   (McLuhan, 1951) and *Understanding Media* (McLuhan, 1964). Postman's shift
   from *Teaching as a Subversive Activity* (Postman & Weingartner, 1969) to
   Teaching as a Conserving Activity (Postman, 1979) parallels Mumford's, as the
   earlier book celebrates the electronic media in the manner of McLuhan, whereas
   the later one is quite critical of television's effects on culture and cognition.
   Although Postman's shift has also been viewed as a political one, it actually maintains a consistently liberal orientation that would place him closer to Mumford
   than McLuhan in his ideology.

REFERENCES

Beniger, J. R. (1986). *The control revolution: Technological and economic origins of the information society.* Cambridge, MA: Harvard University Press.

Bolter, J. D. (1984). *Turing's man: Western culture in the computer age.* Chapel Hill: University of North Carolina Press.

Bukatman, S. (1993). *Terminal identity: The virtual subject in postmodern science fiction.* Durham, NC: Duke University Press.

Carey, J. W. (1989). *Communication as culture: Essays on media and society.* Boston: Unwin Hyman.

Carey, J. W. (1997). *James Carey: A critical reader* (E. S. Munson & C. A. Warren, Eds.). Minneapolis: University of Minnesota Press.

Caro, R.A. (1975). *The power broker: Robert Moses and the fall of New York.* New York: Vintage.

Eastham, S. (1990). *The media matrix: Deepening the context of communication studies.* Lanham, MD: University Press of America.

Eisenstein, E. L. (1980). *The printing press as an agent of change.* New York: Cambridge University Press.

Ellul, J. (1964). *The technological society* (J. Wilkinson, Trans.). New York: Vintage. (Original work published 1954)

Geddes, P. (1904). *City development: A study of parks, gardens and culture institutes: A report to the Carnegie Dunfermline Trust.* Edinburgh, Scotland: Geddes and Colleagues.

Geddes, P. (1915). *Cities in evolution: An introduction to the town planning movement and to the study of civics.* London: Williams & Norgate.

Giedion, S. (1948). *Mechanization takes command.* New York: Oxford University Press.

Goody, J. (1977). *The domestication of the savage mind.* Cambridge, MA: Cambridge University Press.

Goody, J. (1986). *The logic of writing and the organisation of society.* Cambridge, MA: Cambridge University Press.

Goody, J. (1987). *The interface between the written and the oral.* Cambridge, MA: Cambridge University Press.

Gray, C.H. (Ed.). (1995). *The cyborg handbook.* New York: Routledge.

Haraway, D. J. (1991). *Simians, cyborgs, and women: The reinvention of nature.* New York: Routledge.

Havelock, E. A. (1963). *Preface to Plato.* Cambridge, MA: The Belknap Press of Harvard University Press.

Havelock, E. A. (1976). *Origins of western literacy.* Toronto, Canada: The Ontario Institute for Studies in Education.

Havelock, E. A. (1978). *The Greek concept of justice: From its shadow in Homer to its substance in Plato.* Cambridge, MA: Harvard University Press.

Havelock, E. A. (1986). *The muse learns to write: Reflections on orality and literacy from antiquity to the present.* New Haven, CT: Yale University Press.

Hawley, A. H. (1986). *Human ecology; A theoretical essay.* Chicago: University of Chicago Press.

Innis, H. A. (1950). *Empire and communication.* New York: Oxford University Press.

Innis, H. A. (1951). *The bias of communication.* Toronto, Canada: University of Toronto Press.

Kirk, G. S. (1983). *The nature of Greek myths.* New York: Penguin Books.

Kuhns, W. (1971). *The post-industrial prophets: Interpretations of technology.* New York: Weybright & Talley.

Levinson, P. (1988). *Mind at large: Knowing in the technological age.* Greenwich, CT: JAI Press.

Levinson, P. (1997). *The soft edge: A natural history and future of the information revolution.* New York: Routledge.

Luccarelli, M. (1995). *Lewis Mumford and the ecological region: The politics of planning.* New York: Gufolford.

McLuhan, M. (1951). *The mechanical bride: Folklore of industrial man.* Boston, MA: Beacon Press.

McLuhan, M. (1962). *The Gutenberg galaxy: The making of typographic man.* Toronto, Canada: University of Toronto Press.

McLuhan, M. (1964). *Understanding media: The extensions of man.* New York: McGraw-Hill.

McLuhan, M., & McLuhan, E. (1988). *Laws of media: The new science.* Toronto, Canada: University of Toronto Press.

McLuhan, M., & Parker, H. (1969). *Counterblast.* New York: Harcourt Brace & World.

Meyrowitz, J. (1985). *No sense of place.* New York: Oxford University Press.

Miller, D. L. (Ed.). (1986). *The Lewis Mumford reader.* New York: Pantheon.

Miller, D.L. (1989). *Lewis Mumford: A life.* New York: Weidenfeld & Nicolson.

Mumford, L. (1922). *The story of Utopias.* New York: Boni & Liveright.

Mumford, L. (1924). *Sticks and stones: A study of American architecture and civilization.* New York: Boni & Liveright.

Mumford, L. (1926). *The golden day: A study in American experience and culture.* New York: Boni & Liveright.

Mumford, L. (1929). *Herman Melville.* New York: Harcourt Brace.

Mumford, L. (1931). *The brown decades: A study of the arts in America, 1865-1895.* New York: Harcourt Brace.

Mumford, L. (1934). *Technics and civilization.* New York: Harcourt Brace.

Mumford, L. (1938). *The culture of cities.* New York: Harcourt, Brace.

Mumford, L. (1939). *Men must act.* New York: Harcourt, Brace.

Mumford, L. (1940). *Faith for living.* New York: Harcourt, Brace.

Mumford, L. (1941). *The south in architecture.* New York: Harcourt, Brace.

Mumford, L. (1944). *The condition of man.* New York: Harcourt, Brace and Company.

Mumford, L. (1945). *City development.* New York: Harcourt, Brace.

Mumford, L. (1946). *Values for survival: Essays, addresses, and letters on politics and education.* New York: Harcourt, Brace.

Mumford, L. (1947). *Green memories: The story of Geddes Mumford.* New York: Harcourt Brace.

Mumford, L. (1951). *The conduct of life.* New York: Harcourt, Brace.

Mumford, L. (1952). *Art and technics.* New York: Columbia University Press.

Mumford, L. (1954). *In the name of sanity.* New York: Harcourt, Brace.

Mumford, L. (1956a). *From the ground up.* New York: Harcourt, Brace.

Mumford, L. (1956b). *The transformations of man.* New York: Harper.

Mumford, L. (1961). *The city in history: Its origins, its transformations, and its prospects.* New York: Harcourt Brace & World.

Mumford, L. (1963). *The highway and the city.* New York: Harcourt Brace & World.

Mumford, L. (1967). *The myth of the machine: I. Technics and human development.* New York: Harcourt Brace & World.

Mumford, L. (1968). *The urban prospect.* New York: Harcourt Brace & World.

Mumford, L. (1970). *The myth of the machine: II. The pentagon of power.* New York: Harcourt Brace Jovanovich.

Mumford, L. (1972). *Interpretations and forecasts.* New York: Harcourt Brace Jovanovich.

Mumford, L. (1975). *Findings and keepings: Analects for an autobiography.* New York: Harcourt Brace Jovanovich.

Mumford, L. (1979). *My works and days: A personal chronicle.* New York: Harcourt Brace Jovanovich.

Mumford, L. (1982). *Sketches from life: The autobiography of Lewis Mumford.* New York: Dial.

Novak, F.G., Jr. (Ed.). (1995). *Lewis Mumford and Patrick Geddes: The correspondence.* London: Routledge.

Nystrom, C. (1973). *Towards a science of media ecology: The formulation of integrated conceptual paradigms for the study of human communication systems.* Unpublished doctoral Dissertation, New York University, New York.

Ong, W.J. (1967). *The presence of the word.* Minneapolis: University of Minnesota Press.

Ong, W.J. (1977). *Interfaces of the word.* Ithaca, NY: Cornell University Press.

Ong, W.J. (1982). *Orality and literacy.* London: Methuen.

Postman, N. (1970). The reformed English curriculum. In A.C. Eurich (Ed.), *High school 1980: The shape of the future in American secondary education* (pp.160-168). New York: Pitman.

Postman, N. (1979). *Teaching as a conserving activity.* New York: Delacorte.

Postman, N. (1982). *The disappearance of childhood.* New York: Delacorte.

Postman, N. (1985). *Amusing ourselves to death.* New York: Viking.

Postman, N. (1992). *Technopoly: The surrender of culture to technology.* New York: Alfred A. Knopf.

Postman, N. (1999). *Building a bridge to the eighteenth century: How the past can improve our future.* New York: Alfred A. Knopf.

Postman, N., & Weingartner, C. (1969). *Teaching as a subversive activity.* New York: Delta.

Postman, N., & Weingartner, C. (1971). *The soft revolution: A student handbook for turning schools around.* New York: Delacorte.

Smith, M.R. (1994). Technological determinism in American culture. In M.R. Smith & L. Marx (Eds.), *Does technology drive history?* (pp. 1-35). Cambridge, MA: MIT Press.

Stamps, J. (1995). *Unthinking modernity: Innis, McLuhan, and the Frankfurt school.* Montreal, Canada: McGill-Queens University Press.

Strate, L. (1994). Post(modern)man, or Neil Postman as a postmodernist. *ETC.: A Review of General Semantics 51*(2), 159-170.

Strate, L. (1996). Containers, computers, and the media ecology of the city. *media ecology* [online]. Available via World-Wide Web: http://raven.ubalt.edu/features/media_ecology.

Veblen, T. (1899). *The theory of the leisure class: An economic study of institutions.* New York: MacMillan.

4

Jacques Ellul: Technique, Propaganda, and Modern Media

Randolph Kluver

Nanyang Technological University

Jacques Ellul is widely acknowledged as a major social theorist for his insightful and intriguing analyses of the sociological and political systems of the modern world, but his deep concern with issues of human communication is almost unknown among writers within that discipline. More than 30 years after his major writing, there have only been a handful of responses to Ellul within the discipline of communication (see, e.g., Christians, 1976, 1981, 1995; Christians & Real, 1979; Real, 1981). Nevertheless, Ellul's insight into the nature of mass media, media ecology, and modern society provides a welcome challenge to the presumptions that underlie media consumption. In many ways, Ellul articulated key themes that would not be prominent in mainstream communication studies for some years, and placed media processes at the forefront of social analysis.

In this chapter, I describe the key concepts that underlie Ellul's work, *la technique* and propaganda, and demonstrate the utility of Ellul's foundational concepts for media ecology. By demonstrating the utility of Ellul's thought for understanding contemporary society and the role of media in society, I also hope to illustrate Ellul's relationship to other key thinkers in the media ecology tradition.

BIOGRAPHY

Jacques Ellul was born in France and educated at the University of Bordeaux and the University of Paris. Like many of his generation, Ellul was affected by the global forces that were shaping Europe during the 1930s and 1940s, including fascism, communism, and socialism. While still a teen, Ellul had two conversions, one to the worldview of Karl Marx, who explained for Ellul the relationship between economic power and social structure, and one to Jesus Christ, who explained for Ellul the nature of humans and the larger existential questions of life. For the rest of his life, Ellul fashioned a dialectic outlook of these two commitments, as he saw the two were not reconcilable. From Marx, he gained a coherent framework for interpreting and understanding economic and social reality, and from Christianity, he gained a vision of what society and human life should be like, as well as a hope for the future of humanity (Clendenin, 1989, pp. xxi-xxiii).

Ellul received a doctorate in law in 1936 and took up teaching. He was deeply disturbed by the rise of the fascist movements in Europe, and was fired by the Nazi-influenced Vichy government in France. Later, after his father had been arrested, he fled Bordeaux and served in the French resistance movement to the Vichy regime. Believing that the chaos of the war had left France a "blank slate" in terms of its existing social and political structures, he later had a brief stint as a deputy mayor of Bordeaux. As the same social structures reasserted themselves, however, he became convinced that worthwhile political action was impossible in the face of the overwhelming strength of recurrent social forces.

Ellul became a professor of law and politics at the University of Bordeaux, and spent the rest of his career there writing on the problems of modern society, particularly concerning technique, propaganda, and the totalizing nature of mass society. His earliest well-known work, *The Presence of the Kingdom* (Ellul, 1948/1989a), laid out his convictions concerning the role of Christian intellectuals, and also foreshadowed many of the themes for which he would later become famous.

For the rest of his career, Ellul embodied his own social and intellectual principles. He remained engaged in organizations to curb youth crime and delinquency as well as environmental activism. In line with his total disillusion with social order, his approach to youth gangs was not to make the youth "adjusted," but rather "positively maladjusted" to the society of the time. Most of Ellul's writings (some 50 books, and more than 1,000 articles, both academic and popular) revolved around the interrelated issues of communication, technology, and propaganda. After a lengthy illness, Ellul died in 1994.

TECHNIQUE, PROPAGANDA, AND MEDIA

Ellul's greatest concern was not with mass media, but rather with the dramatic changes he witnessed in modern society, of which the mass media are a critical part, but more particularly, the ways in which society became "dehumanized" by technology, politics, and media. Although he died before the advent of current studies on "information society," he nevertheless anticipated much of the analysis that would follow. Ellul's central argument is that the technological methods and mindset of the contemporary world have created a technical milieu, in which human society, thought processes, and communication are altered. In his view, the complexities of modern society both necessitate the rise of technology and in the process, dehumanize experience. Contemporary mass media, in the pursuit of ever more efficient channels of influencing humans, undermine democracy and critical intelligence. Informed debate about significant issues is replaced by propaganda, and meaningful human communication is replaced by clichés, half-truths, symbolically powerful catchwords, and ultimately, images. Ellul argues that images and other technically superior information delivery systems and message formats usurp human discourse about values, goals, and means.

La Technique

Ellul is chiefly known for two key concepts, *la technique* and propaganda. The first, *la technique*, Ellul sees as a self-directing and self-augmenting social process. In order to distinguish the unique concept expressed in French as *la technique* from the more innocuous English words technique or technology, I use the italicized *la technique* in this chapter to refer to Ellul's concept. Ellul does not argue against technique or technology itself, but rather the human mindset that replaces critical moral discourse with technological means and values. The processes inherent in a technologically advanced society create a social value of efficiency. A contemporary example would be genetic cloning. Once we have given primary consideration to technological questions (can it be done?), we lose all sight of axiological questions (should it be done?) and ultimately begin asking purely technical questions (what is the most efficient way it can be done?). Recently, scientists in Europe have dismissed moral criticism of human cloning by arguing that because the technology exists, cloning will inevitably be accepted in society, vividly illustrating Elluls' major contention. When any realm of human life is subjected to *la technique*, the efficiency and efficacy of those processes guarantees the eventual abdication of humanistic and moral criteria in favor of technical standards. Ellul argues that the efficiency paradigm, or the default tendency to turn all tasks over to a more efficient technology, ultimately disqualifies moral discourse from public policy, leading directly or indirectly to the dehumanization of society.

Ellul (1954/1964) argues that "the technical phenomenon is the main preoccupation of our time; in every field men seek to find the most efficient method" (p. 21). As a result, numerical and technical criterion take precedence, over and above any critical or moral criterion. He argues that a human can "decide only in favor of the technique that gives the maximum efficiency" (p. 80). He then argues that all of human life has been given over to *la technique*, including economics, politics, social, and commercial organization, and human influence. This argument, developed primarily in *The Technological Society* (Ellul, 1954/1964), is the cornerstone for several of his most important later works, including *Propaganda: The Formation of Men's Attitudes* (Ellul, 1962/1965, hereafter *Propaganda*) and the *Technological System* (Ellul, 1977/1980).

In the field of communication, *la technique* has also overtaken public discourse, especially in the media. "New media are essentially and primarily technological media" (Ellul, 1977/1980, p. 9), and hence the characteristics of modern mass media are the same characteristics of technological society as a whole. Scientific discovery of human motivational forces, primarily from the fields of psychology, sociology, and human relations, provides the techniques which drive modern media systems. These "sciences" exist for the value they provide in understanding and influencing humans, and in turn, modern research into the effectiveness of media channels becomes the "scientific" basis for stripping humans of their critical discernment. Psychology becomes advertising, and sociology becomes marketing.

PROPAGANDA

The second critical concept that defines Ellul's vision of modern society is propaganda. Among communication scholars, *Propaganda* (Ellul, 1962/1965) is the best known, and in this work, he argues that *la technique* has invaded the realm of politics and persuasion, and that those responsible for public discussion of issues, such as the media systems and the government, now use the techniques of propaganda to override rational discourse and critical thinking. The power of the mass media, with their ability to sway human intention, has merged with an unrelenting social science that provides unprecedented understanding of human motives, and thus has achieved a power over individuals unrivalled in human history.

At the time of Ellul's writing, most writers on propaganda relied on a limited definition of the concept, comprising primarily rhetorical and media techniques, such as those employed by the Nazi party in pre-World War II

Germany and propaganda studies consisted primarily of somewhat simplistic models of influence (Sproule, 1987). Ellul (1962/1965) dismisses this is an oversimplification of propaganda and defines propaganda as: "a set of methods . . . to bring about the active or passive participation in its actions of a mass of individuals, psychologically unified through psychological manipulations and incorporated in an organization" (p. 61). Rather than a limited set of rhetorical techniques, propaganda is comprised of a host of social scientific insights and techniques, including the mass diffusion of media, to engender compliance among a largely acquiescent audience. It is important to note that Ellul doesn't adopt a technologically determinist position, but rather argues that humans willingly give technology and technological methods sway over human affairs.

As previously noted, Ellul's primary area of interest was the relationship of the state to the individual human, rather than media. However, the role of mass media is critical to Ellul's argument, as the media are the primary means of disseminating collective convictions and realities. In a modern society, the mass media have become the means by which collective life is lived and the collective consciousness is shaped. Moreover, the centralized nature of the mass media means that rather than encouraging thought, the media instead have been a crippling force of social control. Ellul (1954/1964) argues that if an individual "listens regularly to the radio, reads the newspapers, and goes to the movies," then he is led to act from motives that "are scientifically directed and increasingly irresistible" (p. 372).

Because all media types uphold and reinforce certain social assumptions and realities, the individual never finds anything in his or her experience to contradict the assumptions of the mass society. Ellul (1954/1964) compares this to a convergence of theater projectors, "each of which has a specific color, intensity, and direction, but each of which can fulfill its individual function only on the basis of the object illuminated" (p. 391). Moreover, the degradation of modern communications to technique means that mere technicians become the most important communicators of social issues, illustrated, for example, by the celebrity (god-like) status accorded to famous newscasters. Because political discourse, for example, is mediated primarily through nonpolitically astute journalists (anchors), they achieve an inordinate power in framing public policy. As Lovekin (1991) argues, "the announcer, the celebrity, is one type of twentieth century shaman, extolling the virtues of technique while at the same time representing them" (p. 195).

The end of propaganda is not understanding and acceptance, but rather compliance. Ellul argues that it does not matter if a person agrees with the propaganda, but rather, that they respond to it. Instinct and reflex are the key issues, not understanding. Fast-food chains do not care if you think they have justifiable reasons for a conviction that you can get good food at a reasonable price, but rather that you buy their food. Thus, the social-scientific insights into human fear, lust, greed and anger, to name but a few, are the most efficient means for calling forth certain conditioned reflexes. When a scientific understanding of human motivation is merged with the totalizing and forceful nature of the mass media, the individual succumbs to mass psychology, typically induced by modern mythologies of progress, of liberalism, and of various ideologies. In the modern technological society, what is most important is the mobilization of the society. This mobilization has no specific goal, but is mobilization for its own sake. Ellul (1962/1965) argues:

> To view propaganda as still being what it was in 1850 is to cling to an obsolete concept of man and of the means to influence him. . . . The aim of modern propaganda is no longer to modify ideas, but to provoke action. It is no longer to change adherence to a doctrine, but to make the individual cling irrationally to a process of action. It is no longer to lead to a choice, but to loosen the reflexes. It is no longer to transform an opinion, but to arouse an active and mythical belief. . . . To be effective, propaganda must constantly short-circuit all thought and decision. (pp. 25-27)

Ellul argues that human face-to-face interaction provides the only antidote to the overwhelming power of the mass society. In fact, one of the characteristics of the intrusion of *la technique* into social life has been the systematic degradation of human communication in general, and ultimately the degradation of messages. Ellul (1954/1964) argues that propaganda has resulted in "the reduction of political doctrines to programs, of programs to slogans, of slogans to pictures (the direct reflex-stimulating images)" (p. 365). Particularly as political, commercial, and religious messages are given over to mass channels, they become trivialized. Visual media are but the final stage in the insipidization of human politics, religion, and philosophy. In an earlier work, Ellul (1948/1989a) argued that although mass media had benefits, real communication had been destroyed by the mediating function of modern channels, or the technologies themselves had replaced real mediation between humans (p. 94). The solution was to find a "new language," one that avoided the totalizing effects of mass media, that would allow humans to truly interact, which Ellul located in the agency of the Holy Spirit (p. 106).

As a result of the "technologization" of human communication, Ellul (1977/1980) argues that the symbolic support of human communication is replaced with a technological support (p. 36). Because the mass media (technology) have become the sole mediators between humans, the values inherent in human "communion" have become stripped from our interactions. Moreover, human consciousness is now directly impressed by the mass media, without the mediating thought characteristic of earlier forms of communication.

Ellul argues that it is impractical to attempt to distinguish between propaganda and information. "Information" in a technological society is omnipresent and overwhelms the individual. As information multiplies, it becomes more and more difficult to interpret. Citizens are left with an overwhelming amount of discourse, and so avail themselves of the ready-made interpretations provided by the propagandists, including advertisers, educators, and politicians. Propaganda, moreover, is part and parcel of the overall media environment that we inhabit, and it finds its potency within the characteristics of a modernized, mass culture. For instance, propaganda can only function in an individualistic society, where individuals are separated from the primary social groupings and loyalties that have traditionally provided social guidance and support in decision making. Humans have abandoned the smaller social groupings, such as the village, church, or guild that formerly provided guidance and social support, and have become completely autonomous and self reliant. Paradoxically, when individualism, spurred by urbanization and technologization becomes widespread, a "mass society" is the inevitable outcome. Individuals turn for information and opinions to the media, and thus imbibe the values and opinions of the collective, entirely relying on public opinion (Ellul, 1962/1965, p. 90).

Ellul argues that propaganda is not necessarily political, but is in fact more powerful in its sociological manifestation, by which he means "the penetration of an ideology by means of its sociological context" (p. 63) or the sociological, cultural, and economic structures that impose and reinforce ideology through subtle means. It rarely involves deliberate action and is typically seen as nonpolitical. An example would be popular entertainment, which assumes ideological or cultural stances, such as consumerism, for example, and perpetuates these stances without calling attention to that fact.

Moreover, propaganda is not always agitative, but is also useful for social, economic, or political integration. Propaganda of integration is most effective in a comfortable, cultivated, and informed milieu, and most effective among those who are traditionally considered resistant to it, the intellectuals: "Intellectuals are more sensitive than peasants to integration propaganda. In fact, they share the stereotypes of a society even when they are political opponents of the society" (Ellul, 1962/1965, p. 76). In other words, even those who seem to be most immune to propaganda and mass media are influenced by it, perhaps more profoundly than the rural peasant.

Ellul is concerned primarily with the ways in which *la technique*, manifested as social science and media production techniques, disrupt rational and critical thought. He argues that propaganda ultimately debilitates any society once it has begun, in that the individual loses individual judgment and creativity. "What is it that propaganda makes disappear? Everything in the nature of critical and personal judgment" (Ellul, 1962/1965, p. 169). After becoming acclimated to propaganda, the individual can no longer truly dissent. "His [sic] imagination will lead only to small digressions from the fixed line and to only slightly deviate, preliminary responses *within* the framework" (p. 169). Ellul openly acknowledges the opposition of propaganda to traditional conceptions of discourse and democracy and argues that democracy is indeed subverted in the modern world:

> For it is evident that a conflict exists between the principles of democracy—particularly its concept of the individual—and the processes of propaganda. The notion of rational man [sic], capable of thinking and living according to reason, of controlling his [sic] passions and living according to scientific patterns, of choosing freely between good and evil—all this seems opposed to the secret influences, the mobilizations of myths, the swift appeals to the irrational, so characteristic of propaganda. (p. 233)

At the social level, the consequences are disastrous. Because the media and the totalizing nature of propaganda disallow true competitive discourse, true deliberation ceases. Democratic societies must use propaganda to maintain sovereignty, but in doing so, betray the very ideal of democracy. Ideologies, philosophies, and even religious faiths, including democratic ones, become mere tools of the propaganda mechanisms which dominate social life. "The only problem is that of effectiveness, of utility. The point is not to ask oneself whether some economic or intellectual doctrine is valid, but only whether it can furnish effective catchwords capable of mobilizing the masses *here and now*" (Ellul, 1962/1965, p. 197).

Because the critical element so necessary for persuasive discourse has been lost and given over to the totalizing media and social scientific forces, a populace is left with little power other than to respond to the stimuli. Moreover, the individual or community is left with no resources with which to counter the overwhelming power of propaganda. What little dissent is allowed is channeled into irrelevant issues. The basic values of the society remain unquestioned, and what little clash remains is merely ornamental.

Ellul's critique of media is multidimensional, but I highlight just a few important issues. First, Ellul largely affirms the thrust of critical media research about the inherent centralizing processes of mass media, but would depart from what he would argue as an oversimplification of the critical issues, such as a concern over media monopolies. If all 500 cable channels, all radio broadcasts, and all newspapers affirm certain basic sociological and cultural assumptions and stereotypes, it matters not who owns or controls them. The fact that none of the channels challenge any underlying cultural and political assumptions reinforces the lack of true critique in society.

Moreover, mass media, even though they centralize social processes, also diminish the possibility of true collective action, in the democratic sense, by partitioning society into "audience segments." Ellul (1962/1965) argues that "the more propaganda there is, the more partitioning there is" (p. 213). This partitioning actually increases the hold of propaganda, in that "those who read the press of their own group and listen to the radio of their own group are constantly reinforced in their convictions. . . . As a result, people ignore each other more and more" (p. 213). Dissent thus becomes invisible, with no power to counter the overwhelming media systems.

Finally, *la technique*, particularly the merging of modern scientific methodologies with communicative technologies, has insidious implications for human freedom and democracy. Whereas previous centuries of technique had been bound to machinations and manipulations of the material world, modern media gain entry into the inner life of the psyche, and makes possible the use of the techniques of propaganda on a large scale. Individuals are now subjected to the techniques of media and propaganda constantly, and cannot escape this influence simply by leaving the room. The common response to criticisms of the mass media that "you don't have to watch," does not apply, because leaving the room doesn't remove one from the totalizing influence of the media. If one chooses not to view this particular channel, the same message will be reinforced through every other channel, every newspaper, movie, and book, as well as the entirety of the social structure.

An example of Ellul's distrust of modern media is his discussion on the role of computers in education, and the concerted social push to train all students in technical computing skills. Ellul (1990b) argues that this "educational terrorism" ultimately is detrimental to individuals, and to society, because an overemphasis on teaching technical skills means that students will not learn anything outside of narrow technological boundaries, which means the loss of critical thinking, human creative versatility, and ultimately true diversity (pp. 384-391).

Present throughout much of Ellul's work is a deep concern for human communication, which Ellul clearly wants to connect to its roots, human "communion." Although many of his works address the conflict between true discourse and propaganda, and the conflict between the image and the word, he makes his fullest argument in his work *The Humiliation of the Word* (Ellul, 1981/1985). In this work, Ellul argues that the linguistic and symbolic world that mediated human interaction in the past is increasingly being replaced with images and icons, which rather than serving as short cuts to logic and rationality, rather serve as detours.

Ellul argues that there is a fundamental distinction between the power of the word (language) and the power of the image, including pictures, movies, and graphic illustrations. Each media form has its own characteristics that affect human consciousness. The impact of sight upon human consciousness is fundamentally different from that of hearing, in that sight, which relies heavily on visual images, is the realm of reality, or the immediate experiences surrounding us, whereas hearing (and reading) is the realm of truth. An example is that a picture can convey emotional power, but that power is undirected until the meaning of the picture is explained, through words.

For Ellul, sight is about "reality," or the immediate visual and emotional context. The Word, however, is about truth, or the abstract and logical imperatives for true understanding. Reality is immediate, but it is also deceptive. Sight commits humans to *la technique*, in that it implies mastery and method (Ellul, 1981/1985, p. 11). The meaning inherent in spoken and written discourse is radically different from the emotional power of images. Whereas one can critically evaluate or question language, thereby leaving the listener with a margin of freedom, there is no such recourse when it comes to images (p. 23).

In all of this, Ellul does not dismiss sight, or images, as irrelevant. He merely argues that images must be kept in balance with the word. The inability of the image to convey truth, only reality, means that as mass media become more important in society, citizens are further removed from any means of rational discussion. Because we are "overwhelmed with images," we have become less able to appreciate and respond to any other means of communication. In Ellul's (1981/1985) words, "the evidence of an image makes any other kind of expression useless" (p. 114).

Thus, the visual media, including television and film, have a disproportionately large role in social life. Television serves as a primary means of socialization, ultimately bringing conformism and standardization of social life (p. 140), whereas film breaks down natural resistance to open the viewer up to "influences, forms, and myths" (p. 119). The ultimate outcome for society is "the humiliation of the word," where because of the overwhelming influence of images, even words have lost their meaning, and have become mere slaves to propaganda (p. 156).

It is in his discussion of possibly finding some reconciliation that Ellul's theological assumptions become foregrounded. In fact, it is not possible to fully understand Ellul without appreciating his theological orientation to media form (Gozzi, 2000; Nisbet, 1981, p. vii). Ellul (1981/1985) argues that images have a proper role in human life, in that they do serve to reveal something of reality, as in the visions of prophets. Moreover, because of the certain reconciliation between word and image in the New Creation, it is impossible to dismiss either one or the other from human life (p. 252).

ELLUL AND MEDIA ECOLOGY

Ellul's work touches on a broad range of disciplines, from communication to theology to politics, and in many ways it is this breadth that makes his work relevant to the media ecology tradition. Although he was quite dismissive of the role of mass media, and would likely find much media research trivial and pedantic, his focus on media and their relationship to society in many ways foreshadows and expands on themes critical to that tradition, such as his concern with understanding both the social and political context of mass media, as well as his arguments concerning literacy, discourse, and media. Ellul agrees with the general argument of most media ecologists when he argues that communication technologies have profound consequences for social organization and ethos. Ellul's writing almost undoubtedly influenced McLuhan and others, as McLuhan (1965) wrote that Ellul's work "brings to the forefront issues that are commonly ignored in a mad search for efficiency and method, and in a manner that is both insightful and poetic" (p. 5). Ellul also was obviously influenced at various times by both McLuhan and Mumford. I discuss Ellul's relationship with other significant writers within the media ecology tradition in reference to three key issues, the impact of mass media and propaganda in society, technology, and orality and literacy in human consciousness.

Of course, more than three decades after its publication, Ellul's analysis of modern mass media seems antiquated. Ellul major works were completed at a time before commercial advertising had completely overwhelmed media, although the consolidation of media around the advertising industry had already begun. In a later lesser-known work, *The Technological Bluff*, Ellul (1990b) makes his most trenchant observations of modern society and modern communications technologies. However, many writers later reflected some of the same themes, including Postman. In his classic *Amusing Ourselves to Death*, Postman (1985) argues that the television medium inherently is unsuitable for truly meaningful discourse, such as politics and religion.

Moreover, writers such as Innis and McLuhan argued that in a media-saturated environment, there would necessarily be a convergence of cultural consciousness, or in McLuhan's (1964) term, a *global village*. This argument is foundational to much of critical mass media research, including media ecology. Ellul's perspective is largely in line with this, although he clearly sees it in a negative light. Moreover, Ellul (1977/1980) argues that McLuhan places too much emphasis on media, and is too deterministic, with not enough emphasis on the larger social milieu (p. 9). Specifically, what McLuhan attributes to media, Ellul attributes to technologization. Although many have argued, and still argue, that the more we communicate, the more we will understand one another, Ellul (1962/1965) argues that the more we rely on the technological means of communication, the less we understand at all (pp. 93-95). Media, rather than bringing greater understanding across national borders, function rather to short-circuit deliberative and reflective thought, distracting humans from the real issues that confront them, making it impossible for people to have true communication.

There is little doubt, however, that Ellul is in harmony with other media theorists in his insistence on the ubiquity of media and its necessary degeneration into propaganda. The world of the mass media is appropriate only to reinforce the existing social structures and the existing reality, not to challenge it. Moreover, media convergence is a foregone conclusion, if not in technique, at least in ideology.

A second important connection between Ellul and other theorists in the media ecology tradition is an emphasis on technology as the defining characteristic of modern society. Ellul is typically grouped along with Lewis Mumford in this regard (Strate & Lum, 2000). Mumford (1934) foreshadowed Ellul's arguments when he wrote that machinery (technology) has its own sense of order, control, and efficiency, and indeed, had ideological dimensions. Mumford, however, focused more directly on technology *per se*, whereas Ellul's concern is primarily with *la technique*, or the mode of consciousness inherent in an overreliance on technical means. Mumford identified historical epochs based on the type of technologies that existed (p. 63), whereas Ellul's historical survey focuses not on the types of technologies present, but rather on the consciousness of humans towards their technologies. For Ellul, it matters not whether one relies on microwaves or magic, the key issue is the trust you put in the technology, as opposed to reliance on humanistic values and ethical choices. Earlier generations of technology are not to be characterized so much by the specific characteristics of the techniques themselves, but to the extent that the technological consciousness exists. For example, earlier techniques were clearly not autonomous and self-reinforcing, characteristics of the modern technological society (Ellul, 1954/1964, pp. 23-60). Postman (1992) clearly echos Ellul's understanding of the ways in which technical assumptions overtake cultural values in his work *Technopoly*. In it, Postman argues, as does Ellul, that the autonomous nature of technical discourse feeds on itself, strengthening the claims of technocrats over decisions once regarded as outside the purview of purely technical rationales.

For Ellul, then, technology is not the issue. It is human consciousness. In this sense, it should be said that Ellul is less of a technological determinist than are other media ecologists, for his focus is never on specific techniques or technologies, but rather is always human consciousness, and human response to technologies, including media technologies.

Finally, a third significant concern that unites Ellul and the other writers within the media ecology tradition is the issue of the word, or the means of different technologies of communication. Many writers, including McLuhan (1962) and Ong (1982), argue that there is a profound difference between orality and literacy. Although these theorists vary in their specific emphasis, they typically argue that oral (pre-literate) cultures operate out of a certain frame of consciousness, and that once cultures become literate, a different form of consciousness arises. In other words, the presence of literacy produces real and significant changes in the way we think. In Ong's view, for example, in an oral culture, discourse is of necessity much less complex and abstract. Complexity of thought, and hence, of argument is an impediment, as it is virtually impossible to record it and remember it. It might be an interesting fleeting thought, but it certainly won't make profound cultural changes. Thus, when writing, a technology, is introduced into a culture, it makes available thought structures and processes previously unavailable (Ong, 1982, p. 36).

Ellul differs from this perspective, in that for Ellul, the Word, whether textual or oral, brings a certain critical perspective and presence that an image cannot. For Ong and others, the critical disjunction is between the technologies of orality and literacy. For Ellul, however, the critical disjunction is sensual, between the senses of hearing and seeing (seeing here implying images, rather than text). Ellul argues that all words, whether spoken or written, invite critical reflection and complexity of argument. Images, however, subvert this critical thought and overcome humans with emotions. He approvingly cites McLuhan's analysis of the role of television in affecting human consciousness (Ellul, 1977/1980, p. 73), but profoundly disagrees with what he takes to be a misunderstanding of the connection between the visual and the linear, which Ellul (1981/1985) argues are opposed to one another (p. 26).

Ellul does agree that these different technologies of communication affect human consciousness, but he differs in that his argument is that verbal discourse, with its requirement for sequential, organized thought, lends itself to abstraction and reflection (p. 36). Images, on the other hand, as the immediate and powerful entities that they are, have no means for encouraging, much less demanding, critical thought.

Boorstin (1973) treats the role of images in public discourse also, particularly in the political realm. But a key difference is that Boorstin distinguishes images from propaganda, and relies on a much more limited definition of propaganda than does Ellul. Boorstin's conception of the "pseudo-event," however, clearly can benefit from the fuller conception of Ellul's, as the pseudo-events that Boorstin identifies are for Ellul but techniques, ways of making political discourse have a greater impact. Ellul most likely would approve of Boorstin's contention that modern political discourse is impoverished by these techniques, but would also hasten to add that in the social context in which we live, they are in fact, inevitable.

This brief identification of Ellul within the framework of media ecology thinkers is intended to sketch only the most obvious connections. There remains much work to be done in terms of consolidating the visions of this disparate group of thinkers, as ideas and arguments that are major themes for some are barely dealt with in others. Ellul, whose primary concern are the political and sociological dimensions of the emerging technological mindset, does not give adequate attention to the specific communicative issues that are inherent in his analysis. Conversely, Ellul's larger vision of the impact of technological consciousness is not given adequate treatment by Ong and others. Inevitably, a greater comparison between these writers would illuminate much that has not yet been explored.

CRITICISMS OF ELLUL AND HIS WORK

Despite his obvious relevance to communication as a discipline, Ellul's impact, particularly on North American scholars of communication and media, has been, I think, severely muted. I briefly mention the primary criticisms of Ellul's work in order to illustrate both the weaknesses inherent in it, as well demonstrate that in most of the criticism of Ellul's work, his critics both misunderstand him and misstate his intentions. The first has to do with Ellul's unorthodox methodologies. Ellul is not content to examine one small part of the human situation, or one aspect of communication, and try to understand it systematically and fully. Rather, he makes the most sweeping of generalizations with little empirical evidence. Ellul (1981) clearly lays out his own vision for his scholarship as a type of dialectic, of attempting to understand the whole of a reality by examining its opposites and contradictions (pp. 291-308). As part of this dialectical process, Ellul also continually contrasts sociological analysis with theological argument, which he argues is a vital part of his methodology.

Ellul's methodology is far more reliant on logical processes of deduction, then, than the inductive approach of most contemporary social science inquiry. Moreover, Ellul's work was grounded in a clearly defined moral center, and he passionately argued against what he perceived as fatal characteristics of modern society, which included the detached, impersonal methodologies typically regarded as "scholarly." Ellul has even been compared to the Old Testament prophets he draws from, in his indictment of modern culture (Hall, cited in Christians, 1981, p. 147).

Upon publication of *Propaganda*, for instance, Ellul was severely criticized for both the "whiny" tone of the analysis, and for its glib use of evidence and empirical data. Daniel Lerner (1964), an important propaganda researcher, states that Ellul's work articulates "derivative, overstated, polemical propositions enunciated with great conviction" (pp. 793-794). Lerner further criticizes Ellul's "evasion of . . . data collection and data analysis," and argues that Ellul misuses the more recent tradition of empirical research. Lerner's criticism perhaps overstates its case, but in doing so, it also illustrates Ellul's central thesis, which is that the mindset of "technique" has so altered our perspective that we no longer trust nonempirical, or "nonscientific," studies. Lerner criticizes Ellul for not doing that which Ellul despises, that is, losing oneself in the bureaucratic value system of efficiency and quantification. Lovekin (1991) notes that Ellul's harshest critics often beg the question, in that they "reflect the commonplaces that are technical consciousness" (p. 38). This argument is reinforced by Sproule (1987), who argues that critical propaganda analysis, such as Ellul's, became the standard social science framework for rhetorical inquiry during the 1930s and 1940s, but fell into disfavor at least partially because of a movement towards specialization and empiricism in communications research: "the rationale and paradigmatic starting point of communication research was methodology" (p. 68).

Thus, one reason for Ellul's limited impact on media studies is that scholars with a social scientific bent took exception to the humanistic, critical approach of Ellul, as illustrated by Lerner's (1964) review. Others argued that Ellul's contentions were tautological, assuming the power of propaganda to then prove it.

A second criticism of Ellul is that his contentions don't correspond with our positive responses to technology. The same technological system that Ellul bemoans provides the foundation for innovations and technologies that truly do improve human life, whether it is advanced medical technology in the developed world or new technologies for providing pure water in the developing world. How can the "system" of which Ellul is so contemptuous be the well-spring of such beneficial developments? Put into the context of the media and communications technology, it seems that we use media and communications technology because we like it. Perhaps we enjoy seeing movies, we enjoy watching television, we enjoy using email to communicate with distant friends and relatives. Thus, Ellul's arguments about the downward spiral of technological society don't correspond to the positive benefits we enjoy.

To acknowledge the positive benefits of specific technologies, however, does not undermine his argument about the technological mindset. He clearly argued that "the development of individual techniques is an 'ambivalent' phenomenon," neither inherently good or bad (Ellul, 1963, p. 40; 1990b, p. 37). Ellul, undoubtedly, made use of the best medical technology he could when he was ill, and most assuredly, used the modern media system to disseminate his own writings. In fact, the publishers of his books are part of the media system that Ellul seems to so roundly condemn. Ellul (1992) even recommends "technical analysis" before we can take political action (pp. 44-45). It is not the specific institutions or innovations that Ellul is addressing, but rather the habit and mindset we cultivate that suggests that the technical solution is of necessity the best solution. It is when we place the technical solutions and answers as the primary criterion that we are again placing ourselves in subjection.

A third strain of criticism of Ellul has to do with an inherent pessimism to his work. If the world is as bleak as Ellul argues, then what is the point? Hickman (1985), for example, complains about "some five hundred pages of pessimism" in his critique of *The Technological Society* (p. 218). Moreover, it seems that Ellul proposes no solutions. Upon encountering *Propaganda* or the *Technological Society*, for example, the reader is struck with what seems to be an overabundance of condemnation with little in the way of solution.

It is evident, however, that Ellul indeed saw solution as very much a part of his program of writing. Ellul is keenly conscious of the radical nature of the entrapment within the technological mindset, but also clearly sees an imperative to find solutions. As Christians (1981) points out, it is necessary to read Ellul's entire corpus of works to find his solutions, because he does not outline a detailed plan of action in the books for which he is best known (p. 148). In fact, Ellul in several locations, notably *The Presence of the Kingdom* (1948/1989a), outlines his vision of what is necessary. A first step is realism, or a true understanding of the nature of society. A further step is a "renewed personhood," or a conscious decision to live in the world, but not of it, a clearly Christian conception. Finally, Ellul advocates a life of action, or personal engagement with the real problems humans face.

Ellul is, however, ultimately dismissive of the attempts of humans to alter their own situation, but only because he is fully convinced of the effects of the fall. Despite human alienation from God, which makes merely human efforts ultimately inadequate, Ellul (1948/1989a) argues that we must act to raise human consciousness and establish a more humane order, under the guidance of the Holy Spirit, and outlines a program for action (pp. 113-127). Perhaps the overt theological nature of this work makes it among Ellul's least read works, which contributes to a perception of Ellul as having no positive contribution to make.

The final criticism of Ellul that I wish to address is the charge of technological determinism. Because of Ellul's forceful critique of *la technique*, he is often charged with being "anti-technology," and a strict determinist. Hickman (1985), for example, argues that Ellul's (1977/1980) vision of technological autonomy is a strict deterministic perspective (pp. 217-220). Ellul at times, seems to be deterministic, as he argues at one point that "in the socio-political problems of Western society as a whole, the main if not single determinant factor is the technological system" (p. 55). However, Ellul is neither a neo-Luddite, nor a strict technological determinist, although these perspectives are often attributed to him. He did not advocate a return to primitive technologies, nor a dismissal of modern ones.

Rather, he argues that it is *la technique*, or the technological mindset, that disrupts human reflectivity and the quality of human life. Moreover, it is the "autonomous technology," in which the system takes on a life of its own and develops into a qualitatively different world, that is the critical issue (Ellul, 1954/1964, p. 133-147). Ellul sees that this emphasis on autonomous technology that differentiates the current era from previous eras, which had tools but not "la technique." As Lovekin (1991) has noted, Ellul's "notion of technique as a form of consciousness" remains misunderstood, and hence, unexplored (p. 31).

For Ellul, technology is merely an example of the problem, it is not the problem itself. Thus, charges of technological determinism don't really hold, since Ellul clearly argues that it is the human mindset, human practices, and human responses to technology that have created the social order, rather than technology itself. Ellul (1977/1980) himself rejects overly deterministic accounts of human life (p. 67), and argues that there are always multiple factors precipitating social change, although one factor might be dominant, as is technology in the West since the 1960s. He further argues that "technology exists only because there are human beings participating in it, making it function, inventing, choosing" (p. 84).

These criticisms of Ellul illustrate some of the problems inherent in his work. His writing is sweeping, rather than narrow, thus leading him to perhaps overstate his case. Moreover, if society is systemically corrupted by propaganda and technique, then what hope should Ellul have for his own writings, which are disseminated by the very media system he so forcefully critiques? His arguments are spread over literally dozens of books, leaving little choice but to read all of them to fully understand his work. His vision of technology and propaganda seems to leave little dignity for the individual who does make choices about media consumption and technology, and yet seems to find these liberating.

Despite these weaknesses, however, Ellul's vision is a healthy dose of "realism" for technological and media utopians, who argue that technology and media have inherently liberating effects. At the turn of the century, these voices are clearly in ascendancy, and Ellul's prophetic warnings help us to attain perhaps a more respectful suspicion of the claims that are made for the technologies that truly are transforming every aspect of human life, often with little or no moral guidance.

SUGGESTIONS FOR FURTHER EXPLORATION

This brief introduction to Ellul's major themes hopefully illustrates the ways in which Ellul draws from and inspires other writers and scholars within the media ecology tradition. In this final section, I provide specific guidance for further analysis of Ellul and his works, as well as demonstrate some of the themes that Ellul raises that need to be strengthened by further research, especially in the areas of communication and media.

For those interested in reading more of Ellul's work, three volumes stand out as deserving of further reflection. *The Technological Society* (Ellul, 1954/1964), *Propaganda* (Ellul, 1962/1965), and *the Presence of the Kingdom* (Ellul, 1948/1989a) are foundational for understanding Ellul's work. His volume, *The Humiliation of the Word* (Ellul, 1981/1985) contains his clearest arguments within the media ecology framework, in which he explores image-based consciousness versus text-based consciousness. *The Technological Bluff* (Ellul, 1990b) provides further insight into his understanding of both the false promises of technology and the nature of modern media, in areas such as advertising, sports, and television. *The Political Illusion* (Ellul, 1965/1967) explores the ways in which politics ultimately is entrapped by a larger ideological consciousness. Finally, *What I Believe* (Ellul, 1989b) and *Reason for Being* (Ellul, 1987/1990a) provide further definition of his theological vision, and the way in which Ellul's commitment to orthodox Christianity underlies much of his social analysis.

Despite Ellul's vision of the technological society, many of his ideas remain unexplored by later scholarship. For example, he argues that technological consciousness pervades the modern media industries, just as it does the society at large. In order to validate this claim, we must understand the extent to which "efficiency," for example, underlies the real production processes, editorial decisions, and values orientations of media. Are there better explanations for these processes of modern media industries than Ellul's? Does Ellul's vision of the autonomy of technique help to explain modern media processes in real world contexts, such as broadcast, movies, music, and newspapers, and online media?

Moreover, contemporary analysis of society focuses not on the "technological society," but rather, the "knowledge society," or the "information society." The presumptions are that information technologies have liberated individuals, corporations, and even governments from the constraints of the past. Ellul (1962/1965) argues, however, that information doesn't exist in the neutral form in which we expect it, but comes embedded within propaganda. Ellul clearly did not anticipate the role that computers would play in everyday life, but neither did any other writer of the 1960s. For the most part, information society theorists ignore Ellul's work altogether (as, e.g., Webster, 1995). This, I believe, is a critical error. Serious scrutiny of the "information society" must take into account Ellul's understanding of technology and information as ideology.

The most distressing aspect of this absence of response to Ellul is that so much time has passed, and there has been little application or testing of his ideas. Other theorists have echoed some of Ellul's themes, such as the ideological role of popular entertainment, but have largely done it outside the framework that Ellul proposed, leaving us with little sense of the extent to which his vision of a totalizing media system is at work in modern society.

As such, we are left primarily with Ellul's proclamations, with little or data to judge the veracity of his ideas.

This chapter is offered in the hope that it will indeed prompt greater application and exploration of Ellul's ideas. It is insufficient to merely restate his themes, but it is imperative that we attempt to take those arguments further. Particularly as the media industries themselves undergo massive changes, in terms of industry consolidation and technological convergence, we must take seriously the words of a 20th century prophet so that we do not gullibly fall into the utopian visions and myths of inevitable technological progress that others have charted for us.

REFERENCES

Boorstin, D. (1973). *The image.* New York: Athenaeum.

Christians, C.G. (1976). Jacques Ellul and democracy's 'vital information' premise. *Journalism Monographs, 45,* 1-42.

Christians, C. G. (1981). Ellul on solution: an alternative but no prophecy. In C. G. Christians & J. M. Van Hook (Eds.), *Jacques Ellul: Interpretive essays* (pp. 147-173). Urbana: University of Illinois Press.

Christians, C. G. (1995). Propaganda and the technological system. In T. L. Glasser & C. T. Salmon (Eds.), *Public opinion and the communication of consent* (pp156-174). New York: Guilford.

Christians, C. G., & Real, M. (1979). Jacques Ellul's contributions to critical media theory. *Journal of Communication, 29,* 83-93.

Clendenin, D. (1989). Introduction. In J. Ellul, *The presence of the kingdom* (Rev. Ed.). Colorado Springs, CO: Helmers & Howard.

Ellul, J. (1963). The technological order. In C. Stover (Ed.). *The technological order: Proceedings of the Encyclopaedia Brittanica Conference* (pp. 10-24). Detroit: Wayne State University Press. Reprinted in L. Hickman (Ed.). (1985). *Philosophy, technology, and human affairs.* College Station, TX: Ibis Press.

Ellul, J. (1964). *The technological society* (J. Wilkinson, Trans.). New York: Vintage Books. (Original work published 1954)

Ellul, J. (1965). *Propaganda: The formation of men's attitudes* (K. Kellen & J. Lerner, Trans.). New York: Alfred A. Knopf. (Original work published 1962)

Ellul, J. (1967). *The political illusion* (K. Kellen, Trans.). New York: Alfred A. Knopf. (Original work published 1965)

Ellul, J. (1980). *The technological system* (J. Neugroschel, Trans.). New York: Continuum. (Original work published 1977)

Ellul, J. (1981). Epilogue: On dialectic (G. Bromiley, Trans.) In C. G. Christians and J. M. Van Hook (Eds.), *Jacques Ellul: Interpretive essays* (pp. vi-ix). Urbana: University of Illinois Press.

Ellul, J. (1985). *The humiliation of the word* (J. M. Hanks, Trans.). Grand Rapids, MI: Wm. B. Eerdmans. (Original work published 1981)

Ellul, J. (1989a). *The presence of the kingdom* (Rev. Ed.). Colorado Springs, CO: Helmers & Howard. (Original work published 1948)

Ellul, J. (1989b). What I believe (G. W. Bromiley, Trans.). Grand Rapids, MI: Wm. B. Eerdmans.

Ellul, J. (1990a). *Reason for being* (J. M. Hanks, Trans.). Grand Rapids, MI: Wm. B. Eerdmans. (Original work published 1987)

Ellul, J. (1990b). *The technological bluff* (G. Bromiley, Trans.). Grand Rapids, MI: Wm. B. Eerdmans.

Ellul, J. (1992). Technology and democracy. In L. Winner (Ed.), *Democracy in a technological society* (pp. 35-50). Dordrecht, The Netherlands: Kluwer Academic.

Hickman, L. (Ed.). (1985). *Philosophy, technology, and human affairs.* College Station, TX: Ibis Press.

Gozzi, R. (2000). Jacques Ellul on technique, media, and the spirit. *New Jersey Journal of Communication, 8,* (1), 79-90.

Lerner, D. (1964). Propagandes [Review of the book *Propagandes*]. *American Sociological Review, 29,* 793-794.

Lovekin, D. (1991). *Technique, discourse, and consciousness: An introduction to the philosophy of Jacques Ellul.* Bethlehem, PA: Lehigh University Press.

McLuhan, M. (1962). *The gutenberg galaxy: The making of typographic man.* London: Routledge & Kegan Paul.

McLuhan, M. (1964). *Understanding media: The extensions of man.* New York: Mentor.

McLuhan, M. (1965, November 28). Big transistor is watching you [Review of the book *Propaganda: The formation of men's attitudes*]. *Book Week,* p. 5.

Mumford, L. (1934). *Technics and civilization.* New York: Harcourt Brace.

Nisbet, R. (1981). Foreword. In C. G. Christians & J. M. Van Hook (Eds.), *Jacques Ellul: Interpretive essays* (pp. vi-ix). Urbana: University of Illinois Press.

Ong, W. (1982). *Orality and literacy: The technologizing of the word.* London: Methuen.

Postman, N. (1985). *Amusing ourselves to death.* New York: Viking.

Postman, N. (1992). *Technopoly: The surrender of culture to technology.* New York: Vintage.

Real, M. (1981). Mass communications and propaganda in technological societies. In C. G. Christians & J. M. Van Hook (Eds.), *Jacques Ellul: Interpretive essays* (pp. 108-127). Urbana: University of Illinois Press.

Sproule, J. M. (1987). Propaganda studies in American social science: the rise and fall of the critical paradigm. *Quarterly Journal of Speech, 73,* 60-78.

Strate, L., & Lum, C. (2000). Lewis Mumford and the ecology of technics. *New Jersey Journal of Communication, 8*(1), 56-78.

Webster, F. (1995). *Theories of the information society.* London: Routledge.

5

Ellul as Theologian In Counterpoint

Clifford G. Christians
University of Illinois at Urbana-Champaign

Jacques Ellul is a dialectician. When describing the character of his scholarship, Ellul (1981) makes dialectical thinking central (p. 292). Dialectic for him is not just a mode of reasoning that uses questions and answers or insists on both pros and cons. *Dialegein* means an exchange, to speak in relation, but *dia* also means contradiction. "Put a positive charge next to a negative one and you have a powerful flash, but this is a new phenomenon excluding neither the positive nor the negative pole" (Ellul, 1981, p. 293). Although conventional linear reasoning presumes the principle of noncontradiction (black cannot be white), Ellul's roots in Marx, Kierkegaard, and Barth put him on a different path, with affirmation and refutation not canceling one another. "The negative exists only in relation to a positive; the positive exists only in relation to a negative" (p. 306).

Ellul's sophisticated understanding of dialecticism accounts for its different traditions and emphases. His reflections are rooted in Heraclitus, Hegel and Marx, Kierkegaard, Old Testament Hebrew thought, and Barth's theology.[1] He concludes his essay on the dialectic with this summary, and it indicates why serious work on Ellul needs to include his theological pole alongside his sociological one:

If the technological system is, as I think I have shown, a total system which embraces all activities, which has its own logic, and which progressively assimilates all cultures, then there is no longer any dialectical factor in relation to it. It tends to become a totality, a unity. If, however, we believe that the dialectical process is indispensable to life and history, it is absolutely necessary that this dialectical factor exist. If the technological system is total, then this factor has to exist *outside* it. But only the transcendent is, in the concrete situation in which technology has put us, the necessary condition for the continuation of life, the unfolding of history, simply the existence of man as man. This transcendent, however, cannot be a self-existing and unknown one. It has to be a *revealed* transcendent if man is to have reason and opportunity to launch upon a dialectical course in spite of the autonomy and universality of technology. In saying that, I am in no sense engaging in apologetics, but simply pointing to the unavoidable results of the twofold flow of my research, sociological and theological. (Ellul, 1981, p. 308)

As a sociologist, Ellul insists he is "realistic and specific, using exact methods," whereas as a theologian he is "equally intransigent, presenting as strict an interpretation of revelation as possible." Thus, on one level he wants each side to be "as immune as possible from contamination by the other." But true to the dialectic, "the whole must not be made up of two unrelated parts: there has to be a correlation. . . . The two play their parts reciprocally as in a musical counterpoint" (Ellul, 1981, p. 306).

Dialecticism's double dimension, as immunity and correlation, is not only an intellectual commitment and academic strategy for Ellul, but rooted in personal experience. During his studies at the University of Bordeaux, Marx's *Das Capital* dramatically explained for him the economic upheaval in his home and cruel injustice as he witnessed it among the wharves and docks of Bordeaux while growing up. "When I was nineteen," Ellul (1970a) writes, "I became 'Marxist' and devoted a great deal of my time to the study of his writings. . . . What Marx brought to me was a certain way of 'seeing' political, economic, and social problems—a method of interpretation, a sociology" (p. 5). Then at age 22 he was converted to Christianity: "It was an awesome experience for me. . . . It gave me a response both on the individual level and on the collective level. I saw a perspective beyond history, one that is definitive" (Ellul, 1982, p. 15). Both conversions continued to inspire him until his death on May 19, 1994, although without reconciling them. He was "unable to eliminate Marx, unable to eliminate the biblical revelation, and unable to merge the two. It was impossible for me to put them together. My thinking can be explained by starting with this contradiction" (Ellul, 1982, p. 16).[2] The writing he first undertook in a tentative frame of mind assumed a progressively better structure and came to define the essential character of his work (Ellul, 1970c, p. 201).

In an increasingly secular age and without widely shared theological tools to examine Ellul's scholarship, analysis appropriately begins with his sociology. But in order to assess correctly his contributions to media ecology, Ellul's dialecticism pushes the sociological dimension towards the theological, and theology completes the analysis while restructuring it. Although his concepts of *la technique* and propaganda establish his engagement with media ecology, their dialectical inverses are critical to completing the picture. The totalizing character of *la technique's* efficiency and necessity requires for Ellul a transformation in our being or no solutions are credible. Pervasive propaganda in a mass media age demands freedom to live humanly outside it, but freedom is only possible transcendently. Moreover, critiques from a media ecology perspective that Ellul's sociological work is pessimistic and deterministic, need to be enriched and nuanced by accounting for his dialectical "Yes."

This chapter explicates these claims that Ellul's theology is crucial to understanding him and his role in media ecology. In the process, it demonstrates also that interpreting Ellul's relationship to key figures in the media ecology tradition necessitates his theological component. Marshall McLuhan is Ellul's (1985) entrée to the theoretical framework of *The Humiliation of the Word*, and in privileging verbal communication throughout, Ellul's conclusions overlap with Postman's (1985) *Amusing Ourselves to Death*. In fact, across his work, Ellul cites McLuhan approvingly and quarrels only with particular arguments. Knowing Ellul as sociologist is sufficient to make connections and distinctions. On the other hand, as the exposition presented here indicates, in comparing Ellul with other intellectual forebears of media ecology, such as Lewis Mumford, theological material is essential. Ellul often dismissed his critics for not reading all of his work and not coming to grips with his dialectic thinking.[3] As one of Ellul's best interpreters concludes: "Any attempt to understand his thought that concentrates excessively on one of the two strands or ignores the relation between them is liable to distort his thinking" (Goddard, 2002, pp. 53-54).[4] This exposition of Ellul's theological counterpoint in general and his Barthian neo-orthodoxy in particular, alongside the sociological chapter, enables readers of this anthology to evaluate Ellul in the terms he himself has specified.

COUNTERPOINT

Given his double commitment, Ellul self-consciously adopts a "composition in counterpoint." Sociology, for him, is answered by a biblical or theological analysis—not in the sense of replying, but in taking the other pole seriously. His three classic studies each have a theological counterpart. Ellul's

book (1967) on politics in the modern state *(The Political Illusion)* corresponds to his biblical analysis of II Kings *(The Politics of God and the
Politics of Man, 1972b)*. *The Meaning of the City* (1970b) stands against *The
Technological Society (1964)*. Prophecy in *The Judgment of Jonah* (1971a)
represents biblical communication in contrast to *Propaganda (1965)*. In his
terms, "I confront theological . . . knowledge and sociological analysis without trying to come to any artificial or philosophical synthesis; instead, I try
to place the two face-to-face, in order to shed some light on what is real
socially and real spiritually" (Ellul, 1970a, p. 6; cf. 1981, pp. 304-308). Ellul
allows these two dimensions to live within himself, refusing to inflect one
for the sake of the other. He constructs a theology of confrontation, his
work turning on "the contradiction between the evolution of the modern
world and the biblical content of revelation" (Ellul, 1970a, pp. 5-6).

The Meaning of the City

The Meaning of the City, counterpoint to *The Technological Society*, illustrates concretely Ellul's dualistic construction. In order to describe *la technique* theologically, he traces the city in biblical narrative. His excursion
begins with Cain, builder of the city called "Enoch." Ellul accentuates the
significant fact that this first builder was a murderer. From there in Genesis
through Revelation, the devastating conclusion applies uniformly: All cities
smart under the same malediction; God has cursed every one. This curse
affects the city's fundamental makeup, Ellul declares, tainting "its sociology and the habitat it can provide" (Ellul, 1970b, p. 48). The same judgment,
the same evaluation of the city appears "at every point for seven or eight
centuries" (p. 8). It is the curse expressed from one end of Scripture to the
other by "I will destroy," says the Lord. [5] God has only words of condemnation," Ellul writes, "leading to death. . . . She is condemned to death
because of everything she represents" (p. 45).[6] God rails against the city and
serves notice of a schism: "The city is presented as the place where the conflict between God and the earth is carried to its highest pitch, where all the
powers in revolt gather together. . . . These cities bear in their bosoms all
the hopes of man for divinity" (p. 60). Thus God is forced to curse as
human beings substitute their own Eden for God's. And condemn he
does—so thoroughly, in fact, that the city's very being and fabric are affected. No longer is the city "conceivable separate from the curse" (Ellul,
1970b, p. 60).

In the same manner that *la technique* does not mean machines or
bureaucracies or political propagandas but their underlying ethos, Ellul's
gloominess about the city does not center on smog, garbage strikes, and cor-
rupt government. He is speaking of something else. The city's curse is simply another angle of vision on *la technique*.[7] The domination of means, soci-

ologically speaking, in biblical language Ellul (1951) calls "the state of sin" (1951, p. 16). The city, seen as having a specific being and self-propelling autonomy independent of its inhabitants, is "shut up under evil" (Galatians 3:22).[8]

When describing *la technique* as "sin" and the city as a condensation of human evil, Ellul is talking neither about individual sin nor simple collective responsibility. He explicitly disavows both possibilities. Individuals, he says, are "engulfed by the sin of the city. . . . It draws men into a sin which is hardly personal to them" (Ellul, 1970b, p. 67). And, he notes further, social solidarity (collective responsibility) in sin "is very strong in the Old Testament, but it is not the exact problem of the city" (p. 67). In addition to individual and group sin, there are vicious and uncontrolled forces underlying the city. Theologically speaking, *la technique* is such embedded sin, structured evil that disfigures all of human life. Ellul is deeply impressed with "what the late Paul Tillich called 'the demonic' and what the Apostle Paul referred to as 'principalities and powers.' Ellul, as a twentieth-century man, still has the audacity to believe in these strange critters" (Cox, 1971, p. 354). This domain of Satan is everyone's primary lifesphere without exception; and "in spite of all our efforts and piety," it engages humankind in "a spiritual conflict as brutal as any battle in time of war" (Ellul, 1951, pp. 16, 78).[9]

Ellul describes his counterpoint strategy as a "science of the city." Obviously, this is "not . . . an objective and purely technical science of the city" but a science involved "in a struggle for truth" (Ellul, 1970b, p. 148). The purpose of this science is to disclose the "spiritual nucleus" of the problem of the city, the core from which all other problems radiate. Its fundamental axiom is that, "the reality of the city. . . as a structure of the world, can be understood only in the light of revelation" (p. 153).

In this dialectical method, what we learn "about the city by natural means, by history and sociology, and about man in the city by psychology and the novel," is "connected, coordinated, strongly knotted together, because of its spiritual nucleus. The result is that our natural sources are dependent on revelation" (Ellul, 1970b, p. 148).

This "spiritual nucleus" of which Ellul speaks is the core of hope and meaning that the city offers as the reason for its existence, and in return expecting the commitment of its citizens. It is the questionableness of these claims to meaning which this science is meant to uncover. In Ellul's view, only the gospel has the capacity to unmask the city's claim to provide spiritual fulfillment (i.e., hope and meaning). The entire purpose of this "science" as a struggle for truth is to come to a decision," that is, to give birth to a Christian ethic for the technological city that will challenge its bravado (cf. Fasching, 1981, pp. 10-11).

Carrying out this counterpunctual science of the city is a task that requires two kinds of expertise. The analyst is involved in two different ways of looking at reality, two different languages of analysis. They can have points of correlation, but there can be no necessary and objective transition from one to the other.

> These two levels cannot be combined, nor do they go together natural-
> ly and objectively. For the person who lives on both planes, the two
> proceedings are mutually consistent. As a sociologist and as a Christian,
> I can pursue this twofold quest. I am able to say that man is doing harm
> and that he is a sinner, that he is unfortunate and that he is separated
> from God. But that correlation is already established in my own think-
> ing, by my own life experience. It is not something impersonal which
> can be passed around. (Ellul, 1973, p. 158)

Thus, for Ellul, the task of carrying forward this science of the city is the unique vocation which can only be assumed by those whose lives are informed by a biblical axis.

Barthian Neo-orthodoxy

Ellul's indebtedness to Karl Barth's neo-orthodoxy is crucial for under-standing the theological side of his counterpoint strategy.[10] In fact, the Barthian understanding of God's otherness and His freedom are the crucial components of Ellul's theology. God is most frequently described by Ellul as the Wholly Other and he sees among Barth's contributions to contempo-rary theology "his stress on the Wholly Other God of radical transcen-dence" (Goddard, 2002, p. 64; cf. Ellul, 1986, pp. 44-45). Ellul emphasizes God's sovereign freedom "within Barth's framework of 'the free determina-tion of man in the free decision of God'" (Goddard, 2002, p. 66; cf. Ellul, 1972b, p. 15). As an alternative to the dehumanizing constraints of the tech-nological order, Ellul anchors a genuine human freedom in a pure, transcen-dent God who is totally removed from the necessity and efficiency of *la technique.*

For Barth, human freedom is enclosed in the free decision of God. Reflecting that emphasis, Ellul sees no conflict between human freedom and divine sovereignty. God's purpose is always achieved, but it does not consti-tute for us a fate or necessity. Humankind still has room for working out the freedom given in Christ; in fact, God's activity invests human action with history and a future (Ellul, 1976, p. 14ff).

Ellul never accepts uselessness in human decisions. He insists on leaving for humans a sphere of free decision and therefore of authentic freedom. He is fully aware that all people do not decide freely; even many decisions we think to be free are in reality determined by the forces controlling human life. Ellul never minimizes these. As he says, "necessity still obtains in the course of history. . . . History and society are still very much subject to constraints." All the same, a power of freedom "was unleashed at the cross" enabling us to perform acts of real freedom, ones that will fall, of course, within divine freedom (Ellul, 1972b, p. 187). He insists on the overriding thesis of Barth: "Human freedom cannot encroach upon divine freedom. Always and in every respect the latter precedes the former. Yet, on the other hand, divine freedom cannot destroy and suspend human freedom" (*Church Dogmatics,* vol. I, part 2, p. 170).

This preoccupation with freedom makes Christianity's message essentially one of liberation. This theme recurs constantly in Barth's *Church Dogmatics* and Ellul takes it up with vigor. Liberation, he thinks, provides the present age with a better definition of salvation than redemption does (Ellul, 1976, p. 66). Preaching the Gospel does not aim at achieving political and economic liberation by a change of government. The problem goes deeper than that. Under any government we are in subjection to forces that enslave us. In this tragic situation philosophers prattle about freedom, theologians utter empty platitudes, and revolutionaries suffer from the delusion that they are achieving liberation even as they serve historical determinations; but only Christ, who displayed his own freedom in the temptations, can bring true emancipation. As Ellul insists, our liberator must come to us from beyond the sociological determinations of life and beyond death. Jesus is this liberator through whom we are given, not an attribute or state of freedom, but a new being in freedom (Ellul, 1976, pp. 51-53, 69-72).

The theme of living out this freedom forms the substance of *Ethics of Freedom (Ellul, 1976).* In discussing it, Ellul follows Barth most closely vis-à-vis freedom for God, that is, freedom for the service of God.[11] Failure at this point undercuts all else that we might try to do, including social action. Freedom, as the obedience of free human beings to God, means first and foremost freedom for God. For Ellul, enslavement to sociological determinations does not mean subjection to fate but bondage to sin in its corporate dimension. Thus, liberation in the deepest sense—not as liberation from certain surface forms but as release from the determinations themselves—constitutes for Ellul the Gospel's substance. It means liberation also from the necessities imposed by corporate structures, so that, whether or not the structures are changed, Christians can know and practice an authentic freedom in spite of them.

In theological content, Ellul emulates Barth's doctrine of God as perfect freedom, the source and guarantee of authentic human freedom. In terms of theological method he carries forward the tradition of dialectical theology associated with Karl Barth. Ellul admires Barth's theology for expressing "the remarkable dialectic that appears throughout the Bible, even in the least of its writings" (Ellul, 1972a, p. 9; cf. 1981, pp. 297-304). Ellul was converted through biblical reading. The scriptural canon anchors his second pole.

And in coming to terms with the character of this revelation, once again he follows Barth closely. Barth holds a dynamic concept of Scripture whereby it is God's Word only as God himself speaks through it. As Ellul puts it in interpreting the Second Book of Kings: "We are in the presence of life; God acts, and it is his action itself which is the Word of God" (Ellul, 1972b, p. 14).

In *Ethics of Freedom,* God's freedom to speak through His word is emphasized. Barth devoted a major section of his *Church Dogmatics* (vol. I, pt. 2) to the Word of God's freedom. Applying this doctrine, Ellul expressly follows what he calls "the remarkable analysis" of Barth. "The only true, complete, absolute, and instrinsic freedom is that of the Word of God" which is "the basis and ground of our freedom" (Ellul, 1976, pp. 63-64). In these terms, Ellul derives a decisive conclusion for his own work: "Whenever the witness of holy scripture is received and accepted, man has a freedom and power which . . . correspond to the freedom and power of the Word of God itself" (p. 66).

This biblical dialectic pronounces both the No and the Yes of God's word over the world. It brings both God's judgment and his grace into a dialectic which finds its fullest expression in the death and resurrection of Jesus Christ. The temptation of modern theology, in Ellul's view, is to break apart this constant dialectic of No and Yes and turn it into a dualistic interpretation of history in which the No of God's judgment over the world has been superseded by an unconditional Yes to the world through the resurrection of Jesus Christ. When that happens, he warns, the gospel becomes an ideological self-justification for the status quo. Such a historical dualism breaks apart precisely what must be held together in a dialectical unity (see Fasching, 1981, pp. 6-7).

> We need to maintain a rigorous dialectic. The "Yes" of God is pronounced in relation to a previous "No." Without the "No," there is no "Yes". . . . But just as repentance has always to be renewed in the Christian life, . . . just as Christ is crucified to the end of the world, just so the "No," pronounced by God over man and his works and his history, is a "No" which is total, radical and ever present. . . . We must . . . maintain the dialectic of the "No" and the "Yes". . . . "Yes" makes no sense unless there is also the "No," and I regret to point out that the "No" comes *first,* that death comes before resurrection. (Ellul, 1972a, pp. 23-24)

This Barthian dialectic informs Ellul's theological approach; through it the gospel both judges and renews the world. And neo-orthodox theology generally establishes the biblical side of his counterpoint, while freeing him as sociologist to concentrate on the history and sociology of institutions. With an axis in Marx, he is enormously indebted to classical sociology as a whole, including Max Weber and Emile Durkheim. Although his approach is novel, the problems that occupy him are the scholarly concerns of sociology generally.

TRIUMPH OF MEANS

As he examines social institutions historically and theoretically, Ellul's theological commitments in counterpoint lead him to a distinctive conclusion about the20th century industrial society in which he lived.

For Ellul, the technological phenomenon is decisive. As an explanatory element, he argues, it plays the part of capital in Marx's interpretation of the 19th century. Ellul does not mean that technology has the same function as capital, nor that the capitalist system is a thing of the past. It still exits, but capital no longer fulfills the role Marx claimed for it. Whereas work produces value for Marx, in extremely technological societies the determining factor is *la technique*. This is the force that now creates value and it is not peculiar to capitalism. The characters in the struggle for political and economic power have changed. In his earliest days as a Marxist, Ellul divided society into capitalists and workers, but he recognizes that the situation at present is completely different and operates on a more abstract level. Ellul (1982, pp. 175-177) concludes that we must read the world in which we live in terms of technology, rather than capitalist structures. We now have technological organizations on one side and all humanity on the other—the former driven by necessity and the latter demanding freedom.

From Ellul's perspective, we have now entered a technological civilization. "Technology constitutes an engulfing universe for man, who finds himself in it as in a cocoon" (Ellul, 1965, p. xvii). The technical artifice is not merely one more arena for philosophers and sociologists to investigate, but a new foundation for understanding the self, human institutions, and ultimate reality. Technical efficiency becomes a force so powerful that it casts aside all other imperatives. Unable to establish a meaningful life outside the artificial ambience of a technological culture, human beings place their ultimate hope in it. Seeing no other source of security, and failing to recognize the illusoriness of their technical freedom, they become slaves to the exacting determinations of efficiency.

The transition to a technological society is for Ellul more fundamental than anything the human race has experienced over the last 5,000 years:

> The creation of the technological environment . . . is progressively effacing the two previous ones. Of course, nature and society still exist. But they are without power—they no longer decide our future. There are still earthquakes, volcanic eruptions, and hurricanes. But humanity is no

longer helpless when faced with such disasters. It has the technical
means to respond; . . . and this is why nature is always menacingly present as an environment that is subordinate and no longer basic. The same
applies to society. It remains a secondary environment. . . . Technology
imposes its own law on the different social organizations, disturbing
fundamentally what is thought to be permanent (e.g., the family), and
making politics totally futile. Politicians can decide only what is technologically feasible. All decisions are dictated by the necessity of technological growth (Ellul, 1989, pp. 134-135).[12]

Galileo's Legacy

The more immediate history of the technological society begins for Ellul, as
it does for Lewis Mumford (1934), with the transition from medieval to
modern science in the sixteenth century. The central figure in this shift is the
Italian Galileo Galilei (1564-1642) who mapped reality in a new way. Galileo
divided the world into primary and secondary—matter and mathematics in
the first, separated off from the supernatural and metaphysical in the second.
In *The Assayer* Galileo (1957) writes: "This great book, the Universe . . . is
written in the language of mathematics, and its characters are triangles, circles, and geometric figures" (pp. 238-239). Matter alone mattered to him; all
nonmaterial was considered immaterial. The universe became cold, lifeless
and silent. Galileo's fascination with the Copernican world-picture motivated him to promote heliocentricity not as the calculation of astronomers
only, but as a wide-ranging truth about the structure of reality.

Galileo's extraordinary dualism became the basic axiom of empiricistic
science, separated physics from philosophy, and relegated all supernatural-
ism to the fringes of human experience. Lewis Mumford (1970), who
describes Galileo's approach most graphically as "The Mechanized World
Picture" (pp. 51-76), condemns it as "the crime of Galileo" (pp. 57-65).
Galileo's bifurcation allowed the religious world to start shriveling away. In
Rene Descartes, for example, Galileo's primary and secondary became a
material and spiritual dichotomy. Descartes contended, in effect, that we can
demonstrate the truth only of what we can measure. The realm of spirit was
beyond such measurement, a matter of faith and intuition, not truth. The
physical became the only legitimate domain of knowledge. Descartes' spiritual world was left to speculation by the divines, many of whom shared the
Cartesian bias that theirs was an ephemeral pursuit.

La technique is Ellul's lever for prying open important dimensions of
the scientific paradigm in Galileo and modernity. Ellul recasts the issues in
terms of *la technique* and steers us toward religion as a rich resource for
engaging the issues. With human freedom now in confrontation with technological necessity, Ellul makes clear how pernicious the matter-in-motion
paradigm has become in our modern era.

Certainly, Galileo conceived his model in innocence, and his dedicated protégé could never have anticipated that mastering the physical world would threaten human existence. But Ellul tenders precisely such a prospect, and his thesis is inescapable: To the degree that the technicized dominates, healthy livelihood disappears. Since the 17th century we have systematically traded away the totality of human experience, until the minute portion now remaining has bred a technological morality devoid of all social ends. Lewis Mumford (1952) presents Ellul's concern interrogatively: "Why has our inner life become so impoverished and empty, and why has our outer life become so exorbitant, and in its subjective satisfactions even more empty? Why have we become technological gods and moral devils, scientific supermen and esthetic idiots?" (pp. 137-138).

However important mechanical achievements have been for human survival, Ellul reiterates the painful sacrifice involved of human freedom and wholeness. The mechanical regularity initiated by Galileo, and prized especially since the 18th century, has taken on a life of its own. *La technique*, Ellul contends, creates an omnivorous civilization obeying inherent procedures, a closed organism impervious to external influences. Humans are left to record the results. *La technique* is a self-directing force "essentially independent of the human being who finds himself naked and disarmed before it" (Ellul, 1964, p. 306). There is nothing more dangerous for Ellul than believing that "the human producer is still master of production" (p. 93). Challenges to select the best means for attaining honorable ends are as "out of place in our own day as it would be to fight against a tank with an axe of the Stone Age" (Ellul, 1951, p. 74).

La technique has a self-augmenting quality with technical elements combining out of their own patterns—a process without explicit human participation and direction. Ellul (1964) concludes: "The accretion of manifold minute details, all tending toward the perfect ensemble, is much more decisive than the intervention of the individual who assembles the data, or adds some element . . . that will bear his name" (p. 86). As means triumph, our goals disappear in the busyness of perfecting methods. Because of the "magnitude of the very means at our disposal" we live in a civilization without ends (p. 430).[13] "We have forgotten our collective ends . . . . In this terrible dance of means which has been unleashed, no one knows where we are going; the aim of life has been forgotten . . . . Man has set out at tremendous speed – to go nowhere" (Ellul, 1951, pp. 63, 69). Obviously we still invoke certain lofty ends such as happiness or justice. However, Ellul contends, these goals no longer inspire; their formative power has dissipated. They are dead illusions, impossible to take seriously; certainly "no one would die for them" (p. 67). Meanwhile, means generate fresh means in every field from education to weaponry, raising a problem "absolutely central for our civilization" (p. 61). In Lewis Mumford's (1970) terms, societies dominated by a mechanized world picture finally become saturated by the "pentagon of power"—political absolutism, mechanical energy, mass productivity, pecuniary profit, manipulative publicity.

Revitalization Through Religion

But is Ellul's distress about means and ends a genuine contribution? Means–ends analysis carries a rich tradition in Western thought. Does Ellul add anything significant? In his *Politics* and *Nicomachean Ethics*, Aristotle brought a teleological framework to maturity in Greek philosophy, developing self-realization ethics and insisting that the nature of all things consists in their end or consummation. John Dewey (1922) introduced a second prominent stream by meticulously separating ends and means, regarding morality as conscious deliberation of both, and intelligent conduct as aiming toward a proposed end (pp. 25-38, 225 ff.). In addition to these two options, and not necessarily indebted to either, teleological considerations have surfaced prominently also in other ways across history—in Thomas Aquinas and Max Weber, for example.

Ellul enters this vast and complicated discussion over means and ends by altering the very framework involved. The issues for him are not philosophical questions whether "ends justify means" or "just ends, just means" or even "ends pre-existing in the means." Our existential problem is the very demise of ends themselves; that is the revolutionary situation we now face. Regarding Aristotle, ends cannot be realized within humans because they have become meansified too. Nor, in Dewey's terms, does humanity confront a choice of good ends or bad; collective ends have disappeared altogether. Ellul insists that these two major lines of argument are totally inadequate. They assume a metaphysical angle without justification and their philosophical pursuit condemns us "to understand nothing, in spite of apparent cleverness. In reality today the problem has been absolutely transformed. . . . It must be seen in the light of *la technique* (Ellul, 1951, p. 62).

Human beings, widely heralded as the lofty end, have in actuality become an "available resource," a component, "the means of the very means" that should serve them (Ellul, 1951, p. 63). Overpowered by *la technique*, human beings are "correctly tailored to enter into an artificial paradise" (Ellul, 1964, p. 227), a transformation where flesh-and-blood people become consumer, worker, market, taxpayer—a person in the abstract. Inaccessible inner life stands impoverished, efficiency displaces moral goods, automatisms supplant creativeness, alienating *la technique* precludes personhood—such are the disquieting results when mechanical ordering becomes supreme (Ellul, 1990).

With technicized phenomena taking on a life of their own—that is, moving within a self-contained circle—Ellul's only hope rests in "outside" intervention. He believes strongly that for overcoming our contemporary mechanization, religion provides the greatest restorative power, the most inner nourishment and creative substance. "The bond between values and the sacred," Ellul (1969a) writes, "seems an unbreakable one"; religion is the source of moral imperatives (p. 156). Ellul is motivated toward religion by his commitment to classic sociological theory, where the idea of sacredness is conceptually fundamental. Christianity's earliest history fascinated Marx and Engels. Auguste Comte recommended a "religion of humanity." Durkheim's striking account of social solidarity rests on myth, ritual, sacrament, and totemism. Simmel considered piety essential for adequately understanding social phenomena. Max Weber's studies of charisma and the rise of European capitalism are among his most provocative achievements. Sacredness was a basic idea to mainline sociology during its formative period. Religion was regarded during these decades as ineradicably constitutive of mental and social life.

The classicists' concern was not abstractly intellectual, but intensely personal and moral. They struggled to reconstruct a threatened social system. The ultimate contribution that they envisaged for social science was not an operationally uniform explanation, but social harmony. Everything that endures as extensive, creative, and substantial about classical theory grew not from empiricistic urgings, but out of the realization that society had entered the twilight. By rejecting the notion that sacredness was inherently secondary, religious phenomena were given an opportunity to surface dramatically as a source of social revitalization. They assumed societies to be moral entities and sought to discover a basis for making them truly human. Ellul understands what these sociological theorists intend by their preoccupation with the sacred. As they did for their era, he recognized the threat under which social life existed in the 20th century. He shared their concern for the moral reorganization of society and their lively interest in sacredness as a source of ideas and intellectual direction. Thus, he capitalized on religion as a crucial human enterprise for infusing meaning and fulfillment. Hopes for revitalizing the human spirit are best nourished, he would suggest, at that religious fountain where symbols of human faith provide integration and a sense of purpose.

But Ellul's religious perspective is not a call to stubborn persistence in a noncongenial climate. His concern with religion cannot be rejected as an attempt to resurrect outmoded forms. He realized fully that organized Christianity has failed since the Enlightenment to be a basic ferment and integrating force in social life. He deliberately agreed with those saying that "the era of religion is at an end" (Ellul, 1970b, p. 175). Institutions in themselves cannot be retrieved and reinvigorated, he suggests, because history never repeats the circumstances for which they once supplied a resolution. The Constantinian model of Christendom—that is, a stress on institutional

religion—received little attention from Ellul because he considered this formulation obsolete and he felt the crucial issues lie elsewhere. Visible religious practice was scorned in the classicist era as well, with the French
Revolution adding spectacular de-Christianization decrees in 1793-1794.
Ellul's intellectual courage enabled him, in a similar manner, to reach behind
institutional practice and consider whether the religious ethos might yet
apply.

Although conceding contemporary ecclesiastical impotence, Ellul recognizes that alterations in logos do not ipso facto reconstitute theos. As
Augustine did before him, Ellul found significance in the distinction
between organizational form and organismic reality, basing his intellectual
work squarely upon the latter.[14] As John Dewey (1934) realized in a different context, the predicament of modern "religions" does not preclude
immersing one's viewpoint in "the religious" as a way of invigorating scholarly work on important issues of social solidarity. For Ellul (1970b), we
must find creative ways of including that latter element—the spiritual nucleus radiating through life—or else remain condemned to "every whim of our
instruments," to a "sterility of death" (p. 148).

Ellul affirmed the religious impulse for maintaining vitality in the
human spirit and empowering moral sensitivity in an age where means have
triumphed. Without a definition of authenticity, a final standard of choice
(which religious studies seek to supply), human existence is condemned to
essential arbitrariness, that is, to meaninglessness. Answers to life's discor-
dances are clear, he declares, "only with those who accept a transcendental,
an absolute value which determines all the rest. Everywhere else we wander
about in confusion" (Ellul, 1969a, p. 146). Ellul anticipated chaos when the
"Good Life" has no settled views. He recognized—as Durkheim perceived
so astutely in describing "anomie"—that selfhood disintegrates without a
supreme court of moral appeal. He was emphatic that our concern with
human fulfillment and community include strict attention to the religious—
those concentrations of moral authority that can finally adjudicate among
colliding values and, in doing so, create a sense of appreciation for whatever
serves to strengthen society and culture. Across human history, religion has
focused attention precisely on those symbols of faith ultimacy, ends, and
grounding, which alone can extricate us from our technicized existence.

But Ellul did not simply appeal to the religious in general; he believes
strongly that cultural worthwhileness originates with human beings themselves. For life to be infused with meaning, a revolution of transformed people is necessary.[15] Consonant with Ellul's religious perspective, a genuine
revolution of human beings has a revelational dimension. It must derive outside technicized culture and move us in an opposite direction. Societies, for
Ellul, are not reordered by antipathy to institutions or more energetically
exploiting means but by illumined consciousness. Only a decisive power,

achieving fruition within us yet originating beyond us, can transform the contemporary environment. Anything less cannot penetrate today's overwhelming *la technique*. Spiritual reality cannot be restored by material means. As a theologian in counterpoint, Ellul frames his concerns eschatologically. Once again, wishing to supersede all dichotomies between end and means, he emphasizes a realm where "means and ends are identical," this time combined in persons (Ellul, 1951, p. 79). Only that situation is exactly opposite of ours today; and only at history's apocalyptic finale will ends be fully and openly realized. However, signs can appear now as first fruits of that ultimate eschatological event where ends reign supreme. Human beings, as a matter of fact, can receive, embody, constitute the presence of the end within themselves.

Thus, people should not merely be incited to noble activity, encouraged to achieve some end. In Ellul's (1977) vision, the end has been established and human beings must represent it (p. 24). We are not asked, for example, to bring in justice, but to manifest it. Ellul does not call for a struggle for peace; we have ourselves to be peaceful. The end, established supernaturally, is miraculously available so that we can live authentically, can "be" rather than act. It is not a "question of doing good but of embodying faith, which is fundamentally different" (Ellul, 1970b, pp. 118-119). The critical matter for Ellul, as it was for Max Weber, is withstanding a preemption, protecting us from "the parceling out of our soul, from the supreme mastery of the bureaucratic way of life." Therefore, "so far as the solution is concerned . . . it can only be a solution in terms of life" (Ellul, 1951, p. 18). Life incarnate is our sole escape from the triumph of means.[16]

Necessity and the Fall

A world where means have triumphed is driven by necessity. Necessity is the "converse of freedom" for Ellul and "the primary characteristic of a fallen world. Necessity is both a sociological and a theological concept for him. Technique appears in germinal form as an element in necessity from the Fall onward" (Gill, 1984, p. 110). The key theme in Ellul's theological method is "the dialectical interplay between freedom and necessity, . . . a golden thread" which serves as a "hermeneutical key to his thinking" (Clendenin, 1987, p. xi).

In the contemporary world, *la technique* has become the all-encompassing feature of necessity. "Fallen and closed off from the Wholly Other God, human life is ruled by conditions and determinations" (Gill, 1984, p. 110). The fallen world obeys its own imperatives, rather than those of goodness or justice. While refusing to call it fate or view "society mechanistically," Ellul (1976) insisted that "there are necessities which we cannot escape" (pp. 37-50). Their supreme manifestation is our bondage to *la technique*.

This universe of necessity is not a world of technological artifacts, but the imperial dominance of technical modes of thought over the human orders of culture, morality, politics and education. When we claim ultimacy and universality for *la technique*, and worship it as unassailable, then its fallenness is most dramatic. We imbue technology with an aura of holy prestige, and it is this social transformation that enslaves us.

On the sociological level, Ellul insisted on a fundamental realism about the crushing invasion of *la technique*. Where the utter harshness of our contemporary predicament nudges us toward superficiality and retreat, Ellul crusaded instead for ruthless honesty. On the theological level, as Ellul contended in *The New Demons*, the fallen world of necessity must be desacralized. We must smash our modern idols, expose false claims made in the name of *la technique* and demythologize today's illusions about technological prowess. Our promotion of revolution as a moral imperative must start with a drastic assessment which shatters all divinatory claims by the technological and bureaucratic domains.

Ellul opposed the farrago of cheap solutions offered by the accommodationism of the mainstream churches and technical experts. Christianity, caught in Constantinism by the fourth century and "mongrelized since the seventeenth," marries the status quo and thereby does not lead the rescue. Ordinary democratic liberalism vaunts its pride in scientific progress. These religious or political rhetorics ultimately offer only cul-de-sacs (Ellul, 1975, ch. 1).[17]

The petite activism of the do-gooders may create some movement at the margins and on the surface. But Ellul insists that "the forces which are of decisive importance in our world situation, . . . the constituent elements," are nowhere touched by them (Ellul, 1951, p. 33). Most turbulence, he contends, does not produce worthwhile changes, but only entrenches existing institutions and canonizes the powerful. Both ecclesiastical and political reform in themselves are futile; by dealing with images on the periphery they dissipate their energies over fictitious disputes, false answers and inadequate definitions. "What a fraud, what a swindle," Ellul (1973) says with scorn, "when the only decisive result is the relentless strengthening of the State" under the guise of liberating oppressed peoples from tyranny (p. 278).

But desacralization does not mean capricious iconoclasm just for indignation's sake; rather it means we must resolve to seal off misleading exits. Authentic revolutions cannot occur until all reasonable possibilities are blocked, and unless we recognize that conciliation is impossible (Ellul, 1971b, pp. 245-246). If we assume that we only need to eliminate defective parts, or more tightly organize the social order, or balance political and economic disproportions, or fill visible gaps, we will pursue these reforms, rather than seriously engage the pervasive malaise of our time. Technology removes humankind's ancient constraints, but it does not make us free.

Destruction of *la technique* rather than administrative reform of technology must be the starting point of change (Ellul, 1991).

Those who attack Ellul's pessimism fail to realize that his vigorous desacralization is but one element in a larger perspective, the first step in a longer journey. Ellul's exposé of crisis does not focus on doubt and despair, but on salvation. "Desacralizing," Ellul (1975) writes, "can be done only if, along with it, one supplied a reason for living adequate to sustain life, and an answer really satisfying and clear" (p. 208). We must break the impasses we have created; we must finally resolve the questions we have raised. All appearances to the contrary, Ellul (1951) is searching for an ameliorative option capable of "communicating good and granting life . . . a true change which would put things right" (p. 31). The end, anthenticated supernaturally, is available so that through its power we can live in a new mode of being. Forces supremely revolutionary arise outside of technicized nature and move in an opposite direction; they "belong to another city," have "another Master" (Ellul, 1970b, pp. 118-119). Anything less cannot penetrate overwhelming technique. A spiritual reality cannot be restored by material means. And when addressing a Christian audience, Ellul (1969b) uses explicitly theological terms: "Only in the light of Jesus Christ's sacrifice of himself can man be compelled to live as man" (p. 167). The intervention of God's Spirit, resurrection power, enables us to incarnate freedom and overcome evil.

In Ellul's dialectic, the "No" of condemnation becomes the "Yes" of redemption. The divine Wholly Other is present as the antithesis to the closed order of necessity. The "freedom of the Wholly Other" is the center and initiator of human freedom but "cannot be assimilated by sociological forces." God's independence is the guarantor of ours (Ellul, 1972b, p. 142). "The end is already present in the world . . . it is not the result of our activity. It is here already as a secret force, both evoking and also provoking our means. We have to be obedient to the end, not as a goal to be reached, but also and at the same time as a given fact, something already there, a presence which is active too" (p. 136).

CONCLUSION

Ellul and Mumford shared the conviction that within the technological order, life was mechanized and dehumanized. They agreed that the core problem was the "uncritical worship of technology as that sacred power that falsely promised to fulfill all human needs and desires even as it led us down the path of self-destruction" (Fasching, 1997, p. 2). Mumford and Ellul both held that the machine itself is not demonic but "the cult of the machine"; therein lay the demonic power that sustained "the myth of the

mega-machine." They shared a common goal "of demythologizing technical civilization and restoring technology to a modest but constructive role
in a larger, more organic vision of human life and the human good"
(Fasching, 1997, p. 2).

Mumford parted with Ellul, however, in developing a humanistic rather
than a theistic response to the threat of technology. Several humanists res-
onate with Mumford's resourceful continence: "The next move is ours,"
Mumford (1970) concludes; "the gates of the technocratic prison will open
automatically, despite their rusty hinges, as soon as we choose to walk out"
(p. 435). Our chief accomplishment, he argued, is not our machines and
organizational wizardry, but the creation of our own humanity. At this crucial point, Ellul's paradigm is incommensurable with Mumford's. In Ellul's
view, only by retaining the God-principle can we protect humanistic values;
without a personal absolute, society consistently erects arbitrary ones.

Ellul enriches the analytic power of the media ecology tradition through
his sociological concepts, *la technique* and propaganda. He interacts with
McLuhan and he complements the work of Neil Postman. Ellul's technical
artifice resonates with Harold Innis's empire and monopoly of knowledge.
But his distinctive contribution is the necessity of transformed humanity for
genuine revolution. However, this very gift to media ecology scholarship is
ambiguous and controversial. Recovering in coherent fashion what he
means by transformation and true freedom requires an elaborate content
analysis of the majority of his work. Ellul understood the problem at an
early date in his career, but only after two decades did he begin to recognize
the solution with equal clarity. Those who only read his pre-1971 writings
might be easily misled, for his most famous works, which appeared before
then, contain little suggestion of any solution.[18]

Nor does Ellul's dialectical mode always function unerratically. In *The
Meaning of the City*, for example, Ellul used an overarching dialectic
between Babylon and Jerusalem. Yet his emphasis throughout rested on the
first pole. Not until the final pages does the "City of God" receive its due,
and an ongoing tension between the "Yes" and "No" was virtually nonexistent anywhere in the book. With sovereign efficiency impounding everything under necessity, liberation is the only alternative. The problem is
tyranny; opposing tyranny is freedom. But that solution appeared at the far
end of an unrelenting paradigm.

Thus, the tendency of readers to find judgment without grace arises at
least in part from Ellul's method. In *The Ethics of Freedom*, Ellul (1976) he
concentrated on solutions which come from individual awareness and never
reconciled them with social and collective awareness very well, although he
mentioned these about halfway through the book (p. 270). Moreover, his
sometimes peculiar definitions (such as the activistic flavor he gives to
prayer, waiting, and the incognito) can easily be misinterpreted as dou-

bletalk. He often formulated his ideas in an unqualified fashion. Labeling him a dogmatic rationalist is certainly inaccurate for a dialectician and usually arises from those fixating on one side of his argument. Yet Ellul himself did not always help matters; his sweeping scope tended to downplay the nuances and countervalences.[19]

Detractors have tended to assume, though unjustifiably, that Ellul made his choices for essentially theological reasons, whatever their sociological disguise. However, Ellul's audience did increasingly become a Christian one, and he assumed that role without reservation. In the process, his confrontation with contemporary culture could be relegated to the fringes more easily. In *The Ethics of Freedom*, for instance, Ellul (1976) insists on a strict correlation between explicit belief and authentic freedom. Faith alone permits and enables us to realize Christian freedom (p. 89).

> Christians, like all other men, are still subject to pressures, temptations, determinations, and necessities. The Christian, like everyone else, obviously knows what it is to be hungry. His distinctive gift, however, is that of participation in the secret lordship which enables him to give a different reply from that of all others in the same conditions, and which allows him to introduce a lever of freedom into the dense mass of constraints. We believe that this is possible for him alone because necessities have been overcome only once in Christ, and therefore this is a possibility only in express association with the work of Christ. (p. 87)

Ellul as sociologist engages media ecology through technical artifice as the contemporary human environment. However, his distinctive contribution is rooted in his theology, that is, transformed beings are *sine qua non* for revolutionary change. But to be taken seriously as a theologian in counterpoint, Ellul's parochial appeal to Christians only and his ill-functioning dialectic need to be fundamentally reconstructed. When the dialectical yes and no operate simultaneously so that fallenness is located within the larger context of creation, Ellul's insistence on transformed life is more believable. Even within Ellul's explicitly Christian framework, there are broader appeals to the positive working of God's providence outside true belief. In terms of his own neo-orthodox commitment, Barth distinguishes between a de jure state of affairs—the covenant as God's all-inclusive pre-temporal "Yes" which obtains for all persons—and de facto knowledge of it which only believers possess (*Church Dogmatics*, vol. IV, part 2; see Outka, 1981, pp. 210-215).

The discontinuity between believer-freedom and every other kind is not as complete as Ellul suggests, even within his own Christian worldview. In fact, there is often solidarity and agreement among disparate worldviews. The transformed life Ellul affirms is distinguished because it is a qualitatively new event; it must be understood in terms internal to itself; it retains its own integrity; it remains irreducible to anything else. In constructing the character and rationale of this concept, a theological framework is inescapable. And Ellul's normative version can deliver such a concept, provided the counterpoint and dialectic of his model are reconstituted and invigorated. In the process, clearly Ellul's theology must meet the standard of religious diversity to be credible.[20] In order to sharpen dialogue and enhance media ecology as a whole, Ellul's theistic approach to technology warrants its own depth and integrity, but out of a commitment to academic pluralism.

ENDNOTES

1. Ellul (1981) included in his overview additional references where he has elaborated further on his methodology through the 1970s (p. 308). See also Goddard (2002, pp. 52-57) for a summary and citations on Ellul's dialectic.

2. Jacques Ellul was born into the Serbian aristocracy and was a member of a wealthy shipbuilding dynasty until the worldwide depression in 1929 plunged his family into poverty. As he roamed the ocean wharves of Bordeaux during his teenage years, he confronted first-hand the death and stark exploitation of this port city's longshoremen and sailors. In his struggle with the personal questions that arose from these experiences, Ellul found Marx deficient. He could not explain "my human condition, my mortal nature, my capacity to suffer or love, or my relationship with others" (Ellul, 1982, p. 15). Meanwhile, he disdained the Communist Party membership for its trivial agenda. As Ellul (1991) puts it, "my relations with communists was poor. They viewed me as a little bourgeois intellectual . . . and I regarded them as insignificant because they seemed not to have any true knowledge of the thinking of Marx. They had read the 1848 *Manifesto* and that was all. I broke with them completely after the Moscow trials" (p. 2). But he continued to take Marx's thinking seriously, and could not escape Marx's insistence that considering God's existence was useless. Moreover, Marx's "rejection of all dimensions other than economic or political" (Ellul, 1982, p. 15) meant that no reconciliation with the Bible would work and simplistic integration impossible. He remained torn between the two all his life, and his dialectic always included a basic confrontational dimension (Ellul, 1988).

3. Ellul wrote in 1981, "I have not actually written a wide variety of books but rather one long book in which each 'individual' book constitutes a chapter. It's a gamble and a little insane to believe that there will be some readers patient enough to see how my thirty-six works actually belong together" (Ellul, 1998, p. 22). As Goddard (2002) notes, "In this brief statement, Ellul encapsulates the difficulty faced by those who wish to understand his thought. Although perhaps a little extreme to claim that 'as demanding a task it may be, his work really must be read in its entirety' [Goddard quoting John Boli-Bennett], it is the case that if any aspect of Ellul's thought is to be seriously examined and properly interpreted, it must be set within the context of the whole Ellul corpus" (p. 52).

4. According to Goddard (2002), "This is the limitation of the excellent" dissertation by Ronald Ray in 1973 "which only examines Ellul's ethics and, on the other side, the problems" with David Lovekin's (1991) *Technique, Discourse, and Consciousness: An Introduction to the Philosophy of Jacques Ellul* and D. J. Wennemann's dissertation in 1991, *The Meaning of Subjectivity in a Technological Society: Jacques Ellul's View of Man as Dialogic Agent*, "arise from their explicit refusal to take his theology seriously as theology" (p. 54).

5. Ellul takes pains early in *The Meaning of the City* (pp. 8-9) to deny that "this harmonious teaching throughout the Scriptures" is the result of a skeptical agrarianism, something accidental to the narrative, or imposed only by eccentric exegesis. It is so pervasive, so "complete and coherent," with such an "undeniable bearing on man's life, his destiny, his relations with God" that it is a veritable "doctrine."

6. Although the etymology of *iyr* (Hebrew for "city") is unknown, Ellul (1970b) suggests it is "probably a Canaanite word adopted by the Hebrews when they came to Palestine, and began living in cities." The connotations given, albeit often unclear, are "enemy," "burn," "angry," "foreboding" (p. 10).

7. Not only is the city connected as counterpoint to the technological society, but to the state "as its hub," as the "synthesis of the state's power." All the "vigor of the state is concentrated in the great city" (Ellul, 1970b, p. 50).

8. Ellul (1970b) strengthens his observations by wide-ranging reference to the New Testament. Jesus, for example, shows no conciliation toward the city. "He never proclaims grace for man's work. All he recognizes is its devilish quality" (p. 113). After his baptism, Jesus is taken — significantly enough, by the devil — to Jerusalem. "This is his first contact with the city – a contact marked by Satan's stamp. It is impossible to affirm that the city here has any positive value; it is rather the instrument of temptation" (p. 114). Jerusalem as the ultimate biblical city commits the ultimately tragic crime, Jesus' crucifixion, and receives an unprecedented destruction in 70 A.D. (pp. 135-138, 145). Moreover, the New Testament affirms the city as an agent of war: War is an urban phenomenon, as the city is a military phenomenon. Perfecting one leads to perfecting the other" (p. 51). Notably also, both times the New Testament speaks of "the fallen angel" it refers to him as "the angel of a city" (p. 45).

9. Ellul constantly refers to modern warfare to show the brutality and power of *la technique* as structural evil.

10. For Ellul (1976), most of the important theological issues today "are implied, outlined, and. . . . discussed in the *Church Dogmatics* (p. 8). For a detailed account of the major themes in Barth's *Kirchliche Dogmatik* and how Ellul uses them in his work, see Bromiley (1981, pp. 32-51). Darrell Fasching includes Karl Barth with Rudolf Bultmann (1952, 1957), Reinhold Niebuhr (1960, 1941/1943/1964) and Paul Tillich (1951/1957/1963/1967) as the dominant theologians of the 20th century. A common theme among them is "the transformation of society brought about by the emergence of modern technology," but it was most natural for Ellul to align himself with the Barthian emphasis on God's freedom and otherness (see Fasching, 1981, pp. 4-6).

11. Regarding Barth on divine and human freedom, Ellul acknowledges that "Karl Barth has dealt very thoroughly with the matter at various points in the *Church*

Dogmatics, and since . . . I am in full accord with his presentation, there seems to be no point in repeating it" (Ellul, 1976, p. 120). *The Ethics of Freedom* has 41 references and Barth runs second only to Karl Marx, whose view of alienation is analyzed in detail in the first part of the work.

12. Ellul (1989) devotes a chapter to each of the three major periods of human existence: "The Prehistoric Period and the Natural Environment" (pp. 104-114); "The Historial Period and the Social Environment" (pp. 115-132); "The Posthistorical Period and the Technological Environment" (pp. 133-140).

13. By "end," Ellul (1951) writes, "I mean the collective ends of civilization, for individuals still have their own ends, for instance to succeed in a competition or to get a higher salary, and the like" (p. 63).

14. Augustine's distinction between the church as organism and organization is delineated in his confrontation with the purist Donatist sect, and in his argument in the *City of God* (Chapters 19-22) that Christianity is not responsible for the Fall of Rome.

15. Ellul was interested in revolution throughout his career and along both poles; see *Presence of the Kingdom, Violence, Autopsy of Revolution, Critique of the New Commonplaces, Hope in the Time of Abandonment, The Subversion of Christianity,* and *Anarchy and Christianity.*

16. See Ellul's (1951) retort to the criticism that he is attempting to revive a misguided Protestant individualism (pp. 82-85). Nor is Ellul's (1968) individualism libertarian. Such individualism, he says, is "outdated" and "it is useless to try to retrieve it" (p. 748). Nor does he intend a retreat into "purely personal consolations"; he is well aware that this is a "suicidal solution" (Ellul, 1951, p. 103). Any judgment to be moral, must by definition involve choice; genuine choosing can be initiated only by persons who have been transformed supernaturally. From there, communities will follow inevitably. The consequences will be, in Ellul's (1976) vision, "the emergence of social, political, intellectual, or artistic bodies, associations, interest groups—totally independent" of technicized forces and thus capable of opposing them (p. 221). As these renewed humans combine into new patterns not under *la techniques'* tutelage, this reordered consciousness will begin choking out the monolithic structure of technological necessity.

17. *False Presence of the Kingdom* is entirely devoted to a critique of Christendom, especially French Protestantism. He attacks political liberalism particularly in *Autopsy of Revolution* (Chapter 4).

18. Books focusing more on hope and solution began appearing after that time: *Autopsy of Revolution* (Ellul, 1971b), *Hope in the Time of Abandonment* (Ellul, 1973), *Ethics of Freedom* (Ellul, 1976), and *Living Faith* (Ellul, 1983). However, Ellul's most important and popular trilogy appears before the more hopeful emphasis: *Technological Society* (Ellul, 1964), *Propaganda* (1965), *Political Illusion* (1967).

19. In his translator's Preface to *Living Faith,* G. W. Bromiley speaks of Ellul's style and methodology as a "dangerous combination of hyperbole and paradox;" yet through it all is "the incontestable erudition, the penetrating insight, and the passionate fervor that make Ellul worth reading" (Ellul, 1983, p. vii).

20. In principle this is not a difficult standard for Ellul to achieve. He defends universal salvation even more strenuously than does Karl Barth (Ellul, 1983, pp.

188-209). In his *Un Chrétien pour Israël*, Ellul argues that Judaism is another community that can introduce freedom into a technical civilization besides Christians.

REFERENCES

Bromiley, G. W. (1981). Barth's Influence on Jacques Ellul. In C. G. Christians & J. Van Hook (Eds.), *Jacques Ellul: Interpretive essays* (pp. 32-51). Urbana: University of Illinois Press.

Bultmann, Rudolf (1952). *Theology of the New Testament.* (K. Grobell, Trans.). London: SCM Press.

Bultmann, Rudolf (1957). *History and eschatology.* New York: Harper Torchbooks.

Clendenin, D. B. (1987). *Theological method in Jacques Ellul.* Lanham, MD: University Press of America.

Cox, H. (1971). The Ungodly City: A Theological Response to Jacques Ellul. *Commonweal*, 94, 352-357.

Dewey, J. (1922). *Human nature and conduct.* New York: Henry Holt.

Dewey, J. (1934). *A common faith.* New Haven, CT: Yale University Press.

Ellul, J. (1951). *The presence of the kingdom* (O. Wyon, Trans.). Philadelphia: Westminster.

Ellul, J. (1964). *The technological society* (J. Wilkinson., Trans.). New York: Knopf.

Ellul, J. (1965). *Propaganda: The formation of men's attitudes* (K. Kellen & J. Lerner, Trans.) New York: Knopf.

Ellul, J. (1967). *The political illusion.* (K. Kellen, Trans.). New York: Knopf.

Ellul, J. (1968). *A critique of the new commonplaces* (H. Weaver, Trans.). New York: Knopf.

Ellul, J. (1969a). *To will and to do* (C. Edward Hopkin, Trans.). Philadelphia: Pilgrim Press.

Ellul, J. (1969b). *Violence: Reflections from a Christian perspective* (C. G. Kings, Trans.). New York: Seabury Press.

Ellul, J. (1970a). From Jacques Ellul. In J. Y. Holloway (Ed.), *Introducing Jacques Ellul* (pp. 5-6). Grand Rapids, MI: William B. Eerdmans.

Ellul, J. (1970b). *The meaning of the city* (D. Pardee, Trans.). Grand Rapids, MI: William B. Eerdmans.

Ellul, J. (1970c). Mirror of These Ten Years. *The Christian Century,* 87, 200-204.

Ellul, Jacques (1971a). *The judgment of Jonah* by (G.W. Bromiley, Trans.). Grand Rapids, MI: Eerdmansj.

Ellul, J. (1971b). *Autopsy of revolution.* (P. Wolf, Trans.). New York: Knopf.

Ellul, J. (1972a). *False presence of the kingdom* (C. Edward Hopkin, Trans.). New York: Seabury Press.

Ellul, J. (1972b). *The politics of God and the politics of man.* (G. W. Bromiley, Trans.). Grand Rapids, MI: William B. Eerdmans.

Ellul, J. (1973). *Hope in the time of abandonment.* (C. Edward Hopkin, Trans.). New York: Seabury Press.

Ellul, J. (1975). *The new demons.* (C. Edward Hopkin, Trans.). New York: Seabury.

Ellul, J. (1976). *Ethics of freedom.* (G. W. Bromiley, Trans.). Grand Rapids, MI: William B. Eerdmans.

Ellul, J. (1977). *Apocalypse: The book of Revelation.* (G. W. Schreiner, Trans.). New York: Seabury Press.

Ellul, J. (1981). On dialogue. In C. G. Christians & J. Van Hook (Eds.), *Jacques Ellul: Interpretive essays* (pp. 291-308). Urbana: University of Illinois Press.

Ellul, J. (1982). *In season and out of season: An introduction to the thought of Jacques Ellul.* New York: Harper & Row.

Ellul, J. (1983). *Living faith: Belief and doubt in a perilous world.* (P. Heinegg, Trans.). New York: Harper & Row.

Ellul, J. (1985). *The humiliation of the word.* (J. M. Hanks, Trans.). Grand Rapids, MI: Eerdmans.

Ellul, J. (1986). *The subversion of Christianity* (G. W. Bromiley, Trans.). Grand Rapids, MI: William B. Eerdmans.

Ellul, J. (1988). *Jesus and Marx : From gosepl to ideology.* (J. M. Hanks, Trans.). Grand Rapids, MI: William B. Eerdmans.

Ellul, J. (1989). *What I believe.* (G. W. Bromiley, Trans.). Grand Rapids, MI: William B. Eerdmans.

Ellul, J. (1990). *The technological bluff.* (G. W. Bromiley, Trans.). Grand Rapids, MI: William B. Eerdmans.

Ellul, J. (1991). *Anarchy and Christianity.* (G. W. Bromiley, Trans.). Grand Rapids, MI: William B. Eerdmans.

Ellul, J. (1998). *Jacques Ellul on religion, technology, and politics: Coversations with Patrick Troude-Chastenet.* (J. M. France, Trans.). Atlanta, GA: Scholars Press.

Fasching, D. J. (1981). *The thought of Jacques Ellul: A systematic exposition.* Toronto: Edwin Mellen Press.

Fasching, D. J. (1997). Lewis Mumford, Technological Critic. Special Issue of *The Ellul Forum,* 18, 9-12.

Galileo, G. (1957). *Discoveries and opinions of Galileo.* (S. Drake, Trans.). Garden City, NY: Doubleday.

Gill, D. W. (1984). *The word of God in the ethics of Jacques Ellul.* Metuchen, NJ: The Scarecrow Press.

Goddard, A. (2002). *Living the word, resisting the world: The life and thought of Jacques Ellul.* Cumbria, UK: Paternoster Press.

Lovekin, David (1991). *Technique, discourse, and consciousness: An introduction to the philosophy of Jacques Ellul.* Bethelem, PA: Lehigh University Press.

Mumford, L. (1934). *Technics and civilization.* New York: Harcourt Brace.

Mumford, L. (1952). *Art and technics.* New York: Columbia University Press.

Mumford, L. (1970). *The myth of the machine: The pentagon of power.* New York: Harcourt Brace Jovanovich.

Niebuhr, R. (1960). *Moral man and immoral society.* New York: Charles Scribner's Sons.

Niebuhr, R. (1964). *The nature and destiny of man.* (2 vols.). New York: Charles Scribner's Sons. (Original works published 1941, 1943)

Outka, G. (1981). Discontinuity in the Ethics of Jacques Ellul. In C. G. Christians & J. Van Hook (Eds.), *Jacques Ellul: Interpretive essays* (pp. 177-228). Urbana: University of Illinois Press.

Postman, N. (1985). *Amusing ourselves to death.* New York: Viking.

Tillich, P. (1967). *Systematic theology* (3 vols.). Chicago: University of Chicago Press. (Original works published 1951, 1957, 1963)

Wenneman, D. J. (1991). *The meaning of subjectivity in a technological society: Jacques Ellul's view of man as dialogic agent.* Ph.D. Dissertation. Marquette University.

6

Harold Innis' Legacy in the Media Ecology Tradition

Paul Heyer
Wilfrid Laurier University, Canada

Here it is worth recalling that Harold Innis's principle that new
communication technologies not only give us new things to
think about but new things to think with.

— *Neil Postman (1982)*

This chapter tells the story of the legacy of Harold Adams Innis, one of the
most original and profound thinkers in North American communication
and media studies in the 20th century. More specifically, it chronicles and
analyzes how Innis' scholarship in political economy and communication
has contributed to the rise of media ecology as an intellectual tradition and
a theoretical perspective.[1]

His name may not be as well known as that of his University of Toronto
colleague and spiritual descendent, Marshall McLuhan, but Harold Innis'
(1894-1952) influence on contemporary critical media and communication
studies has been no less profound. Among media scholars in the United
States, Daniel Czitrom (1982) is certainly not alone when he observes that
for the "most radical and elaborate American media theory, one must look
to the work of two Canadians, Harold Adams Innis and Marshall

McLuhan" (p. 147). James Carey (1989) sees this patrimony in more asymmetric terms when he notes that it is Innis's work, not McLuhan's, "which is the great achievement in communications on this continent" (p. 142). Neil Postman (1992) is of similar bent when he declares Innis "the father of modern communication studies" (p. 9). Within the tradition of media ecology, Innis' legacy therefore looms large in the pantheon of luminaries discussed in this book.

To fully appreciate Innis' contributions, it is necessary to survey his intellectual development: from the early researches in political economy to his later forays into the then largely uncharted realm of communication studies and to consider some of the formative influences, personal as well as scholarly, that shaped his thought. Most of this chapter, however, focuses on his later work in critical media studies and communications history. My goal is to help readers attain a better grasp of this contribution, both on its own terms and with respect to the relevance it has had for the emerging tradition of media ecology.

Innis' later work can be seen as characterized by three related themes: First, he develops an outline for the study of what is now known as communications history or media history, a field for which he remains the definitive cartographer; second, he elaborates several theoretical concepts for the study of communication and culture, such as medium, time-bias, and space-bias, the oral tradition, and the monopoly of knowledge; and third, he suggests how his approach to history and perspective that recent commentators have referred to as media ecology or medium theory can inform a critique of culture and technology in the contemporary world.

Of course, as with any major thinker, there can be no substitute for reading the primary sources. Unfortunately, Innis' later writings are often as difficult, notoriously so, as they are rich. Students can perhaps gain some solace from the fact that the nature of the difficulty is stylistic rather than conceptual, which places almost everyone on equal footing—there are no interpretive experts when it comes to Innis, and his basic concepts are accessible enough. However, I suggest certain strategies for reading, or rereading him that might make Innis more approachable—and possibly engaging—for potential readers.[2]

THE ROAD TO POLITICAL ECONOMY

He was a child of the soil, not the polis. Born in 1894, the same year as Aldous Huxley and Oliver Wendell Holmes, Harold Innis would go on to become one of Canada's most revered scholars. Legend has it that the name on his birth certificate reads "Herald." If so, it would aptly foreshadow both the new directions in political economy his early work would make possible as well as the continually expanding vistas inspired by the communications project that consumed him prior to his premature death from cancer in 1952.

His was a life intimately tied to many of the major circumstances of the first half of the 20th century. Innis both witnessed and commented on major innovations in transportation and communication. The world that unfolded before him was one of rail travel reaching its height, the electrification of everyday life, Golden Age of radio, the emergence of television, and the military and personal holocaust of two world wars—the first of which he experienced as a soldier.

He hailed from the small town of Otterville in the farm country of southwestern Ontario. Ninety miles to the east stood the provincial capital and largest city, Toronto, where he would eventually attend university, although this possibility seemed unlikely in the earth-clotted years of his early youth. His life then was tied to the land.[3]

Farming experiences including the reality of unpredictable weather and markets that behaved similarly, impinged on his consciousness at an early age. He attended a classic one-room schoolhouse and was greatly encouraged in his educational pursuits by a mother who was well-educated by the standards of the day. He was eventually able to attend high school, in part because the family had three other children to help with the chores. His commute there was on the Grand Trunk Railway, not an insignificant biographical fact. Exposure to this mode of transportation and communication, and the impromptu narratives about it that he gleaned from railway people, opened his mind to historical and geographical ideas that would resurface more fully in his academic career.

In time, his thirst for learning led him to the Baptist affiliated McMaster University, located then in Toronto, today in Hamilton, Ontario. History and political economy became his preferred subjects—James Ten Broeke and W. S. Wallace his favorite teachers. The former's reflective question regarding the nature of knowledge, "Why do we attend to the things to which we attend," always remained in the back of Innis' mind, eventually gracing the preface to his 1951 classic, *The Bias of Communication* (Innis, 1951/1995); Wallace's contention that although the economic interpretation of history is not the only interpretation, it is the most revealing, was one that had more immediate ramifications for Innis' graduate studies and early career. However, before that possibility could present itself, a war did.

Upon graduation from McMaster, he enlisted in the army and the experience would test his fiber to the full. His posting with the signal corps may have significance in light of his later work in media history. World War I was a verifiable cross-section of the history of technology and communications, employing everything from pack animals to aircraft for transport, and carrier pigeons to the wireless for communication. He was sent to the front almost immediately and became a player in one of that theater of the horrific's major acts, the battle of Vimy Ridge. While on a reconnaissance patrol an artillery shell exploded close enough to seriously damage his leg. His war was over.

He convalesced in England before returning home. During that time he read economics and, in response to the devastation the war was wreaking on a whole generation of young Canadians, worked on a master's thesis, *The Returned Soldier*, which was accepted by his *alma mater*, McMaster University. The next logical step, given the debating skills he honed while an undergraduate, seemed to be a career in law, although he was still fascinated by economics. To satisfy this urge he decided to spend the summer of 1918 at the University of Chicago studying the "dismal science." The subject, in the hands of one of his teachers, Frank Knight, was anything but. Innis was inspired, although far from satiated. The planned law career soon went on what would become permanent hold and he enrolled full-time in the economics PhD program.

During Innis' Windy City period, when his primary interest was in political economy and economic history, there was possibly another more immediate intellectual influence. America was discovering itself. Its history, geography, and literature were now deemed worthy of serious scholarly study. Canada had yet to make that leap. When it eventually did a decade later, Innis emerged as a key figure challenging the British-oriented European bias that had ruled the pedagogical roost since colonial times. Encouraging him in this direction was his PhD supervisor at Chicago, the economic historian Chester W. Wright, who urged him to pursue a Canadian dissertation topic. *A History of the Canadian Pacific Railway* was the result. While at Chicago, Innis also got a chance to teach several introductory economics courses and saw in this experience the career that would later be his destiny. Part of that destiny included a fulfilling marriage to one of his former undergraduate students at Chicago, Mary Quayle.[4]

Upon graduation, he took up a post in the Department of Political Economy at the University of Toronto, despite several American possibilities—by the mid-1930s Chicago would repeatedly and unsuccessfully attempt to woo him back to its fold with generous offers. In 1923 his dissertation was published as a book (Innis, 1923/1971). A turgid study, it nonetheless charts in an unprecedented way how, in forging a nation, a transportation system (responsible for moving people, goods, and information) such as the Canadian Pacific Railway had to both overcome and adapt to the options proffered by geography.

In assessing the influence of the railway, Innis soon realized that in Canada, prior to spikes and ties, paddles and portages made possible the fur trade, which helped open the land and encouraged immigration and agricultural development. Research for this project would culminate in 1930 with the publication of *The Fur Trade in Canada* (Innis, 1962b), generally considered his magnum opus in political economy. The project took him to archives, to be sure, but also beyond, to the land where the history he sought to study had unfolded. He traveled by steamer and canoe along original routes, eventually charting how, through exploration, commercial rivalries, and settlements, the waterways used in the fur trade for transport and communication were the conduits through which had flowed the lifeblood of a gestating nation.

The study of other staple resources, such as timber, minerals, fish, and wheat, would preoccupy him over the next decade, giving rise to his "staples thesis"—how dependency on such resources often gives rise to economic monopolies and regional disparities that favor metropolitan centers. In 1940 he expanded his purview beyond Canada with the publication of *The Cod Fisheries: The History of an International Economy* (Innis, 1954). In exhaustive and insightful detail he shows how the codfish industry was about more than fish: It created international rivalries as well as commercial rivalries within nations. This led to the opening of trade routes (that served as lines for transportation and communication) and settlements, which prompted wars, treaties, and economic policies among a diversity of nations.

COMMUNICATIONS HISTORY

By the outbreak of World War II, many honors had come to Innis. He was by now full professor and head of his department. During the war he was distrustful of those politicians and civilians who administered to the conflict on the home front. He chose instead to remain at his post and defend the right of scholars to teach and publish, even if some of their views were deemed unpopular. In 1941, he helped found the Economic History Association and its signature publication, *The Journal of Economic History*. He also continued to research and publish in political economy. However, within that discipline he perceived in embryonic form a new subfield deserving to be birthed and nurtured.

If the study of staples had led him to touch on the importance of the transportation of goods and information, the study of one of those staples, pulp and paper, opened a door to the newly emergent field of communication studies. He simply followed pulp and paper through its subsequent stages—the newspaper and journalism, books, and advertising. In other words, from looking at a natural resource based industry, he turned his attention to a cultural industry in which information, and ultimately knowledge, was a commodity that circulated, had value, and empowered those who controlled it. He began by taking a series of voluminous notes that would eventually comprise a large and as yet unpublished compendium known as his "History of Communications" manuscript.[5]

A major declaration of his newfound interest can be found in the essay, "The Newspaper in Economic Development," which opens his *Political Economy and the Modern State*, first published in 1946. Innis looks at three centuries in the evolution of the press in 34 pages. It could have been a 300-page book if all the revealing connections were fully contextualized and extended to completion, as he had done earlier with fur and fish. The newspaper, however, was only one of a number of media he wanted to explore, so the approach is very much slash and burn. The swath he cut through the subject, nevertheless presents it in a new light. He was aware that previous histories covered similar ground, but they had emphasized the political influence of the press in history, especially regarding issues pertaining to the presence or absence of a free press.

Aspects of the medium that interested him included the power of advertising, which increased with the rise of the penny press in the first half of the nineteenth century. Advertising, he notes, helped keep the cost of the papers down while expanding the range of goods and services that would attract consumers. Of the penny press itself, we learn of its general influence and the essay goes on to discuss related issues such as the advent of the steam driven press and the importance of the telegraph (and later the submarine cable) in making available a greater supply of news and giving rise to news agencies such as the Associated Press.

Not surprisingly, given his experiences in World War I, he notes how, beginning with the American Civil War, the marriage of telegraphy and journalism not only speeded up the demand for news from increasingly greater distances, it yielded a condensed style of exposition accessible to a wider readership. These shifts, including the use of bold headlines, accelerated with the rivalry between and Joseph Pulitzer and William Randolph Hearst that began shortly before the turn of the century—doubtlessly he would have been fascinated by a film such as Orson Welles' 1941 film *Citizen Kane*, which dramatizes this period.

Turning to the early 20th century, Innis examines the rise of tabloids, starting with the New York *Daily News* in 1919 and Hearst's *New York Mirror* in 1924. He notes how at this time, even department store advertising became news and the newspaper declined as a political force. There are numerous and impressive other details of press history embedded in his cryptic prose, including a brief passage on the role of the radio and how it became an effective vehicle for dictator, a notion that McLuhan (1964) would explore at greater length in *Understanding Media*.

Another factor influencing Innis's turn toward communications, especially its role in the history of civilizations, ancient and modern, was the influence of classical scholarship. The classics department at the University of Toronto was one of the most prominent in North America. Innis might never have pursued this line of inquiry were it not for the collegial presence of leading figures in the field such as Charles Norris Cochrane, Edward Thomas Owen, and Eric Havelock. Cochrane was especially influential. Hailing from Protestant rural Ontario and a graduate of the University of Toronto, he also served in the army during World War I. His *Christianity and Classical Culture* (Cochrane, 1944), published a year before his death, along with his efforts to make knowledge gathered in the university more accessible, inspired Innis. In 1950, the debt is formally acknowledged in the preface to *Empire and Communications*: "An interest in the general problem was stimulated by the late Professor C. N. Cochrane and the late Professor E. T. Owen" (Innis, 1950/1975, p. xiii).

In 1947, Innis was appointed dean of the graduate school and shortly thereafter came an offer from Oxford University to give a series of lectures on a subject of his choosing relevant to the economic history of the British Empire. Sponsored by the Beit Fund, these lectures were to be delivered the following year and would eventually be published as *Empire and Communications*. Drawing from his 'History of Communications" manuscript, plus adding to it material on ancient and classical civilizations, the lectures were organized in a comparative and systematic way, with the Innisian style much in evidence. Underpinning the wide ranging historiography was a series of concepts relating to communication and culture that would later compel separate elaboration in the *Bias of Communication*, published a year later.

Although based on lectures, *Empire* evidences the structural form and detailed analysis that one would expect from a major text dealing with comparative history. Following the introduction, there are chapters on Egypt, Babylonia, the oral tradition and Greece, the written tradition and Rome, the role of parchment and paper in the Middle Ages, and the early history of print media. Perhaps because the book is based on a series of lectures, the writing is more accessible than Innis's other media related essays. This is not to imply that *Empire* is an easy read—the many references and intellectual range can challenge even the informed reader. Yet here, more than in any of his other books, the reader is given a helpful assist into the main body of the work by means of a cogent nine page introduction. Students who wish to explore any aspect of Innis's communications writings could do no better than to start with this introduction.

TIME, SPACE, AND THE ORAL TRADITION

Although *Empire and Communications* explores the newly emergent field of media history using a series of signature Innisian concepts, it is in the more renowned *Bias of Communication*, where the concepts themselves—

as opposed to the historical case studies they illuminate—take center stage. In elaborating these concepts Innis' writing is the opposite of lucid. It contrasts with his early work in political economy, where despite the reader being overwhelmed with details, the arguments stay their course. In the later work, it is detail that gets sacrificed to concept and the line of argumentation is rarely direct. Exasperation can easily befall the reader when, without transition, a revealing connection is broached only to be followed in the same paragraph by a leap of millennia and the introduction of a new topic. Be that as it may, where does this leave the student who is trying to make sense of such a gnomic and willow-o'-the-wisp form of exposition? Hopefully with a willingness to connect the dots, so to speak, over a broad range of Innis' observations. Spending a lot of time over singular passages can invite frustration.

One possible reason why his later communication studies are so note-like is their *programmatic* nature: they outline a vast new terrain for serious scholarly research. With an urgency perhaps fueled by a sense that his health was failing, Innis must have felt that sketching the temporal and conceptual breadth of it was more important than attempting a detailed study along the lines of his earlier projects in political economy.

Not surprisingly, Innis does not provide us with ready definitions for some of his key terms. The very title of his most influential book links the term *bias* to communication in an unusual way. Normally, we think of a bias the way Webster does, as a "prejudice" or "a personal and sometimes unreasoned judgment." Innis does in fact occasionally use the term in this way, for example, when he notes that he has a "bias" that favors Canadian nationalism or prefers the oral tradition. More recently, when we think of the term in relation to the media it evokes notions of biased reporting that slants news coverage toward a particular point of view. Yet surprisingly, Innis never seems to use the term in this way. He is less concerned with issues of content—what could be described as media bias—and more concerned with the influence *the form of communication might exert over its content*—what we might want to label "medium bias." The way Innis uses the term *bias of communication* can therefore be seen as a less flamboyant precursor to McLuhan's legendary phrase, "The medium is the message."

The title essay in the book by the same name, *The Bias of Communication*, tries to show rather than explain how this concept will be used to assess the relationship between media and culture, from the clay tablet to the table radio. It unpacks a repertoire of concepts—McLuhan would call them "probes"—that are used throughout the rest of the book to examine this relationship. Two of the most fundamental are time-bias and space-bias. All past civilizations, according to Innis, have sought in various ways to control time and space. When these two concerns are in balance, social stability results. When one or the other is overemphasized, collapse is inevitable—as was the case with the overly "space-biased" Roman Empire described more fully in *Empire and Communications.*

For Innis, in a given civilization it is the dominant medium of communication that "favors" certain forms of temporal or spatial orientation over others. For example, durable media that are difficult to transport, such as stone, clay, and parchment, impart a bias toward time rather than space. They "facilitate" an emphasis on custom, genealogical continuity, and the sacred. This impedes individualism as a dynamic for innovation but permits it to flourish in terms of expressive communication. "Time-biased" civilizations usually feature hierarchical social orders that allow an elite group, Babylonian priests or the Catholic clergy of the Middle Ages, to form a powerful class with exclusive access to a monopoly of knowledge.

At first glance, this link between the dominant medium of a civilization and its cultural orientation, might seem simplistic, or even deterministic. A closer reading of Innis' argument, however, will reveal that when he employs the term medium of communication, it usually does not mean only the raw material used—stone, clay, parchment, or paper—but also the *form* of communication embodied in that medium—hieroglyphics, cuneiform, or alphabetic writing. *It is therefore both the medium per se, coupled with form of communication, which predisposes the society in question to organize and control knowledge in particular ways.* Egypt and Rome, for example, both employed papyrus, but their communications, and its consequences, were quite different because the same medium utilizing different scripts is, in effect, not exactly the same. For Innis, this interest in media and communication was not the study of an autonomous aspect of culture, but an outgrowth of his earlier interest in political economy in which material factors play an important role. An obvious example of this is his concern with the economics involved in the production of a given medium and the role that medium plays in regulating the division of labor in the society employing it.

The first civilizations to be construed by Innis as time-biased were, in effect, the world's first civilizations—Sumeria, Egypt, and Babylonia. The first and third employed clay, the second (in its first incarnation), stone. He outlines the calendrical systems each developed and the role of religion in controlling the categories of time necessary to the maintenance of their respective social orders. And, political economist that he was, more than just the medium of communication had to be considered: "In a system of agriculture dependent on irrigation the measurement of time becomes important in predicting periods of floods and the important dates of the year, seed time and harvest" (Innis, 1951/1995, p. 65).

Other historical examples follow. Perhaps the most notable being his take on the European Middle Ages. Being under the sway of Catholicism, which used parchment (animal skins that were durable but expensive to produce) as a dominant medium, medieval culture was exceedingly time-biased.

Calendrical time reckoning was expanded to include the daily measurement of time using, at first, the water clock, and then eventually, mechanical devices that brought the hour as we know it into general use and regularized the work day. This regularization of time began in the monasteries but eventually became part of the daily life of towns by the fourteenth century. One of Innis's key sources here is Lewis Mumford's (1934) *Technics and Civilization*.

Eventually, the rise of paper and then printing brought secular interests in conflict with those of the church. Among other things, this precipitated a struggle between church and state for control over time, which Innis explores with reference to Henry VIII and the Tudor legacy.

For Innis, time is an aspect of cultural orientation that the modern world needs to appreciate more fully. In "The Problem of Space," as the title of this essay in *Bias* forewarns us, space is something we have in excess that needs to be checked. As in the case of time, it has a long history. A concern with space arises when a civilization aspires to establish an empire. In assessing situations where the relationship between time and space shifts toward an emphasis on the latter, Innis again uses examples from the Near East, Greece, Rome, and the medieval to modern transition. In each instance imperial aspirations are facilitated through the use of a light portable medium, especially papyrus or paper, suitable for administration over distance.

For example, with the advent of print, which Innis sees as the defining technology of early modernism, a spatial bias in late medievalism was accelerated. However, unlike McLuhan (1962), whose landmark study, *The Gutenberg Galaxy*, argues that beginning in the 15th century print *brings into being* almost everything we associate with modernity—nationalism, individualism, the scientific method, and a visual orientation in our cultural logic—Innis sees print as *extending* these elements. They had, he observes, already been asserting themselves a century earlier with the widespread manufacture of paper. Print was also not the only medium contributing to a spatial bias of modernity. He adds to the mix the role of the compass in the age of discovery, the telescope in opening up astronomical knowledge, and the role of mathematics and perspective in art and architecture.

In extending the notion of space bias to the 20th century, Innis only touches on the topic of electronic media, save for a few observations on radio and a brief mention of television, which only came to Canada in December 1952, somewhat ironically 1 month after his death. What he does suggest, is that such media exacerbate the spatial bias inherent in print. In the guise of giving greater access to and democratizing knowledge, they tend to perpetuate modes of domination that in many ways resemble what took place in previous eras.

One consequence of space-biased media that he laments, is the way it diminishes the importance of the oral tradition. In time-biased societies, primary orality—to use Walter Ong's term—is for Innis a form of communication that, if not inherently democratic, has strong leanings in that direction. It favors dialogue and resists the formation of monopolies of knowledge until the heavy hand of the state overcomes that resistance in civilizations using durable media. Throughout his writings, Innis makes constant reference to the positive aspects of orality, largely basing his assumptions on the Greek experience prior to the end of the fifth century BC.

Innis (1950/1975) was acutely aware that any understanding of orality, when archivally informed, will be imperfect: "The task of understanding a culture built on the oral tradition is impossible to students steeped in the written tradition" (p. 55). Still, the task of constructing a framework for orality must be undertaken. What results could be called, following sociologist Max Weber, an "ideal type": an inductively derived model valuable as a tool in understanding the phenomenon as a general historical category, although it might not conform precisely to any specific historical example.

Occasionally, Innis' ideas about orality are construed as possessing a näivité that overstates its virtues. True enough, but the oral tradition he venerates most is one that owes a debt to phonetic literacy: "The alphabet escaped the implications of sacred writing. It lent itself to an efficient representation of sounds and enabled the Greeks to preserve intact a rich oral tradition" (Innis, 1950/1975, p. 53). It is this kind of "balance" (an important Innisian notion) between speech and writing that he seeks to recapture, not some lost idyllic state, when, for example, in his comments on educational reform in the *Bias of Communication* he urges teachers to "link books to conversation and oral education" in ways that can "provide a link between a written and an oral tradition" (Innis, 1951/1995, p. 214).

MONOPOLIES OF KNOWLEDGE
AND THE CRITIQUE OF CULTURE

Innis saw his work in media history as providing the foundation for a critical assessment of a world ravaged by two global conflicts and now beset upon by the mechanizing tendencies of mass media and unchecked commercialism. He notes that although modernity has unleashed upon the world great benefits, it has not delivered on all its promises: "The conditions of freedom of thought are in danger of being destroyed by science, technology, and the mechanization of knowledge, and with them Western civilization" (Innis, 1951/1995, p. 190). He questions the arrogance that assumes we are somehow outside history or have finally transcended it. Today, as was the case with Egypt, Babylonia, and Rome, we too might be headed for a fall, since the "biases" that made those ancient civilizations vulnerable to collapse, are not altogether absent from our own. "Monopoly of knowledge" thus becomes a crucial term in Innis' later writings. Not surprisingly, he provides no formal definition save to suggest that it is an extension of "concepts in the special field of economics, and in particular the concept of monopoly," to the field of knowledge (cited in Drache, 1995, p. 85). The term is used broadly, to cover what we would normally classify as knowledge per se, literacy and science, for example, and what is more generally assumed to be information, such as economic records and census data. Sometimes more specific economic factors, such as transportation and the organization of markets, are subsumed under the monopoly of knowledge rubric.

Historical case studies provide him with several precedents prior to a brief but suggestive assessment of his own time. For example, in Greece, the relative ease in learning the alphabet, compared to the protracted apprenticeship necessary for literacy in Egypt and Babylonia, did not favor monopolistic control, at first. The initial situation of balance between Greek oral and literate traditions, however, eventually ended with the rise of complex written laws leading to "oppressive features in judicial control and the levying of tribute" (Innis, 1950/1975, p. 82). Rome followed suit, and although literacy was widespread there, the empire used the vast collection of written works it had acquired more for status display than for learning; writing itself became increasingly directed toward the codification of more complex laws. The subsequent Middle Ages, with its "monopoly of knowledge built up under ecclesiastical control," was even more restrictive (Innis, 1950/1975, p. 139). Here the scribe/priests controlled not only the acquisition of literacy and production of parchment, but the copying of texts deemed to be "knowledge" and the suppression or destruction of those held to be otherwise.

Paper eventually challenged the parchment-dependent monopoly of knowledge of the Church, and by the sixteenth century print had made scribes, both monastic and secular, virtually obsolete. But since, in Innis' view, monopolies of knowledge appear to be inevitable to the process of historical formation, what typography giveth, it would also taketh away. Censorship laws and the economic monopolies enjoyed by various publishers became a problem, a result of the "enormous expansion of the printing industry and an emphasis on freedom of the press, which favored the growth of monopolies" (Innis, 1950/1975, p. 167).

Innis deals only briefly with the 20th century. In a revealing essay, "Technology and Public Opinion in the United States," in the *Bias of Communication*, he looks at the "monopoly position of the Associated Press" and its subsequent collision with William Randolph Hearst, along with Hearst's own newspaper chain-building aspirations. In his last book, *Changing Concepts of Time*, Innis (1952/2004) chronicles a shift in the mass media that has generated much comment in recent years. Where once media monopolies could be directly linked to political interests, now there was another agenda, one he saw powerfully influencing Canada: "We are fighting for our lives. The pernicious influence of American advertising reflected especially in the periodical press and the powerful persistent impact of commercialism have been evident in all the ramifications of Canadian life" (Innis, 1952, p. 19).[6] This is not exactly a "monopoly of knowledge" per se, although he still uses this term in an all inclusive way, but something more along the lines of an attempt at information control or propaganda on behalf of American capitalism.

Nowhere are these themes broached more forcefully than the opening essay in *Changing Concepts*, "The Strategy of Culture." Here, Innis speaks about issues pertaining to culture that are much in the news today in debates surrounding what the North American Free Trade Agreement and the World Trade Organization should be empowered to adjudicate. He is speaking to the Canadian case circa mid-20th century when he observes how American cultural industries are overwhelming and impeding the development of those industries in Canada. Today other countries are echoing this concern, especially with respect to media Innis did not consider—television and motion pictures.

Part of the danger Innis associates with the spread of American cultural influence is the United States' rootedness in militarism. In *Changing Concepts of Time*, he discusses this in the essay, "Military Implications of the American Constitution," which is unsettling and prescient in light of today's geopolitics. Playing the role of an outsider peering in at American culture, a role he likens to Alexis de Tocqueville, the Frenchman, and Lord Bryce, the Englishman, Innis traces the history of American militarism by looking at policies of the presidency from George Washington to the eve of Dwight D. Eisenhower.

Beyond nationalist agendas, however, modern culture, grounded as it is in machine industry and specialism, harbors another danger: mechanization. Innis regards it as a process operating and originating in technology, a process that has now permeated almost every facet of our daily lives. His work here shows strong kinship with a tradition of technological criticism that includes writers such as Siegfried Giedion (whose 1948 book *Mechanization Takes Command* is not cited), Jacques Ellul (1964), who wrote after Innis, and Lewis Mumford (1934). When discussing the impact of mechanization on culture, his most immediate influence and a source cited with much approval, is Graham Wallas' (1934) *Social Judgment*.

Following Wallas, Innis attributes to mechanization a de-emphasis on oral communication: "Reading is quicker than listening and concentrated individual thought than verbal exposition and counter exposition of arguments. The printing press and the radio address the world instead of the individual" (Innis, 1950/1975, p. 191). Innis also cites Schopenauer's warning regarding books as an impediment to thought. He might also have mentioned Kierkegaard and Nietzsche, who espoused a similar view—in their books of course. It may seem ironic that an academic as dependent on the printed word as Innis would chastise the hand on which so much of his handiwork depended. His views do seem extreme, but he is no Luddite regarding either books or machines. His goal is *balance*. Although he offers only a few ambiguous answers, the abiding question is clear enough: Since the gains wrought by communication technology and mechanization have been accompanied by losses, how can we minimize the latter and still make full human use of the former?

INNIS' ENDURING INFLUENCES ON THE RISE OF MEDIA ECOLOGY

Following Innis' death in 1952, most eulogies honored him for his work in political economy. Even in Canada, numerous colleagues were perplexed by his later communication studies. Some saw it as an indulgent preoccupation of his later years—a foray into a field nonexistent in Canada then that seemed to pose a cloudy barrier to his true, staples theory persona. But there were notable exceptions and communication studies at the University of Toronto did not die with Innis. Enter Marshall McLuhan, who became an insistent if somewhat controversial champion of Innis' legacy. His reputation far eclipsed Innis' and for a time became almost synonymous in the public mind with the field of media studies. It also drew considerable commentary. One critique in particular linked the legacies of Innis and McLuhan together in a way that greatly raised the stature of Innis and helped place his work at the forefront of an emerging media ecology tradition.

In 1967, James Carey, then at the University of Illinois, published an essay in the *Antioch Review* titled "Harold Adams Innis and Marshall McLuhan." At the time, an article about Innis sans the comparison with McLuhan would have generated little interest, as Carey must have known. His respectful but stern critique of McLuhan is accompanied by an assessment of Innis that argues not only for Innis' priority in recognizing the centrality of communication technology, but also that he did a better job at comprehending it. Although conceding important similarities between the two Canadian communication theorists, Carey defines clearly an important difference in their respective agendas: "Whereas Innis sees communication technology principally affecting social organization and culture, McLuhan sees its principal effect on sensory organization and thought" (cited in Rosenthal, 1969, p. 281).

In each subsequent decade, Carey would publish essays that discuss Innis in a variety of ways: his relationship to the Chicago School, American geographic thought, and more recent trends in communication studies. Most Innis commentators of the past and current generation, including the present writer, regard Carey's work both as a benchmark in Innis scholarship and a starting point for further assessments of his legacy. Carey's appreciation of Innis, however, is not limited to commentary. As indicated by the title of his 1989 essay collection, *Communication as Culture*, Carey has incorporated Innisian notions into an original perspective on media and modernity. Of note is his essay in that volume, titled "Technology and Ideology: The Case of the Telegraph," which provides a revealing assessment of an important communication technology Innis only mentions in passing. Most recently Carey has contributed a foreword to the 2004 edition of Innis' *Changing Concepts of Time*.

The resurrection of Innis's communication studies in light of popular interest in the subject generated by McLuhan, which Carey had undertaken, was expanded on by William Kuhns in his book, *The Post-Industrial Prophets*. Kuhns links the work of Innis and McLuhan to a burgeoning 20th-century intellectual tradition that assesses, both in a pessimistic and optimistic way, the impact of technology on the natural and social environments and the ways in which technology itself has become an environment. A pantheon of key thinkers is created and examined. It includes, on the pessimistic side, Lewis Mumford, Siegfried Giedion, and Jacques Ellul; and on the optimistic side, Norbert Weiner and Buckminster Fuller. Innis and McLuhan are assessed with respect to the contribution they make to the study of media environments, with Innis leaning toward the critical side of the pantheon and McLuhan associated with the less cautionary more futuristic oriented thinkers.

By the 1980s, numerous further assessments of Innis had helped solidify his position as a major figure in communication studies. Applications of his ideas began to displace mere interpretations. Following Carey's lead, Daniel Czitrom, Neil Postman, and Joshua Meyrowitz applied Innisian concepts to areas Innis only broached in passing, or not at all. Their respective projects also resurrected McLuhan (whose stature had waned in the 1970s), and helped establish the tradition of media ecology.

Czitrom's (1982) *Media and the American Mind* adopts an intriguing and effective two-part structure. The first part examines the formative technological and institutional development of three significant communication media in American history: the telegraph, which initiates the electric age, early motion pictures, and broadcast radio. The second part then looks at three major traditions in communication thought. The first is the work of Chicago School scholars Charles Horton Cooley, John Dewey, and Robert Park, who explored the "holistic nature" of modern media; the second, involves the "effects" approach, in which Paul Lazarsfeld looms as the primary figure in a tradition responsible for the prevailing, empiricist paradigm in contemporary American communication studies; and the third, is the historically informed work of Innis and McLuhan which examines the impact of media on social and psychological organization.

In the mid-1980s, after almost a decade of thinking about the relationship between contemporary mass media, especially television, and everyday life, Joshua Meyrowitz published *No Sense of Place: The Impact of Electronic Media on Social Behavior*. Two major sources have influenced his project: on the media side, McLuhan and Innis; on the (micro) social side, Erving Goffman (1959), noted for his study of social behavior in face-to-face "situationist" contexts. Meyrowitz intersects these two disparate traditions in a detailed and compelling analysis that considers everything from gender roles to political image making. The legacies of McLuhan and Innis, along with the related work of Edmund Carpenter (1960, 1972), Jack Goody (1968, 1977), Eric Havelock (1963, 1976), and Walter Ong (1967, 1982)—sometimes referred to as the "Toronto School" of communication studies—provided Meyrowitz (1985) with the mainframe of an approach he calls "medium theory," defined as the "historical and cross-cultural study of the different cultural environments created by different media of communication" (p. 29).

Finally, among the growing legion of media scholars sourcing Innis, no one has put forth the message as eloquently and prolifically as the late Neil Postman (1931–2003). *The Disappearance of Childhood* (Postman, 1982) marked his shift from writing primarily about education, to exploring the role of media in contemporary culture through a historically informed perspective. He followed with *Amusing Ourselves to Death* (Postman, 1985), *Technopoly* (Postman, 1992), and *Building a Bridge to the 18th Century* (Postman, 1999), thereby becoming one of the most insistent and popular critics of the impact of technology on our time. In so doing, he has continued to inspire students of media ecology to take "as a guide the teachings of Harold Innis," who "stressed that changes in communication technology invariably have three kinds of effects: They alter the structure of interests (the things thought about), the character of symbols (the things thought with), and the nature of the community (the area in which thoughts develop)" (Postman, 1985, p. 23).

CONCLUSION

In his later work, Innis was certainly not a historian's historian. His conceptual framework eschewed detailed analysis in favor of broad generalizations that encompass entire epochs. He also did not set out to do history for its own sake, but instead used the past to measure the present. And always, his background in political economy, touched on only briefly in this chapter, ensured that material factors such as staple resources and transportation and communication technologies would be accorded a dominant role in historical transformation.

To this project he brought a dialectical understanding of change, whereby new media challenge old, and in the resulting collision of communication and culture, social formations—sometimes entire civilizations—rise and fall. In assessing this push and pull he employed a series of revealing concepts: time bias, space bias, the oral tradition, monopolies of knowledge, and the mechanization of culture.

But with Innis the whole is always greater than the sum of its parts. His project, call it communications history, medium theory, or an early version of media ecology, is *programmatic*. It remained incomplete during his lifetime, and probably would have stayed that way even if he had lived another 10 years because it is inherently open-ended—the sketch map for a new scholarly subcontinent that invites further exploration rather than strives for closure. Nietzsche once observed, and Foucault following him, that those who wish to honor their work should challenge and extend it, not dwell on interpretations. Most likely Harold Adams Innis would have felt the same way.

ENDNOTES

1. Materials used in this chapter were previously published in Paul Heyer (2003). Reprint permission has been granted by the publisher.
2. For a general orientation to Innis' scholarship see for example Christian (1980, 1981), Drache (1995), Havelock (1982) and Heyer (2003). For a solid introduction to some of Innis' major writings chronologically, see Innis (1923/1971, 1930, 1930/1962b, 1940/1954, 1942, 1945, 1946, 1950/1975, 1951/1995, 1952, 1962a), and Innis, Harvey, and Ferguson (1969); note that the year before the slash in some of these entries indicates the entry's original publication date.
3. For fuller biographical details see Creighton (1978) and Heyer (2003).
4. Mary Quayle Innis' influence is documented more fully by J. David Black (2003).
5. For a full assessment of this project see William J. Buxton (2001).
6. See also the new edition of *Changing Concepts of Time* (with a foreword by James W. Carey).

REFERENCES

Black, J. D. (2003). The contributions of Mary Quayle Innis. In P. Heyer, *Harold Innis* (pp. 113-121). Boulder, CO: Rowman & Littlefield.

Buxton, W. J. (2001). The bias against communication: On the neglect and non-publication of the "Incomplete and Unrevised Manuscript" of Harold Adams Innis. *Canadian Journal of Communication, 26*(2/3), 114-117.

Carey, J. (1967). Harold Adams Innis and Marshall McLuhan. *Antioch Review, 27*(1), 5-39.

Carey, J. (1989). *Communication and culture: Essays on media and society.* Boston: Unwin Hyman.

Carpenter, E. (1960). The new languages. In E. Carpenter & H. M. McLuhan (Eds.), *Explorations in communication: An anthology* (pp. 162-179). Boston, MA: Beacon.

Carpenter, E. (1972). *Oh, what a blow that phantom gave me!* Toronto, Canada: Bantam Books.

Christian, W. (1980). *The idea file of Harold Adams Innis.* Toronto, Canada: University of Toronto Press.

Christian, W. (Ed.). (1981). *Innis on Russia: The Russian diary and other writings.* Toronto, Canada: The Harold Innis Foundation.

Cochrane, C. N. (1944). *Christianity and classical culture.* London: Oxford University Press.

Creighton, D. (1978). *Harold Adams Innis: Portrait of a scholar.* Toronto, Canada: University of Toronto Press. (Original work published 1940)

Czitrom, D. J. (1982). *Media and the American mind.* Chapel Hill: University of North Carolina Press.

Drache, D. (Ed.). (1995). *Staples, markets, and cultural change: Harold Innis.* Montreal, Canada: McGill-Queen's University Press.

Ellul, J. (1964). *The technological society* (J. Wilkinson, Trans.). New York: Vintage Book

Giedion, S. (1948). *Mechanization takes command.* New York: Oxford University Press.

Goffman, E. (1959). *The presentation of self in everyday life.* New York: Doubleday.

Goody, J. (1968). *Literacy in traditional societies.* London: Cambridge University Press.

Goody, J. (1977). The domestication of the savage mind. Cambridge, England & New York: Cambridge University Press.

Havelock, E. A. (1963). *Preface to Plato.* Cambridge, MA & London: Belknap Press of the Harvard University Press.

Havelock, E. A. (1976). *Origins of western literacy.* Toronto, Canada: The Ontario Institute for Studies in Education.

Havelock, E. (1982). *Harold A. Innis: A memoir.* Toronto, Canada: The Harold Innis Foundation.

Heyer, P. (2003). *Harold Innis.* Boulder, CO: Rowman & Littlefield.

Innis, H. A. (Ed.). (1930). *Peter Pond: Fur trader and adventurer.* Toronto, Canada: Irwin & Gordon.

Innis, H. A. (1942). The newspaper in economic development. *Journal of Economic History, 2/s,* 1-33.

Innis, H. A. (1945). The English press in the nineteenth century: An economic approach. *University of Toronto Quarterly, 15,* 37-53.

Innis, H. A. (1946). *Political economy and the modern state.* Toronto, Canada: The University of Toronto Press.

Innis, H. A. (1952). *Changing concepts of time.* Toronto, Canada: The University of Toronto Press.

Innis, H. A. (1954). *The cod fisheries: The history of an international economy.* Toronto, Canada: University of Toronto Press. (Original work published 1940)

Innis, H. A. (1962a). Essays in Canadian economic history (M. Q. Innis, Ed.). Toronto, Canada: The University of Toronto Press.

Innis, H. A. (1962b). *The fur trade in Canada.* New Haven, CT: Yale University Press. (Original work published 1930)

Innis, H. A. (1971). *A history of the Canadian Pacific Railway.* Toronto, Canada: University of Toronto Press. (Original work published 1923)

Innis, H. A. (1975). *Empire and communications.* Toronto, Canada: University of Toronto Press. (Original work published 1950)

Innis, H. A. (1995). *The bias of communication.* Toronto, Canada: The University of Toronto Press. (Original work published 1951)

Innis, H. A. (n.d.). A history of communications: An incomplete and unrevised manuscript. Montreal, Canada: McGill University McLennan Library.

Innis, H. A. (2004). *Changing concepts of time.* Boulder, CO: Rowman & Littlefield.

Innis H. A., Harvey, D.C., & Ferguson, C. B. (Eds.). (1969). *The Diary of Simeon Perkins.* Westport, CT: Greenwood Press.

Kuhns, W. (1971). *The post-industrial prophets: Interpretations of technology.* New York: Weybright & Talley.

McLuhan, M. (1962). *Gutenberg galaxy.* Toronto, Canada: University of Toronto Press.

McLuhan, M. (1964). *Understanding media.* New York: McGraw-Hill.

Meyrowitz, J. (1985). *No sense of place: The influence of electronic media on social behavior.* New York: Oxford University Press.

Mumford, L. (1934). *Technics and civilization.* New York: Harcourt Brace.

Ong, W. J. (1967). *The presence of the word: Some prolegomena for cultural and religious history.* New Haven, CT: Yale University Press.

Ong, W. J. (1982). *Orality and literacy.* London: Methuen.

Postman, N. (1982). *The disappearance of childhood.* New York: Delacorte Press.

Postman, N. (1985). *Amusing ourselves to death.* New York: Viking Penguin.

Postman, N. (1992). *Technopoly: The surrender of culture to technology.* New York: Knopf.

Postman, N. (1999). *Building a bridge to the eighteenth century: How the past can improve our future.* New York: Knopf.

Rosenthal, R. (Ed.). (1969). *McLuhan pro and con.* Baltimore: Penguin.

Wallas, G. (1934). *Social judgment.* London: Allen & Unwin.

7

Marshall McLuhan: The Modern Janus[1]

James C. Morrison

Emerson College

Media ecology means that if print, or if the written word, is in danger, it
can be rescued by some other medium. Or propped up. And don't just
let something like that go down the drain without any counteractivity.

— *Marshall McLuhan, at Teachers College,*
Columbia University, July 17, 1978

This chapter presents the ideas of perhaps the most influential and well-
known, and certainly the most controversial, of media ecologists, whose
work synthesized the field and helped attract the focus of public attention.
Marshall McLuhan is generally considered to have coined the phrase *media
ecology* in the late 1960s (Gencarelli, 2000, p. 91) and can be considered its
godfather, for his seizure of the public imagination during the 1960s brought
wide public attention to its ideas for the first time. However, the slogans and
formulas he used to promote media ecology have been subject to much misunderstanding, which persists today. The purposes of this chapter are to help

---

The figures in this chapter are reprinted from McLuhan, M., & McLuhan, E. (1988). *Laws of
Media: The New Science.* Toronto: University of Toronto Press. Reprinted with permission of
Eric McLuhan.

dispel common misconceptions of McLuhan's work, clarify it for those who are struggling with its challenges, and introduce it to those engaging it for the first time.

In this chapter I explore the following main points:

1. McLuhan's identification as a promoter of television was an ironic reversal of his personal attitude toward it, primarily because in his public analysis he refused to adopt a moralistic stance about its content, in favor of a more objective understanding of the symbolic form of the medium.
2. McLuhan was firmly in the tradition of 20th-century Modernism and developed in his work parallels with modern, post-Newtonian science, yet his intellectual roots were firmly planted in ancient and medieval rhetoric.
3. The relevance of his work is being justly appreciated even more today than ever before, now that his ideas are being manifested in global telecommunications, the Internet, and the World Wide Web.

AN UNLIKELY ASCENSION

In 1965, Richard Schickel wrote a generally favorable article about McLuhan titled "Marshall McLuhan—Canada's Intellectual Comet" (Marchand, 1998, p. 186), and for much of a decade he blazed across the skies, prompting both wonderment and disdain. No comparable intellectual comes readily to mind, though others such as Clifton Fadiman and Bennett Cerf had previously attained celebrity on TV game shows.[2] McLuhan was the first and only media ecologist to achieve the possibly dubious distinction of being a pop icon whose name was on virtually everyone's lips—a figure whose ideas and persona were recognized by a large portion of the public, whether involved in intellectual pursuits or not.

Herbert Marshall McLuhan was born on July 21, 1911 in Edmonton, Alberta, Canada. His father was a real estate and insurance salesman and his mother an elocutionist who traveled about North America teaching and giving dramatic readings. He earned bachelor's and master's degrees in English literature from the University of Manitoba, and in 1934 he entered Trinity Hall at Cambridge University. He received the baccalaureate in 1936 and in that year became a teaching assistant in the English Department of the University of Wisconsin, where for the first time he encountered students whose exposure to popular culture overshadowed much interest in the High Culture in which McLuhan had been educated. Out of self-preservation, he decided to learn about popular culture and to use on it the analytical techniques he had learned at Cambridge as a way of bridging the gap between himself and his students, as well as inculcating into them literary methods on the path of least resistance (Marchand, 1998, pp. 48–49).

Meanwhile, by 1937 he became a convert to Roman Catholicism and he was hired as an instructor in English at the Jesuit St. Louis University (pp. 50–53). After marrying Corinne Keller Lewis in 1939 he returned to Cambridge for 2 years as a PhD candidate. He then went back to St. Louis University and, upon receiving his doctorate in 1943, was promoted to assistant professor. While there he became interested in the work of two writers whose ideas about technology would contribute to his own, Lewis Mumford and Sigfried Giedion (Marchand, 1998, pp. 77–78). He began publishing literary criticism in such journals as *The Sewanee Review* and *The Kenyon Review,* associated with the Southern Agrarian/New Criticism movement led by Alan Tate, John Crowe Ransom, Cleanth Brooks, and Robert Penn Warren (pp. 75–77).

Almost immediately, he struck up a personal relationship with the English critic, novelist, and painter Wyndham Lewis (1927), whose *Time and Western Man* McLuhan had read at Cambridge and which he claimed had had a profound influence on him (Marchand, 1998, p. 79). Lewis was teaching at Assumption College in Windsor, Ontario, and their friendship led to McLuhan's being offered the position of chair of the English Department there (Marchand, 1998, p. 81). According to McLuhan's first biographer, Lewis was influential in several respects. He reinforced McLuhan's artistic and cultural attitudes regarding the positive values of almost brutal clarity and precise definition, and the pernicious influence of advertising and popularized science. He also demonstrated for McLuhan the value of unremitting analysis of a hostile environment in maintaining intellectual integrity (Marchand, 1998, p. 84). Furthermore, a sentence in Lewis's (1948) *America and Cosmic Man* alluding to the international connectedness fostered by telephones and air transport may have inspired McLuhan's conception of the "global village" (Marchand, 1998, p. 83).

In Spring 1946, McLuhan received an offer to teach in the English Department of St. Michael's College of the University of Toronto, like Assumption, run by the Basilian teaching order of priests. Besides serving as an irritant to many of his colleagues, he was able to turn his series of lectures on contemporary American culture illustrated with slides of advertisements, comics, newspaper articles, and other cultural artifacts into his first book, *The Mechanical Bride: Folklore of Industrial Man* (McLuhan, 1951). The book was not widely reviewed and sold only a few hundred copies, although it did get reviewed in *The New York Times* (Cohn, 1951, October 21), but unsympathetically. When it was remaindered he bought up 1,000 copies, distributed some to bookstores personally, gave copies away to friends, and even resorted to selling some to students in his courses (Marchand, 1998, p. 119).

About this time, he became part of an informal discussion group that met in the coffee shop of the Royal Ontario Museum about 4 p.m. every day and "talked until the place closed" (Carpenter, 2001, p. 251). The group included anthropologists Edmund Carpenter and Dorothy Lee, planner Jacqueline Tyrwhitt, architectural historian Sigfried Giedion, sociologist Ashley Montagu, and political economist Karl Polanyi, all of whom had profound influences on McLuhan's thinking regarding the connections between communication and culture (Theall, 2001). In April 1949, the political economist Harold Innis visited the group and spoke on the cultural impacts of the press and radio (Marchand, 1998, p. 121). McLuhan borrowed freely from Innis's work and wrote a foreword to an edition of his *Empire and Communications* (Innis, 1972, pp. v–xii). But Innis and McLuhan never became close friends, and in his foreword McLuhan saw fit to point out what he considered the limitations of Innis's approach. Although the supposed influence of Innis on McLuhan has been stressed by his biographers (Gordon, 1997; Marchand, 1998), those closest to him intellectually at the time note that the regulars in the group made greater contributions to the evolution of McLuhan's thinking (Carpenter, 2001, pp. 248–252; Theall, 2001).

In 1953, he and Carpenter received a Ford Foundation grant to establish a series of interdisciplinary seminars on media and culture, from which emerged the journal *Explorations*, where the seminal articles in McLuhan's brand of media ecology were published. While Carpenter functioned as editor-in-chief, McLuhan edited the last of its nine issues, which appeared in 1959. It was then that he received a grant under the National Defense Education Act from the National Association of Educational Broadcasters to develop a syllabus for 11th-graders in media awareness. Although the curriculum the report suggested was much too advanced for the students for whom it was intended (Marchand, 1998, p. 157), this project allowed McLuhan to develop further his explorations along paths blazed by the participants in the culture and communication seminar. It eventually led to the writing of *Understanding Media: The Extensions of Man* (McLuhan, 1964) and served as a springboard for his subsequent output concerning media, particularly the effect of television on individuals and society.

In this latter respect, McLuhan's career is fraught with irony, for his reputation is closely associated in the popular mind with a medium—television—whose effects he thoroughly mistrusted and even decried. Some supporters and virtually all his critics have seen him as a television "guru," a proselytizer for the electronic faith, whose attitude toward electronic media was akin to that of psychedelic shaman Timothy Leary, with whose philosophy his was sometimes confused: "Turn on, tune in, and drop out."[3] But when we examine the entire range of McLuhan's thought about the impacts of media on society, we can see that his image as an enthusiast for electronic media obscures his deep distrust of the social and psychic changes he saw them making.

Once, while watching television with his friend and University of Toronto colleague Tom Langan, McLuhan said, "Do you really want to know what I think of that thing? If you want to save one shred of Hebrao-Greco-Roman-Medieval-Renaissance-Enlightenment-Modern-Western civilization, you'd better get an ax and smash all the sets" (Gordon, 1997, p. 301). And he displayed a like attitude in advice to his son Eric regarding one of Eric's daughters in a 1976 letter: "Try not to have Emily exposed to hours and hours of TV. It is a vile drug which permeates the nervous system, especially in the young" (Gordon, 1997, p. 212).

Such irony can be attributed, perhaps, to one of the very points McLuhan was making about media: the almost ineluctable force of the dominant communication medium of the time, despite the best conscious effort to counteract it. Of course, it must be observed that television was totally suited to McLuhan's favorite mode of communication—oral expostulation—and he exemplified those very characteristics of a "cool" image needing completion by the audience that he himself noted as being particularly suited to television (see the subsequent section on Media Hot and Cool for a discussion of this notion).

A comparison might be made with another figure prominent in a prior communications shift, between the manuscript era in Europe and the age of print. In 1494, Johannes Trithemius, the Abbott of Sponheim Abbey, near Mainz, Germany, published *De Laude Scriptorum* (*In Praise of Scribes*), intended as a defense of the monastic practice of copying manuscripts, in the face of the challenge brought to scribalism by the printing press. But in order to reach the widest possible audience, so that his ideas might have the greatest effect, he had the book printed, thus using the very medium he was arguing against (Eisenstein, 1979, pp. 14–15). But this was not his only foray into mass publishing. In fact, according to a modern editor of his work, Trithemius gave so much business to one Mainz printing establishment that "it could almost be called the Sponheim Abbey Press" (Arnold, 1974, p. 15, cited in Eisenstein, 1979, p. 15).[4]

Similarly, McLuhan appeared frequently on television to spread his message, as a result of the intense interest created by the publication of *Understanding Media*. This interest was abetted in no small part by the efforts of two Californian self-styled "genius scouts," Gerald Feigen and Howard Gossage. Feigen and Gossage promoted McLuhan by getting him lucrative corporate speaking engagements and arranging a series of cocktail parties in New York, where he was introduced to prominent publishers of major magazines. Through these latter contacts he met the "new journalist" Tom Wolfe, who lent his considerable cachet to promoting McLuhan (Marchand, 1998, pp. 182–187; Wolfe, 1968). Such notoriety was in distinct contrast to his life as an obscure English professor in a Canadian university on the margins of American culture. Such a position McLuhan considered an advantage, because he could observe the culture as an alien environment, not being part of it.

McLuhan's fortunes and visibility had actually begun a transformation in 1962 with the publication of *The Gutenberg Galaxy*. The book had a measurably greater impact than *The Mechanical Bride,* winning the 1962 Governor General's Award in Canada for Non-Fiction and getting reviewed in such prestigious intellectual journals as *The New Statesman* and *Encounter.* The latter review inspired the historian Elizabeth L. Eisenstein to read the book and embark on her own magnum opus, *The Printing Press as an Agent of Change* (Eisenstein, 1979, p. x).[5] His heightened visibility led to his publishing an article in *The Times Literary Supplement* (*TLS*) and being included in another *TLS* article featuring avant-garde thinkers that the editors felt were "breaking new ground" (Marchand, 1998, p. 166). He also received a consulting assignment for Henry Luce's *Time, Life,* and *Fortune* that increased his cachet in New York publishing and advertising circles (Marchand, 1998, pp. 166–168). But the *Galaxy* itself had its greatest impact not on the general public, but among other intellectuals.

Certainly, this result was partly the consequence of the book's use of erudite sources, as a reflection of the years of scholarly research that went into its creation. Even though McLuhan (1962) wrote the book in what he characterized as a "mosaic" style (p. iv) meant to reflect the modes of awareness fostered by electronic technology, his intent was to call attention to the erosion of the inherited values of print culture:

> We now live in the early part of an age for which the meaning of print culture is becoming as alien as the meaning of manuscript culture was to the eighteenth century. "We are the primitives of a new culture," said Boccioni the sculptor in 1911. Far from wishing to belittle the Gutenberg mechanical culture, it seems to me that we must now work very hard to retain its achieved values. (p. 135)

But after the publication of *Understanding Media* in 1964, McLuhan became a denizen of the very medium whose effects he wanted to counteract, perhaps a prime example of Daniel Boorstin's (1961/1992) definition of a celebrity: "a person who is known for his well-knownness" (p. 57). The apogee (or nadir) of such status was probably reached when McLuhan became the subject of a Henry Gibson "poem" on the quintessential television program, *Rowan and Martin's Laugh-In*: "Marshall McLuhan, what are you doin'?" (*Playboy* interview, 1969, p. 54). The title of the 1969 *Playboy* interview —"Marshall McLuhan: A Candid Conversation With the High Priest of Popcult and Metaphysician of Media"—is emblematic of his elevation into the contemporary pop pantheon alongside such figures as

Leary, the Beatles, the Maharishi Mahesh Yogi, Peter Max, Mary Quant, Twiggy, Roy Lichtenstein, and Andy Warhol. This was a most ironic position for someone who declared at that time, "I find most pop culture monstrous and sickening. I study it for my own survival ("On the Scene," *Playboy*, 1967, February, cited in Marchand, 1998, p. 49).

THE NEW MEDIA AGE

McLuhan's apotheosis occurred at a time when television was just coming into its own in defining, promoting, and disseminating the pop culture of the post-World War II generation. By the time *Understanding Media* was published in 1964, television had become a modern combination of the national hearth and the theater in the home. Several epochal televised events had attracted huge television audiences and brought them together simultaneously in common, emotionally charged experiences as no mass audience had ever before: the appearances of Elvis Presley (beginning in 1956) and the Beatles (1963 and 1964) on *The Ed Sullivan Show*; the first presidential campaign debates, between Vice President Richard M. Nixon and Senator John F. Kennedy (1960); President Kennedy's funeral, and the live, on-screen murder of the suspected assassin, Lee Harvey Oswald, by Jack Ruby (1963). As a consequence, the concept of an "electronic global village" was already a matter of felt experience by the time McLuhan announced it in *The Gutenberg Galaxy* (1962) and amplified it in *Understanding Media* (1964), *The Medium Is the Massage* (McLuhan & Fiore, 1967), and *War and Peace in the Global Village* (McLuhan & Fiore, 1968/1997).

Naturally, as McLuhan's comet shone, he was bound to attract many critics as well as supporters.[6] Although he was championed by many public intellectuals, his ideas soon drew the scorn of others, and probably more disdain than support among the academic establishment. At the University of Toronto in particular, the reaction against McLuhan's celebrity got to the point that he warned his graduate students to erase any trace of his work in their theses and dissertations, to avoid reprisals by their review committees.[7] According to Eric McLuhan, "[t]here were at least two concerted efforts (quiet ones, of course) to collect enough signatures to have his tenure revoked" (personal communication, August 1998). During the 1970s, despite a vigorous publishing output and a cameo appearance in Woody Allen's *Annie Hall*, McLuhan's comet seemed to fade from our ken. Perhaps his ideas had received such emphatic attention and exposure, initially because they appeared so revolutionary, that eventually they became overexposed and co-opted. Although his collaboration with his son Eric (McLuhan & McLuhan, 1988) on *Laws of Media*, published posthumously, represented a brilliant capstone to his intellectual career, the book was not widely understood or appreciated (see Sturrock, 1989), being aimed primarily at an academic audience (E. McLuhan, personal communication, August 1998) and returning to the intensely intellectual mode that characterized *The Gutenberg Galaxy*. By the time *Laws of Media* appeared, hardly anyone was paying attention any more. In fact, his death on the last day of 1980 seemed to be the occasion of reactions more along the lines of "Whatever happened to him, anyway?" than the felt loss of a contemporary figure.[8]

But since the public's growing consciousness of the Internet and the World Wide Web, starting in the mid-1990s, McLuhan's reputation has experienced an astounding upsurge. The apparent reason for this revival of interest is that the creation of global television networks such as Cable News Network (CNN) and the burgeoning of the World Wide Web have manifested to anyone with eyes and ears the trends he tried to make us aware of 30 years before. The globalization of consciousness he alerted us to and the cultural effects he spoke of are now a matter of everyday concern. Adopted as the "patron saint" of *Wired* magazine (see Wolf, 1996a, 1996b), he has been the subject of more than a dozen publications since 1989, including a recent intellectual biography written with the cooperation of the McLuhan Foundation Trust (Gordon, 1997), a revised edition of the first biography (Marchand, 1998), an interactive CD-ROM (Southam Interactive, 1996), a six-tape video production combining biography with some of his television appearances and taped lectures (McLuhan-Ortved & Wolfe, 1996), a work specifically outlining the relevance of his ideas to the Internet and the World Wide Web (Levinson, 1999), a thorough re-examination of his intellectual heritage by a distinguished scholar who was his first doctoral student advisee (Theall, 2001), an exploration of his use of the concepts of acoustic and visual space (Cavell, 2002), and a 90-minute Canadian Film Board production illustrating his ideas for a new audience (McMahon & Flahive, 2002).

What is more, our enhanced appreciation of his thought has doubtless been reinforced by the growing attention paid to multilinear structures of discourse fostered by hypertext. We now recognize that McLuhan thought and wrote in a manner akin to Theodor Holm Nelson's (1992) concept of hypertext: multilinear, associative lines of thought that stress connections among multifaceted phenomena that our print-oriented consciousnesses can normally deal with only by abstractly categorizing them and reeling them out in a fixed linear sequence. Although identified in the public mind with television, McLuhan was aware from the beginning of the growth of computer networking and referred to it regularly throughout his work, and only now can we appreciate the fruits of that awareness. As a thinker, McLuhan was both a man of his time and ahead of it—and the Janus-like figure (Levinson, 2000, p. 19)[9] he strikes demands that we closely examine what he actually said and avoid the mistake of seeing him as a shill for the trendy, the new, and the "technological."

MEDIA AS ENVIRONMENTS

McLuhan's aim was not to be the prophet of a coming electronic Utopia, but to jolt people into an awareness of the psychic and social effects of electronic media, so that we might be prepared to come to terms with them. His further aim was to create awareness that all human "artefacts" (to adopt the Anglo–Canadian spelling McLuhan naturally used)—any arts or techniques, whether involving communication or not—create a background or complex of environmental conditions and related technologies of which we are mostly unaware, because we take them as givens. As he wrote in *Culture Is Our Business*, "Fish don't know water exists till beached" (McLuhan, 1970, p. 191). Of course, he is speaking metaphorically of humans, who are blissfully unaware of the environments created by our technologies until something goes wrong with them, such as pollution.

It is in this sense that McLuhan was most explicitly a media ecologist, trying to create an awareness about the largely unnoticed effects of electronic technologies in much the same way that Rachel Carson (1962) exposed the unintended environmental effects of pesticides in *Silent Spring*. A previously obscure research scientist for the U.S. Department of the Interior, Rachel Carson stunned the world in the early 1960s with a series of articles in *The New Yorker* outlining a devastating empirical case that the pervasive use of organic pesticides, most particularly dichloro-diphenyl-trichloroethane (DDT), was responsible for declining populations of higher order wildlife and the endangerment of a large number of species, particularly the bald eagle. The articles were subsequently collected in a book that shocked the conscience of industrialized society and almost single-handedly launched the environmentalist movement. Like McLuhan, she was vilified for both her motives and methods by the protectors of the status quo (see Graham, 1976), but her case eventually prevailed, and without her pioneering work, the creation of the U.S. Environmental Protection Agency in the following decade is all but unconceivable. If Marshall McLuhan can be considered the Rachel Carson of media ecology, then Rachel Carson is the Marshall McLuhan of environmentalism. Seeing McLuhan in his true light as a technological environmentalist exposes the narrowness of his misperceiving critics who saw him as a booster of pop culture and television; in truth, he was no more so than was Rachel Carson a promoter of DDT.

But being in the humanities, where no established procedures of verification or falsification exist, McLuhan was working in a profoundly different mode of perception, that informed by literary criticism—most particularly, Practical Criticism, with whose founders I. A. Richards (1925/n.d., 1929/n.d.) and F. R. Leavis (1930, 1932) McLuhan studied at Cambridge. Significantly, according to his son Eric, *Understanding Media* "was deliberately titled in order to place it beside [Cleanth] Brooks' and [Austin]

Warren's *Understanding Poetry* [1938], a key text in introducing Practical Criticism to these shores" (online posting to mediaecology@ube.ubalt.edu, November 19, 1999).

The essence of Practical Criticism is the interfusion of sound and sense, and of form and content—the notion that a work of verbal art communicates through the shape of the language and the way that shape subliminally alters our consciousness. Verbal artistry lies in having the style of the utterance enact in the audience a psychic response that mirrors or reinforces its sense. This makes artistic productions experiences in their own right that aim to change the audience's consciousness, rather than informing, persuading, or indoctrinating them. Both the details of the author's biography and any intentions we might infer on his or her part are irrelevant, in light of the work's effect on the reader. In summary, the medium is the message, and the audience, as participants in the fulfillment of the medium's purposes, become part and parcel with both medium and message. In the final analysis, the audience is the message.

Obviously, such a participatory mystique cannot be verified in the same sense as what Thomas Kuhn (1996) terms "normal science"; it can only be appreciated and experienced by training the aesthetic perceptions of the observer. However, such an appreciation can be taught, and the principles that underlie it are capable of demonstration and persuasion. But the evidence used in such inductive processes has its roots not in the logical positivism of science but in the humanistic tradition embodied in the three branches of the medieval trivium—grammar (study of language and literature), dialectic (logic and disputation), and rhetoric (persuading an audience through the shape of language). This triptych was the foundation for McLuhan's (1943) study of the English Renaissance writer Thomas Nashe in his PhD dissertation. Today, it is little appreciated that the trivium formed the structure of higher education in the West from before the time of Cicero up through the latter part of the nineteenth century, when American universities began to adopt the fragmented departmental structures established by the German *Wissenschaft* concept of the university (Kernan, 1990, pp. 34–35). In *Laws of Media,* Marshall and Eric McLuhan (1988) outline this history as follows:

> Following the Greek rhetorician Isocrates, Cicero, and after him Quintilian, established the basic pattern for Western civilized education, reaffirmed by St. Augustine four centuries later as the alignment of encyclopedic wisdom and eloquence. . . . For more than fifteen centuries, most of our Western history, the Ciceronian program, itself a retrieval of the old Greek liberal educational system, the "egkuklios paideia" (*vide* Marrou, *A History of Education in Antiquity*) was the basis of liberal education and Christian humanism. With print, via Gutenberg, the visual stress of the alphabet gained new ascendancy.

Spearheaded by the French dialectician Peter Ramus, a new battle of the Ancients (rhetoricians and grammarians) and Moderns (dialecticians) was waged, and dialectic "Method" obsolesced tradition. (pp. 124–125)

For McLuhan, in sympathy with his religious convictions, in the beginning truly is the Word—and in the end, as well as in between. Indeed, this had been the stance of Western education from its beginnings up through all but the last 125 years, but our subsequently compartmentalized system of knowledge—not only in the sciences and social sciences but the humanities as well—has alienated us from the wellsprings of this tradition. Such an assumption that knowledge is a series of fragmented "disciplines" rather than a unitary whole serves to make McLuhan appear an oddball, even a crank and a "visionary," simply because he chose to retrieve the core values of Western culture and discuss how they have been conditioned by our evolving technologies, particularly those that most directly affect the essence of what makes us human—language. In light of the intellectual traditions not only of the West but of all great cultures, it is we who are the oddballs in thinking that knowledge and experience can be subdivided and dissected without somehow once again being made whole.

STYLE AND SUBSTANCE

To redress this imbalance, McLuhan wanted us to appreciate that human technologies, like all our other artifacts, are "outerings" of our human faculties, or "utterings" (to refer to the word's Middle English roots). Technologies, whether they be devoted to communication or not, are thus extensions of our humanity, not the cold, alien, external forces envisioned by the paranoia of bad science fiction. Seen as utterings, technologies are utterances, rhetorical figures that can be read and analyzed for their cognitive, social, and cultural effects. To this end, McLuhan adopted a distinctly aphoristic style to convey his ideas—one consciously embodying the concept that the medium is the message. Its means is not to follow a continuous, linear, and unbroken line of thought, but to create a tessellated pattern of ideas, with each of the tiles in the mental mosaic reflecting a particular facet of the overall pattern. Like fractals, a field that gained currency only after McLuhan's last work (see Briggs, 1992; Gleick, 1987), the overall pattern is contained in miniature in each of the parts. He took as model the English Renaissance essayist Sir Francis Bacon, whose approach he thought incited independent thought much more than those authors who strive for a smooth, continuous, and homogenous line of argument:

> Francis Bacon never tired of contrasting hot and cool prose. Writing in
> "methods" or complete packages, he contrasted with writing in apho-
> risms, or single observations such as "Revenge is a kind of wild justice."
> The passive consumer wants packages, but those, he suggested, who are
> concerned in pursuing knowledge and in seeking causes will resort to
> aphorisms, just because they are incomplete and require participation in
> depth. (McLuhan, 1964, p. 31)

McLuhan chose this style because he also saw it as organic to the modern
era, in which the virtually instantaneous nature of electronic communication
stresses and fragments the smooth continuities of thought fostered by the
visual bias of print. Hence, his use of slogan, aphorism, *bon mot*, repetition,
and probe as ways of jolting his audience into new modes of awareness necessary for perceiving such changes in their cognitive environment. As Eric
McLuhan describes it in the preface to *Laws of Media*,

> The style of *UM* [*Understanding Media*] had been deliberately chosen
> for its abrasive and discontinuous character, and was forged over many
> redraftings. It was designed deliberately to provoke the reader, to jar the
> sensibilities into a form of awareness that better complemented the sub-
> ject-matter. This is poetic technique (science, if you will) of a high sort—
> satirizing the reader directly as a means of training him. (McLuhan &
> McLuhan, 1988, p. viii)

He observed that the great symbolist and modern artists were creating
insights into the age by discontinuities, for which he liked to claim, "[t]hat's
what Symbolism means—it comes from the Greek *symbaline*—break things
into single bits and reassemble them into patterns" (Stearn, 1967, p. 282).[10]
According to his view, Mallarmé, Joyce, Pound, Eliot, Pablo Picasso, Marcel
Duchamp, and the other great artists were creating insights into the modern
world and its relationships with the past not by smoothing over transitions
from one idea to another, or by providing perspective from a fixed point of
view, or by creating a consistently toned discourse—all mental habits fostered by print. Rather, they were presenting the observer with fragmentary
images of reality and forcing him or her to become a participant in the
process of piecing them together in a pattern of significance. Hence, in order
to make sense of the modern world, McLuhan himself would take a similar
approach.

McLuhan's probes are aimed not at deductive logic, which he saw as satisfying the purely visual conception of a pleasing arrangement of elements,
but at training the perceptive mind in pattern recognition. Such recognition
reveals the grounds of perception, against which the figure of concentration
stands out. In the case of any medium, its manifest content, of which we are
conscious and on which we tend exclusively to focus, is the figure, while the

grounds are the total environment created by the system of services and dis-services any technology creates.

But why should these methods of discontinuity be appropriate to the modern age and the supposed clash between print and electronic sensibilities? The answer to this question hinges on two ideas: (a) there are fundamental differences between oral and literate cultures, and (b) electronic communication is retrieving patterns of thought and culture fostered by orality. The first idea can be explored in modern ethnographic, literary, and linguistic research done on comparisons between primary oral cultures and writing cultures, which is explored more fully in other chapters in this volume. The second idea depends on the contrast McLuhan posits between the sense of "acoustic space" predominant in oral cultures and the "visual space" characteristic of writing and print cultures (Carpenter & McLuhan, 1960). To McLuhan, these ideas are intimately connected, and they lead to his assertion that television, as an "audile–tactile," rather than a "visual" medium, is leading to a recursion of many of the cognitive, social, and cultural forms of orality.

SYNESTHESIA

At the heart of McLuhan's understanding of the effects of media on consciousness is the process of synesthesia, the free interaction among the senses and the mind's normal means of translating the percepts of one sense into those of another. For example, reading is the process of translating symbols, into which speech or concepts have been decoded, back into their originals, although some symbols, such as punctuation, are not conceptualized or voiced, either internally or aloud.[11] McLuhan (1964) posits the existence of what he terms the "sensorium," the collection of the inputs from all five sense organs mediated by a sixth sense, called the "haptic" sense (p. 107). McLuhan identifies the haptic sense with tactility, which includes the sense of touch but extends beyond it as the facility for "interplay" among all the senses:

> It may very well be that in our conscious inner lives the interplay among our senses is what constitutes the sense of touch. Perhaps *touch* is not just skin contact with *things*, but the very life of things in the *mind?* The Greeks had the notion of a consensus or a faculty of "common sense" that translated each sense into each other sense, and conferred consciousness on man. (p. 108)

The ideal state of consciousness is one in which the components of the sensorium remain in balance with one another, "presenting the result continuously as a unified image to the mind. In fact, this image of a unified ratio among the senses was long held to be the mark of our *rationality* . . . ." (p. 60). This he distinguishes from the literate Westerner's narrower concept of rationality, which he considers to be based on purely visual mental structures fostered by the extension, lineality, and homogeneity of the phonetic alphabet, as intensified by print. An ideal culture would be one whose artefacts—language, music, dance, plastic arts, education, and so forth—promote this balanced ratio of the senses. But man the tool-making animal is constantly creating technologies as means of amplifying or extending one of his natural senses or faculties, thus throwing the sensorium out of balance. Because the body (which for McLuhan implicitly includes the mind) seeks to maintain a constant state of equilibrium, or homeostasis, this imbalance among the senses is alleviated in the sensorium (but as we will see, only at a price) through what he terms a process of "closure" (p. 45).

This closure is achieved by numbing the particular sense being amplified or extended, so that it apparently—but not really—is brought back in ratio with the others. For example:

> Battle shock created by violent noise has been adapted for dental use in the device known as *audiac*. The patient puts on headphones and turns a dial raising the noise level to the point that he feels no pain from the drill. The selection of a *single* sense for intense stimulus, or of a single extended, isolated, or "amputated" sense in technology, is in part the reason for the numbing effect that technology as such has on its makers and users. For the central nervous system rallies a response of general numbness to the challenge of specialized irritation. (p. 44)

In the case of reading, alphabetic writing is so efficient in encoding speech, readers of it become almost exclusively dependent on the eye, and the resources of the ear are correspondingly diminished. Alphabetic writing, because of its regularity and efficiency in encoding speech, becomes an extension of the eye, obviating the need for a fund of oral memory to convey meaning. Plato (trans. 1961) discusses this effect in the *Phædrus*, where he recounts the story of the god Theuth presenting writing, only one of his clever inventions, to the king of upper Egypt, Thamus, claiming that it is an aid to memory and wisdom. Thamus replies,

> by reason of your tender regard for the writing that is your offspring, [you] have declared the very opposite of its true effect. If men learn this, it will implant forgetfulness in their souls; they will cease to exercise memory because they rely on that which is written, calling things to remembrance no longer from within themselves, but by means of external marks. What you have discovered is a recipe not for memory, but for reminder. And it is no true wisdom that you offer your disciples, but only its semblance, for by telling them of many things without teaching

them you will make them seem to know much, while for the most part they know nothing, and as men filled, not with wisdom, but with the conceit of wisdom, they will be a burden to their fellows. (p. 520)

Thus, a new ratio of the senses is created, in which the eye comes to dominate. Hence, the medium of writing and, *a fortiori*, print, carries with it a lesson, which is not to rely on the ear for confirmation of truth, but to depend on the eye instead. "Seeing is believing," whereas in oral cultures, hearing is believing, because you can always cross-examine a person, but, as Plato has Thamus say in the *Phædrus* you cannot interrogate a text.

But more important, this lesson works not manifestly but subliminally. The lesson referred to above has been termed differently by Harold Innis (1951) as the "bias" of communication media, whereas Neil Postman (1985, pp. 16–29) has referred to their "epistemology." However one refers to this lesson, its significant characteristic is that it operates subconsciously, or it could not work at all. The conventional notion is that all media are neutral vessels which we simply fill with content and disseminate to an audience. However, McLuhan considers this view naive: while our conscious minds are occupied by the manifest content, our subconscious is left vulnerable to the subliminal effects of the medium. His favorite analogy, borrowed from T. S. Eliot, was that the content is the juicy hunk of meat the media burglar uses to distract the watchdog of the mind (McLuhan, 1964, p. 18). Unconsciously, our sensorium becomes molded by the medium and thus becomes the filter through which we select percepts and experience "reality." Without such filters we would go insane from an overload of input. Concomitantly, we come to identify the characteristics of our particular filter with rationality itself—or, at the very least, with the "natural" structures of knowledge, wisdom, and truth. Those with differing, competing, or conflicting filters are seen as lacking those qualities which our filters have persuaded us are "universal." Hence, clashes of cultures, whether these be ethnic, ideological, or generational.

Print is biased toward smooth continuity, linearity, sequentiality, homogeneity, and efficiency, whereas the biases of other scripts, and of the discontinuous electronic universe, tend in opposite directions. Hence, it is understandable why McLuhan's critics have found it difficult or impossible to comprehend or accept both his medium—aphoristic probes arranged in a mosaic structure—and his message, because of the way our minds have been shaped by typography, invisibly and subliminally. It is also easier then to understand why both his critics and some of his cybernaut enthusiasts—whose mental filters have been shaped just as strongly by electronics—have mistakenly seen his probes as an enthusiastic embrace of electronic media, rather than as the purely detached and descriptive efforts they actually are. Although his intent was always to help preserve the positive cultural values that have been fostered by writing and its amplification via Gutenberg technology, he has been mistaken by both camps as a celebrant of the electronic galaxy, simply because he tried to shock people, by means of the probe, out of their complacent unawareness of the ways in which media "massage" consciousness.

This numbing, or "auto-amputation," is the price we pay for extending our senses through technologies, for it can be achieved only by making us unaware of the effect of the technology on our entire sensorium. Hence, technologies create perceptual environments that we take to be "real," because of the numbness or narcosis they engender in us in order to be accommodated in the sensorium. Thus, the most potent effects of technologies are those of which we are the least conscious, because of the natural evolutionary process of adaptation to the environment.

McLuhan's definition of a medium, then, is the unconscious effects of our adaptation to the environments created by our technologies. The particular bias of perception or consciousness carried by each technology—the very aspect of which we are the least aware—is what has the most telling effect on us, much greater than any "content" the medium may convey. Thus, "the medium is the message" because the contents of a medium vary and may even be contradictory, but the medium's effects remain the same, no matter what the content. In fact, the content serves as a distraction from awareness of how the medium is molding consciousness. This underlines not only how media steal into our consciousness but also the fact that they can do so only because of the mind's continual desire for contentment, completion, or closure. And behind this desire lies the process of synesthesia, the normal process of sensory equilibrium that remains subliminal in just about everyone, but that can break through to the surface of consciousness in some individuals, known as synesthetes, for some of whom letters and numbers appear in consistently different colors, while for others tastes evoke geometrical shapes (see E. McLuhan, 1998, pp. 160–179, and Cytowic, 1993/1998).

Although closure may seem to be advantageous, in terms of adaptability to changing environments, in reality it works to our disadvantage, particularly because we are unconscious of its operation. Under conditions of closure we are most susceptible to media "fallout," or negative effects on the mind. Such negative effects occur when the bias of a dominant medium, particularly a communications medium, is subliminally incorporated into consciousness but is at variance with the achieved value system of a culture, undermining it from below the conscious level of awareness. Such a state is responsible for, as McLuhan and Fiore (1968/1997) phrased it in the subtitle of *War and Peace in the Global Village*, the kinds of "spastic situations" cultures find themselves in when an established dominant medium of communication is being challenged by the introduction of another medium with an entirely different set of biases. Such major situations have happened in the West on three notable occasions: first, when the oral and tribal ancient Greeks adapted the Phoenician syllabary to create the first completely phonetic alphabet; second, when the manuscript culture of medieval Europe was overthrown by Gutenberg's creation of an efficient system for printing with movable types; and subsequently from the invention of the telegraph through today, when print culture is being challenged by the pervasive adaptation of the electromagnetic wave spectrum to telecommunications, in a recursion of the state of tribalism typical of orality.

MEDIA HOT AND COOL

But what is this quality of tribalism? What does it have to do with oral communication? What has caused its disappearance? Why should it be recurring, in different forms today? McLuhan (1964) explains why in the distinction he draws between "hot" and "cool" media:

> A cool medium like hieroglyphic or ideogrammatic written characters has very different effects from the hot and explosive medium of the phonetic alphabet. The alphabet, when pushed to a high degree of abstract visual intensity, became typography. The printed word with its specialist intensity burst the bonds of medieval corporate guilds and monasteries, creating extreme individualist patterns of enterprise and monopoly. But the typical reversal occurred when extremes of monopoly brought back the corporation, with its impersonal empire over many lives. The hotting-up of the medium of writing to repeatable print intensity led to nationalism and the religious wars of the sixteenth century. . . . Similarly, a very much greater speed-up, such as occurs with electricity, may serve to restore a tribal pattern of intense involvement such as took place with the introduction of radio in Europe, and is now tending to happen as a result of TV in America. Specialist technologies detribalize. The nonspecialist electric technology retribalizes. (pp. 23–24)

McLuhan borrowed his terminology from the evolving vocabulary of popular slang, especially of jazz in the late 1940s and 1950s (p. 27). A hot medium is one in relatively high definition, which provides information in sharply defined packages that demand relatively little participation on the part of the observer for completion. Similarly, hot jazz consisted of tightly scripted arrangements in which each player had a highly defined part to play, with any improvisation relegated to a set number of bars in spotlighted solos. By contrast, the cool jazz that emerged in the late 1940s from such innovators as Charlie Parker, Miles Davis, and Dizzy Gillespie evolved into an almost entirely participatory style, in which the theme was stated briefly at the beginning and recapitulated at the end, but in the middle the players were responsible for mutually creating the work almost entirely through improvisation, with each player having a role in the group composition rather than a sharply defined part in an arrangement. By parallel, relatively cool media are of lower definition and require greater participation and interactivity to complete the experience; we cannot use the term *observer* but must consider him or her a *participant*.

For instance, a conversation is a relatively cool medium because it requires much participation in the completion of the experience: Those involved interact with one another in facial expressions, body language, and mutual give and take, and in some cultures even use other senses such as touch and smell of the breath to complete the sense of communion. By contrast, print is a relatively hot medium because it completely occupies only one sense—sight—while translating both speech and writing into that sense, of which process we are normally unconscious. Manuscripts, while translating speech into writing, and are thus hotter than speech, are still cooler than print, because of their greater degree of tactility and closer ties to the world of orality: it was only in the late stages of manuscript culture in Europe that words were separated from one another on the page, and decipherment of the meaning required much interaction with the text and reading aloud to oneself, as well as to others (McLuhan, 1962, pp. 82–99).

The telephone is a cool medium because it transmits a signal of relatively low definition: The frequency range is limited, and one has to participate in the completion of the message to a much greater degree than even in face-to-face conversation. This is perhaps why the use of the cell phone in automobiles has been attributed to an increased accident rate, even when hands-free phones are used: The users' energies are so involved in completing the aural message that their concentration on visual tasks is impaired. By contrast, radio, especially FM and now-emerging digital radio, is a relatively hot medium, because it strives to provide a complete signal that requires no completion on the part of the listener. Of course, AM talk radio is a relatively cool subset of the radio spectrum, because of the comparatively low definition of the signal, encouraging participation and interaction to a much greater degree. This difference points to the fact that different media are either hot or cool only in relation to the culture and the media environment into which they are introduced: Radio in the Europe of the 1930s, as exploited by Hitler, was a distinctly hotter medium than in the hotter typographic environment of England and the United States since the end of World War II, where it has been relegated to the status of entertainment (McLuhan, 1964, p. 31).

Film represents another relatively hot medium, particularly because of its relationship with mechanical technology. Although a film is projected on a screen through a series of wheels, shutters, and sprockets, the viewer is presented with a series of fully completed images at a rate of 24 frames per second. Like print, the film image is distanced and objectified from the observer, who sees it as a reflection of light on a surface, as opposed to the light that is projected through the TV screen, which is more comparable to the light streaming through a stained glass window.

Television is a decidedly cooler medium than either film, writing, or print, because it requires so much participation on the part of the viewer in completion of the image. Like cartoons, television provides a relatively indistinct and low-definition image, and the viewer's eyes are constantly exploring the contours of the quickly changing television image in an attempt to reconstruct it on the fly, as it were. As a result, watching television requires a maximal amount of participation in depth in the recreation of its images, erasing the objectified relationship between user and medium fostered by print and, as a consequence, undermining the cognitive structures of individualism, detachment, and privacy that print made possible.

RETRIEVALS OF ORALITY

It would be useful at this point to explore more fully the technological basis for such claims. With electronic channels of communication, as distinguished from pre-electronic, there is a virtually instantaneous discontinuity of presence of the communicator. Telecommunication not only obliterates the equation between communication and transportation, but also disembodies the source or sender of the message. As Tony Schwartz (1973) describes it in *The Responsive Chord*, electromagnetic waves, like sound waves, are propagated circularly (actually spherically), not linearly in a single direction, so their mode of transmission is akin to both orality and aurality (pp. 11–13). What is more, the source of the message is everywhere within the range of the transmission virtually at once—around a sphere, to echo Pascal (1669/1961), whose center is everywhere and whose circumference nowhere.[12] Disembodiment of the source both decentralizes communication and creates a pervasive discontinuity in the identity of the source. In a sense, the source is tessellated throughout the receiving zone of the transmission: Wherever there is a receiving set, the source is recreated.

Far more than radio, television adds to the tessellating effect by providing a mosaic mesh that requires the perceiver to participate in completing the image. To McLuhan, this makes TV an "audile–tactile" medium, much more than a "visual" one; visuality is the process of translating the products of the other senses into a symbolic code that is decoded strictly through the eye. Thus, reading is a process of internally processing coded shapes for sound back into speech, the prior medium that serves as the content for writing (as writing is the content for print). Similarly, in parallel with Bishop Berkeley's theory of vision, gazing on graphics that depict three-dimensional objects through vanishing point perspective on a two-dimensional surface is likewise a process of mental decoding.

According to Berkeley (1709/1929), what our eyes perceive is a mosaic of flat planes with no real depth whatsoever, but in processing these percepts our minds create depth of field by correlating these planes with our kinesthetic experience of touching objects in space. According to McLuhan, we decode the lines in a perspective graphic to re-present three-dimensional space because we have learned to do something similar with print. Whereas reading decodes abstract and arbitrary shapes into speech, visualizing three dimensions on a flat surface decodes flat lines into space. Cultures whose eyes have not been trained to translate one sense into another by print, whose primary means of storing the contents of their "tribal encyclopedia" (Havelock, 1963) is oral and aural rather than visual, do not use perspective in their art, which more closely approximates tactility by seeing objects from many directions, and sometimes different time frames, simultaneously. In a sense, the eye is encouraged to act like a hand, turning the object around so that all aspects of it are experienced, caressing all its curves and angles in a sensual communion. Cubism in Western art tries to approximate this process on a flat surface, by breaking with vanishing point perspective and rendering all views of the object simultaneously.

To McLuhan, when we watch television the eye must continuously explore and recreate the contours of the image, as the hand would a piece of sculpture. This creates a situation of maximum participation in depth, participation not in the content of the image, but in its assembly by the human sensorium. The contrast with the process of reading is clear. In reading, the eye and brain are involved not in completing constantly changing, complex images but in decoding and interpreting a series of relatively simple, already completed shapes whose succession and combination constitute meaning, and whose pace of scanning is entirely under the control of eye–brain coordination.

The alphabet is the most efficient facilitator of this process because it comes closest to creating a homologue, or phonologue, between its code and the phonemes that constitute the speech it encodes. As distinguished from "unvocalized syllabaries" (such as Phœnician, Hebrew, and Arabic) and hybrid systems (such as Egyptian hieroglyphics and Mandarin script) that combine pictograms, ideograms, and rebuses, alphabets process speech most efficiently because letters have the lowest level of ambiguity in encoding the particular sounds the reader is meant to reproduce mentally (Havelock, 1976, pp. 22–38). What is more, the letters of the alphabet, being meaningless in themselves, are atomistic, not holistic, and meaning resides only in their combinations and permutations. Hence, there is no need and little inducement to contemplate them for their own sake, unless they are illegible or if one is a calligrapher or typographic designer. Even in these cases, the letters do not carry any significance beyond themselves, do not signify some other concept. Instead, they are processed in a succession that creates signification by the continuity with which their lexical and semantic units and structures can be processed by the mind. Reading is most effective and efficient in languages that use an alphabet when there are few or no obstacles to the continuous processing of the symbols—sequentially, linearly, and homogeneously.

The more ambiguous or self-meaningful the signs, and the more discontinuous the process of decoding their sequence, the more one's sensorium has to participate in choosing the correct signification. Under such conditions, the sequence of signs is rendered into a kind of reminder, or *aide-mémoire*, that requires a memorized, supplementary base of knowledge acquired orally in order to complete the process of signification. Thus, to use Eric Havelock's (1976) term, there attaches to such a system a higher degree of "residual orality"—speech apart from the actual speech being coded, needed to complete the thought recorded. Take the case of Chinese characters, which are common to the many mutually unintelligible spoken dialects in China, some of which are used as well in Korean and Japanese. Although a given character may signify the same concept in each of these different languages, its decoding excites entirely different vocables. If the character is an ideograph—that is, it represents a concept rather than functioning as a true sign—the discontinuity between sound and shape is even greater. For example, the Mandarin character for *good* is pronounced [*hau*], but it consists of the combination of the characters for *woman*, pronounced [*ny*], and *child*, pronounced [*dzə*] (Ong, 1982, p. 87). In such cases, reading is not a process of decoding so much as decipherment.

This difference creates entirely different noetic processes in the minds of readers of alphabets on the one hand, who are involved in a process of relative and maximal continuity, and readers of other scripts, who are constantly filling the intervals between symbolic units to complete semantic connections. In much the same way, in completing the images projected by the cathode-ray tube, viewers are similarly "connecting the dots" in a discontinuous process.

Schwartz's (1973) explanation of how our eyes act like ears when watching TV also helps to demystify McLuhan's concept of it as an "audile" medium. Schwartz makes us aware of the fact that there is no such thing in nature as "sound"—only a series of intervals between maximum and minimum pressurizations of a physical medium, to which our eardrums sympathetically vibrate. Sound occurs when the eardrums send electrical signals analogous to these vibrations to our brains, which process and combine the succession of positive and negative pressures into what we conceptualize as frequencies of relatively higher and lower pitch (p. 12).

Similarly, when we watch TV, the cathode ray tube presents us not with a series of completed images (as does motion-picture film), but with only one dot of illumination at a time. The scanning gun does this so swiftly that we are as insensible of its motion as we are of the successive levels of pressure on our eardrums. The eye then must act like an ear in receiving this succession of light "pressures," and the sensorium interprets the pattern among unexcited (dark) and excited (illuminated) dots as a recreated image (pp. 14–16).

Shades of light and dark in a black-and-white image are determined by blending different proportions of fully illuminated and totally unilluminated dots. In color TV, each dot has a red, green, and blue phosphor, and color is determined by what combination of adjacent dots have which of their phosphors illuminated. The dots themselves are not continuous but discrete; they exist in a mosaic-like mesh pattern, and the sensorium is required to process the pattern of their illumination—to fill in the spaces between them to complete the perception of an image.

In both unmediated perception and in still and motion-picture images this is manifestly not the case—the image the brain perceives is instantaneously total. In film there is no inherent motion in the images themselves; the motion one perceives is provided by the brain, which reconciles differences between the positions of objects in successive frames and thus recreates motion by analogy. Film is thus also discontinuous, but the brain is not required to work nearly as hard to reconstruct the illusion, since it is required to process only 24 completed images each second. With TV, the brain has a tremendous amount of processing to do—recreating a new image out of the pattern of hundreds of thousands of illuminated and unilluminated pixels every 1/60th of a second on every other line of dots on the screen. With computer monitors the work is at least doubled, since the lines of pixels are not interleaved, as with TV, but are all illuminated within that same 1/60th of a second, and with monitors with higher refresh rates, 1/75th of a second and even faster. It is no wonder, then, that we should feel zombified by TV and fatigued after using computer monitors—our brains are so absorbed in recreating the succession of images.

One might fairly ask, what happens to television when it achieves higher rates of resolution, as in high definition television, which in its digital format has more than 1,000 lines of noninterlaced resolution? Indeed, McLuhan himself anticipated this question as far back as his 1960 "Report on Project on Understanding New Media," written for the National Association of Educational Broadcasters on a grant from the Office of Education, U.S. Department of Health, Education, and Welfare:

> . . . Engineers claim that a thousand-line television image would provide almost as high definition as the present movie image. Supposing that an

equally high definition of retinal impression were achieved for television, what would be the effect of its multi-point mosaic structure over and above the retinal impression? (McLuhan, 1967, p. 154)

One might expect a glib answer such as, "That would make television a hotter medium, like film, and reverse the effects of 'normal' television," but McLuhan never imposed a doctrine in the manner of a catechism. Rather, he asked such questions as probes for exploration, and expected people to come to their own conclusions. Later in his career, he devised a means of systematizing this process by retrieving the ancient concept of simultaneous causality, which had been overshadowed by the positivist concept of efficient causality, fostered by the linearity of print. This system, embodied in what he called a tetrad, is discussed in the following section.

NONLINEAR CAUSALITY

McLuhan's explorations of the consequences of man's creating and adopting technologies involves a reversion to the fourfold principle of causality, which prevailed in the West until about the 17th century. McLuhan's probes aim at pattern recognition as the means for understanding the interrelationships between culture and communication. They are not linear or syllogistic explanations of the focus of inquiry but multifaceted explorations, analogous to the way that a cubist painting presents many sides of the object at once. Hence, they do not promote single points of view but invite many views simultaneously, while abandoning the smooth spatial continuities implied in vanishing-point perspective, or visual space, in favor of the sometimes jarring discontinuities of acoustic space. They forsake the exclusive dependence on efficient cause as a means of explaining phenomena, in favor of formal cause, which McLuhan equates with pattern recognition.

From the ancients up to the Enlightenment, causality was recognized not as the linear, direct actions of a billiard-table universe, but as having four aspects, all of which occur simultaneously. This conception of causality was derived from Aristotle. In the *Metaphysics* we read,

> On the other hand if there are several sciences of the causes, and a different one for each different principle, which of them shall we consider to be the one which we are seeking, or whom of the masters of these sciences shall we consider to be most learned in the subject which we are investigating? For it is possible for all the kinds of cause to apply to the same object; e.g. in the case of a house the source of motion is the art and the architect; the final cause is the function; the matter is earth and stones, and the form is the definition. (Bk. III, ch. 2, sec. 996b)

Aristotle's medieval followers, while retaining "final cause," termed "source of motion" as "efficient cause," "matter" as "material cause," and "form" as "formal cause." For medieval philosophers, this fourfold conception of causality, applied to the Book of Nature, was "in perfect correspondence" (McLuhan & McLuhan, 1988, p. 218) to the fourfold exegesis of the Book of Scripture, as set out by St. Bonaventure:

> Just as there is an immediate and literal sense of the profane text, but also an allegorical sense by which we discover the truths of faith that the letter signifies, a tropological sense by which we discover a moral precept behind the passage in the form of an historical narrative, and an anagogical sense by which our souls are raised to the love and desire of God, so we must not attend to the literal and immediate sense of the book of creation but look for its inner meaning in the theological, moral and mystical lessons that it contains. The passage from one of these two spheres to the other is the more easily effected in that they are in reality inseparable. (Gilson, 1938, p. 17, cited in McLuhan & McLuhan, 1988, p. 218)

So, according to McLuhan, formal cause corresponds with the literal level, material cause with the figurative (allegorical) level, efficient cause with the tropological (moral) level, and final cause with the anagogical (eschatological) level (McLuhan & McLuhan, 1988, p. 218). This schema provides justification for rejecting the moralism of media analysts who focus upon the content conveyed by media, or the figure, and overlook the ground, or effects that media convey. It also demonstrates the insufficiency of Claude Shannon and Warren Weaver's (1949) influential linear transmission model of communication in truly understanding media:

> It is hardly surprising then that present-day media analysts find it impossible not to moralize, or that they substitute moralism for understanding. Old Science affords only abstract method and the Shannon–Weaver[13] pipeline and its variants—both of these are based on left-hemisphere elaborations of efficient cause and lack the ground that is supplied by formal cause and by interaction with the other causes. Since the four levels, like the four causes, are simultaneous, it is obvious that to perform any one level to the exclusion of the others, as a visual figure minus a ground, is to produce grievous distortion. This goes far towards explaining ... the helplessness of Old Science or philosophy to deal with the new transforming ground of electric information. (McLuhan & McLuhan, 1988, p. 218)

Efficient cause is the basis of modern logical positivism and its extensions, such as the social "sciences." The positivistic ideology has by no means stopped there, and has extended itself into the humanities, forming the basis for the attitudes of those critics of McLuhan who claim that he has-n't proven his case. The vocabulary of proof has no real place in the human- ities, nor in the social sciences or even the "hard" sciences, as the New Science of Einstein, Planck, Bohr, Schrödinger, and Heisenberg has mani- festly shown (McLuhan & McLuhan, 1988, pp. 39–66), and as confirmed in chaos theory (see Gleick, 1987). It is the vocabulary of formal logic, of closed systems, not of living, open systems, where the proper aim of argu- ment is not to establish proof but to increase the likelihood of assent (Toulmin, 1958). McLuhan's critics and some of his "disciples" have concen- trated on the "content" of his work in a positivistic vein, and have ignored the grounds of awareness his approach attempts to establish.

Thus, as an example, complaints about his "misreadings" of Shakespeare or Joyce entirely miss the point—in place of the standard, and standardized, "interpretations" based on positivistic models of evidence and "proof," he offers re-readings whose aim is to reveal the ground of effects fostered in the minds of the authors by media change that are either latent, as in Shakespeare, or manifest, as in Joyce. The critics are most unconsciously revealing the visual bias underlying their misperception of McLuhan's intent when they say they don't see the connections McLuhan does. His aim was to get entirely beyond the visual principle—at the very least, in order to appreciate it for what it is—and to encourage people to realize that the elec- tronic age of instantaneous awareness and involvement dethrones efficient causality and restores formal causality as the means of understanding, or re–cognizing, patterns of relationships within the conscious field. Far from being outside the mainstream of modern thinking, McLuhan is clearly with- in the flow of contemporary currents of thought. His theories have particu- larly found confirmation in brain hemisphere research conducted by Robert H. Trotter (1976) among the Inuit, which mirrors the anthropological research of Edmund Carpenter (Carpenter & McLuhan, 1960) he con- tributed to the Toronto seminars in the early 1950s (McLuhan & McLuhan, 1988, pp. 67–91).

In substitution for Old Science, McLuhan and his son Eric propose a New Science, echoing the title and influence of the *Scienza Nuova* of 18th- century social theorist Giambattista Vico. This process consists of a series of four questions that can be asked of any human artifact, in order to probe its sociocultural effects, called the tetrad:

> More of the foundation of this New Science consists of proper and sys- tematic procedure. We propose no underlying theory to attack or defend, but rather a heuristic device, a set of four questions, which we call a tetrad. They can be asked (and the answers checked) by anyone, anywhere, at any time, about any human artefact. The tetrad was found by asking, "What general, verifiable (that is, testable) statements can be made about all media?" We were surprised to find only four, here posed as questions:

- What does it enhance or intensify?
- What does it render obsolete or replace?
- What does it retrieve that was previously obsolesced?
- What does it produce or become when pressed to an extreme? (p. 7)

To see how these questions might apply, let us see several of the tetrads presented in *Laws of Media*. To stress the multilinear, simultaneous, multicausal quality of the tetrad, it is presented as a four-part schema (Fig. 7.1), rather than a linear, unidirectional sequence, which would be a distortion in the direction of efficient causality:

Fig. 7.1. The schema used in McLuhan and McLuhan's (1988) *Laws of Media* (pp. 132–214) to represent the simultaneous action of four-fold causality in creating media effects. Read clockwise from the upper left, the abbreviations are for enhancements, reversals, obsolescences, and retrievals.

The parts of the tetrads reproduced in Figs. 7.2–7.4 are configured to correspond to the diagram in Fig. 7.1.

Fig. 7.2. Perspective in Painting. (From McLuhan & McLuhan, 1988, p. 132)

To these, the tetrad presented in Fig. 7.5 might be added.

just as the fast
Gutenberg press enlarged
the reading public,
now the speed of printing
becomes the speed of light
(via photographic
process)

With reader as
publisher, the
reading public
disappears.

the speed of
the printing
press

the oral
tradition

everybody becomes
a publisher

the assembly-line book

you make your own book:
books no longer uniform and
repeatable

The (tribal) committee, via
position papers (the happening)
Familiarity breeds. Consensus,
e.g., the 'Pentagon Papers.'

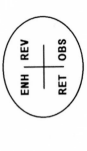

ENH | REV
RET | OBS

Fig. 7.3. Xerox. (From McLuhan & McLuhan, 1988, p. 145)

Using McLuhan's tetrad provides a useful heuristic for organizing thought about transformations within the media environment. Once its possibilities have been explored by applying it to relatively established media, its usefulness can be extended by turning attention to newly emerging media: video games, publishing on demand, DVDs, the format war between Digital Versatile Disc–Audio and Sony's Super Audio Compact Disc, file swapping over the Web, online gaming, digital newspapers, magazines, and scholarly journals, and other emerging technologies. It is in such nascent fields that media ecology becomes most useful, for it is there that we can inject a measure of anticipation of effects and a degree of control we might not otherwise have. As the McLuhans (1988) phrased it in *Laws of Media,* "There is no inevitability where there is a willingness to pay attention" (p. 128).

Orson Welles's
Invasion from Mars

world reverses
into talking picture:
audience as actors
participating in their own
audience participation

'diffusion' broadcasting:
the multilocational

access to entire planet
everybody
everywhere

Global Village Theatre

tribal ecological environment:
trauma, paranoia

wires and connections
and physical bodies

RADIO was an invasion of Western
culture, phasing out 2,500 years
of culture and literacy. It
brought to the surface an
instinctive' tribal sensitivity
to the dangers of alcohol…
a hypersensitivity to 'the
Demon RUM.' Radio
was the hidden
ground to the
figure of
retrieved
Prohibition.

end of rational and lineal:

end of Euclidean space:

end of Western time
and space

Fig. 7.4. Radio. (From McLuhan & McLuhan, 1988, p. 172)

understanding of media
as outerings or utterings:
extensions of
human nature   New Science

physics as   rigid dichotomy of
natural philosophy   C.P. Snow's "Two Cultures"*

Fig. 7.5. McLuhan's laws of media. Snow (1959) claimed that the modern
intellectual world is irretrievably divided between two mutually
uncommunicating cultures, the scientific and the humanistic.

CENTERS AND MARGINS

The instantaneous and discontinuous nature of electronic communication
means that no longer can political entities operate from a centralized bureau-
cracy that projects its power from the center out to the margins. With the
existence of an electric grid, any margin can itself become a center, and so we
end up with a world of centers without margins, with profound implications
for such print-fostered institutions as the nation-state, whose authority and
influence become threatened from two directions at once: from within by
increasingly Balkanized, fragmented groups, which are newly empowered
by the ability to communicate electronically and reinforce their identities;
and from without by the formation of larger, transnational, corporate
agglomerations that can instantly move both money and information across
borders without hindrance by traditional controls of customs and tariffs (see
Deibert, 1997). All this has been made possible by "the cosmic membrane
that has been snapped round the globe by the electric dilation of our various
senses" (McLuhan, 1962, p. 32).

McLuhan's electronic global village is no Utopia of harmonious con-
cord, but a place where total involvement in depth with one another is more
likely to breed conflict and terror:

So, unless aware of this dynamic, we shall at once move into a phase of
panic terrors, exactly befitting a small world of tribal drums, total inter-

dependence, and superimposed coexistence. . . . Terror is the normal state of any oral society, for in it everything affects everything all the time. (p. 32)

The virtually instantaneous nature of global communications means that the closer we get the more people identify with ethnic, linguistic, religious, or other affinities as a way of counteracting the psychic threats of such hyper-involvement.

Although McLuhan (1962) definitely is in sympathy with preserving the "achieved values" of "mechanical Gutenberg culture" (p. 135), the possibility lies open of his being receptive, had he lived longer, to a configuration of media that might promise to recapture such a balance among the senses in an achievement of a higher state of consciousness. In a remarkable passage ending the chapter on "The Written Word" in *Understanding Media,* McLuhan (1964/1994) expresses this possibility in a way untypical of his usual detachment:

Our new electric technology that extends our senses and nerves in a global embrace has large implications for the future of language. Electric technology does not need words any more than the digital computer needs numbers. Electricity points the way to an extension of the process of consciousness itself, on a world scale, and without any verbalization whatever. Such a state of collective awareness may have been the preverbal condition of men. Language as the technology of human extension, whose powers of division and separation we know so well, may have been the "tower of Babel" by which men sought to scale the highest heavens. Today computers hold out the promise of a means of instant translation of any code or language into any other code or language. The computer, in short, promises by technology a Pentecostal condition of universal understanding and unity. The next logical step would seem to be, not to translate, but to by-pass languages in favor of a general cosmic consciousness which might be very like the collective unconscious dreamt of by Bergson. The condition of "weightlessness," that biologists say promises a physical immortality, may be paralleled by the condition of speechlessness that could confer a perpetuity of collective harmony and peace. (p. 80)

The question thus arises: What are the prospects for such a restoration through evolving forms of computer-mediated communication, such as multimedia, hypermedia, and virtual reality?

Perhaps an answer to this question is possible if we are willing to probe and explore what is going on with these new media—how they affect the sensorium. To do so we need to ask some further questions. What are their cognitive effects? Does virtual reality take us towards or away from true synesthesia? Are hypermedia the revenge of text upon television, as the hypertext author Michael Joyce (1988) has put it, or do hypertext and hypermedia simply turn text into television? Do hypermedia turn image and sound into simply other forms of text to be manipulated as such, as Jay David Bolter (1992) claims (p. 39), or do they do just the opposite—relegate text to the status of image? If the latter is the case, are virtual reality and hypermedia overstimulating the right hemispherical cortex of the brain, hindering communication between right and left cortices? What changes in educational curriculum would be needed to compensate for such an unbalanced state of affairs? If current multimedia and hypermedia systems are unsatisfactory in achieving synesthesia, what changes and developments would have to be made in order to do so?[14] McLuhan has shown that the best means of arriving at answers to such questions is to use the probe and the tetrad, rather than depending on ideologies or moralistic fretting over content.

Use of such means reveals that McLuhan was not really a media "prophet," nor did he mean to be one. The prophetic mode, when it comes to media and other technologies, participates in the fallacies of futurology, which for the most part consists of falling in love with, or cowering in fear of, technologies and projecting unreal "what-if" scenarios into the future. This approach lacks insight because it overlooks the ground in favor of the figure—it ignores the environmental effects of technological change. McLuhan's approach is quite the opposite; as he expresses it himself in the *Playboy* interview, when asked about his prediction of the Balkanization of the United States, "Actually, in this case as in most of my work, I'm 'predicting' what has already happened and merely extrapolating a current process to its logical conclusion" (*Playboy* interview, 1969, p. 68).

Unlike such computer "visionaries" as Michael Dertouzos (1997), who was confident in telling us *What Will Be*, McLuhan always focused on What Is, and therein lies his value; for instead of focusing on an uncertain future, he gave us heuristics by which we can examine what is, so as to determine for ourselves what *should* be. Through such methods as the probe and tetrad we have means of evaluating our current situation and anticipating effects in real time. Those who embrace McLuhan as a visionary, or patron saint, of the electronic future are thus just as misled as those for whom he represents nostalgia for an unreal past, for they miss the critical dimensions of his method.

SUMMA MEDIALOGICA

Despite his reputation as a media guru, oracle, seer, and prophet, Marshall McLuhan was quite the opposite—a media ecologist grounded in the hereand-now, whose major purpose was to jolt people into an awareness of the effects of media fallout on our collective consciousness. This misperception, on the part of detractors and some supporters alike, has three major causes: his use of the most advanced technology available—television—to spread awareness of its effects; the aphoristic style of expression he chose as a means of inquiry; and his avoidance of the strictures of logical positivism in making his case. Rather than being a lone, idiosyncratic figure peddling intellectual snake oil to the masses, he is actually part of a rich, although often neglected, school of inquiry into the relationships between orality and literacy, encompassing many fields. His methods are really an outgrowth of the education in Practical Criticism he received at Cambridge in the 1930s, which he applied ever afterward in trying to get people to recognize all technologies as media and all media as outerings or extensions of ourselves. Once they are thus perceived, we can have some control over them, just as we can rhetorically control our other utterances. Rather than being a prophet of a New Age of media bliss, McLuhan used poetic technique and provided the probe, figure–ground analysis, and the tetrad as heuristics for determining the effects of media change, so as to anticipate and counteract the worst of them.

ENDNOTES

1. It was only upon editing the first volume of the *Proceedings of the Media Ecology Association* (http://www.media-ecology.org/publications/proceedings.html) that I realized my indebtedness to Paul Levinson for suggesting this metaphor. In 2000 he had used this image in a presentation he delivered at the inaugural convention of the Media Ecology Association, which I attended. In adapting this chapter from my own paper presented at the 57th annual conference of the New York State Communication Association (Morrison, 2000), my change in title accorded exactly with Levinson's phrasing and meaning. Janus, one of the Roman Numina, or Powers (gods preceding the Pantheon Rome inherited from the Greeks), was the god of good beginnings and endings. The two doors of his temple opened east and west, towards the beginning and ending of the day, and between them stood his statue, with one old face and one young. The month January, marking the end of the old year and the beginning of the new, is named for him (Hamilton, 1942/1953, pp. 44-45). Thus, Janus looks both to the past and future and unites them in a common vision.

2. McLuhan's celebrity came after that of such public intellectuals as Clifton Fadiman, Franklin P. Adams, Mortimer J. Adler, and Bennett Cerf, all well-known figures with literary credentials. Fadiman was book editor of *The New Yorker* from 1933 to 1943, master of ceremonies of *Information Please*, a popular radio show from 1938 to 1948, a member of the editorial board of the Book-of-the-Month Club from 1944 to 1993, member of the Board of Editors of *Encyclopædia Britannica* from 1959 to 1998, and a widely published anthologist. Adams, perhaps the "godfather" of the modern popular newspaper column and a panelist on *Information Please*, was also a poet and wit whose name became

somewhat of a household word from the 1930s through the 1950s. Adler, philosopher, educator, prolific author, and editor for *Encyclopædia Britannica,* was co-founder with Robert Maynard Hutchins of the Great Books program at the University of Chicago and edited with Hutchins the 54-volume *Great Books of the Western World,* as well as other projects (*Encyclopædia Britannica Online,* 2001). His pipe-smoking demeanor was prominent in widespread print advertisements for the series for many years. Cerf was co-founder of Random House, publisher of both popular and "serious" contemporary literature and ideas (including the Modern Library), celebrated for successfully overturning in court the ban of publication of James Joyce's *Ulysses* in 1933, a significant victory for literary expression and free speech. However, Cerf's public persona as a wry but likeable sophisticate was more widely established as a panelist in the television game show *What's My Line?* in the mid-1950s to 1960s.

3.   From the late 1950s to the early 1960s, Leary, in partnership with his colleague Richard Alpert, conducted at Harvard both formal and informal experiments with the hallucinogenic drug psilocybin, which they saw as both a therapeutic tool and a means of self-realization. When their unauthorized use of the substance with graduate students became known, they were fired. Leary became a counterculture figure and proselytized for use of both psilocybin and lysergic acid diethylamide (LSD) as means of transcendence, influencing many pop music figures and their fans (*Encyclopædia Britannica Online,* 2001).

4.   The first book printed by movable types of individual letters, the famous 42-line Bible produced by the firm of Schöffer and Fust, using technology attributed to Johannes Gensfleisch zum Gutenberg, was published in Mainz in 1456, so the town can be considered the cradle of the printed book in the West.

5.   Eisenstein has always been careful to dissociate herself from McLuhan's methods and to distinguish her efforts from McLuhan's pronouncements about the changing relationships between orality and literacy in Western culture. Her examination, rather, has been primarily of the effect of printing on the scholarly activities of already literate, Latin-reading and -speaking élites, rather than on any psychic effects of expanding literacy among middle and lower classes (1979, xii-xiv). Her quarrel with McLuhan lies not in the notion that Gutenberg technology was a profoundly catalytic agent in early modern Europe. Rather, she objects to his methods and to his lack of historiological precision in specifying differential effects of printing in varying locales and periods (Eisenstein, 1979, pp. 129 ff.). By mentioning the embarrassment she has experienced in being associated with McLuhanism by her colleagues (p. xvii), she becomes emblematic of McLuhan's difficulties in being accepted by specialists in traditional academic disciplines.

6.   The most comprehensive collections of commentaries on McLuhan are Stearn (1967) and Rosenthal, (1968). The former seems more balanced, because it provides McLuhan and his supporters virtually equal space with his detractors. The last chapter is an interview between McLuhan and the editor, in which McLuhan provides his most conclusive refutation of his critics' misconceptions. As a habit, McLuhan tended simply to ignore his critics in public and change the subject, so this interview provides a rare insight into his thinking. Rosenthal (1968) seems much less balanced, and the tone of the editor's introduction gives the

volume the appearance of a debunking exercise, despite the appearance of several significant supportive pieces. There is some overlap between the two volumes in selections, both positive and negative.

7. Bruce Powe, in a comment made during a panel discussion on "McLuhan's Life" at the reThinking McLuhan Conference, York University, North York, Ontario, March 21, 1997.

8. This was, prophetically, the theme of a *New Yorker* cartoon, published years before his death, whose caption read, "Are you sure it isn't too early to ask, 'What ever happened to Marshall McLuhan?'" (Gordon, 1997, p. 301).

9. Daniel J. Czitrom (1982, p. 165) also uses this image to describe McLuhan, but in a different sense: to express what he sees as McLuhan's paradoxical fusion of detached, scientific observation and court-jester trickery.

10. McLuhan's etymology seems off here. According to *Webster's Ninth New Collegiate Dictionary* (1991, p. 1195), the root meaning of *symbol* is the ancient Greek word *symballein,* meaning "to throw together," leading to *symbolon,* a "token of identity verified by comparing its other half," then to the Latin word *symbolum,* meaning "token, sign, symbol."

11. Victor Borge's comedy routine "Phonetic Punctuation" reveals, through a dramatic reading in which the punctuation marks are given their own oral sound effects, just how unconscious we are of the difference between how we process these kinds of symbols and those that have "content." But of course in "silent" reading, we attempt to process both kinds of symbols alike, although researchers have discovered that our vocal chords and other organs for speech undergo microtremors as we read silently, even though we may not be aware of them (Chaytor, 1945, p. 7, cited in McLuhan, 1962, p. 86).

12. "C'est une sphère infinie don't le centre est partout, la circonférence nulle part" (p. 87). McLuhan made this connection in McLuhan and Forsdale (1974), cited in Benedetti and deHart (1997, p. 46).

13. For Claude Shannon and Warren Weaver (Shannon & Weaver, 1949), "their main concern was to work out a way in which the *channels* of communication could be used most efficiently. For them, the main channels were the telephone cable and the radio wave. They produced a theory that enabled them to approach the problem of how to send a maximum amount of information along a given channel, and how to measure the capacity of any one channel to carry information. . . . Their basic model of communication presents it as a simple linear process. Its simplicity has attracted many derivatives, and its linear, process-centered nature has attracted many critics" (Fiske, 1982/1988, p. 6). See also McLuhan and McLuhan (1988, pp. 86-91).

14. Eric McLuhan (1998) addresses these issues in *Electric Language*, an update of *Laws of Media* in a format that mimics multimedia, although he ultimately decries interactive multimedia and virtual reality as false synesthesia.

REFERENCES

Benedetti, P., & deHart, N. (1997). *Forward through the rearview mirror: Reflections on and by Marshall McLuhan.* Cambridge, MA: MIT Press.

Berkeley, G. (1929). An essay towards a new theory of vision. In M. W. Calkins (Ed.), *Berkeley: Essay, principles, dialogues; with selections from other writings* (pp. 3-98). New York: Scribner's. (Original work published in 1709)

Bolter, J. D. (1992). Literature in the electronic writing space. In M. C. Tuman (Ed.), *Literacy online: The promise (and peril) of reading and writing with computers* (pp. 19–42). Pittsburgh, PA: University of Pittsburgh Press.

Boorstin, D. J. (1992). *The image: A guide to pseudo-events in America* (25th anniversary ed.). New York: Random House. (Original work published in 1961)

Briggs, J. P. (1992). *Fractals: The patterns of chaos; A new aesthetics of art, science, and nature.* New York: Simon & Schuster.

Carpenter, E. (2001). That not-so-silent sea. In D. Theall (Ed.), *The virtual Marshall McLuhan.* Montreal, Québec & Kingston, Ontario, Canada: McGill–Queen's University Press.

Carpenter, E., & McLuhan, M. (1960). Acoustic space. In E. Carpenter & M. McLuhan (Eds.), *Explorations in communication* (pp. 65–70). Boston: Beacon Press.

Carson, R. (1962). *Silent spring.* Boston: Houghton Mifflin.

Cavell, R. (2002). *McLuhan in space: A cultural geography.* Toronto, Canada, Buffalo, NY, & London: University of Toronto Press.

Cohn, D.L. (1951, October 21). A touch of humor wouldn't hurt. *The New York Times.* Retrieved November 6, 1997 from http://www.nytimes.com/books/97/11/02/home/mcluhan-bride.html

Cytowic, R.E. (1993/1998). *The man who tasted shapes.* Cambridge, MA: MIT Press.

Czitrom, D. J. (1982). *Media and the American mind: From Morse to McLuhan.* Chapel Hill: University of North Carolina Press.

Deibert, R. J. (1997). *Parchment, printing, and hypermedia: Communication in world order transformation.* New York: Columbia University Press.

Dertouzos, M. (1997). *What will be: How the new world of information will change our lives.* New York: HarperCollins.

Eisenstein, E. L. (1979). *The printing press as an agent of change.* Cambridge, England: Cambridge University Press.

Fiske, J. (1988). *Introduction to communication studies.* London & New York: Routledge. (Original work published in 1982)

Gencarelli, T. F. (2000). The intellectual roots of media ecology in the thought and work of Neil Postman. *New Jersey Journal of Communication, 8*(1), 91–103.

Gleick, J. (1987). *Chaos: Making a new science.* New York: Viking.

Gordon, W. T. (1997). *Marshall McLuhan: Escape into understanding; A biography.* New York: Basic Books.

Graham, F., Jr. (1976). *Since silent spring.* New York: Fawcett.

Hamilton, E. (1953). *Mythology.* New York: Mentor. (Original work published in 1942)

Havelock, E. A. (1963). *Preface to Plato.* Cambridge, MA & London: Belknap Press of Harvard University Press.

Havelock, E. A. (1976). *Origins of western literacy.* Toronto, Canada: Ontario Institute for Studies in Education.

Innis, H. A. (1951). *The bias of communication.* Toronto, Canada: University of Toronto Press.

Innis, H. A. (1972). *Empire and communications* (Revised by Mary Q. Innis with a foreword by Marshall McLuhan). Toronto, Ontario, Canada: University of Toronto Press.

Joyce, M. (1988). Siren shapes: Exploratory and constructive hypertexts. *Academic Computing, 3*(4), 10–14, 37–42.

Kernan, A. (1990). *The death of literature*. New Haven, CT & London: Yale University Press.

Kuhn, T. S. (1996). *The structure of scientific revolutions* (3rd ed.). Chicago & London: University of Chicago Press.

Leavis, F. R. (1930). *Mass civilisation and minority culture* (Minority pamphlet no. 1.). Cambridge, England: Minority Press.

Leavis, F. R. (1932). *New bearings in English poetry: A study of the contemporary situation*. London: Chatto & Windus.

Levinson, P. (1997). *The soft edge: A natural history and future of the information revolution*. London & New York: Routledge.

Levinson, P. (1999). *Digital McLuhan: A guide to the information millennium*. London and New York: Routledge.

Levinson, P. (2000). McLuhan and media ecology. *Proceedings of the Media Ecology Association 1*, 17–22. http://www.media-ecology.org/publications/proceedings/v1/levinson01.pdf

Lewis, W. (1927). *Time and western man*. London: Chatto and Windus.

Lewis, W. (1948). *America and cosmic man*. London: Nicholson & Watson.

Marchand, P. (1998). *Marshall McLuhan: The medium and the messenger* (rev. ed.). Cambridge, MA: MIT Press.

McLuhan, E. (1998). *Electric language: Understanding the message*. New York: St. Martin's.

McLuhan, H. M. (1943). *The place of Thomas Nashe in the learning of his time*. Unpublished doctoral dissertation, Cambridge University, Cambridge, England.

McLuhan, H. M. (1951). *The mechanical bride: Folklore of industrial man*. New York: Vanguard Press.

McLuhan, M. (1962). *The Gutenberg galaxy: The making of typographic man*. Toronto, Canada: University of Toronto Press.

McLuhan, M. (1964). *Understanding media: The extensions of man*. New York, Toronto, Ontario, Canada, & London: McGraw-Hill.

McLuhan, M. (1967). Is it natural that one medium should appropriate and exploit another? In G. E. Stearn (Ed.), *McLuhan: Hot & cool; A primer for the understanding of & a critical symposium with a rebuttal by McLuhan* (pp. 146–157). New York: Dial.

McLuhan, M. (1970). *Culture is our business*. New York: McGraw-Hill.

McLuhan, M. (1994). *Understanding media: The extensions of man* (with a new Introduction by Lewis H. Lapham). Cambridge, MA: MIT Press. (Original work published in 1964)

McLuhan, M., & Fiore, Q. (1967). *The medium is the massage: An inventory of effects* (J. Agel, Prod.). New York: Bantam.

McLuhan, M., & Fiore, Q. (1997). *War and peace in the global village: An inventory of some of the current spastic situations that could be eliminated by more feed-*

forward (coordinated by Agel, J.). San Francisco: HardWired. (Original work published in 1968)

McLuhan, M., & Forsdale, L. (1974). Making contact with Marshall McLuhan. In L. Brown & S. Marks (Eds.), *Electric media* (pp. 148–158). New York: Harcourt Brace Jovanovich.

McLuhan, M., & McLuhan, E. (1988). *Laws of media: The new science.* Toronto, Canada: University of Toronto Press.

McLuhan-Ortved, S. (Producer), & Wolfe, T. (1996). *The video McLuhan* [videotapes]. Available from: Video McLuhan Inc., 73 Sighthill Avenue, Toronto, Ontario M4T 2H1, Canada.

McMahon, K. (Director), & Flahive, G. (Producer). (2002). *McLuhan's wake* [film]. Available from the National Film Board of Canada Library: 22-D Hollywood Avenue, Ho-Ho-Kus, NJ 07423.

Morrison, J. C. (2000). Marshall McLuhan: No prophet without honor. *New Dimensions in Communication, v. XIII.* Proceedings of the 57th Annual Conference of the New York State Communication Association, Monticello, New York, October 8–10, 1999, 1–28.

Nelson, T. H. (1992). Opening hypertext: A memoir. In M. C. Tuman (Ed.), *Literacy online: The promise (and peril) of reading and writing with computers* (pp. 43–57). Pittsburgh, PA: University of Pittsburgh Press.

Ong, W. J. (1982). *Orality and literacy: Technologizing the word.* London & New York: Routledge.

Pascal, B. (1961). *Pensées.* Paris: Garnier. (Original work published in 1669)

Playboy interview. (1969, March). Marshall McLuhan: A candid conversation with the high priest of popcult and metaphysician of media. *Playboy,* pp. 53–54, 59–62, 64–66, 68, 70, 72, 74, 158.

Postman, N. (1985). *Amusing ourselves to death.* New York: Penguin.

Richards, I. A. (n.d.). *Principles of literary criticism.* New York: Harcourt, Brace & World. (Original work published in 1925)

Richards, I. A. (n.d.). *Practical criticism.* New York: Harcourt, Brace & World. (Original work published in 1929)

Rosenthal, R. (1968). *McLuhan: Pro & con.* New York: Funk & Wagnalls.

Schwartz, T. (1973). *The responsive chord.* Garden City, NY: Anchor/Doubleday.

Shannon, C. & Weaver, W. (1949). *The mathematical theory of communication.* Urbana–Champaign: University of Illinois Press.

Snow, C. P. (1959). *The two cultures and the scientific revolution.* New York: Cambridge University Press.

Southam Interactive. (1996). *Understanding McLuhan* [CD-ROM]. (Available from Voyager, on-line at http://store.yahoo.com/voyagerco/ltcmcluhh.html)

Stearn, G. E. (Ed.). (1967). *McLuhan: Hot & cool; A primer for the understanding of & a critical symposium with a rebuttal by McLuhan.* New York: Dial.

Sturrock, J. (1989, February 26). Wild man of the global village. *The New York Times Book Review.* Retrieved November 6, 1997 from http://www.nytimes.com/books/search/bin/fastweb?getdoc+book-rev+book-r+10110+0++

Theall, D. F. (2001). *The virtual Marshall McLuhan.* Montreal, Canada: McGill–Queen's University Press.

Toulmin, S. E. (1958). *The uses of argument.* Cambridge, England: Cambridge
    University Press.
Trotter, R. H. (1976). The other hemisphere. *Science News, 109,* 218.
Wolf, G. (1996a, January). Channeling McLuhan. *Wired* 4.01, pp. 128–131, 186–187.
Wolf, G. (1996b, January). The wisdom of saint Marshall, the holy fool. *Wired* 4.01,
    pp. 122–125, 182, 184, 186.
Wolfe, T. (1968). What if he is right? in *The pump house gang.* New York: Farrar,
    Straus & Giroux.

8

Neil Postman and the Rise of Media Ecology

Thomas F. Gencarelli
Montclair State University

One might say that the first media ecologist to hail from New York was Samuel Finley Breese Morse. Morse—an artist, inventor, entrepreneur, New York City mayoral candidate, and teacher of art at New York University (*Samuel F. B. Morse Biography*)—is, of course, best known for his invention of the telegraph, the media technology that ushered in the electronic revolution in human communication. After securing a patent on his invention in 1840, Morse sent the first telegraphic message from Washington, DC to Baltimore on May 24, 1844. The now-famous message—"What hath God wrought?"—constitutes a media ecological question if there ever was one. In choosing these four words from among all possibilities, Morse expressed both his sense of wonder at this new medium that would enable our communication to transcend the previous limits of space and time, but also his wonderment about its consequence.

It is, however, Lewis Mumford who is generally recognized as the first New Yorker *cum* media ecologist (Nystrom, 1973; Strate, 1996; Strate & Lum, 2000). Mumford fits this bill for two reasons. The first is that the main theme running through his prodigious body of work is the influence of technology on human civilization (see especially Mumford, 1934, 1952)—specifically its indirect and often hidden influence rather than that which is intended and expected. The second is that he was born in Flushing, in the city's outer borough of Queens, and was influenced by Manhattan "at a time when new forms of architecture, transportation, and communications were forcibly transforming not only the face of his city, but also the very fabric of its culture" (Strate & Lum, 2000, p. 58).

Marshall McLuhan, the founding father of media ecology himself, also spent significant time in New York. McLuhan found himself in the orbit of New York's intellectual and academic circles first during the 1950s, when his work was championed by Louis Forsdale, professor of English education at Columbia University's Teacher's College, and later as a result of the celebrity that followed publication of his *The Gutenberg Galaxy* (McLuhan, 1962) and *Understanding Media* (McLuhan, 1964). This included a year as a visiting professor at Fordham University (along with his colleague Edmund "Ted" Carpenter [see Carpenter & McLuhan, 1960] who later became a permanent New York resident). It was during this time that a number of media practitioners and academics in the then burgeoning field of media studies also came under his spell and influence.

These scholars, teachers, and media professionals include such notables as John Culkin, a Jesuit who left Fordham to establish the media studies program at the New School for Social Research (now the New School); Tony Schwartz (1973), author of *The Responsive Chord* and a recording engineer/producer who worked in advertising and produced the infamous "Daisy" commercial for Lyndon Johnson's 1964 presidential campaign; Gary Gumpert (1987) of Queens College of the City University of New York, who first met McLuhan while a doctoral student at Wayne State University, where he produced and directed a television program on his work; Paul Ryan (1973), also of the New School, a video artist, former assistant to McLuhan, and author of *Birth and Death and Cybernation;* and, finally, a young graduate student of Forsdale's named Neil Postman.

It is Postman who seized on the tumble of words "media ecology" that may or may not have spilled out of McLuhan's incessant wordplay at some point in the 1960s—recognizing in the term an encapsulation of and springboard for our thinking about our media of human communication. At the same time, Postman latched onto McLuhan's ideas in general, as they fit into, furthered, and served as a catalyst for the evolution of his own thinking as a self-proclaimed "educationist" and student of the English language. (Postman received his EdD in English education from Columbia in 1958.) And although his 45-year career speaks volumes with respect to his own character and gifts as a writer, teacher, and public intellectual, it might also be said that Postman has spent this career legitimizing, grounding, clarifying, and extending McLuhan's probes.

In the process, Postman comes to play perhaps the primary role in the founding of what we today commonly refer to, recognize, and understand as media ecology. It is Postman who institutionalized the term when he established the PhD program in Media Ecology at New York University in 1970. The term and a definition of it first appear in print in the published version of a speech he made in 1968, entitled "The Reformed English Curriculum" (Postman, 1970).[1] In sum, it is Postman whose name is most closely associated with media ecology and all that to which the term refers. And it is the roots, the evolution, and the totality of his contributions to our understanding of media that add up to a general theory of media ecology as a cohesive, powerful, and generative perspective on media and culture and media *as* culture.

The purpose of this chapter is to outline and explain this general theory of media ecology as it is embodied in the work and thought of Neil Postman. To achieve this aim, the chapter is divided into two parts. The first part presents the evolution of Postman's thinking through an analysis of his 15 most prominent works and what each of these has to offer. (In all, Postman has authored, co-authored, or co-edited 25 book-length works. These include 13 books for which he is the sole author, 10 books he co-authored, and two books he co-edited.) The second part of the chapter then isolates and examines the recurring themes found in these works, as well as the salient ideas imbedded within these themes. It is argued that these themes and ideas constitute the fundamental philosophical underpinnings of the conceptual framework known as media ecology as it is comes to us via Postman.

To begin, however, I must also point out that I have grouped the books in Postman's *oeurve* into a series of distinct phases; four to be exact. I do so on the basis of Postman's own acknowledgment of a career spent writing about things that interested him, but also of moving on when the subjects he was studying no longer held his interest (Gencarelli et al., 2001, p. 135).

And yet these phases do not include all of Postman's books. Postman's (1961) very first book, *Television and the Teaching of English,* might be said to preface his entire career. However, this book stands alone, not because of its subject matter or ideas, but because it is chronologically separated from the rest of the books considered here by his next seven books: the "New English" series of textbooks published by Holt, Rinehart and Winston. These books include Postman's (1963) *The New English: A Forward Look* the prelude to the series; *Discovering Your Language* by Postman and Harold and Greta Morine (1963); three books by Postman and Howard Damon, *The Uses of Language* (1965c), *The Languages of Discovery* (1965a), and *Language and Systems* (1966); and Postman's *Exploring Your Language* (1966a) and *Language and Reality* (1966b).

The "New English" textbooks are omitted from the present analysis not because they are of any lesser importance in Postman's development as an author, but because they are conceived and presented as English education textbooks.[2] *Television and the Teaching of English* (Postman, 1961), however, is one of Postman's most significant works, and must be included and discussed here before moving on to those works that comprise the four main phases of his career.

TELEVISION AND THE TEACHING OF ENGLISH

The cover of *Television and the Teaching of English* (1961) lists as its authors Neil Postman *and* the "Committee on the Study of Television of the National Council of Teachers of English." Postman is given credit by name as the primary author since he is the one who actually carried out the book's research and writing. However, it must be noted that he is not particularly nor ultimately responsible for the book's structure and purpose.

The chair of the National Council of Teachers of English Committee was Louis Forsdale. And in the book's foreword, Forsdale explains that the members of the committee "conceived of the project" and worked closely with the author "at every point in the venture" (p. vi). He also expresses gratitude to Postman for working in "such good humor with eight 'bosses'—members of the Committee—who developed the general plan of the book and who criticized its several drafts" (p. vii).

Television and the Teaching of English is an attempt to offer English educators, at all levels of curriculum, the knowledge and the tools—including "methods, materials, and activities" (p. 2)—to provide a "television education" for their students. The book was conceived at exactly that cultural moment when television had successfully taken its first steps, and was now on a roll, making significant inroads into American life. Hence, the book's rationale is a response to the impact that television was already having on the educational system in the United States, as well as on the culture this education is intended to serve.

Postman explains, in the introduction, why the responsibility for this education falls upon English educators such as himself:

> The ultimate purpose of this book is to contribute to the "television education" of our students. The immediate goal of the book is to offer motivation, aid, and confidence to teachers of English who wish to help their students obtain that education.
>
> Teachers of English are singled out because it is they who have the major responsibility for teaching students how to develop those skills that will enable them to respond with satisfaction and intelligence to diverse communication forms. The English teacher, more than any other, is concerned with those media through which our language and literature are given form. (p. 1)

The book is important to the present analysis for the following two reasons. First, it explains the roots of Postman's abiding interest in media. Postman is first and foremost an educator—one dedicated to language, literature, and the culture of print literacy. Thus, although most academic programs and works that focused on media at the time approached the subject from a sociological perspective (or, in the case of the violence studies, from a sociopsychological perspective), Postman begins instead from his predispositions as an educator with a literate bias. His concern, in this first phase and as a continuing thread in his career, is the threat television poses to literacy. Although he and the committee try to remain neutral—even positive—about introducing television into the English curriculum, Postman's primary concern is television's presence and magnetism and what this might portend for the future of education—an institution that has always been built on the edifice of the word. More importantly, he is concerned about the medium's consequence for the entirety of the human endeavor should it come to overwhelm and supplant our modern print-literate foundations.

Second, *Television and the Teaching of English* makes its contributions to the early discussion of the history of the medium and its industry, its effects (citing Klapper [e.g., 1949, 1960] and Schramm [e.g., 1954], among others), and its genres (or what Postman calls here its "literature"). However, it is in the book's opening chapter that its most lasting and significant contribution appears. For it is here that Postman first lays out the basic blueprint for media ecology.

The chapter begins with the example of a teacher who could still recall a world without television facing the first generation of students who had never known such a world. From this nod to the importance of history and the perspective it brings, Postman goes on to outline the history of all of our forms of human communication: a now taken-for-granted schema that includes the epochs of speech, writing, print, and what Postman refers to in this book as the "communications revolution." The latter refers to a period beginning "toward the middle of the nineteenth century, when a more or less continuous stream of media inventions began to make accessible unprecedented quantities of information and created new modes of perception and qualities of aesthetic experience" (Postman, 1961, p. 11). In his later writings, this period is of course refined and redefined as the "electronic age"—with the added realization that *all* of the major innovations in communication history were "revolutionary," in that all transformed our human species.

Equally important is the fact that this articulation of the four eras in the history of human communication and their revolutionary consequence appears at approximately the same time the seminal works on the individual eras first appear and have their impact: for example, Ong's (1967) championing and popularizing of the work of Milman Parry and others on orality,

Havelock's (1963, 1976) analysis of the origins of Western literacy in the Greek alphabet, and McLuhan (1962) and Eisenstein's (1979) treatises on the impact of the printing press. It thus stands as one of the earliest presentations in print of this complete media historical view.

PHASE 1: LANGUAGE AND EDUCATION

The first significant phase in Postman's career is comprised of the largest number of books—six—all of which are about either language or education or both. This focus, and the extent of his output during this stage, are, however, critical factors in any assessment of how his thinking evolved, of his contributions overall, and of his media ecology.

Four of these books were written with Charles Weingartner:[3] *Linguistics: A Revolution in Teaching* (1966), *Teaching as a Subversive Activity* (1969), *The Soft Revolution: A Student Handbook for Turning Schools Around* (1971), and *The School Book* (subtitled: *For People Who Want to Know What All the Hollering is About*) (1973b). A fifth book was co-edited by Postman, Weingartner, and Terence Moran—a former doctoral student of Postman's and later his colleague in the Department of Culture and Communication at New York University: *Language in America: A Report on our Deteriorating Semantic Environment* (1969). The sixth book represents Postman's first foray as solo author: *Crazy Talk, Stupid Talk* (1976).

These works are presented here in the order that they were published.

Linguistics: A Revolution in Teaching

Linguistics: A Revolution in Teaching (Postman & Weingartner, 1966) is, like *Television and the Teaching of English*, a book about media and education. However, the emphasis of this book is the primary media of education: verbal language in its oral, written, and print forms.

Linguistics was published at the height of a linguistics movement in public education. In fact, at the time, Postman and Weingartner were serving together as directors of the "Linguistics Demonstration Center" at New York University. Thus, one possible reading of this book is that Postman took advantage of what was then the cutting edge of English education theory, while also gravitating back, after *Television and the Teaching of English*, toward what he had initially set out and been trained to do.

However, a pair of alternate readings better accounts for the significance of this work in the chronology of Postman's developing thought. The first of these readings is that *Linguistics* serves as almost a reaction to *Television*

and the Teaching of English. It is a blatant step back from the idea of incor-
porating television into English education. Instead, it is a reaffirmation of
the importance of language instruction—not only because such instruction
accounts for two of the three "r's," but because the effective, successful, and
engaged grasp and use of language is central to *all* of education and its outcomes. That is to say, beyond the general subject areas that are at the forefront of what we are meant to learn and know through education, it becomes
incumbent on us to study and understand the very *means* by which we learn
and know. And it is essential that we realize the ways in which the medium
that is our language impacts, controls, dictates, and even limits both *what* we
can know and how we can *know* it. As Postman and Weingartner write, in
their attempt to define the linguistic enterprise:

> What is needed is a definition of linguistics that transforms the subject
> into actions that result in improved language and learning behavior.
>   By "improved language and learning behavior," we mean improve-
> ments in the ways in which students *use* language (i.e., in reading, writ-
> ing, speaking, listening), along with a knowledge of how to go about
> learning that which is yet to be learned. We believe linguistics can con-
> tribute importantly to these goals *when it is defined as the use of scien-
> tific processes of inquiry into the role of language in human affairs.* (p. 29)

A second reading recognizes that 1966 was a time when academic theory across a number of disciplines was still influenced by a structuralist paradigm. And linguistics—a structuralist approach to the language arts, how
language works, and how we might more effectively achieve those ends for
which we use it (i.e., articulating our experience to ourselves and others,
making ourselves understood, persuading others, etc.)—is a matter of
uncovering the otherwise invisible underlying and governing principles of
language. It is about the rules and rudiments of language, which are ostensibly beyond meaning but which allow meaning (or which explain the problems we have in making and apprehending meaning).

In the simplest terms, Postman and Weingartner call our attention in
Linguistics to the *medium of* language as opposed to the usual, more obvious and surface state of affairs that is our preoccupation with the things we
say, hear, read, and write when we use and rely on language.

The core of their argument is revealed in the appearance of yet a second
primary influence on Postman's thinking. This is the introduction, in
Chapter 6, of the subfield of linguistics known as "General Semantics." In
this chapter, Postman and Weingartner trace the intellectual history of theory in language, thought, and behavior—including the contributions of,
among others, Ogden and Richards (1923), Cassirer (1946), Peirce (1932),
Russell (1953), Whitehead (1959), Wittgenstein (1933), Langer (1942), Sapir
(1921), and Whorf (see Carroll, 1956), as well as Johnson (1946) and

Hayakawa (1943). Ultimately, then, their take on this history arrives at the founding figure of general semantics: Alfred Korzybski (1941).

According to Postman and Weingartner (1966): "If Korzybski's system has one central point it is that language should bear close correspondence to 'reality'" (p. 131). And it is this one sentence that represents the key to *Linguistics*. The book represents Postman's first attempt to answer the following questions, which he will return to again and again: In what ways and to what extent does language allow us to re-present reality—to create a "map" of it, in Korzybski's words? At the same time, in what ways and to what extent is the mediation of reality and experience through language *removed* from reality? Finally, to what extent are we cognizant of the fact that language can and does lead us in both of these directions, of how, when, and why it does so, and of the problems that inevitably arise when and if these matters are lost on (or invisible to) people?

Language in America: A Report on Our Deteriorating Semantic Environment

Language in America (Postman, Weingartner, & Moran, 1969) is subtitled "A Report on Our Deteriorating Semantic Environment," a subtitle that has a significance for two reasons. First, it introduces this book as a continuation of Postman's interest in general semantics. But whereas *Linguistics* sought to establish and explain the purpose and value of general semantics as a theoretical approach (and then only within the larger framework of the book's thesis), the intent in *Language in America* is more direct and immediate: It is to examine language in action and put the general semantics approach to a real-world test. Second, the subtitle denotes the fact that this is the first major work with Postman's name on the cover to focus on what is arguably *the* core idea in media ecology: the conceptualizing of media—in this case, language—as environments. And although this conceptualization owes a debt to Innis (1950, 1951), and his articulation of media bias and the importance of equilibrium, the book stands as the first major work by anyone to offer this idea at its center.

Language in America is also a collection of essays. Postman and his co-editors solicited some 22 essays on variations of the theme from a host of writers and thinkers with something of significance to say on these variations. Authors and titles run the gamut from African-American actor Ossie Davis on "The Language of Racism" to newspaper columnist Pete Hamill on "The Language of the New Politics" to anthropologist and social critic Ashley Montagu on "The Language of Self-Deception." The fact that the book is a collection, however, means that Postman's contribution, beyond his work as an editor, amounts mainly to his penning of his share of the introduction and his own lead essay, "Demeaning of Meaning."

In the book's introduction, Postman and his colleagues (1969) write that *Language in America* is, as "presumptuous as it might sound . . . about human survival" (p. vii). It is so, they argue (invoking Korzybski), because language itself is

> . . . the key to human survival. It is, as Korzybski said, our map for charting what is happening both inside and outside of our skins. When the map is inaccurate or inappropriate, our chances for survival are decreased. And not only at the physical level. We can talk ourselves into emotional death, or moral insensibility. We can even impose on language the Sisyphean task of exorcising the demon of uncertainty. Indeed, it may be that this is the primary and most dangerous function of all human symbols—to create the illusion of security in an environment of unremitting change.
>
> In any case, it is clear that with and through language man codes the realities in which he must survive. It is equally clear that language is man's unique instrument for survival—at any level—if he knows that it is and if he constantly checks the results it produces. (p. ix)

This excerpt speaks to how we use language to negotiate and manage our relationship with the environment in which we live. As such, it draws the connection between a medium—in this case, language—and that which we have always typically understood to be our environment. The remainder of the introduction and Postman's essay on "Demeaning of Meaning," however, go beyond this simple and obvious enough connection. Both make the case that (a) language is not something distinct and separate from this environment but is *part of it*, just as we ourselves are, and that (b) language can in fact be said to constitute or create an environment *in its own right*. We co-exist within a "world" of our own creation; a world we create by means of language, and which includes our culture, our social structure with its mores, norms, and codified law, and our technology. And as is the case with the natural environment, we are wholly influenced by this world at the same time that we try to bend and shape it to our ends.

"Demeaning of Meaning" serves as a *de facto* second introduction to the book, and also offers a subtitle that references the environment: "Or, What's the Language-Pollution Index Today?" However, although this essay is expressly about the medium of language, the book's main focus, Postman does not stop on this note. Instead, he begins to introduce here the notion of *all* of our media of human communication as environments, and even includes some of these environments within his argument.

As an example, he equates the saying of things we do not actually believe with "waste" and "garbage"—therein introducing the analogy of "the pollution of our semantic environment." And while still relying on the definition of the "communications revolution" from *Television and the Teaching of English*, he goes on to write about the semantic environment of mass media:

> In considering the ecology of the semantic environment, we must take into account what is called the communication revolution. The invention of new and various media of communication has given a voice and an audience to many people whose opinions would otherwise not be solicited, and who, in fact, have little if anything to contribute to public issues. Many of these people are entertainers, such as Johnny Carson, Hugh Downs, Joey Bishop, David Susskind, Ronald Reagan, Barbara Walters, and Joe Garagiola. Before the communications revolution, their public utterances would have been limited almost exclusively to sentences composed by more knowledgeable people, or they would have had no opportunity to make public utterances at all . . .
>
> Another problem created by the communications revolution is generated by the sheer bulk of the media. Even if the press, radio, and TV were largely devoted to the dissemination of opinions of our most well-informed citizens, a substantial amount of garbage would still be present. Even smart people run out of things to say—in fact, usually sooner than they anticipate. But if one must write a column everyday, or an article every week, or answer complicated questions in thirty seconds, one is soon responsible for more nonsense than can be retracted in a lifetime. In other words, big media demand lots of stuff, fast, and they don't especially discriminate among kinds of stuff. (pp. 14-15)

"Demeaning of Meaning" also foreshadows considerations that will be revisited in Postman's later books like *Amusing Ourselves to Death*, with its illustrations about the language of religion and politics, and *Technopoly*, with its brief illustrations about the language of science.

In sum, *Language in America* is a groundbreaking work in Postman's media ecology. The term media ecology does not appear in it. The word ecology appears by itself only twice—in reference to an "ecological imbalance" in our semantic environment in "Demeaning of Meaning" (pp. 14, 18). Meanwhile, Postman's (1970) speech, "The Reformed English Curriculum," will itself appear in print within a year of the book's publication. What is groundbreaking, then, is the introduction of this fundamental concept in media ecology: that media are environments, and that consequences arise when there are problems in these environments.

Teaching as a Subversive Activity

Teaching as a Subversive Activity (Postman & Weingartner, 1969) is the book that put Postman on the map as a public intellectual and an educational theorist. The book became a best-seller among academics and students in schools and programs of education across the United States, due to the fact that it is, first and foremost, a book about the state of public education in the United States at the time, and because its intent is to offer prescriptions to improve education and its outcomes.

As such, the book takes something of a turn away from the lines of thought presented in the present analysis. Yet this does not mean that there is no media ecology here. Chapter VII on "Languaging" distills and re-presents many ideas from both *Linguistics* and *Language in America*. Chapter X on "New Languages: The Media" reintroduces the case, from *Television and the Teaching of English*, of the four communications revolutions. (Note that the fourth of these is *still* called the "communications revolution.")

Taken as a whole, however, *Teaching as a Subversive Activity*'s primary contributions to media ecology are two. The first is that Postman and Weingartner go beyond the case for the inclusion of television into the mission of a general education, and now lay claim to the need to examine and understand *all* media at the base of this mission. Stated as such, this line of thinking becomes the first published argument for a program of media education or media literacy. As the authors write:

> The fact that the new media are inseparable from the changes occurring in the environment requires that the school's virtually exclusive concern with print literacy be extended to include these new forms; in other words, the magnitude of the effect of new media, still in the process of being assessed, requires that any attempt to increase the relevance of education include substantive consideration of them. (p. 161)[4]

Subversive Activity's second contribution to media ecology is in its introduction of H. Marshall McLuhan and his ideas. The references to McLuhan here represent Postman's first explicit nod, in the books under examination in this essay, to his influence. And quite a nod it is: McLuhan looms large in this work, both explicitly and implicitly.

The initial citation of McLuhan comes on the fourth page of the introduction, as Postman and Weingartner develop their argument for why the institution of education requires change, and why such change requires thinking and initiatives that are so radical and revolutionary as to be considered "subversive."[5] McLuhan is quoted as saying that the institution of schooling must be changed if it becomes "irrelevant" (p. xiv) and his *Understanding Media* (McLuhan, 1964) is cited as an example of the kind of "shock therapy" that might help push the educational system toward revitalization (p. xv).

However, these two brief references are only the beginning. The book is laced with McLuhan's ideas and aphorisms, with arguments built from and around them, and with their connection to the ideas of theorists from a range of disciplines, including education, linguistics, and psychology. For example, the chapter on "The Medium is the Message, of Course" explains and expands on the famous adage in the title, but also introduces McLuhan as an educationist. According to the authors, he is an educationist because his ideas are an extension of the ideas of other educational theorists, but also because he himself extended the purview of what we need to know and why we need to know these things. Chapter II begins with the following:

> One of the most dangerous men around at the moment—dangerous because he seems to be subverting traditional assumptions—is Marshall McLuhan. Nonetheless, as of this writing, he is capturing the attention of intellectuals and the press as few educationists have ever done. One of the reasons is the seeming uniqueness of his remarks. Another is the unconventional manner in which he conducts his reflections. And a third is that he is not generally thought of as an educationist ...
>
> But McLuhan is an operational educationist nonetheless. Moreover, some of his "probings," as he calls them, are unique mostly in their metaphorical verve. (For an educationist, he expresses himself in an uncommon flow of puns and poetry.) Many of his observations are reaffirmations of ideas previously expressed by other educationists—for example, John Dewey and A. N. Whitehead—ideas which were, and still are, ignored by those who could most profit from them. We are especially in McLuhan's debt for his restatement, in alliterative language, of Dewey's belief that "we learn what we do." McLuhan means much the same thing by his famous aphorism, "The medium is the message" ... From this perspective, one is invited to see that the most important impressions made on the human nervous system come from the character and structure of the environment within which the nervous system functions; that the environment itself conveys the critical and dominant messages by controlling the perceptions and attitudes of those who participate in it. (pp. 16-17)

Three more of McLuhan's metaphors are invoked in Chapter III: the "label-libel" gambit, the "rear-view mirror" syndrome, and the "story line" (pp. 25-29). Label-libel refers "to the human tendency to dismiss an idea by the expedience of naming it. ... If you know about it, you needn't think of it any further" (p. 25). The rearview mirror concept refers to the contention that "most of us are incapable of understanding the impact of new media because we are like drivers whose gaze is fixed not on where we are going but on where we came from" (p. 26). The story line metaphor comes into sharp relief through McLuhan's insistence that "the electric age has heightened our perception of structure by disrupting ... the *lineality* of information flow (emphasis added)" (p. 28), and the belief (and play on words) that we are not so "ABCED-minded as before, not so sequential and compartmentalized" (p. 28) as a people whose lives and thought were governed by the dictates of print.

Finally, the chapter on "New Languages: The Media" begins with what the authors pose as McLuhan's extension of the Sapir-Whorf hypothesis: "the view that language structures our perception of 'reality'" (p. 160). And it is here that the clearest connection is drawn between *Subversive Activity*'s two contributions to media ecology. That is, via McLuhan, Postman and Weingartner urge us to recognize that not only language but *all* media structure our perception of reality. As a result, and extending the contributions of *Linguistics* and *Language in America*, not only the study of language but *all* "media study becomes critical in the new education" (p. 160).

The Soft Revolution: A Student Handbook for Turning Schools Around

The Soft Revolution (Postman & Weingartner, 1971) is also a book about education, albeit it differs from *Subversive Activity* in two ways. First, it is directed to a readership of students rather than professional educators. Second, it is presented in a playful way, much like *The Medium is the Massage* (McLuhan & Fiore, 1967), which arguably influenced it. *The Soft Revolution* has no table of contents, no index, no bibliography. Its pages are replete with multiple type fonts, illustrations, reprinted cartoons, and brief, sometimes single page "chapter-ettes."

The title, *The Soft Revolution*, can be explained as follows. The book comes on the heels of *Subversive Activity*'s call for changes in the educational system in the United States that would subvert the ossified practices of the time and thus be considered downright "revolutionary." However, its target audience is students, and its release comes soon after the May 1970 riots and shootings at Kent State effectively ended the decade of student uprisings in support of the Civil Rights movement and against the Vietnam War. As a release meant to appeal to students during these tenuous times, then, the book is a call to incite, not a violent revolution against the educational system, but a "soft" one. A soft revolution is intended "to help all of us get it all together in the interests of our *mutual* survival" (Postman & Weingartner, 1971, p. 4). As the authors explain:

> The basic metaphor of a soft revolution is judo. As the term suggests, its primary use is in the defense of self against system. When you are using judo, you do not oppose the strength of your adversary. You use your adversary's strength against himself, and in spite of himself (in fact, *because* of himself). You do not need judo when your strength is greater than your adversary's. In that case you can, if you wish, smash him to bits. But that is clearly not the situation in relation to change in educa-

tion. The bureaucracies that govern educational institutions, while not as powerful as certain others in our society, still have the forces of precedent, law, academic prejudice, economic coercion, tradition, and inertia behind them. (p. 5)

The value of this book as a work within the canon of media ecology arises late on—in, oddly enough, a chapter entitled "Nader's Raiders" (pp. 138-146). After an introduction that credits Ralph Nader as "one of America's most effective soft revolutionaries" (p. 138) because of the way he uses the system of laws in the country to "call attention to the ways in which powerful corporate interests hustle consumers" (p. 138), Postman and Weingartner present a proposal for a university program that might "mobilize the talent and energy of graduate students to provide our nation's first line of defense against ignorance and charlatanism" (p. 139) in *all* areas of daily life. Their description of such a program then follows—taken from the actual prospectus for the PhD program in Media Ecology at New York University. It includes Postman's first use and definition of the term media ecology in one of his book-length works:

> Media ecology is the study of transactions among people, their messages, and their message systems. More particularly, media ecology studies how media of communication affect human perception, feeling, understanding, and value; and how our interaction with media facilitates or impedes our chances of survival. The word *ecology* implies the study of environments—their structure, content, and impact on people. An environment is, after all, a complex message system which regulates ways of feeling and behaving. It structures what we can see and say and, therefore, do. (p. 139)

The remainder of the chapter outlines the course of study for this program, focusing on four components: "Media History, Media Literacy and Creativity, Media Research, and Media Perspectives and Criticism" (p. 140). With respect to media history, the authors propose that students should "study the history of technology and communication, as well as 'inquire into' the future of both" (p. 140). The future is included as part of the continuum of history in the hope that students might make use of their historical knowledge—for instance, "to solve a particular problem dealing with the future" (p. 140). "Multi-media literacy" is a matter of understanding "the structure of various media" (p. 141). Media research is directed simply toward those areas of communication and media research that remain "uncharted." Here, McLuhan is cited—pointing out that until a few years prior, "one could not find a single paragraph written about the effects of the printed page on perception" (p. 143). Finally, "the most singular feature" of such a program is "continuous participation in media criticism" (p. 143).

The School Book: For People Who Want to Know What All the Hollering is About

Whereas *Teaching as a Subversive Activity* is addressed to educators, and *The Soft Revolution* is for students, *The School Book* (Postman & Weingartner, 1973b) is written for the benefit of the general citizenry. Together, these three books comprise a coherent trilogy about the school reform movement of the time in that they seek to reach out to *all* of the constituencies that would need to be involved in bringing about such reform.

Of all of Postman's books, *The School Book* is the one that, at face value, is least about the principles and purposes of media ecology. That is to say, media ecology is more implicit in this work than it is explicit and obvious. Nonetheless, the book fits the bill as a contribution to the development of media ecology in three respects.

The first of these is found in the chapter on "The Reading Problem." Here, the authors point out that what the education profession decries as the problem that students do not read is really a larger matter: that of the imminent decline of literate culture in the face of the electronic. As they write:

> Even if Marshall McLuhan did not exist, the electric plug would. And one need not be a media determinist, apostle, or anything else to point to the obvious fact that print has less importance in the conduct of our lives today than it has ever had. (p. 83)

The chapter goes on to make the case that is the basis for Postman's career-long argument on behalf of print literate culture—for all print has brought of value to the course of the human experience, for all it has allowed, and for all of the reasons we need it to maintain, if not improve the health of our collective existence. In this way, this chapter also marks the beginning of a shift in Postman's orientation. It is from here on that his "subversive" tendencies, very much a product of the tenor and tumult of the times—of 1960s culture—begin to shift toward an interest in "conserving"—conserving, that is, the hallmarks of print literacy in light of the electronic onslaught.

In "People," Postman and Weingartner list the names of "some seventy people who have made contributions to current thinking about schools" (p. 198) and provide a brief description of the contributions of each. This list is of obvious importance to media ecology in that it includes John Culkin and Marshall McLuhan. (The latter in fact receives the lengthiest biographical treatment.) However, it also includes a number of educational theorists (Adelbert Ames, John Dewey, Paulo Freire, Ivan Illich, Jonathan Kozol, Maria Montessori, and Henry Perkinson) and psychologists (Bruno Bettleheim, Jerome Bruner, Erik Erikson, R. D. Laing, Abraham Maslow,

Jean Piaget, Carl Rogers, and B. F. Skinner) who were not only participants in "the great school debate" (p. 198) but whose work can be said to be essential reading in media ecology.

Crazy Talk, Stupid Talk: How We Defeat Ourselves by the Way We Talk, and What to Do About It

Crazy Talk, Stupid Talk (Postman, 1976) marks a break from Postman's troika of books about the educational system with Charlie Weingartner and his return to his preoccupation with language and the general semantics approach. It also marks the coming to the forefront of his voice as a writer, his sense of humor, his ability as a storyteller, and his gift for the anecdote and example.

Like *Linguistics*, the book is infused with the principles of general semantics. But whereas *Linguistics* is a scholarly work targeted to English educators, *Crazy Talk, Stupid Talk* borrows a page from *The School Book*'s appeal to the general citizenry. That is, at the same time it is Postman's first solo book, it also becomes his first truly populist work. As a result, it sets the terms and tone for the remainder of what will become his unique contribution to media studies: the media ecologist as public intellectual. It might also be said that his impact comes to rival McLuhan's in this regard, as he becomes a clarifier and filter of many of McLuhan's ideas, bringing them to an even wider audience.

What are "crazy talk" and "stupid talk"? According to Postman, stupid talk is

> . . . talk that has (among other difficulties) a confused direction or an inappropriate tone or a vocabulary not well-suited to its context. It is talk, therefore, that does not and cannot achieve its purposes. To accuse people of stupid talk is to accuse them of using language ineffectively, of having made harmful but correctable mistakes in performance. It is a serious matter, but not usually dreadful. (p. xi)

Crazy talk is

> . . . almost always dreadful . . . crazy talk is talk that may be entirely effective but which has unreasonable or evil or, sometimes, overwhelmingly trivial purposes. It is talk that creates an irrational context for itself or sustains an irrational conception of human interaction. (pp. xi-xii)

In short, crazy talk "reflects 'bad' purposes"; stupid talk "defeats legitimate purposes" (p. 74). An example of stupid talk is answering the phatic greeting "Hi! How's it going?" with a laundry list of all that is wrong or right in one's life at the moment. An example of crazy talk comes from Paul Blobel who, in defending himself at Nuremberg against the charge that he was responsible for the massacre of 30,000 Jews and Russians at Babi Yar in the present-day Ukraine, explained that "Human life was not as valuable to them [i.e., the Russians and Jews] as to us. Our men who took part in these executions suffered more than those who had to be shot" (quoted on p. 78).

Part I of *Crazy Talk, Stupid Talk* takes an in-depth look at our semantic environment, a subject that received its initial treatment in *Language in America* (Postman, Weingartner, & Moran, 1969). The semantic environment is the context in which crazy talk and stupid talk take place, or which itself causes such talk. In Postman's words:

> The metaphor of a semantic environment . . . says that communication is not stuff or bits or messages. In a way, it is not even something that people do. Communication is a situation in which people participate, rather like the way a plant participates in what we call its growth. . . . If there is no sun or water, there is nothing much the plant can do about growing. And if there is no semantic environment, there is nothing much we can do about communicating. If communication is to happen, we require not merely messages, but an ordered situation in which messages can assume meaning. (pp. 8-9)

Following this conceptual orientation, Part I then offers an attempt to define the whole of our semantic environment according to (a) the purposes of our talk, (b) our relationships (the immediate and obvious context in which we talk), and (c) the content that is our talk. And although Postman cites Paul Watzlawick only once, on p. 218, with his concepts of "first order and second order thinking" from his book *Change* (Watzlawick, Weakland, & Fisch, 1974), *Crazy Talk, Stupid Talk* is undoubtedly influenced by Watzlawick's seminal work, *The Pragmatics of Human Communication* (Watzlawick, Beavin-Bavelas, & Jackson, 1967). The chapters on relationships and content as components of the semantic environment parallel Watzlawick et al.'s concepts of content and relationship "levels" of communication. Likewise, Watzlawick and his colleagues refer to the relationship level of communication as "context."

In Part II, Postman offers a classification and analysis of the various categories of crazy talk and stupid talk. In the chapter "The Communications Panacea," for example, he dissects as limited and even mistaken thinking the assumption that fully open, forthright communication is always what is needed, and the *only* thing needed when problems arise in our relationships. In "IFD Disease," inspired by Wendell Johnson's (1946) *People in Quandaries,* Postman explains how the way we talk to ourselves about ourselves and our lives in "ideal" terms can lead to "frustration" when things do not work out according to that talk, and that the result is often our "demoralization." The chapter on "Reification" addresses the often and easily overlooked fact that we confuse words with things. In Postman's (1976) words, this confusion is perhaps "our most seductive form of stupid and crazy talk, since its origins are deeply imbedded in the structure of language itself" (p. 135). Finally, in the chapter on "Eichmanism," Postman holds up Adolph Eichmann, administrator of the Nazi concentration camps, as the poster boy for the kind of crazy talk that results when "maintaining our role and status in a situation is apt to be more important to us than the overall purpose of the situation itself" (p. 179).

In summary, if the antidote to the symptoms and raging maladies of crazy talk and stupid talk is our recognition and comprehension of the semantic environment in which talk takes place, then this is what Postman is exhorting us to pay attention to and do: to better understand and use language through a heightened awareness of the context in which we use it—or, to paraphrase McLuhan, of how *context* is the message. This is what Postman (1976) refers to as "meta-semantics":

> Meta-semantics is the discipline through which we make our minds behave themselves. It is the best way to regulate and minimize the flow of our own stupid and crazy talk, and to make ourselves less accessible to the stupid and crazy talk of others.
>
> The fundamental strategy of meta-semantics is to put ourselves, psychologically, outside the context of any semantic environment so that we may see it in its entirety, or at least from multiple perspectives. From this position—or variety of positions—it is possible to assess the meaning and quality of talk in relation to the totality of the environment in which it occurs, and with a relatively high degree of detachment. We become less interested in participating in semantic environments, more interested in observing them. (pp. 236-237)

There remains, however, one final and essential point in the present discussion of this book. Toward the end of the book's final chapter, "Minding Your Meaning," Postman offers a passage that harkens back to the shift from the "subversive" to "conservative" that begins in *The School Book*. This passage segues into his next work and what I am arguing is also the next phase of his career. As he writes:

> You may have also gathered from what has gone on before that I place a high value on social order and its four pillars—empathy, tradition, responsibility, and civility. I realize that these words are extremely abstract and therefore not easy to define. I am using them here to suggest the socially conservative idea that there is something worth preserv-

ing in most semantic environments. What I have been calling "semantic environments" are, after all, situations shaped by long human experience, and their purposes and language are on no account to be taken lightly or to be revised precipitately. (pp. 250-251)

It is with this passage in mind that I move on to phase two of Postman's career, and his next book, *Teaching as a Conserving Activity*.

PHASE 2: THE RISE OF MEDIA ECOLOGY

The second phase of Postman's body of work is characterized by the three books that can be said to constitute the central works in his development of media ecology. The first of these books is not always recognized as such, in part because of its title: *Teaching as a Conserving Activity* (Postman, 1979). The second book is Postman's argument about the nature and notion of childhood in an age of electronic mass media: *The Disappearance of Childhood* (Postman, 1982). The third book is Postman's (1985) best-selling and most widely known work, *Amusing Ourselves to Death*.

Teaching as a Conserving Activity

Teaching as a Conserving Activity (Postman, 1979) is, despite its title, the media ecology primer. It is as much about media as it is about education and teaching. Eight of the book's 12 chapters after the introduction are wholly about media, media education, and/or media ecology. The remaining four chapters include considerations of media as part of their argument.

The book begins with Postman decrying "the beginning of the end of the education reform movement" (p. 4) and explaining what happened—wherein despite all the good intentions, inspired movers and shakers, progressive and provocative ideas, and herculean efforts, no change was ever really realized. And it closes with the elegantly stated declaration that: "In the end education is an act of faith in the power of ideas to have consequences unforeseen and immeasurable" (p. 230). In between, Postman acknowledges that his arguments are a reconsideration of his perspective in *Teaching as a Subversive Activity*—perhaps because he has changed, perhaps because things have changed, perhaps because he has always recognized the value of the other side of an argument, or all of the above. He also writes his first book that is expressly about media education.

In "The Thermostatic View," Postman revisits the term *ecology*, as he begins to construct his argument about media ecology. In his view

. . . ecology is not essentially about DDT, caterpillars, and the effect on muskrats of diverting a stream. Ecology is about the rate and scale and structure of change within an environment. It is about how balance is achieved, a balanced mind and society as well as a balanced forest. It is, therefore, as much about social institutions, bulldozers, freeways, artifacts, and ideas as it is about natural processes, trees, rivers, and the survival of herons. As a matter of fact, the Greek word from which "ecology" is derived does not direct our attention to the natural environment at all. We first come across it meaning house or household, and Aristotle's use of the word is in political terms: The stability of one's household is weakened as the state increasingly intervenes in social affairs. (pp. 17-18)

He then goes on to cite Norbert Wiener's (1950) principles of cybernetics, and make the balance-oriented argument that: *"Education is best conceived of as a thermostatic activity"* (Postman, 1979, p. 19). It is Wiener who provides the metaphor of the thermostat:

Cybernetics . . . is the science of control and equilibrium, the study of "feedback," which . . . calls our attention to the means by which we maintain balance in a system. To Norbert Wiener, who invented the science of feedback, the clearest example of cybernetics-in-action—that is, the principle of oppositional complementarity—is a thermostat, a mechanism for triggering opposing forces. (p. 19)

Postman's application of this metaphor to education then offers an explanation for his shift in ideology—a shift toward education as a matter of preserving or *conserving* those things that a culture might otherwise leave behind:

From this point of view . . . education tries to conserve tradition when the rest of the environment is innovative. Or it is innovative when the rest of the society is tradition-bound. It is a matter of indifference whether the society be volatile or static. The function of education is always to offer the counterargument, the other side of the picture. The thermostatic view of education is, then, not ideology-centered. It is balance-centered. (pp. 19-20)

"The Thermostatic View" thus presents a philosophy of education that has, as its central concern, a balance within the culture/society it is intended to serve. Such balance requires us to question and counter the prevailing tendencies of the culture/society at the time. As a result, the primary purpose of education becomes a matter of rescuing and maintaining what is lost to these tendencies; what is ignored, invisible, or left behind. And to Postman, this purpose is as an "either–or" proposition: education must be a conservative response to forward-looking times or vice-versa.

It is clear that this line of thinking is rooted in his experience and disillusionment with the forward-looking education reform movement, which was itself influenced by the social revolution of the 1960s. At the same time, however, it gradually becomes clear that he is building a case that is not just about education, but about media and education. For the question the reader is left with at the end of "The Thermostatic View" is: What *is it* that needs to be balanced in our culture/society? Or as Postman articulates it: "What specific cultural biases, if left unchecked, will leave our youth with incompetent intellects and distorted personalities?" (p. 25).

The answer to this question is the biases of "The Information Environment," which is the title of the ensuing chapter. As Postman writes, "it is always necessary to provide a balance to the information biases of a culture" (p. 46) and "it is the main business of education to know what these biases are and to know what to balance them with" (p. 46). But the basis for *this* argument adds yet a third balance theory to the notions of ecological balance and a balance between conservation and innovation. Although Harold Innis (1951) and his book *The Bias of Communication* are cited only toward the end of the chapter (p. 45), Postman's argument is grounded in and building toward Innis' warning (albeit short of the same overtone of impending doom): that the seeds of destruction of a civilization or culture are to be found in the tipping of the scales of that civilization/culture's media bias to the point at which equilibrium is irrevocably disturbed.

It is with this addition of Innis, and the intersection of these three balance-centered theories, that Postman finally and fully arrives at the idea that is central to both his theory of education and his theory of media, and by which he constructs the conceptual bridge that connects the two. This is the idea of the ecology of, or balance in our mediated environment. And we find in *Teaching as a Conserving Activity* yet another definition of media ecology:

> Media ecology is the study of information environments. It is concerned to understand how technologies and techniques of communication control the form, quantity, speed, distribution, and direction of information; and how, in turn, such information configurations or biases affect people's perceptions, values, and attitudes. (p. 186)

It must be emphasized, however, that there are *two* components to this media ecology, this endeavor to find balance. The first is a need to understand media, and especially the biases of the primary medium of a culture and its age. To this end, Postman presents the four-part schema for analysis from the passage cited above: that an understanding of media requires attention to (a) the form of information a specific medium provides; (b) the quantity and/or magnitude of this information; (c) the speed at which the information travels; and (d) the extent to which the information can be accessed, and by whom. He then concentrates, in the chapter "The First Curriculum," on the medium that is "surely the single most powerful new element in our new information environment, television" (p. 47).

As Postman explains, television is the *first* curriculum because it teaches children about their world and things in it before they enter into the institution that is formal, public education. As he argues in the chapter "The Technical Thesis," and with support from Mumford (1934) and Ellul (1964):

> We have a generation being raised in an information environment that, on one hand, stresses visual imagery, discontinuity, immediacy, and alogicality. It is antihistorical, antiscientific, anticonceptual, antirational. On the other hand, the context within which this occurs is a kind of religious or philosophic bias toward the supreme authority of technicalization. What this means is that as we lose confidence and competence in our ability to think and judge, we willingly transfer these functions to machines. Whereas our machinery was once thought of as an "extension of man," man now becomes an "extension of machinery." (Postman, 1979, p. 100)

The second component of Postman's media ecology is one he intimates at the end of the chapter "The Thermostatic View." For his media ecology—for this culture and this age—requires that we take a look back: to language education and the culture of print.

The Disappearance of Childhood

The Disappearance of Childhood is Postman's (1982) first book that is not expressly about education. Instead it is an application of his theory of media ecology to the life's world surrounding education; to the culture in general. It is about the idea that our information or media environment not only influences culture, but creates and *is* culture. More specifically, the book is about two ideas. The first idea is that the stage in life we recognize and refer to as childhood is a product of typographic culture. Childhood began because print created a line of demarcation that kept children away from information that could then only be accessed by literate adults. The second idea is that our electronic media, and especially television, have erased this line once again—and along with it the modern notion and experience of childhood.

Accordingly, the book is divided into two parts. The first part makes the argument for the "appearance" of childhood and the roots of this appearance in the invention and diffusion of typography. The second part makes the argument that childhood is disappearing because of the availability, accessibility, and impact of electronic media. Clearly, the first of these arguments is the more audacious one, as it implies that childhood is the byproduct of a technologically deterministic cause. Thus, it is this half of the book that requires greater attention and scrutiny here, to summarize and adequately explain its carefully reasoned argument.

In Chapter 1, "When Their Were No Children," Postman traces the idea of childhood as we understand it across the history of Greek and Roman culture and the Middle Ages. As he points out, the Greeks "paid scant attention to childhood as a special age category" (p. 5); that their "words for *child* and *youth* are, at the very least, ambiguous, and seem to include almost anyone between infancy and old age" (p. 6). He adds that among surviving Greek statuary "none is of a child" (p. 6). Finally, he makes the argument that

> the Greek preoccupation with school must not be taken to mean that their conception of childhood parallels our own. Even if we exclude the Spartans, whose methods of discipline, for example, would be regarded by the modern mind as torture, the Greeks did not approach the disciplining of the young with the same measure of empathy and understanding considered normal by moderns. (pp. 7-8)

The Romans, Postman goes on to note, "borrowed the Greek notion of schooling and even developed an awareness of childhood that surpassed the Greek idea" (p. 8). Principal among their advances was the connection between childhood and the concept of shame. As he writes in italics: "*without a well-developed idea of shame, childhood cannot exist*" (p. 9). And although the Romans did not necessarily practice the rearing of their children with a mind to this connection, Postman argues that it becomes the basis for the dividing line that creates the concept of modern childhood: "the need to be sheltered from adult secrets, particularly sexual secrets" (p. 9).

With respect to childhood during medieval times, Postman sums up the consequence of this historical period with the following passage:

> Every educated person knows about the invasions of the northern barbarians, the collapse of the Roman empire, the shrouding of classical culture, and Europe's descent into what is called the Dark and then Middle Ages. Our textbooks cover the transformation well enough except for four points that are often overlooked and that are particularly relevant to the story of childhood. The first is that literacy disappears. The second is that education disappears. The third is that shame disap-

pears. And the fourth, as a consequence of the other three, is that childhood disappears. (p. 10)

From this point, Postman makes the following case in "The Printing
Press and the New Adult" and "The Incunabula of Childhood": If childhood must obviously be understood in relation to adulthood, and if the
adult world changed drastically with the invention of the movable-type
printing press, the eventual spread of literacy, and the cultural revolution of
print literacy, then clearly the idea of childhood must have changed with this
historical moment also. It is here that Postman is greatly influenced by his
reading of fellow media ecologist Elizabeth Eisenstein's *The Printing Press
as an Agent of Change* (1979); a book that predates his by only 5 years. He
also, however, brings Innis, Mumford, and Lynn White, Jr. (1962) into the
argument.

In "The Incunabula of Childhood," Postman (1982) deftly invokes the
etymology of the term "incunabula" and uses it as a metaphor. He notes that
the literal translation of the term is "the cradle period." And he writes that
by the time print moved out of its incunabula, its cradle, "the idea of childhood had moved in" (p. 37). That is, by the end of the 16th and 17th centuries, "childhood was acknowledged to *exist*, to be a feature of the natural
order of things" (p. 37). Children were separated at this time as a class of
people "because it became essential in their culture that they learn how to
read and write, and how to be the sort of people a print culture required"
(pp. 37-38).

With all of this as a foundation, Postman then turns to the argument that
is the real purpose of his book: his concern about contemporary electronic
media culture and its implications for the existence of childhood as a necessary stage in modern life. Childhood is necessary because it continues the
ongoing cultural pattern wherein each generation is brought up to take its
place in an adult world, the purpose of which is to improve on the civilized
legacy and civilizing benefits of print literate culture, and wherein each generation becomes itself responsible for the succeeding generation. In
Postman's words, however

> television erodes the dividing line between childhood and adulthood in
> three ways, all having to do with its undifferentiated accessibility: first,
> because it requires no instruction to grasp its form; second, because it
> does not make complex demands on either mind or behavior; and third,
> because it does not segregate its audience. With the assistance of other
> electric, nonprint media, television recreates the conditions of commu-
> nication that existed in the fourteenth and fifteenth centuries.
> Biologically we are all equipped to see and interpret images and to hear
> such language as may be necessary to provide a context for most of these
> images. The new media environment that is emerging provides every-

> one, simultaneously, with the same information. Given the conditions I have described, electric media find it impossible to withhold any secrets. Without secrets there can, of course, be no such thing as childhood. (p. 80)

As he writes in conclusion: "It is not conceivable that our culture will forget that it needs children. But it is halfway toward forgetting that children need childhood. Those who insist on remembering shall perform a noble service" (p. 153). Thus, it might be said that *The Disappearance of Childhood is* a book about education after all. It is so because it is about what we need to know to instill in our children an understanding and appreciation of our culture, how to live productively and successfully in it, and how to ensure its continuity into the future.

Amusing Ourselves to Death: Public Discourse in the Age of Show Business

Like *The Disappearance of Childhood, Amusing Ourselves to Death* (Postman, 1985) expressly addresses one of the salient consequences of our contemporary media environment. It is about the impact of television on the discourse by which our culture maintains itself and by which we try to move it, in positive ways, into the future. In short, the book is about how all serious discourse, when filtered through television, becomes bound up in television's need to attract and hold our attention; to entertain, divert, and amuse us. And it is equally about the consequences of this fact.

Amusing Ourselves to Death also represents the pinnacle of Postman's career as a public intellectual. It became a best-selling book not only in the United States, but in countries around the world—especially western Europe. The primary reason for its popularity in western Europe is that it came to print at exactly that moment when a number of European countries were in the throes of redeveloping parts of their television systems toward the commercial U.S. model. Many cultural and political leaders and intellectuals were understandably concerned about the implications of this transition for the continuance—if not the very existence—of their individual cultures, as well as for informed political life in their countries. Postman spoke directly to their concerns.

Amusing Ourselves to Death is also the book that influenced Roger Waters—former lead singer, bass guitarist, and principal songwriter for the rock group Pink Floyd—to scrap the record he was working on, and with which he had become disenchanted, and return to the studio with a new set of ideas and inspiration. This inspiration came after he read Postman's book on a transatlantic flight. The album would eventually become his 1992 release, *Amused to Death*.

Like its predecessor, *Amusing Ourselves to Death* is divided into two parts. The first part lays out the media ecological foundations for Postman's argument that our contemporary media environment, epitomized by the medium of television, is one in which the crowning achievement of print culture—serious civic, political, and social discourse—is becoming debased and diminished. For Postman, this state of affairs is more the result of the nature and characteristics of the medium of television than it is about the ways we have adopted and adapted the medium as a profit-driven business. For Postman, television evolved into what it has become simply because we eventually and inevitably learned to make the best use of what it is for; what it is best at providing. The second half of the book then considers those arenas of public discourse that have been impacted by television's place at the forefront of our media culture, and how these have been impacted. This includes the reducing of all television fare to entertainment, the discontinuity and fragmentation of television's content, the "humiliation" (to use Ellul's [1985] word) of religion and politics on television, and the Faustian bargain of educational children's television.

The book begins, famously, with Postman's juxtaposition of the two "dystopian" prophecies that arose out of 20th century literature—Aldous Huxley's (1932) *Brave New World* and George Orwell's (1949) *1984*. Postman poses the question (in his foreword, which he wrote in 1985) whether it is the Huxleyian nightmare that has actually come true. For we never came to be controlled by the totalitarian, all-seeing and knowing oppressive force of Orwell's imagination. Instead, as Postman offers and Huxley warned, we have come to welcome and willingly accept that which oppresses us. We find ourselves lulled into a kind of somnambulant state wherein we are so consumed with the pursuit of our pleasure that we pay little mind to the ways in which, and the fact that we are controlled. We become ultimately responsible for our own control. And it is not the Orwellian big brother always watching us, but the loyal, lovable family member *we watch*—the television—that becomes the primary means by which we fall victim to this control. As the primary medium and cultural force of our time, television most powerfully communicates our culture—it most powerfully *is* our culture—at the same time it reduces all it touches to mere amusement. As a result, our cultural life's world amounts to little more than amusement also.

It is Part II of the book, with its examples and anecdotes, that is arguably the more accessible read for the trade audience that read it. But it is Part I that provides the added value for media ecologists. The first two chapters in Part I do not so much extend Postman's media ecology as clarify it. In "The Medium is the Metaphor," an obvious enough extension of McLuhan's adage "the medium is the message," Postman makes the case that all media are metaphors in that their biases—and our expression of bias when we favor or privilege one over all others—tell us about ourselves and our age. In "Media as Epistemology," he elaborates on this idea to examine how the primary medium of any culture becomes the primary factor in determining what people will know, what they are interested to know, and what they *can* know. In Chapters 3 and 4, "Typographic America" and "The Typographic Mind," Postman again looks back to print as a metaphor and explains its epistemology. These two chapters then provide the base for the final chapter in Part I, "The Peek-a-Boo World." Here, Postman makes his case for television as a metaphor, and for its epistemology, at the same time that he makes his transition into the rest of the book. As he writes, invoking the whole of the electronic revolution

> . . . this ensemble of electronic techniques called into being a new world—a peek-a-boo world, where now this event, now that, pops into view for a moment, then vanishes again. It is a world without much coherence or sense; a world that does not ask us, indeed, does not permit us to do anything; a world that is, like a child's game of peek-a-boo, entirely self-contained. But like peek-a-boo, it is also end-lessly entertaining.
>
> Of course, there is nothing wrong with playing peek-a-boo. And there is nothing wrong with entertainment. As some psychiatrist once put it, we all build castles in the air. The problems come when we try to *live* in them. The communications media of the late nineteenth and early twentieth centuries, with telegraphy and photography at their center, called the peek-a-boo world into existence, but we did not come to live there until television. Television gave the epistemological biases of the telegraph and the photograph their most potent expression, raising the interplay of image and instancy to an exquisite and dangerous perfec-tion. And it brought them into the home. (pp. 77-78)

In sum, television becomes "the command center of the new epistemol-ogy" (p. 78). There is no subject, from any realm of contemporary life, that escapes the medium's reach and grasp, and once grasped, that is not shaped by it. Even if this shaping means minimizing or debasing entire subjects and their importance. Consequently, a citizenry that looks to television for most, if not all of its serious public discourse, finds itself more consumer than cit-izen, more amused than interested and enlightened, and more lulled than stirred to action.

PHASE 3: TRANSITION, AND THEN TECHNOPOLY

The third phase of Postman's writing begins with *Conscientious Objections* (Postman, 1988) and *How to Watch TV News* (Postman & Powers, 1992).

However, it culminates with the book *Technopoly: The Surrender of Culture to Technology* (Postman, 1992).

Conscientious Objections: Stirring up Trouble about Language, Technology, and Education

Conscientious Objections (Postman, 1988) was originally published in the attempt to capitalize on the widespread success of *Amusing Ourselves to Death*. It appears in print only three years after the publication of its predecessor, while that book's impact is still being felt and debated, and while Postman's star is still shining brightly, particularly in western Europe.

The book is a collection of 18 essays. Of these, eight are reprintings from previous publications. Four are identified as speeches. Two are acknowledged as summaries of his two previous books, *The Disappearance of Childhood* and *Amusing Ourselves to Death*. In explaining and justifying a coherence among these selections, Postman writes, in his preface, that there is "a theme to these essays, or, to be exact, three themes that make a single whole," and that together "have formed the core of my academic interests for thirty years" (p. xii).

The first of these themes is his objection to the "triumphs of one-eyed technology" (p. xiii). By "one-eyed," he means technology that cannot "see" context, history, or consequence, but only "what is directly in front of it" (p. xiii). More important than this explanation, however, is the fact that this introduction of the book's first theme (and presumably it is first for a reason) represents a shift in terminology, and perhaps fixation, from the specific "medium" to the more McLuhanesque "technology." In his own words, Postman continues to be preoccupied with "where we are being taken, and in whose interests, by the unfettered development of technology" (p. xiii).

The second theme, borrowing once again from Ellul (1985), is the "humiliation of the word" (Postman, 1988, p. xiii). And the third theme is education—"a subject never far from the issues raised by technology and language" (p. xv). The essay on "Defending Against the Indefensible," for example, looks back to Postman's writing about language and education—and, strangely enough at this point in his career, to the subversive leanings of *Teaching as a Subversive Activity*. As he notes, the title "derives from a phrase in George Orwell's famous essay 'Politics and the English Language',", where he "speaks of the dangerously degraded condition of modern political thought, and proceeds to characterize its language as mainly committed to 'defending the indefensible'" (p. 20). Postman borrows on this idea to argue that we need to teach our young to develop defenses against such language and its consequences, and free themselves, in the words of Cicero, from "the tyranny of the present" (p. 22).

With respect to the essays that extend Postman's work, "Social Science as Moral Theology" is the most important essay in this book. It is the essay that opens the book, and a work that Postman once remarked in a doctoral seminar is "the best it gets" with respect to his writing. In this essay, he argues that the social sciences are not science, that they should not be confused with science, and that they should not be held up to the same criteria as the natural and physical sciences in an attempt to justify and accord respect to the learning and knowledge they produce. To use his word, they are more correctly and appropriately a matter of "storytelling." As he writes about people who practice social science—himself included:

> I call the work these people do storytelling because this suggests that an author has given a unique interpretation to a set of human events, that he has supported his interpretation with examples in various forms, and that his interpretation cannot be proved or disproved but draws its appeal from the power of its language, the depth of its explanations, the relevance of its examples, and the credibility of its theme. And that all of this has an identifiable moral purpose. The words "true" and "false" do not apply here in the sense that they are used in mathematics or science. For there is nothing universally or irrevocably true or false about these interpretations. There are no critical tests to confirm or falsify them. There are no postulates in which they are imbedded. They are bound by time, by situation, and above all by the cultural prejudices of the researcher. Quite like a piece of fiction. (p. 13)

According to this argument, it does not matter whether one's form of support in his or her research is the statistical treatment of quantified data or a carefully reasoned argument. These are simply the forms by which we choose to tell our stories and provide value and resonance for those who would choose to read and use them. In Postman's words, then, the true purpose of so-called social scientists, as "our culture's most important tellers of psychological and social tales" (p. 16), is to serve as "creators and narrators of social myth" (p. 17) whose intent, first and foremost, is not to "contribute to our field, but to contribute to human understanding and decency" (p. 17). For the media ecologist, specifically, the purpose is "to tell stories about the consequences of technology; to tell how media environments create contexts that may change the way we think or organize our social life, or make us better or worse, or smarter or dumber, or freer or more enslaved" (p. 18).

Finally, the essay entitled "The News" takes on television news with the understanding that news, in principle, is the most important information people can seek out about the society in which they live, and that its function is to help them live their lives as contributing citizens. In this respect, the essay not only looks all the way back to a series of chapters on news from Postman's "New English" textbook, *Language and Reality* (Postman, 1966b). It also looks forward to his next book.

How to Watch TV News

How to Watch TV News (Postman & Powers, 1992) is co-authored with Steve Powers, a long-time radio and television news reporter and personality in the local New York market and one of Postman's former PhD students. It is also Postman's only true "trade" book—a book marketed to a general readership.[6] The book purposefully pairs an academic, known primarily at the time for his media criticism, with a professional television and radio newsman, in order to balance the suspected bias of each, to offer the reader the strengths and knowledge of each, and to target the book's basic argument to the widest possible readership (not to mention anyone and everyone who might benefit from it).

The basic argument, however, stems from the fact that both authors are, from their respective sides of the professional fence, in agreement about the nature and consequence of television news. As they write in the book's preface: "We came to the conclusion some years ago that what television news says it is presenting and what it actually delivers are two different things" (p. x). As a result, their book is about two things. First, it presents an explanation of what television news actually *is* delivering versus what those who produce and present it purport to be delivering. Second, it provides viewers with a series of lessons intended to help them recognize and use television news for what it is *and* what it is not.

In "Are You Watching Television or Is Television Watching You?" for example, Postman and Powers make the point that although viewers typically regard television as an appliance that exists to provide *them* with information and entertainment, it is, as an industry, a tool by which advertisers are provided with entry into the privacy of our homes, so that *they* can gain access to the attentions of potential customers. The chapter on "What Is News?" does not so much answer the question as pose the importance of asking it, and expose the problems that result from trying to answer it; from trying to define what news is and should be. Chapter 3, "Getting Them into the Electronic Tent," introduces the means by which news professionals entice viewers to tune into *their* news—since, if the news of the day is pretty much the same no matter who reports it or how, the reasons to choose one network or station's news program over another's must be manufactured. Chapters 4–6, take a look "behind the scenes" at the workings of a news department, the people who make the news, the jobs these people do, the constraints, pressures, and motivations they face, and the relationship of the news endeavor to the larger corporate structure within which it exists. Media ecology rears its head in an obvious way in Chapter 8, entitled "The

Bias of Language, the Bias of Pictures." Here, the point is made that television news—like news delivered via any medium/mass medium—presents a *mediated* reality. As Postman and Powers write: "All news shows, in a sense, are re-creations in that what we hear and see on them are attempts to represent actual events, and are not the events themselves" (p. 97). The chapter goes on to explain the ways in which this bias manifests but also hides itself. Finally, the chapter "What Can You Do?" offers a list of eight recommendations by which people might make the most of their news viewing.

In the end, *How to Watch TV News* stands, like *Conscientious Objections*, as a follow up to *Amusing Ourselves to Death*. However, this is true not only to the extent that the book presents another critical treatise about television's impact on contemporary life. The primary argument in *Amusing Ourselves to Death* is that television is at its best when it serves to entertain. But *How to Watch TV News* is for those who do not heed this lesson. If upwards of 75% of people in the United States use television as their primary, if not their only source of news, then the purpose of this book is to provide such people—who continue to look to television for that for which it is least or worst suited—at least *some* means to negotiate the medium, and this particular component of its messages, to a successful and healthy ends. In this sense, it, too, is a book about media education.

Technopoly: The Surrender of Culture to Technology

The argument in *Technopoly* (Postman, 1992) is an elegant one, much like the argument in *The Disappearance of Childhood*. It is simply this: As human civilization has developed, we have evolved through three distinct cultural stages. The first of these is a culture of tool-making. The second is a *technocratic* culture. And the third stage—the one we are presently living through—is *technopoly*. In this book, Postman seeks to make clear exactly what it is that defines the second and third stages, what the difference is between them, and why we need to know these things—that is to say, what are the consequences of the fact of life in a technopolistic world.

What is equally important about this book, however, is that it brings to fruition and to the forefront Postman's preoccupation with technology. To the extent that Postman has always been a McLuhanite, he finds some merit in McLuhan's equating of the concepts of medium and technology.[7] Both are "extensions of man" that we interpose between ourselves and our environment in order that we might extend our potential, if not our ability to manipulate, affect, and transcend limits—both our own limits as humans and those forced on us by our environment. This focus dates back to the chapter "The Technical Thesis" from *Teaching as a Conserving Activity*. It is acknowledged first among the themes that cut across the essays in *Conscientious Objections*. But as Postman wrote in his preface to *Conscientious Objections*, it has *always* been an implicit, running theme across his entire body of work. For although he starts out as a student of the English language, his approach has always been to place language into its context as a medium of human communication, and as a technological innovation. This inevitably led him to a focus on our electronic technologies of mass communication, and to place these into the context that is the history of all forms of human communication. And it led him to look to scholars like McLuhan, Mumford, and Ellul, who extend and expand this context to the history, purpose, and consequence of all human invention.

The three stages outlined in *Technopoly* begin with our roots as simple tool-makers, seeking to solve our immediate problems and to exert some control over our world. As Postman writes about such cultures (and some do still exist, although they are no doubt disappearing from the face of the earth)

> the main characteristics of all tool-using cultures is that their tools were largely invented to do two things: to solve specific and urgent problems of physical life, such as in the use of waterpower, windmills, and the heavy-wheeled plow; or to serve the symbolic world of art, politics, myth, ritual, and religion, as in the construction of castles and cathedrals and the development of the mechanical clock. In either case, tools did not attack (or, more precisely, were not intended to attack) the dignity and integrity of the culture into which they were introduced. With some exceptions, tools did not prevent people from believing in their traditions, in their God, in their politics, in their methods of education, or in the legitimacy of their social organization. These beliefs, in fact, *directed* the invention of tools and limited the uses to which they were put. (p. 23)

Technocracy, on the other hand, comes about not only as we become makers of advanced and intricate tools and technologies, but as these tools and technologies lead to radical changes in both the natural order of things and in our human species. In Postman's words, in a technocracy: "Tools are not integrated into the culture. . . . They bid to *become* the culture" (p. 28). He then proposes that it is three inventions that arose out of Europe during medieval times that are primarily responsible for bringing about the technocratic age in the West: the mechanical clock, the printing press with movable type, and the telescope. The mechanical clock is responsible as a result of the fact that it atomized time and regimented daily life (a point he derives from Mumford's [1934] book, *Technics and Civilization*). The printing press is responsible because of the vast and powerful changes it engendered in wresting existing knowledge from the Church, in ushering the laity out of the

Dark Ages, and in altering the epistemology of the times. It is the telescope, however, that Postman most emphasizes as an agent of change, in that it destroyed the belief "that the earth was the stable center of the universe, and therefore that humankind was of special interest to God" (p. 29).

Technopoly is the inevitable end game of this trajectory, this collision course between our humanity as we were granted it and humanity as we have made it. Technopoly is technocracy run amok; it is "totalitarian technocracy" (p. 48). Postman explains it as a life's world that has "as its aim a grand reductionism in which human life must find its meaning in machinery and technique" and in which the result is "the submission of all forms of cultural life to the sovereignty of technique and technology" (p. 52). He goes on to suggest that we find this mindset best expressed in "Taylorism"—the principles of scientific management, from the book of the same name by Frederick Taylor (1947). Taylorism offers

> the first explicit and formal outline of the assumptions of the thought-world of Technopoly. These include the beliefs that the primary, if not the only, goal of human labor and thought is efficiency; that technical calculation is in all respects superior to human judgment; that in fact human judgment cannot be trusted because it is plagued by laxity, ambiguity, and unnecessary complexity; that subjectivity is an obstacle to clear thinking; that what cannot be measured either does not exist or is of no value; and that the affairs of citizens are best guided and conducted by experts. (p. 51)

In short, however, it is Ellul's (1964) concept of *la technique* that is the obvious basis for this vision of humanity in the grips of its own inventions and the extremes to which we have come. Ellul urged us to discern the ways in which the machines we invented in our attempt to exert control over our world have equally come to control us, how embedded in every machine is at least one idea that is distinct from the use for which that machine is intended, and how the human drive to make and use machines and to pursue technological progress is a governing world view—with implications like any other world view.

In summary, given that the present essay has already made the case for the development of Postman's argument for media as culture, the obvious now comes into sharp relief. Following McLuhan's conflating of media and technology, the case for technology is likewise: Technology becomes—it *is* our culture. The culture encompassed within the term *la technique* is one in which, because of our overreliance on and quasi-religious worship of machines, we come to be governed by them, and, as a result, become machine-like ourselves. And both Postman and Ellul take it as their mission to warn us against *this* particular tyranny of the present: the tyranny of our machines.

PHASE 4: A RETURN TO EDUCATION

If the third phase of Postman's career centers on this treatise about technology that is *Technopoly*, and is otherwise made up of books that seem to fit into his *oeurve* only as projects that follow up on the success of *Amusing Ourselves to Death*, the fourth phase of his career presents not only a return to coherence, but a return to his roots as an educationist. The two books in this phase are *The End of Education* (1995) and *Building a Bridge to the 18th Century* (Postman, 1999).

The End of Education: Redefining the Value of School

The title of *The End of Education* (Postman, 1996) is clearly an echo of its time. Postman has always disavowed any connection to or interest in the tenets of postmodernism—notwithstanding the great service Strate (1994) provides to the literature on Postman's contributions when he frames his "perspective on media and technology . . . as a theory of the postmodern" (p. 160). Nonetheless, the title is no doubt influenced by the spate of literature from the last years of the 20th century that addresses one of the outcomes of the postmodern condition and postmodern theory: the idea that we may well have come to an "end" of sorts with regard to the pursuit of truth, the evolution of theory and philosophy, the possibilities of art, and so on (see, e. g., Fukuyama, 1993).

The fact is that Postman does not believe, nor does he argue in this book that we have reached a dead end with respect to education in the United States. As a skeptic rather than a cynic, he still has hope. What he offers is a double-edged point: the play on words presented by the use of the word "end" in the title (and which he acknowledges, in his preface, is a deliberate *double entendre*). That is, on the one hand we are faced with the end of education to the extent that we have lost our sense of the basic purposes of education; of what it is for. On the other hand, this loss opens the door for us to reassess and reintroduce what these "ends" of education really are, or what they should be. As such, *The End of Education* reflects Postman's return to his role as critic of the shortcomings and failures of the educational system in this country, with the purpose (and hope) that his "conscientious objections" and ideas might actually be read and heeded, and even lead to correction and improvement.

The basic thesis of the book is that education in the United States has failed our youth because it does not offer them any inspiring, overarching narrative by which they might make sense of and find meaning in their lives. In short, it provides them with nothing to believe in. In the opening chapter, "The Necessity of Gods," Postman quotes Nietzsche's aphorism: "He who has a *why* to live can bear with almost any *how*" (p. 4). But the crux of the matter is that this search for a *why* in contemporary life—or the vague, empty yearning that results from a lack of such purpose—remains unaddressed by the system of public education in this country, much less by any other realm of contemporary life. Religion is often viewed by the young as a quaint aspect of a culture or cultures whose time is past. In many ways, family and family values have broken down. And although television, entertainment in general, and rampant materialism have transfixed young people and fill this vacuum to an extent, it becomes achingly clear that these diversions amount to little more than a vain attempt to fill the existential hole in their lives.

The question of why it should be left to schools to provide this missing and sorely needed narrative is answered early on in the book. It is not that schools are the *only* wellspring out of which such a narrative might arise. But echoing the poet Emma Lazarus, the fact of the matter is that schools are our means

> to fashion Americans out of the wretched refuse of teeming shores. Schools are to provide the lost and lonely with a common attachment to America's history and future, to America's sacred symbols, to its promise of freedom. The schools are, in a word, the affirmative answer to the question, Can a coherent, stable, unified culture be created out of people of diverse traditions, languages, and religions? (p. 14)

However, the expectation that education should provide this missing narrative is not the entire point. Equally important is the failures of those narratives that education *does* provide. This includes the narrative that education is a means to the end that is growing up and making a living—that education is only necessary in that it is a prerequisite to getting a good, and good paying job. It includes multiculturalism, which Postman sees as the "exclusive preoccupation" with cultural diversity (p. 50), and which he fears is bringing about a reversion to tribalism and ethnic separation. And it includes the idea that training in technology, especially computers, is a paramount responsibility of the educational system—not only because of the ways in which computers and computer networks are assumed to benefit the learning process, but because computers are the key to the economy and jobs of the future, and because no one should be left behind on the proverbial "information superhighway."

It is on this last note that *The End of Education* makes its most salient contribution to media ecology, and also continues the line of argument offered in *Technopoly*. At the end of Chapter 9, "The Word Weavers/The World Makers," Postman presents a list of ten principles, which, he implores us, should be the response to, or at least be included in the story of technology in our schools. They summarize a substantial extent of the framework for media ecology, and much of what has been said here so far:

1. All technological change is a Faustian bargain. For every advantage a new technology offers, there is always a corresponding disadvantage.

2. The advantages and disadvantages of new technologies are never distributed evenly among the population. This means that every new technology benefits some and harms others.

3. Embedded in every technology there is a powerful idea, sometimes two or three powerful ideas. Like language itself, a technology predisposes us to favor and value certain perspectives and accomplishments and to subordinate others. Every technology has a philosophy, which is given expression in how the technology makes people use their minds, in what it makes us do with our bodies, in how it codifies the world, in which of our senses it amplifies, in which of our emotional and intellectual tendencies it disregards.

4. A new technology usually makes war against an old technology. It competes with it for time, attention, money, prestige, and a "worldview."

5. Technological change is not additive; it is ecological. A new technology does not merely add something; it changes everything.

6. Because of the symbolic forms in which information is encoded, different technologies have different *intellectual* and *emotional* biases.

7. Because of the accessibility and speed of their information, different technologies have different *political* biases.

8. Because of their physical form, different technologies have different *sensory* biases.

9. Because of the conditions in which we attend to them, different technologies have different *social* biases

10. Because of their technical and economic structure, different technologies have different *content* biases. (pp. 192-193)

Building a Bridge to the 18th Century: How the Past Can Improve Our Future

The final sentence of the blurb on the inside cover of this book states that it is Postman's most "radical" book yet. Yet this presents a seeming contradiction: How can a book that looks back to the Age of the Enlightenment — the crowning intellectual achievement of a print age and culture—and which seeks to rescue, and preserve or conserve the ideas of that time, be seen as *radical*?

There are two answers to this question. The first is that in an age in which we bow down to the god of progress—and especially to progress through technology, where the mantra is that educational technology will enhance and empower learning and knowledge in ways greater than education has ever been able to achieve so far—any sustained attempt to look backward instead of forward is so out of line with the accepted perspective of the culture-at-large as to be considered downright radical. The second answer is that with this book, Postman achieves a resolution of the career-long tension epitomized in the titles *Teaching as a Subversive Activity* and *Teaching as a Conserving Activity*. Whether it is a function of the times, or simply the end-product of 15 books and 38 years worth of developing and deeply engaged thought, or both, the conservative leanings and arguments of Postman's later career become, with this book, fused with the radical and subversive.

In short, *Building a Bridge to the 18th Century* offers the argument that education has lost its way, in that we struggle not only to stay "in the moment" but to move forever forward in an attempt to remain relevant and engage the students of an electronic age. And that in doing so we have forsaken the hallmarks of the print culture on which modern and public education were built. The obvious and unfortunate consequence of this fact is that we lose, like the rest of the culture, a sense of history and its import. We push literacy further and further toward the dustbin of obsolescence. We find college and university students who think their professors are woefully out-of-sync with the cutting edge of their field when they assign texts that are more than 10 years old. Most importantly, we champion ideas that are fashionable and of the moment at the expense of maintaining and advocating for ideas that are universal, and that are not only of their time but of *any* time, in that they remain powerful, generative, and relevant. And which of course are the very ideas that got us here in the first place.

In this last regard, the book is also a screed against postmodernism, post-structuralism, critical theory, and cultural studies. That is to say, it is a critical response to the late movements in the history of learning and knowledge that seek to move our "great conversation" forward, but that Postman views as absurd and even wrong.

To remedy the problem that is this state of affairs, Postman prescribes that we rediscover and reclaim the legacy, literature, and thought that arose out of the 18th century, and principally out of the explosive (and subversive) period of rationalism known as the Enlightenment. As he writes in Chapter 1:

> The eighteenth century is the century of Goethe, Voltaire, Rousseau, Diderot, Kant, Hume, Gibbon, Pestalozzi, and Adam Smith. It is the century of Thomas Paine, Jefferson, Adams, and Franklin. In the eighteenth century we developed our ideas about inductive science, about religious and political freedom, about popular education, about rational commerce, and about the nation-state. In the eighteenth century, we also invented the idea of progress, and, you may be surprised to know, our modern idea of happiness. It was in the eighteenth century that reason began its triumph over superstition. And, inspired by Newton, who was elected president of the Royal Society at the beginning of the century,

> writers, musicians, and artists conceived of the universe as orderly,
> rational, and comprehensible. Beethoven composed his First Symphony
> in the eighteenth century, and we should not be surprised that Bach,
> Handel, Mozart, and Haydn composed their music in the eighteenth
> century. (pp. 17-18)

This passage comes, however, only after he offers an example that is emblematic of the present-day state of education, ideas, and letters. He has the following to say about Jean Baudrillard and the post-structuralist paradigm:

> Jean Baudrillard, a Frenchman, of all things, tells us that not only does
> language falsely represent reality, but there is no reality to represent.
> (Perhaps this explains, at long last, the indifferent French resistance to
> the German invasion of their country in World War II: They didn't
> believe it was real.) In an earlier time, the idea that language is incapable
> of mapping reality would have been considered nonsense, if not a form
> of mental illness. In fact, it *is* a form of mental illness. Nonetheless, in
> our own time the idea has become an organizing principle of presti-
> gious academic departments. You can get a Ph.D. in this sort of thing.
> (p. 8)

The obvious point of this contrast (and Postman invokes similar contrasts
throughout his book) is this: In contradistinction to what he sees as the
nihilistic, pessimistic, and ultimately dead-end view of the pursuit of reason
that comes to us from Baudrillard, Derrida, Foucault, and company, it is in
returning to and recognizing the value of the traditions and ideas of
Enlightenment thinking that we will surely find a more positive, productive,
and hopeful set of pathways and possibilities.

Building a Bridge to the 18th Century also builds on the entire foundation that is Postman's writing and thinking over the years, in the following
way. The book's chapters are constructed according to the themes that have
been Postman's main preoccupations throughout his writings. The eight
chapters, after the first, address, in order: progress, technology, language,
information, narratives, children, democracy, and education. And the point
of each chapter is to convey what is important—what is worth remembering, learning from, maintaining, and even extending—in the ideas the great
figures of the Enlightenment have to offer us on these subjects.

As such, the book stands as a fitting denouement to Postman's career. It
returns him to education, which is where he began. It emphasizes a bias
toward print-literate culture that is the fount of his conservatism—and even
makes this radical. And in it, he continues to write about all of the things
that matter to him, that matter to our civilization, and that he seeks to make
matter to us—by building on the very foundation of 18th-century ideas that
ultimately made us as civilized as we have become.

THE FOUR THEMES OF POSTMAN'S MEDIA ECOLOGY

In this final section, I extract from these 15 books the main ideas presented in them, and attempt to outline these ideas in a way that connects them together as a coherent thought structure. My intent is to summarize what we understand as media ecology as it comes to us by way of Neil Postman—who, in these very works, developed and gave us this conceptual framework and all it encompasses in the first place. That is, it is my ultimate goal to clarify the "heart" of what media ecology is as it is channeled to us through Postman's intellect, his perspective, his purpose, and, if I may say so, his humanity.

To do so, I present four admittedly overlapping and recurring themes that comprise the primary thrust of Postman's concerns and contribution. Within these themes, I then enumerate the significant, salient, and most often repeated concepts. The four themes include education and media education, language from a media perspective, media and technology as culture, and cultural conservation/conservatism.

Education and Media Education

Postman is first and foremost an educator; in fact, he begins his career as an elementary school teacher. He is also an English educator, to the extent that this is where his scholarly career begins. Finally, Postman can also be considered the founding father of the media education/media literacy movement in the United States.

What is important here, from the perspective of media ecology, is how all three of these are intertwined. Postman is not just a teacher, but a scholar. Yet he is not only a scholar of education, driven by the idea that education is necessary to making us civilized individuals and a civilized whole—and *then* only if we are engaged in this purpose, and continually seek to improve the way we school ourselves and our culture. He is also a scholar of the language through which education is conducted, and which is the basis of all learning and knowledge; the singular tool for human understanding. Furthermore, he is interested in the ways in which language, when reflected on, fully understood, and well used, brings about successful, positive learning and knowledge, rather than the opposite. This is what leads him to study the nature of language, but then also to study the nature of *all* of our forms of communication as a means of comparison and contrast. For each impacts upon the means and ends of education and, ultimately, on its purpose of civilizing us. This is especially true at this juncture in our electronic age.

This is the foundation atop which his media ecology is constructed. And it is from this basic understanding that the following can be offered.

Media Ecology Is Education-Based. Media ecology grows out of a perspective that posits that media both impact education and must also be a primary subject of education.

Media impact education in that each medium directly affects *what* we can know when using and relying on it, but also *how* we can know these things. This becomes obvious when we trace the endeavor to educate across the epochs of orality, writing, and print. Learning in an oral world, for example, requires committing material to memory. There is simply no other means or place to store it. Learning in a world of writing and print, however, means that not only can material be saved for us, in artifacts that we can consult and reconsult, but that we can store a record of our own thinking and ideas. Thus with writing and print, our minds are freed from the need to spend considerable and valuable brain power on the task of memorizing and remembering. We can expend this energy on thinking; on synthesizing, integrating, and extending the information with which we are presented.

This point becomes even sharper when one contrasts education in a print literate age against education in our electronic age—as Postman does beginning with his very first book, *Television and the Teaching of English.* The electronic or "information" age created a literal avalanche of information under which we become buried and out of which we find it very difficult to dig ourselves. Here, discovering what information might be valuable and worthwhile becomes equally difficult and effort-laden a task as what it took to fully commit information to memory in an oral world.

Media must become a primary subject of education for the very same reason. If, to use McLuhan's word, media themselves are "invisible" to us, it becomes the responsibility of the educational mission to make them visible. That is, it becomes tantamount that education be not just about the subjects—the content—we learn, but about *the very nature of the means by which we learn,* whether this means listening to lectures, reading books, or viewing documentaries. Understanding how we learn, how *to* learn, and what the results of such learning are become as critical to our education as any of the various subjects—and perhaps even more so, in that they influence how and why we will hopefully continue to educate ourselves about these things long after our formal education is ended.

Media Ecology Is a Form of Media Literacy/Media Education. Given the above, this argument for the inclusion of a media education within the endeavor of a general education proper constitutes the very first argument for a program of media literacy or media education. Although Postman does not really fully develop this argument until *Teaching as a Subversive Activity* in 1969, it is clear that he is working toward it from his very first book. And it is clear that all of his work in linguistics and general semantics, and the influence of McLuhan among others, amount to steps in this direction.

Interestingly enough, as a philosophy of media education that is fully articulated by the time of *Teaching as a Subversive Activity*, and best articulated in *Teaching as a Conserving Activity*, media ecology predates the recognized British movement in media education that is based out of the British Film Institute (BFI). British media education is in full flight by the end of the 1970s (Mediaed.org.uk, Paragraph 2), around the time that *Teaching as a Conserving Activity* appears. However, the work of critical figures in that movement, such as David Buckingham, do not begin to appear in print until the mid- to late-1980s. (Of course, a key difference is that the British movement is now "an established part of U.K. education" [Paragraph 2]. The same cannot, unfortunately, be said of the situation in the United States.)

Media Ecology, Via Postman, Privileges Print Literacy. The difference between the brand of media education that is Postman's media ecology and other perspectives on media literacy or media education, is that Postman's media ecology centers upon the achievement that is print literacy. This is wholly a function of his embrace of print literacy as the touchstone of our modern system of education, as well as many, if not most of the crowning glories of the civilized, modern world (thus the argument that is *Building a Bridge to the 18th Century*).

Most importantly, print, in Postman's media ecology, becomes the medium against which all other media "are measured, compared, and contrasted" (Gencarelli, 2000, p. 99). It is the vantage point from which he begins, and continues to understand media. And if the word "ecology" in media ecology calls our attention to balance, and Innis' lesson that a culture or civilization must counter the bias that leads it to favor one medium of communication over others, then the following can be said of this privileging: Postman wishes us to balance our headlong rush into the electronic age and future, and the predispositions of its media, with a recognition of the continued promise and value of print.

Language From a Media Perspective

As I pointed out at the very beginning of this chapter, Postman's educational training and terminal degree are in English language education. As I emphasize in the previous paragraphs, he is biased toward print-based language even while he argues for balance; for a media ecology.

What must be further clarified at this point, however, are two matters. The first is that the wellspring of Postman's contributions is based not only in education but in language and language education—that, in fact, the two are inseparable. This explains why I give the second phase in his work the title "Language and Education," why this phase follows a series of textbooks with the title "The New English," and why it begins with a book entitled

Linguistics and subtitled "A Revolution in Teaching." The second matter is that any comprehensive summary of Postman's media ecology requires that we situate print, and Postman's print bias, within a context that recognizes the history of all human language—oral, written, and print—and that also then extends this history to the revolution in communication that is our present-day electronic age.

Language Is a Technology. Postman's take on language begins from the recognition that language is a human invention.

Oral language is not corporeal. It is not built or fashioned out of material. Although, as sound, it leads us to exert pressure on molecules of air, it is not in and of itself a tangible, physical extension of our physical selves. It is, however, a tool. Orality, and later writing, are systems we humans innovated, and that we continue to develop and refine. It becomes especially important to recognize this fact given the extent to which people typically take oral language for granted and treat it as a part of the natural order of things.

An even more essential point is that language is *the* most important and powerful tool in the history of our species. Oral language is what allows for the reflective interiorization of experience that is human thought. As Postman (1996) quotes Socrates in *The End of Education*: "When the mind is thinking, it is talking to itself" (p. 188). It is also the means by which we bridge the gulf between us and are able to share our conscious, individual experience with each other. In addition, once built, this bridge enables the commentary, cooperation, and instruction that become both the critical steps in the advancement of physical tool making and our first steps in civilizing ourselves.

Language Is a Medium. Once we realize that language is invented, we tend to stop taking it for granted and instead think about it in all of its strangeness and wonder. This is the point at which it starts to become visible as a medium, and at which we start to think about how it works, and what its strengths—and, equally importantly, its weaknesses—are.

This explains Postman's preoccupation with linguistics and general semantics. Both are efforts to understand language first in and of itself and second as means to an ends—in order that we might more effectively and successfully use it. They are attempts to understand how and why language works (and sometimes does not), what the underlying principles for its use are, and how it determines but also limits what we can know. For it is only through such an appreciation of the medium that we can expect to achieve the best possible results with respect to its content, and best use it in all of the ways and for all of the reasons we need it. Furthermore, for Postman, the ultimate approach to the linguistic enterprise comes with his discovery of

Korzybski, Johnson, et al., and the general semantics perspective. And the most important principle here is the idea that language does not represent reality but mediates it: that "the map is not the territory."

Going all the way back to *Television and the Teaching of English*, however, Postman also relies on yet another framework for understanding language: the comparative perspective that derives from an historical view of communication. That is to say, an examination of the differences among orality, writing, and print helps to illuminate the nature of each individual media form. For example, it is a strange phrase to suggest that we "think before we speak," since this would entail substantial pauses in conversation, as we finished listening and then thought about our response before offering it out loud. Writing, however, offers us exactly this ability to think slowly and deliberately, to reflect on our thoughts, and to even edit ourselves once a thought is out there and expressed on the page. Similarly, it is important to recognize how the letters of our alphabet represent the sounds made in our spoken language, how the alphabet became the ultimate development in writing systems because of the fact that it connected the spoken and written language in this way, and how, in contrast, the more ancient, ideographic systems of writing such as Chinese do not make this same connection. Speakers of the Mandarin or Cantonese dialects of Chinese share a single written Chinese language. However, while certain characters or parts of characters in the written language do signify sound and inflection, the majority of characters do not have a relationship to the sounds of the spoken words for things and vice-versa. As a result, literate people who speak one or the other dialect read the same language but cannot necessarily understand each other when speaking.

Language Is an Environment. From this discussion about the different forms of language, it follows that each form also creates its own environment in which communication takes place; that each creates its own kind of map of the territory. Speech requires presence and is ephemeral. It is learned informally, for the most part through immersion in a culture in which a particular language is spoken. Writing and reading break this requirement of presence and therein change the space and time bias of speech. You can read Postman without ever having known him, you can do so alone in a library or on a transatlantic plane flight, and you can do so 20 years from now. Writing and reading also require enough formal learning to at least acquire and practice the rudiments. Finally, print democratizes literacy, first by making books a commodity, but eventually by bringing about our modern system of education, built on the edifice of the book, and our first medium of mass communication.

Furthermore, in works like *Language in America* and *Crazy Talk, Stupid Talk*, Postman points out the existence of multiple environments *within* the use of a particular form of language. He refers to these as semantic environments, because they point to the manifold ways people use a particular form of language in ways that separate them, in ways wherein they do not or cannot understand each other, in ways in which language that makes sense to one person does not make sense to another, and in ways where language that has a purpose for one person does not achieve that purpose when received and interpreted by another or others. The recognition of semantic environments makes visible the ways in which meaning is construed and misconstrued, the ways in which it is used for good, bad, and cross-purposes, and the ways in which it is used effectively and ineffectively. This, then, becomes the basis for Postman's argument that general semantics and a language education are of critical importance. It is incumbent upon us to make language work, to its utmost potential, and for our mutual benefit and purposes. It is the best means we have for such purpose. It is also the only means we have.

Media and Technology as Culture

Postman, following McLuhan, uses the words *medium* and *technology* somewhat interchangeably. That all media are technologies goes without speaking. That all technologies are media, however, requires that we recognize both as extensions of our human selves, which we interpose between ourselves, our world, and things in it. As McLuhan put it, media are in fact the extension of our central nervous system; of the advanced and primitive brain, the cerebral and the visceral.

It is also important to point out, at the beginning of this particular section that, beyond his concentration on language in its three forms, Postman's writings primarily deal with only one other medium in any concentrated and sustained way: television. His books on language and education outnumber those works that are expressly about other media by almost two-to-one. But of the books that are not about language and education, there are really only two that look beyond the impact of television as the most powerful and influential invention of the electronic revolution in communication: *Conscientious Objections* and *Technopoly*. The books that focus on television include *The Disappearance of Childhood*, *Amusing Ourselves to Death*, and *How to Watch TV News*. (I would add that *Television and the Teaching of English* spans all three categories: language, education, and media.)

With this in mind, the three key ideas in this section are presented with an emphasis on Postman's preoccupation with and arguments about television.

All Technologies Are Human Impositions into the Natural Order of Things and, as a Result, Change That Order. This idea is best expressed in a sentence that appears more than once in Postman's work, but that appears for the final time in *The End of Education*: "Technological change is not accumulative, but ecological" (Postman, 1996, p. 192).

The fact is that technologies are invented to solve a problem that people have; to make our lives easier or better in some way. This is their explicit purpose. However, when we introduce an atomic weapon into the history of human civilization, we have more than just the newest and most powerful armament in the history of the conduct of war. We have a technology that changes the very nature of war, and of peace. We have a constant and permanent situation in which there is the possibility of the annihilation of our entire species. And if the age of modernity is characterized by the promise that technology will enhance and improve our existence, we were awakened to the dawning of the postmodern condition when the United States dropped its bombs on Hiroshima and Nagasaki and effectively exposed this modern promise for the Faustian bargain it is.

Likewise, when we introduce writing into a world of speech, we do not wind up with a world that now simply has two means of communication at its disposal. Writing re-orients the epistemology of such a world; its ways of knowing and nature of what it knows. And it does so partly because of its own unique nature and partly because it re-orients the nature of speech. Speech does not become obsolete or fall into disuse or disappear altogether as a result of the introduction of writing. It goes through a period and process of adaptation—as do all old media with the development of new media. Socrates lamented that writing would destroy memory and poetry. It did not do so. But it did create a new means by which to store and retrieve memories. It did extend poetry to the page and make it visual. It did lead to an age in which speech was no longer our only means to carry on our traditions, our lore, and our history—in which this was no longer a purpose for which it was needed or best suited. And it did lead to an age in which the most important function of speech is how we use and rely on it to have and maintain relationships.

Television's explicit purpose was to add the dimension of pictures to its audio-only predecessor, radio. In the process, however, it becomes the most effective and powerful marketing tool ever conceived. As Postman argues in *The Disappearance of Childhood*, it also leads to the breakdown of the distinction between the adult world and the world of childhood, in that its omnipresence and ease of use makes the secrets of adulthood readily available to children. And as he maintains in *Amusing Ourselves to Death*, the power of its attractive visuals, engaging stories, and the like—of its vast and seemingly endless ability to entertain and amuse—eventually and inevitably leads to a cultural practice wherein we bend everything television touches to this end.

All Media/Technologies Have an Implicit Bias. All technologies are invented with an explicit purpose. However, Postman urges that it is imperative for us to make ourselves aware of the hidden biases built into these extensions of ourselves—*and* to rely upon and use them accordingly. Such biases are mostly unanticipated and unintended. They tend to take awhile to develop and come to light. Nevertheless, all media and technologies have them.

As Postman points out on numerous occasions throughout his work—and as he again notes toward the end of *The End of Education* (p. 193)—all media have an intellectual and emotional bias, a political bias, a sensory bias, a social bias, and a content bias. Television's intellectual bias, for example, is a function of the fact that its visuals overpower the audio portion of its message—that images are what attract people to television and what television professionals emphasize in the creation of programming, be it entertainment or news. As a result, the power and importance of language is diminished by the televisual. And since ideas are language-based, television's bias skews away from the intellectual.

The emotional bias of television is cut from this same cloth. Visuals evoke a visceral response rather than an intellectual one. People tend to praise television when it moves them, when it is gripping, when they cannot turn their attentions away from what they are seeing—not when it is used to (try to) convey an important idea though language. Television's coverage of the Kennedy assassination, the space shuttle explosions, and the tragedy of September 11th are prime examples of this bias in action.

What Postman means by television's political bias can be explained as follows: Who has access to the medium and what it has to offer? Who is left out and disenfranchised? Broadcast television, because of its ease of use and the fact that it is found in more than 99% of homes in the United States, is our most democratic of mass media. Contrast this against the case of cable television, however, where only two-thirds of U. S. households subscribe and the remaining one-third does not mainly because they cannot afford to do so. Contrast this even further against the number of households who subscribe to a "premium" cable service like HBO, and the numbers are the reverse: Only about one-third of households subscribe or can afford to subscribe to such service. Finally, if we contrast television against personal computer use and subscription to an online service, the democratic bias of broadcast television becomes even more clear, as does the political bias *against* access to computers and online services. (Computer ownership is limited by cost, by the relatively rapid pace at which personal computers become obsolete, and by what is still relatively user-*un*friendly. Internet access from the home is even further limited by the additional subscription cost.)

Television's social bias continues to evolve. The medium's history began with a bias toward family viewing and the stationary object that anchored a living room or family room. However, with the widespread diffusion of television, the growth in the number of channels available through cable and now satellite television, and the addition of technologies such as the remote control, the VCR and DVD player, and the video game system, use of the medium has gradually been transformed from a family-based experience to an individual and more private pursuit.

The content bias of television, for purposes of this chapter, is best characterized by Postman's argument in *Amusing Ourselves to Death*. This argument accounts for the preponderance of entertainment programming on television as well as the rise of the grey area of television content we refer to as "infotainment." It also explains the critical importance of a book like *How to Watch TV News*.

Media Technologies Are Environments. Postman has often referred to a scientific definition of the term "medium" that he and his colleagues came across around the time they were developing the PhD program in Media Ecology at NYU: "A medium is an environment in which a culture develops." The use of this definition as an analogy points to two ideas that hold as true for our media of human communication as they do for the growth of an organism in a petri dish.

The first of these ideas is that media are environments. As are any number of technologies that people do not typically think of as media—think, for example, of a gun or the nuclear weapon I referred to earlier. Media and technologies are environments to the extent that they impact and become part of and permeate the very world in which we live and the ways in which we conduct our individual and collective lives within it. Another way of saying this is that media do not necessarily change everything in our culture, but they do change everything *about* our culture.

This leads to the second idea: In this regard, media do not only impact culture. They become, and *are* our culture. Because of the ways and the extent to which the various symbolic systems we humans have invented are incontrovertibly bound up with how we carry out, maintain, and move forward our existence on the planet, we cannot but arrive at a definition that says that our culture is made up of nothing but and everything that is our communication. And because of the ways and the extent to which particular media become the prominent, most powerful, and even governing media of a place and age, the ultimate point of Postman's media ecology is that we must understand this bias, this environment, this culture—and find our way to counter and balance it.

Cultural Conservation/Conservatism

Postman's Media Ecology Seeks to Counter the Biases of the Electronic Revolution in Communication by Conserving Print Literacy. This is the one key idea that arises out of this theme. It is also the final component of media ecology as it comes to us through the work and thought of Neil Postman.

From the bookends of his career that are *Television and the Teaching of English* and *Building a Bridge to the 18th Century*, as well as from all of the books and words that come in between, it is clear that this final idea is the foundation for *all* of Postman's contributions to our understanding of media. Neil Postman is the very model of a print-literate man. As an educator, this is how it should be, in that ideas are wholly and only language-based, and that the most significant consequence of Gutenberg's invention of the movable type printing press was the rediscovery and extension of the learning and knowledge of ancient Greece and Rome, which reached its pinnacle accomplishments in the contributions of Enlightenment thought. Postman seeks to forcefully remind us about the gifts of print literate culture—using the gift of language itself—and how they are integral to who we have become as a civilized people, to how we got here, and to where we might be headed in the future. This is his bias in a world in which our electronic means of communication—and principally, so far, television—threaten and diminish literacy and all it continues to offer us. And this conserving of print culture is his solution, his argument for balance, given the current place we stand.

CONCLUSION

In summary, it might be said that there is an arc to Postman's work that reaches its zenith not, as many people think, with *Amusing Ourselves to Death*, but with *Teaching as a Conserving Activity*. For it is in *Teaching as a Conserving Activity* that Postman fully realizes his theory of media ecology as the intersection of three theories of balance. The rest, as they say, is merely commentary. These three theories are: (a) the idea of an ecology of or balance in the natural environment; applied to (b) the idea of a balance between conservation and innovation in all aspects of our created culture, but especially in our communication/media/symbolic systems, because these are the key to our conversation about and understanding of such balance and its necessity; and finally (c) the Innisonian warning that it is in our interest or willingness to strike such a balance, or in the lack thereof, that the fate of our contemporary civilization lies.

Finally, it is abundantly clear that Postman's particular and principal bias is that he privileges literacy. But in closing, I must acknowledge one other expression of bias by Postman—this one from the final paragraph of "Social Science as Moral Theology," the essay that opens *Conscientious Objections*. I include this because it stands as an elegant statement of the ultimate purpose of media ecology; of the media ecology "cause." I also offer it because, after all of the words in this chapter about his contributions to our understanding of culture, technology, and communication, it is Postman (1988) himself who, in all of his eloquence, deserves the last word:

> I feel sure the reader will pardon a touch of bias when I say that the stories media ecologists have to tell are more important than those of other academic storytellers—because the power of communication technology to give shape to people's lives is not a matter that comes easy to the forefront of people's consciousness, though we live in an age when our lives—whether we like it or not—have been submitted to the demanding sovereignty of new media. And so we are obliged, in the interest of humane survival, to tell tales about what sort of paradise may be gained, and what sort lost. We will not have been the first to tell such tales. But unless our stories ring true, we may be the last. (pp. 18-19)

ENDNOTES

1. "Media Ecology looks into the matter of how media communication affect human perception, understanding, feeling and value; and how our interaction with media facilitates or impedes our chances of survival. The word ecology implies the study of environments: their structure, content and impact on people. An environment is, after all, a complex message system which imposes on human beings certain ways of thinking, feeling and behaving" (Postman, 1970, p. 161).

2. Three other books are omitted from this analysis.
   The Roots of Fanaticism (Postman & Damon, 1965b) is a collection edited by Postman and Damon and published by Holt, Rinehart and Winston, but not as a part of the "New English" series. This book is out-of-print and all but unavailable.
   Postman and Weingartner's (1973a) *How to Recognize a Good School* was published by the Phi Delta Kappa Educational Foundation and originally distributed on only a limited basis. It is omitted from this analysis, however, for the reason that it mostly reprints and recapitulates what is found in *The School Book* (1973b).
   Myths, Men, & Beer: An Analysis of Beer Commercials on Broadcast Television (Postman, Nystrom, Strate, & Weingartner, 1987) is more of a pamphlet than a book, and was also published and distributed on only a limited basis, by the American Automobile Association's Foundation for Traffic Safety. A substantial extent of this work was written by Lance Strate. However, an alternative analysis could certainly include the work within the third, transitional phase of Postman's career.

3. "Charlie" Weingartner and his contributions to this literature are all too often and unfortunately overshadowed in the light of Postman, who went on to develop the reputation and legacy. This is, in part, the result of Postman's personality

and presentation of self (including his sense of humor and teacher's gift for the anecdote), the later books that he wrote on his own, his gifts as a writer, and the fact that he is credited as first author for the Postman and Weingartner books. Indeed, even the present analysis is guilty of this mistreatment since it considers these works only insofar as they are part of Postman's *oeurve*. However, I would emphasize that Weingartner—intellectual *compadre* and confidant from their days as students under Forsdale—is as responsible as Postman himself for the content of their co-authored works—perhaps more so in certain cases and respects. A recommendation for future research is a study that would parse out the individual contributions of the two men to their collaborative efforts. Furthermore, I would argue that Weingartner deserves scholarly attention in his own right.

4. For those who would claim the term *new media* as a coining of the Internet age, I emphasize Postman and Weingartner's (1969) use of the term here to refer to television and radio—as well as to "the LP record, the tape recorder, the comic strip, the comic book, the tabloid newspaper, the electronic computer, the paperback book (p. 166).

5. It is perhaps useful to point out that, like the use of the term *ecology* in media ecology, the use of *subversive* in the title and thesis of *Teaching as a Subversive Activity* is a sign of the times—of the social and political upheaval of the decade that was the 1960s.

6. It might be argued that *Amusing Ourselves to Death* (Postman, 1985) is a also trade publication, given the size and scope of the general, international audience that read it.

7. Postman (1985) has always been fond of the following analogy, an extension of McLuhan's thought: "A technology is to a medium as the brain is to the mind" (p. 84). The technology is the hardware, or vessel. The medium is the software, or how we come to use the technology.

REFERENCES

Carpenter, E., & McLuhan, M. (Eds.). (1960). *Explorations in communication.* Boston: Beacon Press.

Carroll, J. B. (Ed.). (1956). *Language, thought, and reality: Selected writings of Benjamin Lee Whorf.* Cambridge, MA: M.I.T. Press.

Cassirer, E. (1946). *Language and myth* (S. K. Langer, Trans.). New York: Harper & Bros. (Original work published 1925)

Eisenstein, E. (1979). *The printing press as an agent of social change: Communications and cultural transformations in early-modern Europe.* Cambridge, England: Cambridge University Press.

Ellul, J. (1964). *The technological society* (J. Wilkinson, Trans.). New York: Vintage Books. (Original work published 1954)

Ellul, J. (1985). *The humiliation of the word* (J. M. Hanks, Trans.). Grand Rapids, MI: William B. Eerdman's. (Original work published 1981)

Fukuyama, F. (1993). *The end of history and the last man.* New York: Avon.

Gencarelli, T. (2000). The intellectual roots of media ecology in the work and thought of Neil Postman. *The New Jersey Journal of Communication, 8* (1), 91-103.

Gencarelli, T., Borrisoff, D., Chesebro, J. W., Drucker, S., Hahn, D. F., & Postman, N. (2001). Composing an academic life: A symposium. *The Speech Communication Annual, XV,* 114-136.

Gumpert, G. (1987). *Talking tombstones & other tales of the media age.* New York: Oxford University Press.

Havelock, E. A. (1963). *Preface to Plato.* Cambridge, MA: Harvard University Press.

Havelock, E. A. (1976). *Origins of western literacy.* Toronto, Canada: The Institute for Studies in Education.

Hayakawa, S. I. (1943). *Language in action.* New York: Harcourt, Brace.

Huxley, A. (1932). *Brave New World.* New York: Doubleday.

Innis, H. A. (1950). *Empire and communication.* New York: Oxford University Press.

Innis, H. A. (1951). *The bias of communication.* Toronto, Canada: University of Toronto Press.

Johnson, W. (1946). *People in quandaries.* New York: Harper.

Klapper, J. (1949). *The effects of mass media.* New York: Bureau of Applied Research, Columbia University.

Klapper, J. (1960). *The effects of mass communication.* Chicago: The Free Press of Glencoe, Illinois.

Korzybski, A. (1941). *Science and sanity: An introduction to non-Aristotelian systems and general semantics* (2nd ed.). Lancaster, PA: Science Press.

Langer, S. K. (1942). *Philosophy in a new key: A study in the symbolism of reason, rite, and art.* Cambridge, MA: Harvard University Press.

McLuhan, H. M. (1962). *The Gutenberg galaxy: The making of typographic man.* Toronto, Canada: University of Toronto Press.

McLuhan, H. M. (1964). *Understanding media: The extensions of man.* New York: McGraw-Hill.

McLuhan, H. M., & Fiore, Q. (1967). *The medium is the massage.* New York: Bantam Books.

Mediaed.org.uk. (n.d.). Media education in the U.K. Retrieved November 17, 2003 from http://mediaed.org.uk/posted_documents/mediaeduk.html.

Mumford, L. (1934). *Technics and civilization.* New York: Harcourt, Brace & World.

Mumford, L. (1952). *Art and technics.* New York: Columbia University Press.

Nystrom, C. (1973). *Towards a science of media ecology: The formulation of integrated conceptual paradigms for the study of human communication systems.* Unpublished doctoral dissertation, New York University, New York.

Ogden, C. K., & Richards, I. A. (1923). *The meaning of meaning.* New York: Harcourt, Brace.

Ong, W. J. (1967). The presence of the word. New Haven, CT: Yale University Press.

Orwell, G. (1949). *1984.* New York: Harcourt, Brace.

Peirce, C. S. (1932). *Collected papers of C. S. Peirce.* Cambridge, MA: Harvard University Press.

Postman, N. (1961). *Television and the teaching of English.* New York: Appleton-Century-Crofts.

Postman, N. (1963). *The new English: A forward look.* New York: Holt, Rinehart & Winston.

Postman, N. (1966a). *Exploring your language*. New York: Holt, Rinehart & Winston.

Postman, N. (1966b). *Language and reality*. New York: Holt, Rinehart & Winston.

Postman, N. (1970). The reformed English curriculum. In A.C. Eurich (Ed.), *High school 1980: The shape of the future in American secondary education* (pp. 160-168). New York: Pitman.

Postman, N. (1976). *Crazy talk, stupid talk: How we defeat ourselves by the way we talk and what to do about it*. New York: Delacorte Press.

Postman, N. (1979). *Teaching as a conserving activity*. New York: Delta.

Postman, N. (1982). *The disappearance of childhood*. New York: Delacorte Press.

Postman, N. (1985). *Amusing ourselves to death: Public discourse in the age of show business*. New York: Viking.

Postman, N. (1988). *Conscientious objections: Stirring up trouble about language, technology, and education*. New York: Alfred A. Knopf.

Postman, N. (1992). *Technopoly: The surrender of culture to technology*. New York: Vintage Books.

Postman, N. (1996). *The end of education: Redefining the value of school*. New York: Alfred A. Knopf.

Postman, N. (1999). *Building a bridge to the 18th century: How the past can improve our future*. New York: Alfred A. Knopf.

Postman, N., & Damon, H. C. (1965a). *The languages of discovery*. New York: Holt, Rinehart & Winston.

Postman, N., & Damon, H. C. (Eds.). (1965b). *The roots of fanaticism*. New York: Holt, Rinehart & Winston.

Postman, N., & Damon, H. C. (1965c). *The uses of language*. New York: Holt, Rinehart & Winston.

Postman, N., & Damon, H. C. (1966). *Language and systems*. New York: Holt, Rinehart and Winston.

Postman, N., Morine, H., & Morine, G. (1963). *Discovering your language*. New York: Holt, Rinehart & Winston.

Postman, N., Nystrom, C., Strate, L., & Weingartner, C. (1987). *Myths, men, & beer: An analysis of beer commercials on broadcast television, 1987*. Falls Church, VA: AAA Foundation for Traffic Safety.

Postman, N., & Powers, S. (1992). *How to watch TV news*. New York: Penguin Books.

Postman, N., & Weingartner, C. (1966). *Linguistics: A revolution in teaching*. New York: Delta.

Postman, N., & Weingartner, C. (1969). *Teaching as a subversive activity*. New York: Delacorte Press.

Postman, N., & Weingartner, C. (1971). *The soft revolution: A student handbook for turning schools around*. New York: Delacorte Press.

Postman, N., & Weingartner, C. (1973a). *How to recognize a good school*. Bloomington, IN: Phi Delta Kappa Educational Foundation.

Postman, N., & Weingartner, C. (1973b). *The school book: For people who want to know what all the hollering is about*. New York: Delacorte Press.

Postman, N., Weingartner, C., & Moran, T. P. (Eds.). (1969). *Language in America: A report on our deteriorating semantic environment*. New York: Irvington Publishers.

Russell, B. (1953). *The impact of science on society*. New York: Simon & Schuster.

Ryan, P. (1973). *Birth and death and cybernation: Cybernetics of the sacred*. Newark, NJ: Gordon & Breach.

Samuel F. B. Morse Biography. (n.d.). Retrieved July 21, 2003, from http://www.morsehistoricsite.org/morse/morse.html

Sapir, E. (1921). *Language: An introduction to the study of speech*. New York: Harcourt, Brace.

Schramm, W. (Ed.). (1954). *The process and effects of mass communication*. Urbana: University of Illinois Press.

Schwartz, T. (1973). *The responsive chord*. Garden City, NY: Anchor Books.

Strate, L. (1994). Post(modern)man, or Neil Postman as postmodernist. *ETC.: A Review of General Semantics, 51*(2), 159-170.

Strate, L. (1996). Containers, computers, and the media ecology of the city. *Media Ecology: A Journal of Intersections*. Retrieved July 21, 2003, from http://raven.ubalt.edu/features/media_ecology/articles/96/strate1/strate_1.html

Strate, L., & Lum, C. M. K. (2000). Lewis Mumford and the ecology of technics. *The New Jersey Journal of Communication, 8*(1), 56-78.

Taylor, F. W. (1947). *The principles of scientific management*. New York: Harper & Bros. (Original work published 1911)

Waters, R. (1992). *Amused to death* [audio recording]. New York: Soony Music.

Watzlawick, P., Beavin-Bavelas, J., & Jackson, D. (1967). *The pragmatics of human communication: A study of interactional patterns, pathologies, and paradoxes*. New York: W. W. Norton.

Watzlawick, P., Weakland, J. H., & Fisch, R. (1974). *Change: Principles of problem formation and problem resolution*. New York: W. W. Norton.

White, L. (1962). *Medieval technology and social change*. London: Clarendon Press.

Whitehead, A. N. (1959). *The aims of education*. New York: Macmillan.

Wiener, N. (1950). *The human use of human beings: Cybernetics and society*. New York: Avon Books.

Wittgenstein, L. (1933). *Tractatus logico-philosophicus* (2nd Ed.). New York: Harcourt Brace.

9

James Carey: The Search For Cultural Balance

Frederick Wasser

Brooklyn College,
City University of New York

James W. Carey's influence on media studies and practice began approximately 40 years ago. Communications study was increasingly exhausted in appearance, if not literally so. Administrative research proceeded solely by quantitative measures of narrowly defined issues. An alternative tradition of critical studies had only begun to redefine culture for the mass media age. It still was tied into a reductive mass society paradigm and an overly literary debate about the debasement of "high" culture. Carey insisted that the field take the notion of communication as culture seriously. This gathered together what had been scattered strands into a commonality and reinvigorated the field by clearly marking dead ends.

In doing so, he solidified the insights of cultural studies and media ecology. These approaches were emerging in the 1960s when people such as Raymond Williams and Marshall McLuhan formulated new methods to analyze the insinuation of mass media into all realms of life. They rejected both quantitative and literary analysis of this phenomenon. British academicians labeled their approach as cultural studies. Meanwhile, a group of North Americans identified their field as media ecology. These approaches share many common responses to communications study:

- An interdisciplinary concern with culture, defining culture as a way of life rather than a hierarchy of taste.
- Emphasizing social analysis over textual interpretation of media impact.
- Sensitivity to new formations in media audiences and media technologies.

These are central features of Carey's writings and he has become an important figure for cultural studies, media ecology, and the entire field. He does not identify himself with either media ecology or cultural studies, although he sympathetically places both approaches within the older intellectual tradition of North American pragmatism. Media ecology and cultural studies merely are preliminary to a much larger game. The synthesis remains abstract for Carey until he makes clear what is at stake in media studies, which is the health of the democratic discourse within the nation. This insistence on democracy as discourse is his profound response as the turn-of-our-century trend toward globalization increasingly reveals its lack of public responsibility. The public discourse is a natural result from the trajectory of his writings and speeches since his early essays in the 1960s. Coming out of a Catholic Workers tradition and responding to the national crises of the time, he has used cultural and ecological approaches to ask a mixed audience of academics and media practitioners to understand the implications of communication for a mass democracy.

Because he speaks to this mixed audience, he has articulated a broader humanistic perspective that goes beyond either the interpretation of individual messages or the explanation of specific media effects. Since the 1960s, he has addressed journalists in his essays, and therefore has consistently inquired into the effects that information-technology systems have on every citizen's ability to engage journalistic functions. This inquiry into journalistic function has famously inspired Carey to insist on the centrality of the ritual function of communication. Ritual analysis liberates communication studies from the dead end of mere description and asks how acts of communication facilitate democratic communities. Indeed, Carey's contribution has been a principled insistence that communications is a sphere of moral responsibility. This gives urgency to his ongoing struggle against monopolies of knowledge.

The synthesis he worked out in response to the positivist domination of the 1960s becomes more critical in today's polarization of culture. The challenge has deepened as market values colonize previously autonomous spheres of human life. This is now a culture—where newspapers are addressed to demographics rather than readers—where broadcasting no longer even pays lip service to public interest—where neither the past not the future is respected in the search for a transnational media.

BIOGRAPHY

James Carey was born in 1934, which places him squarely in an academic generation that was already reaching positions of trust during the 1970s crisis of legitimacy reaching across all institutions including higher education. He grew up in Providence, Rhode Island in a milieu that was simultaneously Catholic and sympathetic to socialism. Although somewhat sickly, he participated in the activities of the neighborhood and learned to appreciate the bonds that hold together a working community (Munson & Warren, 1997, p. xii). He received his PhD from the University of Illinois and became a professor there, with brief stints at Pennsylvania State University and the University of Iowa. His longest tenure has been as dean of the College of Communication, University of Illinois at Urbana-Champaign from 1979 to 1992. He left in 1993 to join the faculty at the School of Journalism, Columbia University in New York City. He is still there as of this writing.

Even as a graduate student at the University of Illinois, Carey was encouraged to write both as an academic and as a journalist. His writings appeared in such venues as *The New Republic*, *The Nation*, and *Commentary* through the 1960s and in the ecumenical spirit of Illinois, these pieces furthered his career (James Carey, personal conversation, June 2002). It was natural for the young professor to make his intellectual home in the Association for Education in Journalism (currently called the Association for Education in Journalism and Mass Communication [AEJMC]). He was elected president of the AEJMC in 1978 and takes pride in the fact that this election was prior to his becoming dean. His election and acceptance of the position signaled his own intention to treat journalism as an intellectual pursuit. His present position at Columbia's Graduate School of Journalism allows him to encourage others to pursue this ideal. Indeed, this ideal is the central tenet of his work.

Illinois was at the heart of Carey's career for the better part of four decades, and represents the "place" from which he views American and global development. But, I am not quite sure that his view is rooted in one place. His biography moves between the margin (the American midwest) and the metropolis (New England and New York City) and accordingly, he synthesizes traditions associated with different locations and fields.

METHOD

There was an interdisciplinary approach to communications at Illinois when Carey arrived there and from this, he learned to resist today's academic pressure to specialize and divide. I will never forget how he prefaced his remarks to a disputatious conference panel by saying: "I agree with all of you, even when you disagree with each other." Although some complain that this attitude lacks edge, Carey has counterintuitively used the synthetic approach to safeguard against complacency. He cannot dismiss various ostensibly "wrongheaded" positions easily but must first test them to see if there is a remnant of worth.

The method is historical in the broadest sense of the word. Events and trends are viewed as embedded in a political/social/cultural matrix that precludes separation, isolation, and generalization. Instead, we can seek wisdom from those who have thought about cultural and communication problems as they have emerged and developed. This is intellectual history of a muscular pragmatic sort. Among Carey's numerous essays there is no one piece that states the fundamental principles, and proceeds systematically from there. He has not engaged in field studies or primary data research. This is not suitable to Carey's task. He is an essayist of ideas and has a meticulous knowledge of the thinkers that he discusses. The very fact that this is rare in communications studies makes it all the more important to keep this form vital.

The problems of communication in a democracy are fundamental. Yet, there is a sense that we keep losing the forest for the trees in our primary communications research. Carey has been able in his career to take on the urgent task of reminding us of the forest—which is the temporal dimension of the present. Carey's essays often seek to test new passions against older wisdoms. The form juxtaposes Rupert Murdoch, and Alexis DeTocqueville, Vaclav Havel, and Benjamin Franklin. In any given week of work, he responds against the latest tabloidization of the 10-minute news cycle; weighs in against the careerist pressures on the university; exposes the media erosion of our communal memory.

Carey has been able to give proportion and weight to current media debates through the use of influential distinctions. There have not been major shifts despite the length of his prominence but there has been evolution and elaboration. Already in the 1960s, he had plumbed Harold Innis' application of economic categories to communication. From Innis, Carey adopts a concern with the physical nature of communication. This intimately ties Carey to media ecology and its interest in the technology/culture matrix (Lum, 2000, p. 2). By the 1970s, Carey is thinking about culture in ways that parallel developments in the Birmingham school of cultural studies.

However, at this time, he recuperates John Dewey's thoughts on communication and Clifford Geertz's approach to culture, two strands of influence that tend to be neglected in the radical schools of cultural studies. By 1975, he has worked out Dewey and Geertz to the point where he proposes that we make a further advance on the key question of communication and social control through distinguishing the *ritual* from the *transmission* function of communication. This distinction re-centers journalism for it is within the daily output of journalism that the ritual of democracy becomes visible. This becomes the foundation of Carey's wide ranging articles on technology and communication, on economics and communication, on the legacy of the Chicago School of social thought, on the conflicting determinisms of McLuhan and Mumford et al., on new notions of media serving the monitorial citizen: the omnipresent question of whether these ideas help invigorate the democratic ritual.

The ritual function alerts us that Carey has expanded Innis' insistence on the *physical* nature of communication in order to look broadly at all social relations. Carey requires that cultural analysis be supported by the histories of particular places; in his case, the continental United States. Carey uses the physical dimension to guard both against the excessive idealism of more recent cultural studies and the weightless speculations of McLuhan. These histories uncover the formations of monopolies of communications that are neither natural nor inevitable but the result of specific power structures. In opposition to these monopolies, Carey searches for *media balance*.

This balance is dynamic, not static. The Carey ideal for a democracy is the openness of a conversation, the give and take, and the opportunity to explore. There is room in it for all the forms of media outlets that have sprung to life over the course of history. Unfortunately, the present situation calls into question whether various forms can coexist in dynamic interaction. Carey's essays try to identify the balance between centrifugal and centripetal forces, between global, local and national, between private lives and public life. The chapter takes up these issues in turn. I now look at the cultural turn in communications, then proceeding to the study of technology and ideology. We finally move to his specific concern with media and the conflation of marketplace values with the democratic ethos.

THE IMPORTANCE OF CULTURE

The cultural critique is Carey's foundation. He starts with mass society theory and media criticism. The mass society critique—associated with C. Wright Mills, Dwight MacDonald, George Seldes, Paul Lazersfeld and Robert Merton—articulated the interplay between the organization of mass society and the functions of popular culture. Within this articulation, writers debated how far had popular culture debased all culture with its monolithic imposition of low brow taste and kitsch. Kitsch was perhaps the worse offense because it was the act of mass culture appropriating high culture and popularizing it (such as lifting catchy tunes out of classical symphonies).

Carey (1977/1988b) reviews these arguments and sympathizes with them (as is his wont), only to side step them (pp. 37-45). They have been played out because they were premised on a narrow concept of culture as "taste." Carey follows an expanded notion of culture as a whole way of life, a phrase associated with Richard Hoggart and Raymond Williams. Carey (1977/1988b) delineates this notion by reviewing the anthropology of Clifford Geertz. Geertz (1973) famously refuses to validate any particular explanation of a Balinese cockfight, but engages in elucidating an ensemble of meanings from the living texts of the fight. The resulting "thick" description shows the web of culture and Carey goes on to consider that web in questions of communication.

Carey writes that "[w]hen the idea of culture enters communication research, it emerges as the environment of an organism or a system to be maintained or a power over subject" (p. 65). He goes on to refine this crude notion of culture that implies that culture is separate from the human sphere. The refinement embraces the pragmatic intuition that culture is the realm of meanings created by humans, something that is implicated in the very act of being human.

Environmental questions bring to the surface Carey's problematic yet illuminating relationship with McLuhan. It is McLuhan who uses the environment metaphor to reverse the figure (content) and ground (form) of media. On the face of it, Carey (1967) has criticized McLuhan for being too mechanistic in his treatment of the relation between technology and human biology (pp. 24-29). McLuhan is not yet culturalist enough. However, he has never dismissed McLuhan (Grosswiler, 1998, pp. 134-135). Over 40 years, since his own personal encounter with McLuhan at Illinois in 1960, Carey comes back several times to reweigh McLuhan's views on culture and environment. In "Marshall McLuhan: Genealogy and legacy," he recalls McLuhan's important breakthrough in disputing the once prevalent notion that the problem of communications was solely a problem of transmission (Carey, 1998, p. 300).

Although he does not directly trace out McLuhan's influence on his own work, we can see that by the mid-1970s, Carey is ready to perform his own reversal of figure and ground. This occurs in the 1975 essay about a cultural approach to communications. Here, Carey (1975/1988a) asks us to consider that communication has a ritual function that is as important as its transmission function. Practically all of our acts of communication have meaning beyond the transmission of information. Much of the meaning can be called ritual such as when we exchange and share messages in order to renew fellowship and a sense of belonging. Communion, bonding, social renewal of shared symbols (such as language) are all ritual communications. When we think about ritual generously, we realize that it is present in the daily habit of reading the newspaper and in office chit-chat about the latest movie. It is a large part of who we are. It is secular as well as spiritual, a common lubricant not restricted to a drop of anointed oil.

We are surprised by this distinction because we are used to American puritanical insistence on the practical nature of communication, and because we are living through the global rise of scientific culture. In such circumstances, understanding of communication had hardened: Communication was defined and used as transmission for the purpose of control. The two world wars gave us mathematically driven communication theories and the growth of public relations and other instrumental programs of communication. Yet, the transmission thinkers, concentrating on the separation of signal (directed message) from noise (all other meanings), failed to notice that instrumental communication may materially contribute to the fragmentation of social bonds if it supplants the ritual functions of various media.

The identification of the ubiquitous need for ritual communication becomes Carey's contribution to the increasing academic popularity of social construction of reality theory. He was able to make this contribution because he had made the epistemological break with the dominant philosophical dualism of individual/group that American thought has inherited from Locke, Berkeley, and Descartes. Despite their other differences, these philosophers all postulate that individuals possess reason prior to their socialization. This postulate affirms that reality is independent of the social, of language, of the observer. There are many dissents to the rationalism postulate. Carey's dissent follows John Dewey. In the early part of the 20th century when rationalism was still in full prestige, Dewey declared that at least one type of reality, social reality, had no existence independent of the observer. This is what he meant by stating that "Society not only continues to exist *by* transmission, *by* communication, but it may fairly be said to exist *in* transmission, *in* communication" (Dewey, 1916/1961, p. 4).

Carey is expanding on Dewey when he writes, "communication is a symbolic process whereby reality is produced, maintained, repaired and transformed" (Carey, 1975/1988a, p. 23). The three categories of communication, social life, and reality become deeply dependent on each other, without independent autonomy.

This is almost the same break that Stuart Hall and other researchers at the Centre for Contemporary Cultural Studies at Birmingham were making. This group had extended anthropological methods to industrial countries.[1] They were particularly interested in the many meanings that can be derived from a cultural event. This "polysemic" approach was derived from Stuart Hall's modification of Frank Parkin's model of the encoding and decoding of cultural production and reception. This tool emphasized that a movie, a television news report, or a romance novel was not reducible to a single meaning. Meaning was a site of negotiation with the audience either accepting or modifying the intentions of the cultural producer, or even sometimes inverting these intentions.

TECHNOLOGY AND SOCIETY

This negotiation of meaning had ritual aspects and certainly supported Carey's own concern with the circulation of communication. From the late 1970s on, Carey wrote about and promoted the cultural studies movement. He was so intrigued by the Birmingham group's emphasis on ideological analysis that he titled his own seminal work as on ideology and the telegraph (Carey, 1983/1988d). In turn, the British and Australian scholars associated with this movement became indebted to Carey's historical concern with the physical nature of media (Morley, 1992, pp. 278-279).

This reciprocity of interest should not be overstated. Carey is more of a sympathizer than of a participant in the movement. He has never shown much interest in treating culture as a set of codes to be interpreted. This difference is one of scale. Cultural studies authors such as David Morley, Roger Silverstone, Ann Gray and others, address technological matters as issues of micro-sociology. They ask how people use the TV, the Walkman, and the VCR in their domestic lives. In ideological analysis, the domain of cultural studies often remains domestic. This is in complete contrast to Carey who is always interested in the public and asks the macro questions of how technology, particularly the technologies of communication, shapes society, brings far flung communities together, subjugates the margins to the center, preserves democratic openness. It is indicative that as he cites Carey's influence in the very paragraph, Morley defers further explication in order to move on to the more micro-concerns of the work by Joshua Meyrowitz (1985). Carey wants to understand communication as national culture. This complements other approaches that tend to be less sensitive to national developments. There is a sense that media play a unique role in at least two of the North American countries. Certainly, there is a commitment to the notion that media have to be understood within the national frame.

For example, I feel that Carey created his approach in particular to deal with the post-Vietnam malaise that goes beyond the U.S. foreign policy failures of the 1960s and 1970s. On a deeper level, the failures revealed the American incapacity to benefit from and articulate its own collective wisdom. Somehow if this collective common sense had emerged we would have avoided or mitigated these failures. A hubris was blinding our common sense and Carey is not the only thinker to wonder if this hubris was partially caused by the role of technology in the American imagination.

It must be stated that such a role is premised on understanding technology in a broad way. It is not just a particular apparatus but a cultural system. Thus, automotive technology is the shopping mall, the disappearance of the sidewalk, and an entire subordination of the landscape to the interstate highway system. Communication technology operates the same way, as an environment not as single machines. When television is adopted, we must ask not only for its direct influence on the viewer but about the changes it has forced on print, film, and radio. We must stop thinking of discrete units as we investigate the social impact of media on an entire people.

In 1970, Carey along with John Quirk published an essay that retraced the various hopes and disappointments the philosophers of technology have formulated. They virtually invite us to read this intellectual history as their response to the Vietnam War and the dissolution of the liberal consensus (Carey & Quirk, 1970/1988). In this trajectory, they follow the example of Lewis Mumford and his interest in how successive technologies determined large-scale social/political organizations. Mumford had initially adopted the enthusiasm of such 19th century figures as Patrick Geddes and Prince Kropotkin who had attracted attention by concluding that electrical power would ameliorate the worst effects of the industrial revolution and promote a new sense of regional and national community. Lewis Mumford stated these hopes in his 1934 book *Technics and Civilization*. However, by the 1960s, Mumford had become disillusioned. Electrical power was only amplifying the central authority of the American political establishment. Mumford's disillusionment was a warning to Carey about the hopelessness of technological determinism.

Thus, we see the maturing Carey creating his own cultural approach to communication. He is inspired by Dewey to preach the centrality of culture; he is influenced by Mumford to think about technology as national systems and by McLuhan to reject the proposition that the problems of communication are reducible to scientific categories. However, at this point there are only glimmerings of what is the ideal for modern communication systems. I feel that in actuality Carey has a fully dimensional view of ideal communication systems. This ideality in Carey comes from Dewey and from a Canadian who studied briefly at the University of Chicago before spending his career at the University of Toronto: Harold A. Innis.

Innis lived from 1894 to 1952. He wrote in frustration over British imperialism and subsequent American cold war attitudes that are similar to Carey's disappointment with 1970s politics. Innis had begun as an economist examining the movement of staple goods such as cod and fur when he concluded that the most important staple good was communication. From this realization he saw that the medium in which communication was transported was the key to the power bias of the society. If a medium is time-biased (messages are preserved [transported] over time), power elites will organize society around traditions and centralized ideologies. Historic examples include Pharonic Egypt, medieval Europe, and Mandarin China. If a medium is space biased (messages are easily transmitted (transported) across vast distances) power elites will extend their area of control without much concern for traditions. Our Western society is a very good example of such a space-biased organization.

Innis had been inspired in his own work by Graham Wallas' regret over the decline of the oral in modern society (Innis, 1951/1964, p. 191). Oral communication was valued because it held space and time in rough balance. However, print on cheap mass-produced paper and the subsequent developments of electronic communication has overwhelmingly favored space bias. This bias has led to only a few groups having open access to media and results in their monopolization of knowledge. An open society must have a plethora of communication and a balance that at least resembles the original balance of face to face talk.

This union of economic analysis with cultural/political history struck Carey deeply. However, Innis wrote about media in frustratingly rushed manner and left much work to be done in his wake. For instance, as Innis had only postulated the cultural importance of the telegraph, Carey decided to plumb the issue further and to make it his demonstration of a soft deterministic relationship between the telegraph and social changes. Carey was able to argue that its adoption changed the American view of time, eroded the sense of local control, and delinked market prices from local conditions. An understanding of the "ideology and the telegraph" essay (Carey, 1983/1988d) is rewarding because it continues to serve as a role model of how to uncover the cultural dimensions of technology, avoiding either McLuhan's hard determinism or a Birmingham limited focus on sites of reception.

Carey begins by taking the reader on a drive through the American countryside. He notes the parallel lines of river, canal, railroad track, telegraph and telephone lines (Carey, 1983/1988d, p. 203). (By now, he may have added the long distance fiber optic lines.) In these parallels of transportation and communication, the telegraph represents the clear break, which separates transportation from communication. Messages could now move faster, much faster than humans. The first to take advantage of this phenomenon were the transportation companies. There was early heavy use of the telegraph for railroad scheduling and switching. This use of the telegraph to control the space of the railroad system soon spilled over into control of time. By 1883, the railroad companies (not the government) imposed a standard four-zone division of time on the continent. The spatial dominance of the telegraph led to the demise of local time. This was symptomatic of the monopoly the combination of the railroad and the telegraph had over economics and information.

The telegraph also publicized local variations in prices to the nation. Therefore, local variations started to disappear. The pre-telegraph broker had taken advantage of these variations by transporting goods from areas where the price was low to areas where the price was high. This activity declined since it was a simple matter for anyone to order goods from cheap areas. The futures trader supplanted the broker since the telegraph allowed competition over knowledge. The futures trader would learn of favorable growing conditions in distant parts and would sell receipts for future delivery of wheat to lock in the prices before the bountiful harvest forced prices down. Eighteenth-century capitalism had started the separation between the use of goods and their value. The monopolies of knowledge associated with the telegraph so accelerated this separation in the mid-19th century that Marx was inspired to construct his theory of commodification (Carey, 1983/1988d, p. 221).

ECONOMICS AND COMMUNICATION

It took a student of Innis looking for patterns of cultural determinism to note the correlation between the telegraph and 19th century economic theory. Carey came to Marx through his concern with the physical nature of media. However, he has a different relationship with Marx than either those who pursue political economic analysis of communication or the British cultural studies group (Flayhan, 2001, p. 37). Political economists concentrate on production and ask: who owns media and how do they shape media to be part of the capitalist system? The cultural studies people have become interested in ideological analysis and ask: what is the encoded message of media and how does this message reproduce the values of capitalism? Carey fully participates in the left-wing critique of capitalism but his position is not to be conflated with either ideology or political economy (Pauly, 1997, pp. 11-12). In this aspect, Carey has kept us attentive to the damages of media bias that has been ignored in the partisan bickering of cultural studies.

Raymond Williams specifically separated cultural studies from classical Marxism by rejecting the model of base and superstructure. Marx wrote that the dominant "mode of production of material life conditions the social, political and intellectual life process in general. It is not the consciousness of men that determines their being but, on the contrary, their social being that determines their consciousness" (Karl Marx as quoted by Williams, 1977, p. 75). Williams felt that this became overly reductive in the 20th century, since it reduced culture to an epiphenomenon of economics. He turned to Antonio Gramsci's notion of hegemony to work through how culture and economics are equal players in the "whole way of life" of the human subject. Hegemonic values are inculcated in the various social institutions and become accepted as common sense. Gramsci and Williams argue people will adopt beliefs and attitudes that are independent of their economic understanding if they feel that such values are part of their common culture. This adoption of hegemony theory was decisive in the emergence of cultural studies.

Carey is sympathetic to Williams' critique, particularly in the discourse in which it originated: European critical thought. However, something happened when it crossed the Atlantic. Carey charges that American professors have reduced hegemony so that "race and gender have assumed a position as the new 'base.' . . . culture is now reduced to ideology and ideology is in turn reduced to race and gender" (Carey, 1992/1997c, p. 276). It is not that Carey rejects racial and gender explanations, it is that such explanations have been used as new general totalities and often ignore the specific physicality, continuities and problems of American life. Race and gender politics has actually distracted academics while media corporations have stolen the game and eroded what little sense of public interest we had at the start of media age. Carey has perhaps been too gentle in his critique of this distraction because he dreads the negativism within leftist scholarship but the implications of his unease are clear.

Indeed we can group together Carey's unease with extreme versions of the social construction of reality such as French post structuralism (Carey, 1986/1988c, p. 105), reduction of hegemony to race and gender and even McLuhan's notion of physiological and psychological media changes. In each case, he is responding to an excessive idealism that has effaced the specific contour of the physical situation.

British cultural studies occurs within a society with class divisions that go back before the development of modern media. Hegemonic politics are situated in institutions of long standing and are presented as common sense traditions. In a younger society such as the United States or Canada, institutional prestige is less traditional, less certain. In new societies, values and communal bonds are ritualized through mass media. It is, therefore, vital that critical thinkers confront how media environments have bias, how these bias give opportunities to those who would create monopolies of knowledge. In short, if we wish to uncover the equivalent of hegemonic values in the New World, we must be sensitive to issues of technological systems. It is instructive that mainstream communication analysts and cultural studies ethnographers have emphasized sites of reception, because they both tend to assume the functioning nature of contemporary capitalist societies (even if they challenge the ideologies of such societies). Meanwhile, Innis and Carey focus on conditions of producing and distributing meaning, because they worry that the imbalance of communication is leading to dysfunction.

Technological systems present a conundrum for American media scholars since they are not created to extend the public sphere. They are created and distributed within a marketplace that is decidedly oriented toward private gain. In contrast, communication is public, language and all symbols are that which we share and makes us a community. From this perspective, Carey (1994/1997a) writes that economics and communication "constitute contradictory frameworks. . . . Economics is the practice of allocating scarce resources. Communication is the process of producing meaning, a resource that is anything but scarce—indeed, it is a superabundant, free good" (pp. 63-64). Despite their contradictory frames, the increasing technologization of communication has made it more a source of private gain and less a common sphere of sharing. Carey captures this in noting the unconscious transitions we have made in our language from communication to information, from public to audience.

THE SPECIAL PROBLEM OF JOURNALISM

Carey has decisively repositioned communication as culture. He has opposed it to economics, and refused to let it be reduced to a matter of ideological transmission. He has integrated media studies into a tradition of American thinking about technology. Already these amount to a major influence on the field and many have expressed gratitude. Nonetheless, to leave off here is to miss the punch. These are general categories. Although Carey is not a system builder and each essay and statement stands on its own, the student will wish to explore the specific task that motivates his thought, which is the daily routine of journalism education.

By linking Carey to journalism education rather than journalism per se, we can see exactly how he situates the problems of media within the ritual of American democracy.

Education has been the starting point for many who are prominent in media studies from Dewey and Innis to McLuhan and Neil Postman. Journalism education is a prominent site to resist the pressure to justify education as vocational training. The university is the one space in American society that has so far resisted the marketplace. Although professional training is not necessarily in service of the market nor is it out of place in the academy, there is an easy conflation between professional training and career training for the marketplace. To avoid this conflation there must be an intellectual mission in teaching future journalists and Carey's enterprise in all his media critiques is to illuminate this mission. The problem is the special role of the journalist in servicing the democratic discourse.

For example in 1969, Carey clearly refers to McLuhan's condemnation of print linearity when he questioned the premise of objective reporting. He wrote "the conventions of objective reporting were developed to report another culture and another society [when] daily events . . . could be rendered in the straightforward 'who says what to whom' manner. . . . In such reporting a disorganized, fluid, nonrectilinear [Vietnam] war was converted by journalistic procedure into something straight, balanced, and moving in rectilinear ways, into a war of hills, tonnage, casualties, divisions, and numbers" (Carey, 1969/1997b, p. 140).

This kind of statement made in an essay on the general topic of communications is insightful because it picks out an analogy between the American establishment ideology of the time and the ethos of news reporters. Both groups try to contain the Vietnam war within a "rectilinear" frame. Nonetheless this kind of observation remains merely suggestive and awaits the detailed history that Dan Hallin (1986) provided later in his own work. Carey follows up on his own suggestion in a different manner, by looking at the values that go into journalism school. Are the values here somehow contributing to the mistakes of disengaged news reporting? This question bears fruit in his often cited piece "The Problem of Journalism History" that appeared 5 years later (Carey, 1974/1997d).

The essay begins with the complaint that news history has become too bogged down with the stories of great reporters and editors. Journalism schools were teaching their students the reporting tradition according to the "whig" interpretation. This is a term borrowed from Herbert Butterfield's historiography. A whig history presents the past as a series of events unfolding in a steady progress towards the present as if past actors were aware of the goal of history. In journalism history events were presented as a linear sequence unfolding towards ever greater freedom in reporting and ability of distribute information to a grateful citizenry. In this interpretation, the autonomy of the reporter is always increasing and the government is always cast as the villain.

There are elements of truth to this interpretation and Carey typically refuses to condemn the whig history. He merely characterizes it as played out and no longer useful. The story of accelerating progress ignores the narrowing of the journalistic enterprise in our era. We may have news reports from all over the globe in a matter of seconds but our understanding of the world has not correspondingly deepened. The crusading news editor is now a relic, not a hero. The autonomous reporter has become increasing fearful of presenting any point of view, let alone one not sanctioned by a consensus. Meanwhile, broadcast competition has caused print writers to forego immediacy and visual description, adopting the neutral stance of expert analysis.

A tangible part of the problem is that journalism schools are not paying enough attention to the changing structure of the culture. This essay is a call for a cultural history of journalism to supplant the factual one that was now present in the classroom. In this call, Carey is feeling his way towards implementing the ritual bonds of communication across time into journalism programs. A plea for a cultural history is a plea to train students to enter into the imaginative side of previous events in order to understand the meaning of these events. Only slowly are communication scholars discovering this view of history, one path is through Walter Ong, McLuhan and through McLuhan's discussions of the earlier philosopher of culture—Giambattista Vico (see McLuhan & McLuhan, 1988). Another is through Dewey, Innis, and Carey.

A cultural approach means that journalists cannot think of themselves as scientific observers outside the society about which they report. In other words, journalism has to be more than the instant factoid and static balance between two equally shrill voices; it ought to present the myriad positions that frame current controversies and disputes. Carey scolds journalists who quickly describe the "who, what, when, where" and then are skittish around the "why and how." The point is to convince reporters that their stories are not transparent transmissions of desiccated information and conventional punditry is the frame of the democratic dialogue in which the journalists themselves are engaged.

In "A Plea for the University Tradition," Carey (1978) amplified his argument into an actual plea in the presidential address to the Association for the Education in Journalism. Here he was speaking to a body of teachers who were still unsure of the union between the university and journalistic education, and he decided to treat his own election to the presidency of AEJ as the members' growing awareness of the intellectual possibilities of journalism. He borrowed Innis' title "A Plea for the University Tradition" to argue against separating journalism training from the university, against fragmenting the university into separate professional schools and ultimately against the collapse of the public (Carey, 1978, pp. 853-854).

Although Carey admonishes the specialties of the law school and the medical school, his special target is the journalism school. The reference to Innis was deliberate because media training has a unique place in the university's mission to preserve public memory; this is the place to begin a general reform of the public. He does not burden his audience with the space-time-bias model of Innis but the argument is centrally premised on this model. Carey (1978) tells us that: "Under the force of the media, public opinion lost its anchorage because the press was obsessed with the immediate. The intense concern with the present made the interest in the past and future difficult to maintain . . ." (p. 847). The wisdom of choosing the space-time model for the AEJ is that the one profession that may be the most culpable in depriving the public of its memory is the journalism profession. Thus, although Carey is arguing for a cultural history in journalism, he is arguing that the very profession that currently encourages public amnesia, must restore a sense of time and memory to its own work and to the public discourse.

Education has the greatest possibility for guiding students to the realization that journalism must be a ritual of communication as well as a transmission of information. In this spirit, Carey (1999) is fully allied with Jay Rosen (e.g., 1994) and others who seek to promote a sense of public journalism with practitioners.

CONCLUSION

I find that Carey's essays have an increasingly prescriptive basis. The intellectual task of preserving public culture—always present in his work—has become more prevalent since the AEJ address. It serves as the litmus test of what matters in media studies. For example, while Daniel Dayan and Elihu Katz (1992, pp. 25-53) have developed a descriptive model of media events, Carey takes their model to look at the Senate hearings on the nomination of Robert Bork for the Supreme Court. He finds that the media fully participated in a ritual of degradation and excommunication. That particular media event worked to undermine public culture of civility and toleration. Carey concludes with a strong feeling that the media ought to have resisted the political manipulation of that event.

There are several caveats embedded in the implied prescriptions of Carey's analyses. He believes in the community but he is not a strong proponent of the popular. Indeed popular division and fragmentation, as in various regional movements, are ill-considered reactions to the monolithic nature of global media. To put it another way, he writes very little about people forming alternatives to mainstream media and notions of an "empowered" audience. He writes a great deal about mainstream media returning to its democratic mission. He does not endorse technological determinism; he is a proponent of resisting technological bias toward a monopoly of knowledge. He is concerned with economic determinations of communication but he feels that communication cannot and should not be reduced to economic questions. He keeps returning to the original promise of media in the American experiment.

The very notion of an American experiment that can still be reformed is contrary to a radical political premise. The most prevalent criticism of Carey is as a reforming romantic. Michael Tracey accuses Carey of an Arcadianism, of turning away from the unequal distribution of power (cited in Munson & Warren, 1997, p. xv). Dan Schiller (1996) wonders why Carey assumes that everyone participates in language. "The implications of Carey's notion that language is, simply 'shared,' can hardly be masked: How—and how far—is English shared . . . ? Is standard English an example of Carey's shared language?" (p. 156). It is also instructive to mention Michael Schudson (1998), who started off providing the kind of cultural history that Carey called for and yet now seems to have veered off in another tangent, of debunking the notion that previous eras facilitated democratic discourse more than our current one. Together these state a hard-headed view of our past to overtly or implicitly undermine Carey's pluralist view of history.

They miss the premise of Carey's intellectual history methodology. The empirical question of whether a language community is always characterized by full and open participation is not the point. The pragmatic goal is search for a legacy can bring a useful perspective to our present struggle to build a community. Carey does this by examining and re-articulating the history of social thought concerning community building. Perhaps in this, Carey has more in common with McLuhan than with Mumford or Innis.

McLuhan was less concerned with the material investigation of the media environment than he was with how artists and others responded to their environment. This is evident in his long disquisition on Shakespeare's King Lear in the opening chapter of *The Gutenberg Galaxy* (McLuhan, 1962). Carey uses intellectual forebears to mark the interaction of the communication and social spheres. He uses past thought to illuminate current problems precisely because our discussions all too often are limited by space bias. We tend to forget past hopes and aspirations for a vibrant democracy. Therefore, we become too prone to errors of complacency and cynicism.

Alexis de Tocqueville admired the engaged debates of the 1830s America. Whether the extent of these debates actually can be measured is immaterial to Carey's method. What is material is that Tocqueville is witness to an emerging ideal of a democratic society. In the same manner the Lincoln/Douglas debates are one of the enabling beliefs we have about ourselves. Intellectual histories rather than case studies articulate how media must contribute to the growth of the American community and/or communities.

The nature of Tracey and Schiller's criticism demonstrate that they are refusing to share the purpose of Carey's scholarship. Carey (1991/1997e) once used Benjamin Franklin's phrase "a republic, if you can keep it" as an essay title. It is certainly a motto for his own work, which can be entitled "A public culture, if we can communicate." Thus, the method always prescribes the possibility of communication. This prescription is held on to, as a measure of the distant we have to go. It is of less pragmatic concern the extent that the reality of the past may have been less than ideal.

Carey has taken the implications of the Chicago School and applied them to the age of television. He has raised intellectual goal of journalism education by applying those broad social implications. His contribution to media technology thought is to keep a steady eye on the larger trends in social organization while acknowledging the bulk of the work that goes on in cultural studies and ethnography in micro-sociology. Because of this method, he is able to give interdisciplinary weight to the denunciation of current journalism. Many have seen that current media conglomerates have exchanged the cart for the horse by using news to pursue profits, rather than using revenue to pursue news (see, e. g., Bagdikian, 1983). Others are worried that globalization has facilitated corporate irresponsibility (Herman & McChesney, 1997). Carey pulls these concerns together within a philosophy of media that integrates cultural, political and economic approaches. The public must be educated to demand more of journalism and journalists must be part of that education and must be sensitive to the resulting demands.

We must read him in good faith and this can be drawback. He does not write in an argumentative style that will convince us despite our previous inclination. It is a style that never takes the time to pick apart other positions systematically. Thus, Carey's remarks on the excessive "economicism" of left wing analysis remains elusive. Most of all, he has not fully confronted those questions of popular culture that center on the meaning-making power of media audiences. He, of course, rejects the extreme passivity that McLuhan's media determinism assumes about the audience. On the other hand, there is a tension with a cultural studies approach that posits and honors the readers/audiences as actively involved in creating their own meaning. I infer this tension from Carey's Innis-like insistence on media balance, on reciprocity and full interaction. Is any of this possible when we transfer the site of meaning-making from producer to the audience? No, it is just flipping the monopoly of knowledge back into a private domestic space that defeats the public nature of meaning. This is the corollary of Carey's remarks on the excessive left-wing "economicism" that we can understand once we are reminded that economics is the domain of the private, of the "what's in it for me." In both cases, the private is the enemy of public meaning.

Carey's current work is about the post-network age and the breakdown of national systems of media. The triggering point is once again the role of journalism education. Globalization has accelerated media imbalance, to an annihilation of a long view of time, since companies that operate all over the world can operate without a sense of belonging anywhere. The various outlets of Rupert Murdoch's News Corporation seem more intent on distracting the various citizenries, not engaging them in the problems they ought to be considering. Of course, Murdoch is not the only one. "The various components of CBS and Viacom, like MTV, VH-1, and the UPN network speak to disembodied micro-publics who have no stake in the 'news' they receive and no physical connection to the community who watches it with them. It is as if, [Carey] quips, 'we have a Euro, without having a Europe'" (Alterman, 1999, p. 10).

Carey has turned his attention to the fate of the nation-state. The breakup of national media such as the three broadcast networks in the United States and deregulation of state broadcasting in Europe has fragmented culture into local and transnational entities. Whether either of these is satisfying to the kind of community that once Dewey and now Carey hope for is a very open question. Both have shown alarming tendencies for irresponsibility. Local cultures have shown lack of concern and hostility even to neighbors who happen not to be members of the culture. Global culture is too big for anyone to feel a sense of mutual obligation. Perhaps the nation was a unit that was large enough to provide services to all and to frame a truly democratic conversation.

ACKNOWLEDGMENT

I would like to thank Lynn Johnson-Corcoran, Heidi Kropf, Charles Marlor and John Rutherford of the Central Connecticut State Library for their assistance in helping me research this article.

ENDNOTE

1. While the Birmingham school viewed Britain as anthropologists would, the various members rejected the implicit functionalism of the contemporary anthropology of the 1970s.

REFERENCES

Alterman, E. (1999, October 11). A Euro without a Europe. *The Nation*, p. 10.

Bagdikian, B. (1983). *The media monopoly*. Boston: Beacon Press.

Carey, J. W. (1967). Harold Adams Innis and Marshall McLuhan. *Antioch Review*, 27(1), 5-39.

Carey, J. W. (1978). A plea for the university tradition. *Journalism Quarterly, 55*, 846-855.

Carey, J. W. (1988a). A cultural approach to communication. In J. W. Carey (Ed.), *Communication as culture: Essays on media and society* (pp. 13-36). Boston, MA: Unwin Hyman. (Original work published 1975)

Carey, J. W. (1988b). Mass communication and cultural studies. In J. W. Carey (Ed.), *Communication as culture: Essays on media and society* (pp. 37-68). Boston: Unwin Hyman. (Original work published 1977)

Carey, J. W. (1988c). Overcoming resistance to cultural studies. Reprinted in J. W. Carey (Ed.), *Communication as culture: Essays on media and society* (pp. 89-112). Boston: Unwin Hyman. (Original work published 1986)

Carey, J. W. (1988d). Technology and ideology: The case of the telegrapy. In J. W. Carey (1988), *Communication as culture: Essays on media and society* (pp. 201-231). Boston: Unwin Hyman. (Original work published 1983)

Carey, J. W. (1997a). Communications and economics. In E. S. Munson & C. A. Warren (Eds.), *James Carey: A critical reader* (pp. 60-75). Minneapolis: University of Minnesota Press. (Original work published 1994)

Carey, J. W. (1997b). The communications revolution and the professional communicator. In E. S. Munson & C. A. Warren (Eds.) *James Carey: A critical reader* (pp. 128-143). Minneapolis: University of Minnesota Press. (Original work published 1969)

Carey, J.W. (1997c). Political correctness and cultural studies. In E. S. Munson & C. A. Warren (Eds.), *James Carey: A critical reader* (pp. 270-291). Minneapolis: University of Minnesota Press. (Original work published 1992).

Carey, J. W. (1997d). The problem of journalism history. In E. S. Munson & C. A. Warren (Eds.), *James Carey: A critical reader* (pp. 86-94). Minneapolis: University of Minnesota Press. (Original work published 1974)

Carey, J. W. (1997e). "A republic, if you can keep it": Liberty and public life in the age of Glasnost. In E. S. Munson & C. A. Warren (Eds.), *James Carey: A critical reader* (pp. 207-227). Minneapolis: University of Minnesota Press. (Original work published 1991)

Carey, J. W. (1998). Marshall McLuhan: Genealogy and legacy. *Canadian Journal of Communication, 23*, 293-306.

Carey, J. W. (1999). In defense of public journalism. In T. L. Glasser (Ed.), *The idea of public journalism* (pp. 49-66). New York: Guilford Press.

Carey, J.W., & Quirk, J. (1988). The mythos of the electronic revolution: In J.W. Carey (Ed.), *Communication as culture: Essays on media and society* (pp. 113-141). Boston: Unwin Hyman. (Original work published 1970)

Dayan, D., & Katz, E. (1992). Media events: The live broadcast of history. Cambridge, MA: Harvard University Press.

Dewey, J. (1961). *Democracy and education: An introduction to the philosophy of education.* New York: Macmillan. (Original work published 1916)

Flayhan, D. P. (2001). Cultural studies and media ecology: Meyrowitz's medium theory and Carey's cultural studies. *The New Jersey Journal of Communication, 9*(1), 21-44.

Geertz, C. (1973). *The interpretation of cultures.* New York: Basic Books.

Grosswiler, P. (1998). *Method is the message: Rethinking McLuhan through critical theory.* Montreal, Canada: Black Rose Books.

Hallin, D. (1986). *The "uncensored war": The media and Vietnam.* New York: Oxford University Press.

Herman, E. S., & McChesney, R. W. (1997). The global media: The new missionaries of corporate capitalism. Washington, DC: Cassell.

Innis, H. A. (1964). *The bias of communication.* Toronto, Canada: University of Toronto Press. (Original work published 1951)

Lum, C. M. K. (2000). The intellectual roots of media ecology. *The New Jersey Journal of Communication, 8*(1), 1-7.

McLuhan, M. (1962). *The Gutenberg galaxy: The making of typographic man.* Toronto, Canada: University of Toronto Press.

McLuhan, M., & McLuhan, E. (1988). *Laws of media: The new science.* Toronto, Canada: University of Toronto Press.

Meyrowitz, J. (1985). *No sense of place.* New York: Oxford University Press.

Morley, D. (1992). *Television audiences and cultural studies.* New York: Routledge.

Mumford, L. (1934). *Technics and civilization.* New York: Harcourt Brace.

Munson, E. & Warren, CA, (Eds.). (1997). *James Carey: A critical reader.* Minneapolis: University of Minnesota Press.

Pauly, J. (1997). Introduction/On the origins of media studies (and media scholars). In E. S. Munson & C. A. Warren (Eds.), *James Carey: A critical reader* (pp. 3-13). Minneapolis: University of Minnesota Press.

Rosen, J. (1994). Making things more public: On the political responsibility of the media intellectual. *Critical Studies in Mass Communication, 11*(4), 362-388.

Schiller, D. (1996). *Theorizing communication: A history.* New York: Oxford University Press.

Schudson, M. (1998). *The good citizen: A history of American civic life.* Cambridge, MA: Harvard University Press.

Williams, R. (1977). *Marxism and literature.* New York: Oxford University Press.

10

Symbols, Thought, and "Reality"

The Contributions of Benjamin Lee Whorf and Susanne K. Langer to Media Ecology

Christine L. Nystrom
New York University

Toward the beginning of the 20th century, there arose an idea so powerful and so radical in its implications for our understanding of reality that it transformed every arena of scientific and humanistic study. This idea might most generally be summed up in the word *relativity*. More specifically, it is the idea that the reality humans encounter is not what is out there, but the particular version of what is out there that our instruments of perception, exploration, representation, and communication provide. Because I take this to be the defining idea of the 20th century, as well as the central idea on which media ecology is founded, it is worth saying more about it before turning to the ways in which Benjamin Lee Whorf and Susanne K. Langer transformed it into a cornerstone of media ecology.

THE ROOTS OF RELATIVITY

To begin, it should be said that although the idea of relative realities attained its most powerful expression and impact on human understanding in the 20th century, it did not originate in our own time. Plato knew, in the 5th century BCE, what Einstein demonstrated in 1905: that humans cannot encounter reality directly, but only from some position in relation to it and through instruments of perception and knowing that play an active (and transforming) role in our construction of the known. Plato's allegory of the cave is about as concise an illustration of the relativity of reality, of its social construction, and of the biases of the senses as one is likely to meet in 20th century works on the same subjects. But for all its centrality to Plato's philosophy of knowledge, the allegory of the cave was just that, an allegory, an illuminating tale and not a scientific treatise. Its potential as a serious instrument of thought in itself was swept away, with most things Platonic, by the new broom of the empirical sciences with the coming of the Enlightenment.

The great achievements of Enlightenment science in early modern times, and the steady march of technological progress that resulted, rested squarely on Newtonian assumptions of a fixed and absolute framework of space and time, and of observers entirely capable of neutral and objective reports on what they read in nature's book. Although those assumptions did not entirely banish intimations of relativism in the 18th and 19th centuries,[1] such intimations could not make much headway against the prevailing Newtonian paradigm of scientific objectivism. In that paradigm, the world was held to be ultimately knowable and (at least in theory) knowable in full, through instruments and procedures that in no wise affected the workings of the reality they investigated.

By the closing years of the 19th century, however, the Newtonian paradigm had begun to wobble more than a little under the weight of accumulating anomalies (Kuhn, 1962)—scientific findings that could not be made to fit coherently within the established frameworks, assumptions, and principles of Newtonian physics. These anomalies, arising out of the behavior of both very large bodies, like planets and solar systems and galaxies, and very, very small bodies, like electrons and other subatomic particles, led in the early years of the 20th century to the two great thought experiments that revolutionized not only science but our understanding of human knowledge and of its relationship to reality. The first was Einstein's question, "What would one see if one were riding astride a beam of light?" His answer was that what an observer sees depends both on the observer's position in relation to what is observed and on the speed at which the observer is traveling. Nor is it only the hypothetical *observer* who is affected by relative position and speed of movement. Instruments of measurement are equally affected: clocks slow down and speed up, yardsticks stretch and shrink with changes in speed of travel. Time and space themselves change as a function of the relative movements of objects and observers within them. There is, moreover, no place in which an observer can take a fixed stand *outside* these relationships, no position from which an observer can construct a detached, neutral, objective account of reality without including him or herself within it, as a defining element of that reality. In short, there are multiple realities of which accounts may be given, and each is dependent on the stance of the observer in relation to it.

The second thought experiment was that of Werner Heisenberg, and it emerged from attempts to predict the behavior of electrons in the shells of atoms. The Newtonian paradigm assumed that a complete understanding of the world could be built up, piece by piece, from the application of laws of physics to the interactions among the smallest building blocks of matter, thence to their interactions as larger units, thence to their interactions as still larger units, all the way up to the interactions of such great bodies as planets, stars, solar systems, and galaxies. To maintain that assumption, it was essential that the laws of physics be able to account with perfect precision for the interactions among the simplest building blocks of nature or all the rest would founder. Thus Heisenberg asked, "What would be required to ascertain the exact position and velocity of an electron in the simplest of nature's building blocks, the hydrogen atom, which contains only one electron in its shell?" His answer was that to obtain such information, an observer would need to somehow make the electron visible. This would require bouncing a beam of light off it, because we can only see what light reflects back. But as Einstein had already demonstrated, light itself is composed of particles that affect the position and velocity of what they bounce off. Making the electron visible would alter its position and velocity in such a way that, while one might be calculated with near-perfect precision, the other could not. To put it simply, wherever the electron might be before it is observed, it isn't, when it is observed because the requirements of *observing* change what is observed in ways that cannot be fully accounted for. Heisenberg concluded from this that there is an irreducible amount of uncertainty in our knowledge of the physical world, at least at the subatomic level. Because all the rest of our knowledge is built up from there, we can never attain the full and certain knowledge of reality that the Newtonian paradigm promised. The only reality one can have knowledge of is that reality which the conditions of observing it require. The conditions of observing, moreover—the operations of our senses and the technologies used to extend them; the structures of the media (like light or sound) they require to obtain information—not only limit what we can know, but *alter* the reality observed in ways not fully predictable, so that what we know and what is out there are sometimes subtly and sometimes greatly different things.

From this brief account of relativity as expressed in the physical sciences,[2] it should be clear why I say it is the central idea on which media ecology rests. Media ecology is the study of the ways in which our instruments of knowing—our senses and central nervous systems, our technologies of exploration, the physical media they require (like light, sound, electricity), and the conditions in which they are used—construct and reconstruct what we know, and therefore the realities that humans inhabit. To that extent, media ecology is deeply indebted, for its guiding assumptions and questions, to Einstein, Heisenberg, and their 20th century colleagues in physics, who made relativity the defining concept of the modern era.

But there is something critically important missing from the physicists' account of relativity, and from the definition of media ecology just provided. That something has to do with the meanings of knowledge and instruments of knowing. In Einstein's and Heisenberg's accounts, and in Plato's allegory of the cave, the instruments of knowing referred to are primarily our senses and those technologies used to extend them, and knowledge refers to the sensory data received through such means. But sensory data themselves constitute only a tiny part of what is meant by knowledge. Without some way to record, sort out, categorize, organize, retrieve, and communicate what we see, hear, smell, taste, touch, knowledge would consist merely of a welter of fleeting and fragmented impressions of what lies beyond our skins. To construct and maintain a coherent understanding of sensory experiences, we need something more than our senses. We need to *represent* experience to ourselves, so that what we know can be recalled and reworked and articulated and passed on to others in words, sentences, pictures, graphs, measurements, and other systems of codes and symbols. These systems of representation are no less vital instruments of knowing than our senses and their technological extensions. Codes and symbols also play an active role in constructing the realities we know—or think we do. Indeed, they play an even more significant role than do our senses and technical instruments, because codes of representation, starting with language, not only govern how we record and report what we see, but shape our choices about what to observe, and how to make sense of it. Heisenberg himself intimated as much in his well-known observation that "All we know of nature is a result of the questions we put to it." Questions are a product of language and, in this sense, Heisenberg meant to acknowledge the power of language as an instrument of knowing that transforms our conceptions of reality. Einstein, too, acknowledged the pivotal role of language in shaping constructions of reality when he remarked that the greatest adversary to his theory that space and time are functions of a single phenomenon, spacetime, is language itself, which insists on dividing space and time into two different things.

It was neither Heisenberg nor Einstein, however, who placed at the center of relativity, and of media ecology, the idea that language and, by extension, all symbol systems for representing experience, play a major role in how we construct reality and, as a consequence, conduct our affairs within it. That idea was given its most systematic and forceful expression, not by physicists, but by the linguistic anthropologists Benjamin Lee Whorf and Edward Sapir.

BENJAMIN LEE WHORF AND LINGUISTIC RELATIVITY

The names of Whorf and Sapir are invariably linked in referring to their powerful hypothesis about the role language plays in shaping human conceptions of reality; that is, their thesis is known, alternatively, as the Whorf–Sapir or Sapir–Whorf Hypothesis. I give Whorf precedence here, both in naming the thesis and in singling out his contribution to media ecology, because although Sapir is the better known (and more academically respectable) linguist, it is Whorf who most fully articulated the set of ideas that constitute what has also come to be called the theory of linguistic relativity and the theory of linguistic determinism. The choice between the latter two terms to characterize the Whorf–Sapir hypothesis, incidentally, is not unimportant, because they reflect different readings of the theory and its implications. Before turning to the thesis and its interpretations, however, let me provide a brief sketch of the two men whose names it bears.

Of Edward Sapir, I say very little, not because there is little to be said, but on the contrary, because his contributions to the study of language and culture were so extensive and distinguished that any attempt to sum them up in a few sentences would be both futile and presumptuous. Suffice it to say that he was, in the 1920s and 1930s, a leading linguist of the anthropologically oriented school founded by Franz Boas; an authority on American Indian languages; and a teacher of great distinction at the University of Chicago and, subsequently, at Yale University, where Whorf first came under his tutelage in 1931 (although the two had met and talked several times at professional congresses of linguists in earlier years).[3] Sapir's influence on Whorf's thought and work long predated their meeting, however, because Sapir's (1921) important and widely read book, *Language*, could scarcely have escaped Whorf's attention, addressing as it did many of the issues and languages with which Whorf was already deeply involved. Among these issues was the relationship between language and thought, which Sapir argued were inextricably related, although not *coterminus*, to use his word (p. 15), and between language and culture, which he argued must be considered separately from one another (pp. 218-219). Generally, it may be said that, once they began to work together as teacher and student, Sapir exercised a moderating influence on Whorf's more radical thinking, whereas Whorf apparently persuaded the more scholarly, careful, and temperate Sapir that bolder statements on the relationship between language and thought were warranted.[4]

As for Whorf, he was more than something of an anomaly among linguists. By academic training a chemical engineer, and by his own choice a lifelong employee as a fire insurance claims adjuster and administrator for the Hartford Fire Insurance Company, Whorf had no formal education in linguistics until he enrolled in Sapir's course in American Indian languages at Yale in 1931. But he was a voracious reader with a particular passion and gift for languages, a denizen of museums and libraries with university-quality collections on linguistics and American Indian cultures, and a tireless correspondent with Americanists and linguists throughout the United States and Mexico. By the late 1920s, he had already presented technical papers on such subjects as Toltec history and Aztec linguistics at learned congresses of Americanists and linguists, and his scholarly output and reputation grew steadily throughout the 1930s and 1940s, with many of his technical articles on Aztec, Shawnee, and Hopi linguistics appearing in the professional journals of both linguists and anthropologists and in books compiled by such notable linguists as Harry Hoijer. In the 2 years before his untimely death in 1941, at the age of 44, Whorf brought his ideas before a wider, non-specialist audience in a series of three articles on linguistics, science, and logic published in MI T's *Technology Review,* and it was in these three pieces, together with his widely reprinted 1939 article on "The Relation of Habitual Thought and Behavior to Language," that he gave the thesis of linguistic relativity its most forceful expression.

Linguistic Relativity

In "Science and Linguistics," Whort (1956) put the thesis this way:

> [T]he background linguistic system (in other words, the grammar) of each language is not merely a reproducing instrument for voicing ideas but rather is itself the shaper of ideas, the program and guide for the individual's mental activity, for his analysis of impressions, for his synthesis of his mental stock in trade. Formulation of ideas is not an independent process, strictly rational in the old sense, but is part of a particular grammar, and differs, from slightly to greatly, between different grammars. We dissect nature along lines laid down by our native languages. The categories and types that we isolate from the world of phenomena we do not find there because they stare every observer in the face; on the contrary, the world is presented in a kaleidoscopic flux of impressions which has to be organized in our minds—and this means largely by the linguistic systems in our minds. We cut nature up, organize it into concepts, and ascribe significances as we do, largely because we are parties to an agreement to organize it in this way—an agreement that holds throughout our speech community and is codified in the patterns of our language. The agreement is, of course, an implicit and unstated one, BUT ITS TERMS ARE ABSOLUTELY OBLIGATORY; we cannot talk at all except by subscribing to the organization and classification of data which the agreement decrees.

> This fact is very significant, . . . for it means that no individual is free to describe nature with absolute impartiality but is constrained to certain

modes of interpretation even while he thinks himself most free. . . . We
are thus introduced to a new principle of relativity, which holds that all
observers are not led by the same physical evidence to the same picture
of the universe, unless their linguistic backgrounds are similar, or can in
some way be calibrated. (pp. 212-214)

I cite this passage in its entirety because it contains most of the significant ideas that comprise Whorf's thesis. But it does not contain all of them.
A fuller reading of his collected papers suggests the following elaboration.
Every language is a particular way of cutting up and reassembling the reality experienced through our senses. Our senses alone give no instruction, for
example, about where one thing ends and another begins. We can say, "See
that cup." But no one has ever *seen* a cup that is not part of some larger
whole: cup-in-the-hand, or cup-on-the-desk, or cup-on-the-shelf. The same
is true for the hand, the desk, and the shelf. Each is connected in sensory
experience to something more. But through the agency of *naming* we can
cut the connections, separate the cup from the hand or the shelf, and
through *grammatical conventions,* we can reshuffle nature at will: take the
horns from a goat and the mane from a lion, the head of a man and the legs
of a horse, and imagine a creature to vex our dreams to nightmare. In short,
through words we can make a world our senses cannot enter, a place biology cannot even understand. And words, for all their power, cannot encompass what biology understands. Language *represents* experience, or part of it;
it does not *replicate* experience. Indeed, that is where the power of language
lies: in the fact that it is a code, not a replica of the world known through the
senses. Through words we can construct a universe we cannot hear, see, or
touch. We can call to mind times that do not exist to our senses, the future
and the past, and invent things like cups and tables, unicorns and gargoyles,
that nature has never produced. Because language is a *code,* it operates
according to rules that are not the rules of our creaturely experience, of the
sensory–motor–biochemical world. And that world cannot be made to fit
within the structures and rules of language. The reality given by language is
fundamentally different from the reality given by sense data.

Words and Worldviews

Whorf argued that no two languages cut up reality in exactly the same way.
To begin with, each has a somewhat different lexicon or set of words it uses
to call attention to one or another distinction that is important in the lives of
the people who use that language. And we habitually attend to those distinctions our vocabularies make. There is nothing startling about this observation or about the fact that, even among speakers of the same language, there
may be large differences in vocabulary. One would expect, for example, that

people who ski will use more words for different types of snow than will ordinary city dwellers, for whom the generic "snow" (and perhaps "slush") will suffice; and that people who work with textiles for a living will have a larger set of words for different kinds of weaves and fabric surfaces than those who do not. Nonetheless, it is important to note that the vocabulary distinctions any language provides never reflect the infinite gradations of difference in nature. Each person, for example, is unique in his or her feelings of sexuality and their enactment. At the moment, however, English provides only a small set of words—masculine, feminine, homosexual, gay, queer, lesbian, bisexual—to categorize a much larger spectrum of variations. In so doing, it tells us which differences this culture thinks it is important to pay attention to and which may be safely (for social reasons) ignored. Of greater importance, it suggests that these are the real categories of sexuality into which nature is divided, and this is more Whorf's point: The lexical categories language provides condition the ways in which reality is conceptualized. Still, Whorf gave only passing attention to lexical differences among languages, except to point out that the vocabulary distinctions available to a speech community condition the attention given to differences among things and, conversely, the tendency to treat things named by the same word as the same. Of far greater importance, in his thesis, is the nature of the units into which different languages carve up the world—that is, *how* they construct their words and the grammatical categories into which different phenomena are sorted. English (and most European languages), Whorf pointed out, cuts up reality into hundreds of discrete, autonomous things: cups, tables, chairs, cats, dogs. It also distinguishes grammatically among such "things" *(nouns)* and what we conceive of as actions or processes—running, growing, loving, and going *(verbs)*. Moreover, English has a set of grammatical rules that permits the transformation of almost any verb into a noun; thus loving becomes love, growing becomes growth, and thinking becomes thought. These grammatical features of English, he argued, play an important role in the tendency of English speakers (and speakers of other languages with the same features) both to conceive of reality as a collection of discrete objects and to objectify (i.e., make into things) phenomena that are not thing-like at all. What could be less like a thing and more a dynamic process than, for example, an explosion? English allows us to disguise the process as a thing by the simple technique of assigning it the form of a noun. This in turn leads us to talk and behave as though relationships, activities, and processes exist in the material world in the same way as do other "things" in the grammatical category of nouns, like cats and dogs and apples, and to search for them there—as when people search for love or success or power, or resent their inequitable distribution or mourn their loss.

By contrast, the radically different languages Whorf studied—Shawnee, Aztec, Hopi, Nootka—form their words in a process Whorf called polysynthesis. In those languages, each word consists, not of a single unit with a discrete semantic meaning, like dog, or apple, but of a core semantic root embedded in a relatively large set of prefixes, suffixes, and other morphemes that indicate particular states, relationships, intensities, conditions of observation, and the like. In other words, such polysynthetic languages cut up experience into less autonomous or isolated pieces than does English (and other European languages); they incorporate in their words a larger part of the sensory, social, and interactive surround. This aspect of their grammatical structure, Whorf argued, favors a way of conceptualizing reality that focuses more on relationships and contingencies than on isolated entities and their actions, as English speakers conceive it.

Structure of Grammar and Thought

Such languages as Hopi do not permit, according to Whorf, the objectification of such nonspatial and subjectively experienced phenomena as duration (the sense of the passing of time) or of feelings, wishes, hopes, thoughts, expectations, and the like. Indeed, to speak of these requires an entirely different grammatical form from that used for objects with perceptible spatial features, and the different forms may not be used interchangeably, any more than we may use English verb tenses interchangeably—for example, say "He ran to the store" to indicate something that *will* happen tomorrow. Just as English speakers *must* choose a verb form that indicates whether something has happened in the past, or is happening now, or will happen in the future, speakers of Hopi, for example, *must* choose a verb form that indicates whether the event/thing spoken of lies in the realm of the objective world (i.e., things perceptible to the senses at the moment of speaking) or in the realm of the subjective (i.e., things remembered, imagined, hoped for, but not-now-present-to-the-senses). This grammatical distinction between the objective and the subjective realms extends, in languages like Hopi, even to ways of counting. In English, cardinal numbers (one, two, three, four, etc.) can be used to count both perceptible collections of objects, like chairs in a room or pieces of chalk held in the hand, and purely imaginary collections, like a set of days (which no one has ever seen standing together in a cluster, like so many trees or houses). But Hopi grammatical structure does not permit the use of cardinal numbers for counting such imaginary collections. It requires, instead, the use of ordinals to count remembered or anticipated successions of events. The Hopi speaker cannot talk of 10 days or 6 years, but must speak of the tenth coming of *the* day or the sixth coming of *the* spring. This grammatical requirement, Whorf argues, reinforces a construction of reality in which events-in-time are understood not as a progression of units along some imaginary line extending from the past into the future (as the structure of English leads us to conceive them), but as a continuous *cycle.* In this worldview, such Western conceptions as the idea of progress are not only very difficult to express, but more important, difficult (if not impossible) to *think.* So, too, are such notions (and behavioral compulsions) of English speakers as the preoccupation with saving time, spending time, wasting time, investing time, and the like. Such preoccupations arise in large part from the linguistically founded conception of time as a *thing* that exists in the real world as a set of units that may be counted, collected, stored, and otherwise handled just as any other set of perceptible objects.

The cyclical conception of time codified in the linguistic structure of Hopi is closely related to the cultural history of its speakers. The Hopi are an agrarian people, at least in origin, closely tied to the cycles of the seasons and of planting, reaping, and cultivation of the earth. Thus, the question arises, "Which came first: their language and the habits of thought and behavior it engenders, or their cultural activities, which shaped the development of their language?" This is a question about how language and culture originate and evolve and it has an important place in our attempt to understand ourselves. But it is not a question that Whorf was concerned to address in detail, except to stress that language and culture grow up hand in hand in their origins and evolution and are inextricably intertwined. From the point of view of the present, however, how different languages attained their grammatical structures is largely irrelevant. Every human child is born into a language community that already has a fully developed linguistic system in place. Every child, in the process of learning to speak, learns along with his or her language the particular *way* of cutting up and reassembling reality that the grammatical structure of his or her language requires. Having learned that way, reinforced every time we speak, write, or think, we unconsciously project it onto reality ever after. Thus, to one extent or another, we all become prisoners, not of our senses, but of our language.

Linguistic Relativity or Linguistic Determinism?

The key question is to *what* extent language imprisons thought. As I noted earlier, there are some who have read Whorf's thesis as an argument for linguistic determinism. That is, they understand him to be saying that (a) *all* thinking is linguistic; (b) every aspect of a language imposes equally inescapable constraints on thought, perception, and behavior; and therefore (c) language totally dictates (or determines) thought and culture. Pinker (1994) is one contemporary writer on language and thought who represents Whorf's thesis in this way, and he ridicules the absurdity of such a set of ideas (no doubt to bolster the serious significance of his own, by comparison). Indeed, such a position *would* be absurd. But this is more Pinker's construction than Whorf's. In the long excerpt cited earlier, Whorf is careful to say that the kaleidoscopic flux of our sensory impressions is organized *largely* by the linguistic systems in our minds, and that we cut nature up and organize it as we do *largely* because we are parties to an agreement codified in the patterns of our language. *Largely is* not the same as *entirely,* and Whorf was of the view that underlying all the variations of languages there are more fundamental processes of mind. As Whorf (1956) put it:

> [T]he tremendous importance of language cannot, in my opinion, be taken to mean necessarily that nothing is back of it of the nature of what has traditionally been called "mind." My own studies suggest, to me, that language, for all its kingly role, is in some sense a superficial embroidery upon deeper processes of consciousness, which are necessary before any communication, signaling, or symbolism whatsoever can occur. (p. 239)

Whorf hoped that the study he called *comparative linguistics* might eventually lead to the discovery of a universal set of sublinguistic or superlinguistic mental processes that, transformed as they may be by the varieties of different languages, would provide clues to those commonalities that bind us as members of a single human family. In this respect, he anticipated the Chomskian project of searching for universals underlying the diversity of human tongues. But his own project had a different thrust: to demonstrate that the grammatical structures of widely different language groups provide a ready-made set of patterns that give very different shapes to the habitual modes of perception, conception, and elaborated thought of their speakers.

The phrase that most troubles determinist readers of Whorf's thesis, in the frequently quoted passage cited earlier, has to do with the "absolutely obligatory" terms in which different languages codify thought. If this is taken to mean that *every* aspect of a language is absolutely obligatory, then the thesis is not only deterministic but exceedingly easy to refute, because nothing could be more obvious than the *choices* speakers (and writers) must make in composing every utterance. Nothing obligates me to use the word "use" rather than "choose" or "select" in the sentence I am now writing, and I might have written "instead of" in place of "rather than." Indeed, writing and speaking (not to mention thinking) would be a great deal easier if *all* the terms of language were equally obligatory. But that is not what Whorf says. It is the grammatical structures and categories of language, not word choices, that he characterizes as absolutely obligatory for elaborated thought. The grammatical structure of English, for example, requires us to indicate in the form of every verb the time it refers to—past, present, or future. We cannot choose *not* to do so. The grammar of Hopi, by contrast, has no tenses, but imposes different requirements—among them, not only the use of different verb forms to distinguish between objective and subjective events and phenomena, but the use of different endings to indicate whether utterances are reports, expectations, or generalizations. English grammatical structure requires us to articulate thought in sentences composed of substantives (or subjects) and predicates, leading us to conceive of the world as composed of actors and their actions—even when there are no actors in any sane sense of the word. (What exactly is the "it" that is doing the activity of raining, for example, in the sentence "It is raining"?) Hopi grammatical structure does not require verbs to have subjects, and thus constructs a different picture of reality.

Can we think *outside* the grammatical structures of our own language—fully grasp an alternative reality where time, for example, has no past, present or future? Can a native speaker of English genuinely apprehend, and accept as an entirely reasonable construction of reality, the idea that a rosebush and the *thought of* a rosebush are not two independent things but are simply two different stages of a single phenomenon, so that the one of course affects the other? No doubt one *can* think such thoughts, and Whorf would have been the last to deny it. Were it not possible, he would not himself have been able to make sense of the Hopi or Aztec or Nootka constructions of reality—nor would his readers be able to understand his attempts to explain them. But it is intensely difficult to think in such ways for more than a few moments, and we do not *habitually* do so.

Language and Culture

Habitual thought runs quickly and lightly along the tracks that linguistic structures provide. If it did not, it would be a continuous struggle to think and speak at all and people would find themselves continually at odds with their own culture. For the worldviews languages codify are expressed and reinforced not only in speech but in countless other symbol systems, cultural practices, and social institutions. The objectification of time that characterizes the linguistic structure of English and other Standard Average European languages, for example, gives rise to mechanical clocks, calendars, digital watches, time cards, daylight saving, lateness penalties, datebooks, appointments, and hundreds of other artifacts, practices, and cultural values derived from the projection of time into an imaginary visual space, where it may be carved into units and counted. Of course, linguistic structure alone is not the cause of such techniques and cultural practices. As other media ecologists have pointed out, in particular, Havelock (1976), McLuhan (1964), and Ong (1982), the development of writing systems, beginning some 3,500 years ago, also played a major role in the spatialization and objectification of subjective experience. Writing permits the commitment of thoughts, expectations, feelings and the sense of the passage of time to a fixed, visible form outside the body, as marks on stone, clay, and paper. It projects subjective experience into visual space, and by fixing it there, allows it to be subjected to analysis. One may not be able to see ten sunrises standing in a row like so many trees; but one can certainly see 10 *marks* representing those sunrises on a stone, and count the marks just as one counts any other collection of perceptible objects. It well may be that the availability of writing systems, rather than linguistic structure, is the key factor in the objectification of time and the spatialization of the subjective that characterize cultures that write. Indeed, McLuhan and Ong, among others, have suggested that many of the characteristics of the Amerindian worldview that Whorf attributes to linguistic structure are better explained by the fact that the cultures Whorf studied are (or were then) primarily *oral* cultures; that is, cultures that did not develop writing systems of their own or come to rely on writing until recent times. Whorf did not live long enough to respond to that suggestion. If he had, he might have replied that the development of writing was itself influenced by the structures of the spoken languages of the cultures that played major roles in the evolution of writing from its logographic forms (in Sumeria and Egypt) to its syllabic forms (in West Phoenicia) and ultimately, to its unique alphabetic form (in Greece). Although he did not extend his inquiries back that far, Whorf (1956) does remark that much of the reference to the nonspatial by spatial terms and linguistic structures was already fixed in the ancient tongues, most notably in the Greek-influenced Latin from which most of the spatializing Standard Average European languages derive (pp. 156-157).

Whorf would have been quick, in any case, to grant an important role to writing in the intensification of such pre-existing linguistic biases toward spatialization. He understood that language and other systems of representation interact in exceedingly complex ways with social, environmental, and technological conditions to create and continually transform the ecologies of culture. He says so quite clearly in his brief answer to the question why and how the Western European worldview and the Amerindian attained their distinctively different forms:

> In the Middle Ages the patterns already formed in Latin began to interweave with the increased mechanical invention, industry, trade, and scholastic and scientific thought. The need for measurement in industry and trade, the stores and bulks of "stuffs" in various containers, the type-bodies in which various goods were handled, standardizing of measure and weight units, invention of clocks and measurement of "time," keeping of records, accounts, chronicles, histories, growth of mathematics and the partnership of mathematics and science, all cooperated to bring our thought and language world into its present form.

> In Hopi history, could we read it, we should find a different type of language and a different set of cultural and environmental influences working together. A peaceful agricultural society isolated by geographic features and nomad enemies in a land of scanty rainfall, arid agriculture

that could only be made successful by the utmost perseverance (hence
the value of persistence and repetition), necessity for collaboration
(hence emphasis on the psychology of teamwork and on mental factors
in general), corn and rain as primary criteria of value, need of extensive
preparations and precautions to assure crops in the poor soil and precar-
ious climate, keen realization of dependence on nature favoring prayer
and a religious attitude toward the forces of nature, especially prayer
and religion directed toward the ever-needed blessing, rain—these
things interacted with Hopi linguistic patterns to mold them, to be
molded again by them, and so little by little to shape the Hopi world-
outlook. (Whorf, 1956, pp. 157-158)

Whorf was not in fact a linguistic determinist. He was, rather, an early
media ecologist. He understood and argued persuasively that humans do not
live in the objective world alone, but in symbolic environments of thought,
communication, and culture built on systems of *representing* experience.
The earliest and most fundamental of these systems of representation is language, and Whorf's most urgent and insistent point was that language is not
a neutral container or conveyor of ideas, but an instrument of thought that
has a distinctive structure of its own, and a different structure in different
speech communities. These structures of language are interposed between
people and reality, and just as the astronomer's telescope, the biologist's
microscope, and the physicist's beam of light bring different realities into
view and transform them, so do the different structures of language construct different conceptions of the world. In particular, the structure of every
language codifies a *metaphysics*—a set of assumptions about the nature of
space and time and the relationships among objects and events within them
(or it). These conceptions, in turn, direct attention to certain aspects of experience and suggest different social arrangements, different cultural practices,
different inventions to solve particular problems as we conceptualize them.
Social arrangements, cultural practices, and inventions feed back into the
patterns of language, transforming it, in turn, in a continuous process of language, thought, and culture change.

Whorf himself did not generalize these foundational principles of
media ecology to all systems of representation and communication. His
passion and scholarly concern was language, and except for brief references
to such other symbolic forms as painting, music, dance, and architecture,
and to the medium of radio (relatively new on the scene in Whorf's time),
he did not pursue the question whether different forms of symbolic representation and communication might cut up and reassemble reality in ways
very different from language, in ways specific to the structure of each medium. But Whorf's work played a major role in moving that question to the
forefront of inquiry, and thus laid the groundwork for the development of
media ecology.

SUSANNE K. LANGER AND THE SYMBOLIC
TRANSFORMATION OF EXPERIENCE

One of the first to recognize the significance of the larger question implied by Whorf's work, and to address it systematically, was Susanne K. Langer. In the first of her major works on symbolic philosophy and aesthetics, *Philosophy in a New Key*, Langer (1942) argued that the "new key" of her title (i.e., the new question at the center of philosophical inquiry in the 20th century) is the question, What is the nature of symbolic representation and how does it function, in its various transformations, in the constructive process of human thought and response? In a set of volumes that became the core of her life's work—in particular, *Philosophy in a New Key* and its successor, *Feeling and Form* (Langer, 1953)—Langer set out to give her answer to that question. In the process, she set forth not only a comprehensive theory of symbolism, but an analysis of the different symbolic structures and functions of discursive language and painting, sculpture, architecture, literature, music, dance, drama, and film. Her work had worldwide impact on the philosophy of art, and it is still considered obligatory reading for students of aesthetic philosophy. More to the point, it is obligatory reading for students of media ecology, or should be, because *Philosophy in a New Key*, in particular, advances a number of ideas that are vitally important to the understanding of differences among various codes and modes of representation and their consequences for human thought and response. Here the focus is on the central argument of Langer's work in that volume, rather than on the detailed analyses of music, dance, sculpture, and so on, in *Feeling and Form*.

Signals, Symbols, and Mind

At the core of Langer's thesis is her argument that neither the human capacity for language nor our capacity to express feeling in such forms as ritual and dance is the distinguishing feature of the human mind; rather, these capacities grow out of a more fundamental activity that distinguishes humans from other creatures. That underlying activity of the human mind is the process of abstracting experience and representing it *in symbols that evoke conceptions*—that is, that *call ideas to mind*. This process of transforming experience into symbols is radically different from what other creatures do with signs. Signs (which may generally be defined as the entire set of things which indicate, to some creature or person, something else or some larger state of affairs) serve two quite different functions.[5] One function is to *signal* the existence of some state of affairs, as when a chimp barks to signal the approach of an intruder to the rest of its tribe. Signals serve as behavioral triggers or commands; they function as a stimulus to a conditioned response, so that the receiver behaves in response to the sign as it would in response to the actual presence of the intruder. In this respect, one might say that the meaning of a signal is the *behavior* it triggers. The signal-ic function of signs is widespread among creatures of all kinds and it is entirely utilitarian and survival-oriented. We ourselves may respond to signs as signals, as when we pull to the side of the road at the sound of fire-engine sirens, although the engines are not yet in view. But humans may also respond to signs *symbolically*. In their *symbolic* function, signs do not trigger overt behavioral reactions, but *call ideas to mind*. If the sound of sirens leads someone not to pull over, but to reflect on fire engines and their pretty colors, or on the brave deeds of firefighters, or on the irony that fire both gives life and destroys it, then the observer is responding to the sign (the sound of sirens) as a symbol, not as a signal. While doing so, the per-son is likely to be run down by the engines, but that is not the point. The point is that, in humans, signs may function either as signals or as *symbols:* as instruments for *thinking about* things they call to mind. The meaning of a symbol is not the reaction it calls into behavior, but the *conception* it calls to mind.

So far as is known, other creatures do not use signs as symbols. Chimps or gorillas may be taught to use a particular sign (from American Sign Language, or even on a keyboard) for banana. But it has not yet been demonstrated that they can use these signs as symbols; for example, to reflect on the virtues of bananas or their relative dietary value as compared to, say, fish. Their object in signing "banana" would seem to be to bring the banana into their hands, not the *idea* of bananas into their minds.[6]

Langer's point in distinguishing between the symbolic and signalic func-tions of signs is to rebut the view that human language is merely a complex elaboration on the signalling systems used by other creatures, and, like those systems, serves primarily communicative and utilitarian ends. That line of argument, she contends, leads inevitably to the privileging of discursive, propositional language over other forms of symbolic representation, because it is this form of representation that has made possible logic and sci-ence and all their utilitarian benefits. This view also relegates the arts to a minor and somewhat accidental position in the spectrum of human symbol-ic progress, because they do not seem to serve the destined utilitarian ends on which language is based (according to this view) and to which it must inevitably lead. By arguing that language is *not*, in its origins, an outgrowth of utilitarian signaling, but is, like the arts, a manifestation of the human mind's tendency to transform experience into *symbols*, Langer places the arts and discursive language on a par, as two different forms of that symbolic activity that characterizes all human thought.

Langer argues that the distinctively human need to transform experi-ence into symbols has generated two quite different modes of representation. Both are equally symbolic, and both reflect the higher activities of mind. But the two modes are quite different in their forms and structures, in the spectrum of human sensibility they represent, and in the responses they engender. Langer calls these two distinct patterns of codes the discursive and presentational (or nondiscursive) modes of symbolic representation. Discursive symbolism, according to Langer, is comprised for the most part of true or propositional language and of mathematics. These coding systems differ both formally and logically from the codes of presentational symbolism, which comprise what is usually called the arts: painting, photography, music, dance, sculpture, architecture, literature, drama, and film.

Digital Symbols and Discursive Forms

The major logical difference between the two modes derives from the ways in which they represent their objects, that is, the conceptions they call to mind. The discursive forms of true language and mathematics, to begin, represent ideas in discrete units, sometimes referred to as digital symbols, that have no natural or structural correspondence to what they represent.[7] A digital symbol is a purely *arbitrary* mark or sound associated with a concept and applied to things and events as a name for them. There is nothing about the form of a digital symbol (its particular shape or noise or color or length or size or anything else) that corresponds to any perceptible characteristic of what it stands for. People simply *agree* to use this sound or mark or whatever to stand for something else (conceptions and the objects, events, etc., they denote). One cannot tell by looking at the letters "man," for example, whether the object denoted by those marks is big or little, straight or round, animate or inanimate. One does not change *the form* of the symbol to indicate a change in the form of what it denotes; one does not write MAN in bigger letters to indicate a big man, or use long words for long things and short words for short things. It is purely a matter of convention, of social agreement, to use *this* (digital symbol) to stand for *that* (conception, object, or event). As Whorf and other linguists have pointed out, different cultures have developed, over their long histories, very different agreements and conventions about what sounds and marks will stand for what concepts and name what things. That is why, if a Russian woman tries to describe her cat in *words* (digital symbols), listeners will not understand her (unless they speak Russian), nor a German man who describes his house in his language.

Words are not the only kinds of digital symbols. *Anything* can function as a digital symbol, simply by our agreeing to make it do so. People can agree to let the color red mean stop and the color green mean go, or the sound of a bell mean stop and the sound of a siren mean go. On road maps, we can let the color black mean two-lane roads, the color red mean major highways, and the color green mean throughways or toll roads. How would one know that? *Because the agreements about what digital symbols stand for can be made explicit.* If one looks at the top of the map (the key) it will indicate that black line equals two-lane road. A dictionary is a culture's equivalent of the map key for its lexicon: It makes explicit the concepts that words stand for and gives examples of the things and events that the words name or denote.

The individual units of discursive forms like true language, then, are arbitrary digital symbols that both bring to mind or *connote* certain abstract conceptions (like the conceptions associated with the word "dog," for example) and *name* (or *denote*) things in the world of experience that fit those conceptions (like the specific four-legged, tail-wagging, cold-nosed bundle of fur that barks you a welcome home each evening). But that is only the beginning. To construct their representations of experience, discursive forms also rely on *syntax.*

Syntax is a set of rules for how to indicate the relationships among things denoted by individual words. The important point is that these rules, like word-symbols, are a form of *digital* symbolism, in that the rules are a matter of cultural agreement or convention. Different cultures have different ways to indicate different relations among things. In English, for example, the order in which things are named tells us what is the subject (or doer of the action) and what is the object (or receiver of the action) in some situation. Generally, the rule is, "Name the doer of the action first, then the action, then the thing acted upon." This rule lets us know that when someone says, "The dog chased the cat," they mean the dog was running after the cat (because that's the order in which they named them). In some other languages, the *order* of the words doesn't make any difference. They have a different rule—like "attach a particular ending to a word to indicate that it's the subject, and a different ending to indicate which one is the object." It is possible to make these rules for how to indicate relationships among named things *explicit.* That's what I've just done: told you the rule in English for how to indicate the subject and object. If you study a foreign language by using a textbook, the textbook will teach you the explicit rules for indicating various kinds of relationships in that language.

These characteristics of true language—that it uses digital symbols whose meanings and rules for indicating relationships can be made explicit—give it an enormous capacity for precision in representing experience and communicating it to others. Syntax, in particular, allows the representation of complex *situations* with great specificity and distinction between one situation and another. Syntax allows us to assert that "this pattern of symbols corresponds to that situation in the real world." It allows us to make *statements* that others can decode by following the explicit rules, then verify or refute by looking at the world. But there is a catch.

Truth, Falsity, and Propositions

The catch is that not all statements can be verified or refuted (falsified) by looking at the world. There are some statements, for example, that are not *about* the world outside our skins and what is going on out there. There are many statements, for example, about what *ought* to happen in the world. These are usually called prescriptive statements, to contrast them with descriptive statements. Commands, too, are a form of prescriptive language. Logicians have pointed out that prescriptions, whether they are commands or statements about what ought to or should happen, cannot be verified or refuted by looking at the world because they don't indicate anything that is happening or has happened. One cannot say of such statements that they are either true (meaning, they correspond accurately to something that is happening in the non-word world) or false (meaning they do not correspond to what is happening outside our skins).

Second, we do not always make the meanings of our words so explicit that they indicate very specific things to look at in the world outside our skins. In other words, it isn't always clear what someone intends to *denote* by her words. If I say, for example, "There is a purgle in the top left corner of this page," and you do not know what the word "purgle" denotes, you cannot judge whether one is there or not, because you don't know what to look for or how you would know whether there's one there. The same thing is true about a great many regular words like "ghost," "soul," "intelligence," and "beauty." Unless the speaker makes his meanings so explicit (i.e., makes them public) that we can be sure we are looking for or at the same *thing*, there is no way to determine whether it is there or not. In short, one cannot say a statement is true or false unless one knows precisely what the words used in it *denote*.

The same thing would be true if one doesn't know the rules for decoding the statement as a unit; that is, if it does not follow the conventional rules of grammar or syntax. If someone puts her words in an any-which-way order, one would not be able to tell what she means to assert, or even whether an assertion has been made. We cannot say that something is true or false if we don't know what it means. In order to assert something in English, one must arrange words in such a way as to *predicate* something about a subject; that is, say something *about* it.

Finally, one cannot say that something is true or false unless there is some conceivable way to *test* it; that is, some imaginable procedure one could use to verify or refute it. If I say, for example, "No more than 23 angels can dance on the head of a pin at the same time," and specify precisely what I mean by an angel (e.g., a being exactly like a human, but invisible), and the dimensions of the pin, you would still need to know how you could find out whether that is true or not. If the answer is, "There is no way to find out, because angels never do it when someone is there, or when any kind of mechanical device is around," then it makes no sense to say the statement is true or false because there is no way to verify or refute it.

In the tradition of other symbolic philosophers, Langer uses the term "propositions" or "propositional utterance" to refer to representations that satisfy the foregoing criteria. Propositions are *statements* that can be said to be true or false because (a) they use symbols that have explicit, public denotations; (b) they conform to syntactic rules that can be made explicit; (c) they propose or assert (i.e., predicate) something about something; (d) they are *descriptive*, not prescriptive; and (e) they are in principle subject to tests of refutation and verification.

All this is necessary to understand because Langer argues that *propositional utterance is both the symbolic form and the mission of true language and of discursive symbolism in general.* The discursive forms of symbolic representation, comprised of true or propositional language and mathematics, are the codes through which people conduct rational thought and reasoning, and through which they build up scientific and logical knowledge of the world.

Analogic Symbols and Presentational Forms

True language and mathematics are not, however, the only forms in which the human mind expresses its need to transform experience into symbols. Langer argues that the discursive forms of symbolic representation constitute only a fraction of our total symbolic experience. The larger part takes a different form, which Langer calls the nondiscursive or presentational mode of representation, and it differs from the discursive mode in many important respects. To begin, the presentational forms of representation—like drawings, paintings, photographs, music, dance, and the other arts—are not composed of digital symbols, but represent their objects (that is, what they call to mind) *analogically.* Unlike a digital symbol, which is totally arbitrary, an *analogic* symbol represents in its *form* some important characteristic(s) of the object it stands for, in such a way that when the characteristics of the *object* change, so does the form of the symbol. Pictures, sketches, and drawings are good examples of *analogic* symbols. If I want to send my sister a sketch of a new dining table, and the table is round, the shape I draw must also be round. If the table is square, the shape of the marks I make on the paper must be changed to reflect that difference. If two different tables need to be represented, a cocktail table and a dining table, then shorter marks are made for the legs of the first and longer marks for the legs of the second to correspond to the different lengths of the legs on the objects. The way the path of a road is represented on a road map is also a good example of an *analogic* symbol: the line that represents the road changes in length and direction as the road changes in length and direction. Analogic symbols do not have to represent *every* feature of something to call their objects to mind. Some analogic representations are very detailed, as photographs tend to be, and some (like road maps) are very abstract, meaning they leave out most detail. The important thing in analogic representation is that some features of the *symbol* must correspond to some features of the *object* the symbol calls to mind.

To be more precise, an analogic symbol represents in its form the *structure of relations among parts* that the mind abstracts from *sensory* experience. The familiar visual symbol of the smiley face, for example, brings to mind a human face, not because real human faces are composed of three black dots and a curve, but because the *structural* relationship among the dots and the curve in the symbol corresponds to the *structural* relationship among eyes, nose, and mouth that the mind abstracts from the sensory perception of human faces. And it is the *whole structure* of relations among the elements of the symbol that is significant, that is *meaningful,* not the individual dots and lines of which the symbol is composed. To put it another way, the individual units or elements of which analogic/presentational symbols are composed do not have independent meanings outside the particular structure of relations in which they are presented. The smiley face, for example, is composed (in part) of three dots that are exactly alike, yet the two that are at the top of the drawing call to mind eyes, whereas the one in the center calls to mind a nose. In a totally different arrangement of lines and curves, the same dots might call to mind, instead, the pips on a strawberry, or raindrops falling from a cloud. In short, the elements of which presentational symbols like drawings or musical chords are composed are *not* the equivalent of words, which carry over their meanings from one context to another. It is quite impossible to say what a dot means generally in pictorial representation, or a straight line, or a curve. Similarly, it is impossible to say what the *sound* of a C-major chord calls to mind, or the sound of a piccolo or snare drum, outside of the context of their relations with other chords and instrumental sounds in a particular composition. That is, the individual elements of a complex presentational symbol like a painting or piece of music do not have independent, fixed connotations, as words do. Neither do the elements of a dance, a painting, or a symphony *denote* specific things and events in the experiential world. Musical sounds, for example, in particular combinations and relationships, may *connote* (call to mind) certain ideas and feelings (e.g., rising excitement or a sense of a resolution of tension), but they do not point to this or that event or object in the phenomenal world, as names for them. There are instances in which different musical sounds in a particular piece *are* used to refer to or denote specific things. For example, in *Peter and the Wolf* certain instrumental sounds and melodies denote the character Peter, while other sounds and melodies refer to different characters in the musical story. But people must be *told* this, in *words*, in a written program that accompanies the music. Without that guide, one could not guess from the sounds alone that they *denote* particular characters or events. Nor do the same instruments refer to the same characters and events outside that particular musical composition.

Similarly, the visual composition alone, in Picasso's *Guernica*, for example, does not denote or refer to any particular set of events. Its elements, in their specific arrangements, connote or summon to mind ideas/conceptions/feelings of discord, imbalance, destruction, chaos, grief, but they do not name any particular objects or events to which those feelings (and the symbolic elements of the painting) apply. Indeed, without the *title* of the painting (a word) and an accompanying linguistic text, one would not be able to say what the whole refers to or denotes.

Presentational Forms versus Statements

Because the units of which presentational symbolism is composed have neither fixed connotations nor explicit denotations, there can be no such thing as a dictionary in which one might look up the meanings of dots or lines or curves, or of the sounds produced by violins or piccolos, or of the different positions in which a dancer might hold her arms. Nor is there the equivalent of a grammar book where one can learn the explicit rules for building up the units of visual or musical representation into larger structures of meaning. This is not to say that paintings and symphonies and ballets do not *have* a structure. But it is a kind of structure entirely unlike the structure of propositional language and other discursive forms, and it does not lend itself to analysis into independent parts with fixed meanings and explicit rules for combining those parts into statements. Langer argues that the presentational forms of representation do not *make* statements. They present subjects, structured symbols that call to mind conceptions and feelings, but they do not predicate or assert anything *about* their subjects. A striking landscape photograph, for example, may call to mind many different ideas—about the monumental permanence and substantiality of mountain peaks, the insubstantiality of clouds, and the ever-changing quality of light, or about the relative endurance of nature compared to humankind, or about the magnificence of the Creator's awesome design. But the photograph itself does not assert any of these things. Such is the power of our tendency to think in *language*, as Whorf noted, that we may formulate into sentences the wordless conceptions to which paintings and photographs, music and dance and sculpture give rise. But the statements are not there in the work itself. Even the symbolic form of film, for which the metaphor of a language is often used, does not make statements (although its characters might when they speak). Film is not a medium for messages, assertions, statements, or propositions. Neither is painting, photography, music, dance, architecture, or sculpture. Their symbolic form does not permit them to assert or state anything because their elements do not have fixed connotations or denotations. The structural relations in which they arrange their elements are not the structural relations of linguistic syntax. For these reasons, Langer argues, the presentational forms of symbolism fall outside the realm of expression to which the words true and false apply. If MacDonald's *says*, in a television commercial, that its hamburgers weigh one quarter of a pound (before cooking), that is an assertion in the realm of propositional utterance; it may be subjected to tests of verification or refutation, and on the basis of the outcome one may say that the statement is true or false. But there is no way to test a series of images in which children roll in the grass with a lawnful of puppies in front of a MacDonald's sign, or smile and snuggle against their parents while eating French fries. Such images do not assert anything, such as "MacDonald's provides puppies to play with" or "French fries cause children to snuggle against their parents." Thus, the images themselves cannot be said to be true or false. One may like them or dislike them, be moved to laughter or tears by them, associate good feelings or bad feelings with them. But one cannot argue with them or refute them, because they are not in the symbolic realm of *discourse*. Discourse is defined by a specific set of formal and logical properties of representation, found in a limited set of codes, particularly true language and mathematics. The mode of symbolic transformation that characterizes such other codes as images, music, and dance has neither the forms nor the functions of discourse, argument, or reasoning. For that reason, Langer warns us not to use the metaphor of languages in referring to photography, film, painting, music, or dance, since it implies that these forms are language-like in their structures and functions, and obscures the much more important point that, in fact, they are vitally different.

Presentational Forms and Feeling

If the presentational forms of representation are *not* language-like, if they do not serve the functions of discourse, rational thought, argument, and reason, what functions *do* they serve? What exactly *is* it that they represent, and why do we need them? Langer's answer to these questions is concisely indicated in the title of her sequel to *Philosophy in a New Key: Feeling and Form* (Langer, 1953). To reduce it to a sentence, her argument is that the presentational forms of symbolism articulate the life of *feeling*. They provide, in their structures, symbolic *analogues* of what our eyes can see, what our bodies experience, what our ears hear, and all the feelings, sensory and emotional, that arise from our encounters with the world as very complex biological creatures. We need such modes of expression and communication because

*the ways in which language cuts up and reassembles the world are not the
same as the ways in which we experience the world through our senses.* We
are, despite all our rational linguistic achievements, creatures of biology and
sensation. Our deepest feelings run together, concatenate, reverberate, cross
semantic (and neurological) boundaries in ways that no digital symbol system of words or mathematical symbols can ever adequately represent. In its
technical sense, a digital system of codification is a way of sampling the full
range of some phenomenon, such as a sound wave or a light wave, rather
than reproducing the entire spectrum of variation along the wave.
Propositional language is like that: a sampling of what we experience, a highly selective and compressed code that represents only the peaks and troughs
of the continuous wave of our bio-sensory-motor experience—the bits and
pieces that have proven essential, in the history of our culture, to surviving
and getting on in the world. All the rest of the wave of our creaturely experience is voiceless because it has no words into which to fit. There is no adequate way to speak, in digital, propositional language, about how gravity
tugs at our senses and weighs us down, and how winter and rain and certain
slants of light seem to add to that weight, while the greening and brighten-
ing of spring somehow frees us. The tongue stutters and stammers in our
attempts to express our deep autumnal sense of—of what?—of things passing, slowing, dying, falling, darkening, spiraling down, coming to rest, and
of the inchoate feelings of longing, mourning, yearning that come with the
changing of the light. But the cello's voice in Max Bruch's *Kol Nidre* somehow sings of this, and dance gives expression to our feelings of weight and
weightlessness, falling and rising, tension and release, oppression and freedom, grief and joy.

In short, Langer argues that the presentational forms offer, in their
structures, complex analogues of sensory experience and feeling, of all that
cannot fit within the sparse and parsimonious structures of propositional
utterance. They also call forth a different mode of response. Where true language fosters analytic reasoning and linear thinking—the taking of things
apart and the reconstructing of ideas in logical and grammatical sequence—
the presentational forms foster the instantaneity of *recognition,* of gestalt
apprehension, for the meanings of pictures, music, dance must be grasped
as wholes or they cannot be grasped at all. Propositional utterance—true
language or discourse—fosters the delayed response, not only because its
elements are strung out one at a time in such a way that successive elements
modify the meanings of preceding ones, but because *the criterion of its merit
is its truth or falsity.* That requires time for tests of verification and refutation, the search for evidence in the non-word world to which propositions
purport to correspond. Thus discourse directs our attention outward to the
world beyond our skins. The criterion of merit for the presentational forms,
on the other hand, is not their truth or falsity, but their *consonance with the*

structure of our sensory experience and feeling. They direct attention inward.

The discursive and presentational modes of symbolic representation complement one another. Taken together, they permit us to do what neither mode can do alone: transform the entire range of knowledge and experience, thought and feeling, into symbols, and so give articulated expression to the fundamental activity of human mind.

Codes, Modes, and Media Ecology

Langer wrote *Philosophy in a New Key* in the early 1940s, and completed her analysis of the different forms of presentational symbolism in *Feeling and Form* in 1953. She did not foresee the proliferation of new forms of representation that would emerge with the maturing of television in the decades that have followed, and therefore did not address many of the questions that occupy media ecologists today—for example, how people choose between the different modes of response and assessment required by discursive and presentational symbolism when confronted with mixed forms such as the docudrama and the infomercial. Neither did she speculate on whether the increasing immersion of young people in presentational forms might lead to a rearrangement of habits of thought and response that would leave an older generation of discursively conditioned teachers puzzled and frustrated by their students' apparent difficulties with logic, reasoning, argument, and the niceties of evidence. Of computers and their unique symbolic forms, Langer had nothing to say—although she did move the terms virtual space, virtual time, and virtual reality out of the domain of physicists and into the common parlance of humanistic studies of symbols, codes, and media. Indeed, *Feeling and Form* is almost entirely about virtual space, time and reality and how they are constructed and manipulated in different symbolic forms. Her analysis there is as vital for understanding the role of computer-mediated forms in the construction of reality and response as it is for understanding the more traditional forms of representation and their unique functions.

I have focused on *Philosophy in a New Key* here not only because it is, as Langer herself wrote, a prerequisite for understanding the later work, but because it first charted the ground on which so much of media ecology stands. In it, Langer extended Whorf's insights into the relativity of language to a much larger set of codes and modes of representation. She argued that language is not *the* way in which humans construct reality, but *a* way, and that different systems of symbolic transformation codify different aspects of the spectrum of human experience. She raised for the first time, in a systematic way, the question, How does the *structure* of different symbol systems constrain what they can express, and shape the nature of human response?

As Heisenberg said, all that we know is a result of the questions we ask. Benjamin Lee Whorf and Susanne Langer are foundational to media ecology, not because their analyses of the languages and other symbolic forms they addressed are adequate or complete or even correct in every respect. They are foundational because they asked the right questions.

ENDNOTES

1.   For an excellent compendium of quotes from Enlightenment thinkers who anticipated later ideas on the role of language in shaping conceptions of reality, see Postman (1999).
2.   Comprehensive and quite readable accounts of these ideas can be found in Barnett (1968), Heisenberg (1962), and Matson (1966).
3.   Biographical data in this and the following paragraph were abstracted from Carroll's introduction to and comprehensive bibliography in *Language, Thought and Reality* (Whorf, 1956). All references to Whorf's thought and writing are to Whorf's articles, collected in the same volume (Whorf, 1956).
4.   Although Sapir's (1921) views in *Language* were rather moderately expressed, Whorf quotes him, by 1934, as saying, "The fact of the matter is that the 'real world' is to a large extent unconsciously built up on the language habits of the group. . . . We see and hear and otherwise experience very largely as we do because the language habits of our community predispose certain choices of interpretation" (cited in Whorf, 1956, p. 134).
5.   For clarity of explanation, I have revised Langer's use of "sign" and "signal" in *Philosophy in a New Key* according to her later use of those terms in *Feeling and Form*, and her acknowledgment that this usage is more accurate. See Langer (1953), p. 26, n 1.
6.   There is, of course, a great deal of debate on this issue at present. Here I represent Langer's view of the matter (as well as my own).
7.   Langer does not use the terms digital and analogic symbols, although she does consistently refer to presentational symbols as "analogues." I have introduced the terms digital and analogic for purposes of providing a clearer explanation and more current terminology.

REFERENCES

Barnett, L. (1968). *The universe and Dr. Einstein.* New York: Bantam Books.

Havelock, E. A. (1976). *Origins of Western literacy.* Toronto, Canada: The Ontario Institute for Studies in Education.

Heisenberg, W. (1962). *Physics and philosophy.* New York: Harper & Row.

Kuhn, T. S. (1962). *The structure of scientific revolutions.* Chicago: University of Chicago Press.

Langer, S. K. (1942). *Philosophy in a new key.* Cambridge, MA: Harvard University Press.

Langer, S. K. (1953). *Feeling and form.* New York: Charles Scribner's Sons.

Matson, F. W. (1966). *The broken image: Man, science and society.* Garden City, NY: Doubleday.

McLuhan, M. (1964). *Understanding media: The extensions of man.* New York: McGraw-Hill.

Ong, W. J. (1982). *Orality and literacy.* New York: Methuen.

Pinker, S. (1994). *The language instinct.* New York: William Morrow.

Postman, N. (1999). *Building a bridge to the eighteenth century.* New York: Alfred A. Knopf.

Sapir, E. (1921). *Language.* New York: Harcourt, Brace.

Whorf, B. L. (1956). *Language, thought and reality.* Cambridge, MA: MIT Press.

11

Susanne Langer's Philosophy of Mind

Some Implications for Media Ecology

John H. Powers

Hong Kong Baptist University

As media ecologists begin to build a coherent conceptual framework for developing their theory and research in a programmatic manner (Lum, 2000), one of their most useful intellectual resources may be the nine volumes produced by philosopher Susanne Langer (1895–1985) during the course of a professional career that spanned more than 60 years. Langer was an exceptionally systematic thinker whose interests ranged over a wide variety of topics that are relevant to understanding the nature of symbolic media, the intricate relations that may exist among various kinds of media, and the kind of symbolic activity that characterizes the human mind. The purpose of this chapter is to introduce Langer's ideas and to explore some of their implications for constructing the conceptual foundations for the emerging field of media ecology. I begin with a survey of Langer's major writings in order to provide a sense of the range of topics that she addressed and how they developed over time. Then I extract from her works a number of principles that should prove conceptually useful for the development of media ecology theory and analysis.

LANGER'S MAJOR PUBLICATIONS

Langer is best known for two of her books, *Philosophy in a New Key* (*PNK*; 1942/1957a) and *Feeling and Form* (*FF*; 1953). In *PNK*, Langer argues that the key to understanding our distinctively human mentality is recognizing the mind's relentless power of transforming routine sensory experience into a myriad of different types of symbolic forms. In the course of developing this argument, Langer generates a detailed semiotic theory that first distinguishes signs (the basis of animal mentality) from symbols (the basis for the uniquely human mind) on structural grounds, and then develops a theory of the two different categories of symbols that humans produce, namely, discursive (language in the strict sense) and presentational (virtually all other forms of symbolism). In the second half of the book she explores the nature of language as a system and selects three different forms of presentational symbolism—ritual, myth, and music—for additional consideration.

Based on the theory of symbolism presented in *PNK*, Langer subsequently developed an elaborate analysis of one of the many classes of presentational symbolism, namely, the creative arts—published as *Feeling and Form* and subtitled, *A Theory of Art Developed from Philosophy in a New Key*. Divided into three parts, *FF* first explores what it means to say that a work of art *as a whole* is a singular, unified symbol and then examines the relation such symbols have to the artist's understanding of the many forms of human feeling, of which artistic creations are symbols. The largest part of the book explores the nature of each of the arts separately, arguing that each different type of artistic medium (whether music, painting, architecture, dance, literature, etc.) is uniquely suitable for expressing in symbolic form some specific category of human experience: time, space, ethnic domain, memory, destiny, fate, and so forth. In Langer's terms, each of the arts creates a different form of virtual experience that helps make some aspect of our actual experience more easily perceptible for reflective contemplation and deeper understanding. That is, the art symbol directly presents the artist's idea about the nature of some type of human feeling so that the feeling can be inspected through this symbolic projection. The third part of *FF* steps back from the analysis of each of the arts seriatim and explores what the arts *as arts* have in common that allows them to all be considered collectively as different members of the same general class of presentational symbolism, namely, the *creative* arts.

Were these two books Langer's only publications, she would already have an important role to play in the development of media ecology as a discipline. Her theory of signs and symbols remains the best account of the logical basis of the distinctions between these two types of human expression, and her theory of art not only produces an insightful approach to understanding different classes of artistic media, but also illustrates the kind of careful thought that is required to analyze the many philosophical types of presentational media that exist if we are to understand the *ecology* of media in meaningful detail.

However, as significant as *PNK* and *FF* are in Langer's philosophical canon for media ecologists, they were preceded by two other books that are also important because of the conceptual grounding they provide for the development of Langer's general semiotic theory and subsequent theory of art. Langer's (1930) first book, *The Practice of Philosophy* presents an introduction to philosophy itself. In it, Langer emphasizes that philosophy should not be characterized in terms of the problems traditionally addressed by professional philosophers, such as the nature of truth, ethics, knowledge, or beauty. Rather, philosophy is best understood as the conceptual process that underlies these traditional pursuits, namely, the intellectual activity of exploring the meaning of the terms used in one's discourse about a subject matter, and especially the task of deriving the implications of those meanings for understanding the phenomena they refer to. Applied to the problem of developing a philosophy for conducting systematic theoretical and empirical work in media ecology, for example, Langer's philosophical method would encourage media ecologists to identify a small core of central critical terms, rigorously define them to form a conceptual system, explore the intellectual consequences of those terms and definitions to see where they lead, and, ultimately, to reconstruct the terms if they lead to either conceptual contradictions or empirical anomalies when media ecologists use the philosophical architecture to try to do their work in a programmatic manner. For Langer, intellectual progress in understanding a new area like media ecology depends on a willingness to engage in a fairly extensive amount of careful philosophical construction. In Langer's view, the traditional social sciences have not yet taken up this challenge.

Because of the importance Langer attaches to developing the philosophical foundations of whichever area of inquiry we are involved, *Practice* provides preliminary lessons in how philosophical technique works and explains why training in formal logic is an excellent foundation for conducting the kind of close conceptual analysis she advocates. In the course of this discussion, Langer presents an early version of the semiotic theory that is fully developed in *PNK*.

The role played by logical analysis in the philosophical process was so central in Langer's (1937/1967a) approach to philosophical technique that her next book was *An Introduction to Symbolic Logic (ISL)*. Whereas modern introductions to symbolic logic frequently rush to present the forms of inductive reasoning, patterns of valid inference, truth tables, logical fallacies, and techniques for generating deductive proofs, Langer's *Introduction* begins with a detailed analysis of the concepts which underlie modern logical theory and practice in the first place. Here the reader will find some of our most common words given close philosophical attention: *form* and *content*, *elements* and *relations*, *abstraction* and *interpretation*, *terms* and *degree*, *proposition*, *language*, *structure*, *logical analogy*, *intuition*, *concepts*, *system*, *symbol*, and most important for our purposes, perhaps, the concept of a *medium*. The first 80 pages of *ISL* are so clearly written and so directly relevant to the semiotic theory presented in *PNK* that they should almost be treated as a preparatory chapter for the later book. For many concepts used with only minimal explanation in *PNK* are more fully explained in her discussion of the theory underlying modern logical technique.

In the prefaces to the later editions of *PNK*, Langer indicates that her ultimate interest is in generating a philosophy of mind and that the earlier works should now be seen as stages along the way toward that goal (Langer, 1942/1957a, pp. vii, ix). This can also be said for two little collections of Langer's essays and public lectures that were published after *FF*, namely, *Problems of Art* (Langer, 1957b) and *Philosophical Sketches* (Langer, 1962). *Problems* is a collection of Langer's public lectures presented to widely varied audiences on topics arising from issues in *FF*. Its primary purpose is to clarify issues raised by her art theory on such questions as what the artist "creates" in the so-called creative arts, the nature of artistic abstraction and how it compares with abstraction in the sciences, what the arts have to do with human feeling, why artistic creations must appear to have "living" form in order to be successful, and how the artistic product expresses the artist's ideas about the nature of human feeling. However, because Langer's art theory plays a central role in grounding her theory of human mentality, *Problems* also points the way to issues in the philosophy of mind that were beginning to take on a central role in her thinking.

In contrast to *Problems*, which merely hints at its relationship to Langer's thinking about the origins and development of human mentality, the essays in *Philosophical Sketches* are all quite consciously preliminary versions of her emerging philosophy of mind that was eventually published as *Mind: An Essay on Human Feeling* (Langer, 1967b, 1972, 1982). For Langer, the problem of imagining the origins and evolution of feeling in organic beings is the starting point for her philosophy of mind. *Philosophical Sketches*, therefore, begins with a very accessible chapter on the nature of human feeling as a philosophical problem. This is followed by chapters on topics such as the origins of speech, a new definition of the concept of a *symbol*, the concepts of *emotion* and *abstraction*, the cultural importance of art, the differences between humans living in cities and bees living in hives, how we imagine the person as an individual, and the rise of scientific knowledge. In spite of the fact that Langer's *Mind* volumes have long been available, her *Philosophical Sketches* remain a very useful source of insights because they were written to be accessible to lay readers and therefore avoided much of the detailed argumentation that characterize their fully developed presentation in *Mind*. While the *Sketches* could not stand alone for students interested in Langer's theory of mind because they do not cover many of the truly innovative analyses presented in *Mind*, they remain Langer's most straightforward explanations of several of the crucial ideas upon which her philosophy concerning mind and human symbolic nature rest.

As suggested previously, the capstone of Langer's philosophical career is her three volume philosophy of mind. Arising from her earlier theories of the logic of symbolism and the artistic expression of insights into human feeling, the goal of *Mind* is to provide a new conceptual foundation for research in humanities and social science disciplines such as psychology, sociology, anthropology, communication, and by extension, of course, media ecology. Langer's reason for trying to construct a new conceptual foundation for the human sciences is her belief that these disciplines are making very little intellectual progress in understanding human symbolic mentality because they are built on exceptionally shaky foundations whose most basic concepts are too weak to encompass the nature of human mentality. Langer believes that everything from the biological origins of our mental life to the unique evolution of our symbolically constructed minds should be describable and, eventually, comprehensible within the naturalistic framework of science—but only if that framework is adequate to the living reality of the human symbolic world.

Because *Mind* aims to provide an entirely new conceptual architecture for research in the humanistic disciplines, it is as difficult as it is daring, as important as it is challenging. Divided into five parts (a sixth was unfinished because of Langer's increasing blindness before her death in 1985), *Mind* sweeps up the themes in her earlier works, gives them new meaning and suggests how they might be woven together into a vaster and more insightful approach to understanding distinctively human mental and social phenomena than we have previously had available.

The first two parts of *Mind* are essentially preparatory, with Part 1, "Problems and Principles," establishing the central problem to which any naturalistic theory of mind would have to give scientific access: the evolution of *human feeling* from its pre-human origins in sensory and endogenous experience to the numerous highly evolved and articulate symbolic forms it has today. The problem of feeling is central for Langer because the human sciences have failed to imagine our felt experience without either reducing it to a meaningless epiphenomenon of brain activity or treating it as a mystery that stands outside of the routine evolutionary processes that are otherwise well understood. That is, they have failed to adequately address the longstanding conceptual problems that have arisen from the mind/body/brain problem and that have, accordingly, foiled our best efforts to develop an adequate psychology of human symbolic mentality.

Langer's approach to understanding the relation between our material and mental dimensions is to treat feeling as an *activity* that the organism *does* rather than an entity that the organism *has*. As shown in Figure 11.1, she contends that both our mental feelings (general consciousness, perceptual awareness, logical intuition, and the like) and our material bodies arise as the result of underlying act structured processes (much as the material nature and electrical phenomena associated with a tornado arise only because of an underlying pattern of activity in the atmosphere). What we feel, therefore, is always the same organic activity that continuously produces our material bodies. Moreover, even though the only thing we can feel is our own organic processes once they intensify beyond some minimal threshold, our feelings may be divided into those that are felt as being internally generated (Langer says these are felt as "action") and those that are felt as arising from outside the organism (which Langer identifies as being felt as "impact"). It is this distinction that provides the organic basis for what we experience as subjective versus objective feelings.

In addition to introducing the central problem which her philosophy of mind is designed to solve, Part 1 also inquires into the reasons that the con-

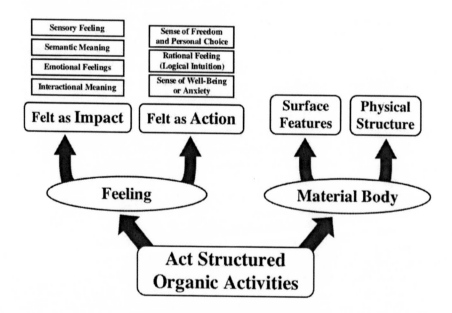

Fig. 11.1. Susanne Langer's act-based solution to the mind/body/brain problem showing how the concept of organic acts produces both our material bodies and the feelings we experience as arising from our material bodies.

temporary human sciences have made so little progress in imagining the nature of human mentality—which may be summarized as their headlong rush to *appear* scientific before they have developed an adequate concept of the mental phenomena they are trying to study. That is, they have failed to patiently do their philosophical homework before developing their "scientific" methodologies. The first Part concludes with a small chapter explaining why artists and their creations may provide the key to unlocking a more adequate approach to imagining human feeling in its naturalistic context—for it is they who have been creating the *images* of human feeling for millennia.

With this groundwork laid, Part 2, "The Import of Art," unfolds the philosophical method Langer will use in constructing the scientific conceptual structure she subsequently develops in Part 3. Because Langer finds the key to understanding human mentality in the creative principles artists spontaneously use as they symbolize their understanding of human feeling, the four chapters of Part 2 abstract those principles in a more concentrated and updated rendition of the ideas first presented in *FF*. The argument in these four formidable chapters may be summarized as follows.

In whichever medium they work, artists project their ideas about the nature of our felt experience into their created works. To be successful in its symbolic mission, the work of art must present a *logically adequate analogy* for whichever aspect of feeling the work attempts to project. Because artistic works operate on the principle of logical analogy, the principles underlying the creation of artistic works are the symbolic counterpart of the organic principles that give rise to feeling in the living individual. Therefore, to the extent that we properly understand the principles by which the arts operate *as arts*, we have a blueprint for constructing a conceptual architecture that is adequate for understanding actual human feeling and its evolution in the human species. The philosophical method, therefore, is to use the principles of arts first discovered in *Feeling and Form* and generalized in the four chapters of Part 2 of *Mind* to guide philosophical thinking about the nature of the organic processes which give rise to actual human feeling.

Part 3 of *Mind* is entitled "*Natura Naturans*," or nature bringing forth, and it moves immediately to the main goal of Langer's philosophy of mind, namely, using the artistic images of human mentality as a guide to developing the principles underlying the biological foundations of mind. Divided into four biologically sophisticated chapters, the argument is difficult to summarize in only a paragraph or two because the implications for theory in the human sciences are so breathtakingly bold.

In essence, Langer argues that because the solution to understanding the biological origins of feeling in the animal kingdom rests on the fact that feeling is an organic activity or process, the first goal of a philosophy of mind must be to produce a better understanding of the nature of actual organic processes. In this regard, Langer develops her *act theory of process* that begins with the empirically testable claim that *all* organically based process-es take the form of acts. The act form has a four-phase structure of impulse, acceleration, climax, and deceleration back to a period of relative inactivity. The four phases of the act form are illustrated in Figure 11.2.

In saying that all organic processes exhibit this form, Langer means that the act form can be empirically found at all levels of organic observation we may choose to investigate, including everything from the cellular, neuronal and muscular levels required to produce even the most basic movement, up to the level of uttering a word, sentence, turn, or conversation-as-a-whole, and even up to the level of one's life as a whole.

After providing evidence for the empirical validity of the four-phase act structure as a fundamental unit of all organic processes, Langer identifies a number of principles related both to the internal dynamics of acts (such as their structural wholeness while their phases unfold and their tendency to press to complete themselves despite encountering obstacles) and to the many different types of relationship (motivational, entrainment, rhythmic, pressive, etc.) that the acts of the organism can have with one another. Along the way, Langer develops act-based theories of the principles of evolution, the progressive individuation of the individual, the nature of social involve-ment, and other similar types of process-based phenomena. What Langer is doing in these four chapters is, in essence, deriving an elaborate set of act-based principles on which all organically based processes operate and evolve. For what Langer is claiming is that in the organic world of which human mental phenomena are a natural evolutionary part, *all explanatory principles are ultimately derivable from principles of acts*. To the extent that communication phenomena are processes in the act concept sense (as they

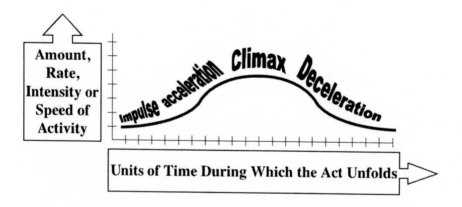

Fig. 11.2. Four phases of Langer's concept of the act form which all organic process exhibit.

clearly appear to be) (Powers, 1981, 1982), the principles Langer provides in Part 3 of *Mind* should be useful in trying to explain them.

Assuming that all explanatory principles in the human sciences are ultimately principles of acts, the question becomes which phenomena we want to explain first. For Langer, the answer is the natural evolution of human symbolic mentality and its unique consequences for our species. Building upon the concepts and principles developed in Part 3, Parts 4 (1972), and 5 (1982) are designed as specific applications of the philosophical act-based system to resolve significant theoretical problems in several areas of animal and human psychology.

Mind's Part 4 (the whole of Volume II), entitled "The Great Shift," turns to the evolution of human symbolic mentality as construed within the structure of her act theory. Divided into seven chapters, Part 4 raises three interrelated problems: (a) how nonsymbolic animal mentality is distinguished from human mind; (b) how human mentality could have evolved from its animalian precursors to its presently unique symbolic form, as expressed most obviously through the evolution of speech; and (c) how the evolution of speech has influenced the subsequent and ever-continuing evolution of human mind.

At each step in the argument, Langer uses principles derived from her act philosophy to develop new interpretations of familiar ethological and evolutionary claims about animal and human mentality. Among the most striking of these reinterpretations may be Langer's claim that, because communication depends on the evolution of human symbolic mentality, only humans communicate. Animal interaction, even complex joint interaction— however sophisticated it may appear to us in its mutual coordination (such as during honeybee recruitment in their hives)—operates on nonsymbolic act-based principles. The goal of these reinterpretations is to piece together a detailed picture of animal mentality—animal perceptions, values, motivations, instincts, and behavioral repertoires—and to characterize exactly how that mentality differs from the symbolic mentality which the human species evolved. Having argued that substantial differences *in kind* exist at all levels between animal and human mentality, Langer next pieces together an act-based theory of how human mentality, and especially speech, might have evolved in the course of natural evolution. Part 4 closes with a chapter of speculations on the differences the newly evolved symbolic mentality may have made in building up what might best be called "the human world." This phrase distinguishes the world as humans experience it symbolically from the nonsymbolic "ambient" that animals inhabit and in which they operate. The seven chapters of Part 4 are a powerful model of how one systematically reinterprets presently available scientific data in act terms for the purpose of beginning to build an act-based theory of important psychological phenomena, and they are especially important for this reason.

Part 5 of *Mind*, "The Moral Structure," comprises the bulk of Volume III, with only a brief concluding essay on "Mathematics and the Reign of Science," standing in for the intended capstone of her career, an essay "On Knowledge and Truth." Even without the fully developed sixth part, Volume III is a grand speculative book outlining a theory of the successive evolution of the human mind and its most fundamental ideas from the origins of speech (treated in Part 4) to the recent rise of the concept of "fact," which is the conceptual basis for all contemporary science.

In her treatment of "The Moral Structure," Langer is not developing a specific theory of proper ethical conduct, as might be expected from her title. Rather, she is developing a general *anthropological* theory of the evolution in human mentality of the *idea* of "*ethos*," or human value. That is, the question addressed in Part 5 is how our species could have developed an ethical or moral consciousness in the first place—however different one culture's specific ethical values may be from another's. Drawing upon vast quantities of anthropological data, Langer pieces together a detailed theory of the organic basis of the historical succession of the various ideas which have led to the contemporary concept of a moral structure for society.

In barest outline, Langer envisions the stages of conception through which generations of human minds must have passed as follows:

1. Primitive animism—the feeling that the world is a plenum of spirits and forces to be dealt with as best one can.
2. Empathetic magic as a way of increasing one's own personal power by enabling the tribe to induce the spirits to act in its own best interests.
3. A crisis in power—the rise of the idea of personal self-identity and a corresponding recognition of the inevitability of one's own individual death, over which no magic has any power.
4. The rise of the great religions as various ways of dealing conceptually with the idea of death—power is taken from the individual and delegated to a highest god who rewards the good and punishes the bad in an afterlife.
5. The replacement of tribal life with city life—cities as a new mode of social organization symbolically mirroring on earth both the increased importance of the individual and the hierarchical conception of the world order reflected in the pantheons of the great religions.
6. The gradual breaking down of the great religious conceptions and the dawning of the rise of scientific and technological ideas.

For media ecologists, one of the special contributions of Part 5 is what it demonstrates about the interralationship between the evolution of human ideas and the symbolic media available to express them. For at each point in the argument, Langer identifies the media involved in the development of the sequence of conceptions leading to the modern world as we know it today.

Although the starkness of this survey of *Mind* belies the richness and detail of Langer's argument, it suggests the breadth of the aspects of human mentality to which she gives very serious attention. If Langer's approach is correct, the evolution of human mind cannot be reduced to simplistic formulations based on "survival needs," and the like. Instead, the story of human symbolic mind pervades every aspect of our mentality. Human mind was forged in the massive evolutionary tensions resulting from the accidents and specializations that first led to speech. No philosophical structure which avoids the complexity of human *conceptual* feeling, or hides it under a simplistic vocabulary, can help us understand the mysteries of human mind— especially as those mysteries are revealed in the discursive and presentational media we hope to understand in terms of their relation to human mental development.

LANGER'S THEORY OF EXPRESSIVE MEDIA: EIGHT IMPLICATIONS

Having surveyed the general progression of Langer's argument through the sequence of her books, this chapter next develops eight implications for understanding symbolic media derived from Langer's writings, especially as viewed from the context of her philosophy of mind. The headings of the following sections are worded as major claims that Langer's books support and that provide organizing centers for elaborating a conceptual structure based on Langer's philosophy of mind. The first principle concerns the nature of a symbolic medium itself.

A Symbolic Medium Is the Content Wherein a Conceptual Form Can Be Expressed

When media ecologists use the term *media*, what might they mean beyond the relatively diffuse notion of the mass media such radio and television, or other electronic media such as telephones, CD players, and the Internet? For Langer, the term *medium* has a relatively technical meaning arising from her logical theory. This theory not only grounds her entire semiotic system, but may also help to explain how media as diverse as good luck charms, routine speech, urban landscapes, and the various modern electronic media all inter-relate with one another. So, in order to begin mining Langer's insights for media ecology, we will look first to her logical theory.

In her *Introduction to Symbolic Logic,* Langer (1937/1967a) argues that the most basic feature of anything that exists is its form. A thing's *form* is its structure—that is, the arrangement of its parts into a particular pattern. Thus, whenever we describe something's form, there are two aspects to con-sider: (a) the *parts* that make up the thing, and (b) the *pattern* or *arrangement* that must exist among those parts before they can be said to be that partic-ular thing. The "parts" out of which something is composed are called its *elements*. The connections among those elements that give the thing its pat-tern are called its *relations*. To emphasize that the concept of *form* is not restricted to material things, but also extends to processes, qualities, events, and the like, Langer uses the phrase *logical form* to designate the "structure" or "principle of orderliness" that characterizes anything that we may be considering. The four phases of the act form precisely illustrate this point.

Based on her definition of *form,* Langer next defines two critical corre-sponding concepts: *content* and *medium*. *Content,* Langer says, is the "medium wherein a form is expressed" (p. 27). By implication, a *medium* is the form's physical embodiment or instantiation on a particular occasion. In material objects the medium is, of course, some sort of physical "stuff." Thus, if the form were that of a cup, the elements would include sloping cylindrical sides, a flat bottom, and a handle on the side. But the cup *form* could be expressed in a wide variety of media, each representing a different content for this form: fine bone china, waterproof paper, brown plastic, tint-ed glass, and clear crystal, among many others. Each of these media is said to *express* the form because it makes the form perceptible.

The distinction between form and content may also be applied in non-material things such as the processes studied by communication scholars. For example, different utterance forms—*speeches, conversations, narratives, greetings, knock-knock jokes, limericks, figures of speech, and store-counter interactions*—can each have dissimilar contents (topic, subject matter, per-sons involved, etc.) and still be recognized as exemplifying the same form. Knock-knock jokes always follow the same pattern, as do limericks, and so forth. In fact, it is their form that identifies one utterance as a limerick and another as a knock-knock joke. Words like *limerick* and *knock-knock* joke are simply the names for these verbal forms.

The ability to discover a common form in dissimilar contents is accom-plished through the process of *abstraction*, wherein the person ignores the features of a particular medium that expresses the form and focuses on only the elements and relations that are expressed *in* the medium. When two con-tents are discovered to share a similar form they are said to be *analogous* to one another. As we shall see below, Langer believes that the human aptitude for consciously producing logical analogies using a variety of artifactual and actional media is the basis for all modes of symbolism. If we were unable to produce such analogies, the overt expression of our ideas in perceptible forms would be impossible.

Abstraction is also the basis for routine concept formation. A *concept* is an abstracted form. That is, once someone has discovered a form through the process of abstraction, the resulting mental formulation is a concept. In *PNK*, Langer distinguishes between concepts and conceptions. *Conceptions* are incompletely abstracted mental formulations that still bear the marks of the concrete instance from which the form was first abstracted. Langer's example of this distinction in *ISL* concerns the concept of "oscillation," which is a type of repeated back-and-forth motion. One person might have encountered oscillation when watching a guitar string vibrate, whereas someone else might associate it with watching an aspen leaf quavering in a Rocky Mountain breeze. What any two people who share a concept have in common is the fully abstracted form without any reference to the personal content. What they will not share is their personal conceptions based on how they imagined the concept.

The importance of concepts is that once a concept has been abstracted, it may be used as a template for use in searching for additional analogies, that is, for more instances of the form. When a conceptual form is used as a template to discover more instances, Langer calls this the *interpretation* of the form. *Interpretation* is the process of using an abstracted form to locate additional examples in other dissimilar contents.

As mentioned previously, Langer contends (in *ISL*, *PNK*, and elsewhere) that all symbolic media operate on the principle of logical analogy. The argument runs like this. The purpose of symbols is to express our ideas in a perceptible medium such as speech, action, or a material substance. Because our ideas can take many different forms, and because it is their form that is important, the symbols we create must be able to express by logical analogy the form of our ideas. That is, for something to be used as a symbol of a particular idea it must be able to express the form of that idea using some principle of logical analogy.

The most commonly recognized symbolic medium, of course, is language, which uses verbal labels provided by the language's vocabulary to name the conceptual elements and relations that form one's ideas. In addition, language uses the principles of grammar and syntax to express the order of elements and relations composing the idea. To the extent that two people share the conceptual labels and the grammar used to arrange those labels into a sentence, they can communicate their ideas because, as Langer (1937/1967a) writes, "Syntax is simply *the logical form of our language,* which copies as closely as possible the logical form of our thought" (p. 31). Thus, what the syntactical structure of language represents "is the order and connection of ideas in our minds" (p. 37). Language creates its analogy with the person's ideas through a system of categorical labels and the principles of syntax, and it can express only those ideas whose form can be analogized using those verbal resources.

Because nonlinguistic media—such as stone in architecture or sculpture, sound in music, and movement in dance and ritual—have their own intrinsic properties as expressive media, each is better suited than language for analogizing different types of ideas. Accordingly, as humans have developed more and more varied ideas, and as new media have become available to express them, people have seized on the opportunities provided by newly invented media to try to express themselves. But the important point for the present theme is that *all* symbolic media are the perceptible content in which different types of conceptual forms can be expressed. To the extent that two people can use a particular medium to perceive the same conceptual form, the medium can be used to create symbols for sharing the formal nature of the ideas expressed.

Sign Meaning May Be Distinguished From Symbolic Meaning on Structural Grounds

In *PNK* Langer uses the logical principles described previously to develop a relational theory of sign and symbol meaning that fundamentally departs from the kinds of theories based on the work of C. S. Peirce that continue to dominate semiotic analysis in communication theory today (e.g., Liska, 1993). Because the difference is both radical and important for the development of media ecology theory, it is useful to briefly review the main point of Peirce's theory before contrasting it with Langer's.

Figure 11.3 illustrates the essential features of Peirce's theory of signs. According to Peirce, the meaning of signs comes into being when a relationship exists among a trio of elements: (a) something that serves as a sign, (b) an organism that interprets the thing to be a sign (the interpretant) , and (c) something else that the sign stands for in some way (the object). Thus, if one person interprets another's smiling facial expression as a sign of happiness, three elements have been brought into simultaneous relationship: (a) the smile used as a sign, (b) the observer as an interpreter of the behavior, and (c) a possible mood state that the interpreter believes the smile to stand for.

In addition to identifying the relational nature of sign meaning, Peirce was also interested in discovering how many different *types* of meaning there might be. As Fig. 11.3 indicates, Peirce believed that all forms of meaning depend on a triadic relationship (thus, the triangular model). However, as the figure also reveals, the overall triadic relationship is composed of at least three sets of dyadic (two-termed) relationships: AB (the relationship between the sign and the interpretant); AC (the relationship between the

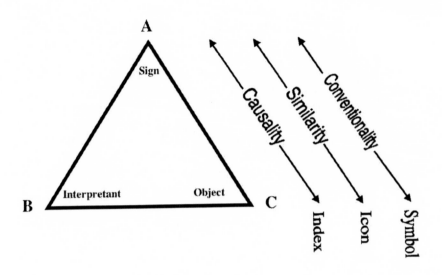

Fig. 11.3 C. S. Peirce's classification of signs based on the three kinds of relationship that may occur between a sign and its object (relationship AC).

sign and its object), and BC (the relationship between the interpretant and the object). Based on his opinion that three different types of structural relationship may arise between a sign and its object—(a) by being *caused* by its object, (b) by being *similar* to its object, and (c) by *social convention* or agreement—Peirce concludes that there are three major classes of signs: indexes, icons, and symbols, respectively.

Although Langer and Peirce both agree that meaning is ultimately a relationship among a set of elements rather than a quality of any one of those elements, theories in the Peircean tradition hold that all meaning relationships are ultimately triadic. That is, indexes, icons, and symbols each require only three elements and three primary relations to bring their various kinds of meaning structures into being. Accordingly, Peircean theories treat symbolic meaning as a subcategory of general sign meaning. Indexes, icons, and symbols are treated taxonomically as three parallel categories of signs which are differentiated based on the type of relation (causality, similarity, and conventionality, respectively) that exists between each type of sign and its object.

Langer differs from Peirce in her analysis of the elements and relations involved in various kinds of meaning structures. As early as 1942, Langer proposed that the difference between sign meaning (Peirce's indexes) and symbol meaning rested on a radical difference between their logical structures—with sign meaning requiring only a triadic (three-termed) relational structure and symbol meaning requiring an irreducibly tetradic (four-termed) relational structure. Thus, signs and symbols are not subtypes of the same basic thing. They are fundamentally different because they *arise from irreducibly different logical structures.* If Langer is correct, the radical difference between the relational structures required for sign and symbol meaning can provide the basis for a new approach to understanding the systematic connections which exist among the variety of symbolic media. That point is explored in a later principle. However, before moving to that step in the argument, it is necessary to examine Langer's approach to the logic of sign and symbol meaning in two additional principles.

Sign Meaning Operates on a Triadic Relational Structure

Although Langer agrees with Peirce that sign meaning (limited, however, only to Peirce's indexical signs) depends on a triadic relationship, her explanation of the *nature* of the relationship between a sign and its object (relationship AC in Fig. 11.3) differs from Peirce's "causal" account. According to Langer, sign meaning is always taken to indicate the *existence*—past, present, or future—of a thing, event, or condition. Therefore, a sign may be defined as *any perceptible artifact or action that can be taken to indicate the existence of some other thing, event, process, or condition.* The key to sign meaning is that (a) signs can be experienced by an organism's sensory organs, and (b) the sign user takes the sign to be related to the existence of something else that is usually less readily perceptible. Langer's name for this aspect of meaning (i.e., the relationship between a sign and whatever it is taken to be a sign of) is *signification*; and so we can say that *the signification of a sign is the presumed existence of a situation which is otherwise less perceptually available than is the sign.*

For a sign to be meaningful, however, it must also be connected to an organism that perceives the possible relationship between the perceptible sign and the covert situation. Accordingly, sign meaning requires a triadic relationship between three elements: (a) the more easily perceptible sign, (b) the less easily perceptible situation, and (c) a being (human or otherwise) who interprets the sign as indicating the existence of the situation. Only when an organism notices the relationship between the sign and the situation do we have an instance of the sign meaning relationship. If someone notices an action or artifact, but fails to correlate it with the existence of something else that is not directly perceived, then the action or artifact is not being interpreted as a sign—and there would be no "sign meaning."

In explaining why one thing can be taken as a sign pointing to the existence of something other than itself, Langer argues that the sign's interpreter presumes there to be a structural relationship between the sign and the situation whose existence it is taken to indicate. Specifically, signs are always presumed by their interpreter to be actual components of whatever situation they are thought to be a sign. Because the sign is taken by its user to be a component of the situation which it signifies, the existence of the sign is taken to mean that the other parts of the situation also exist.[1] Accordingly, the significant relationship between a sign and its object is not one of causality (as Peirce had proposed), but one of a part to a whole. Causality is an incidental feature of some sign-relationships but cannot be used to define all. Social scientists routinely acknowledge this difference when they observe, while interpreting statistical signs, that "correlation does not prove causality." In summary, signs work according to a principle of pairing—the sign is structurally attached to its attributed meaning because they are both component parts of a complex situation.

Langer's theory of sign meaning can readily be applied to understanding routine social interaction, where the signs communicators observe are typically unimportant for their own sake (after all, for example, eye behavior is just eye behavior). But social actors find such behaviors interesting for two reasons. First, they are readily perceptible. Signs given off by others can easily be seen, smelled, heard, or tasted; so they can arrest the user's attention. Furthermore, they are paired by the observer with something that is usually both less readily perceptible (e.g., the motivations, intentions, or values of the other communicator) and more critically important (only if we know what the other's motivations, intentions, or values are can we effectively plan our own communication strategies). Hence, yawns, blushes, or gazes in a particular direction may not be intrinsically significant; but when they are paired by the observer with inner fatigue, embarrassment, or boredom, for example, they can provide information needed for successful communication. Communicators learn to look for relatively insignificant overt signs, but what they care about are the significant covert conditions they assume the signs are naturally paired with.

Symbol Meaning Operates on a Tetradic Relational Structure

Structurally, symbol meaning differs from sign meaning in two fundamental ways: the sheer *number* of elements and relations involved in their respective relational structures, and the *nature* of the elements and relations required to bring each type of meaning into being. Figure 11.4 illustrates both of these points.

As the figure reveals, four elements must be brought into simultaneous relationship before even the simplest type of symbolic meaning comes into being: (a) something perceptible (such as a word, gesture or material artifact) that can serve as a symbol, (b) someone who uses the item as a symbol, (c) a

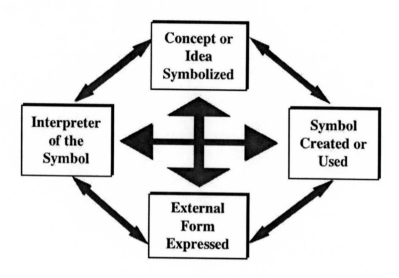

Fig. 11.4. The logical structure of elements and relations involved in symbolic meaning.

concept that the symbol expresses, and (d) some object in the real or imaginary world that the symbol may be said to denote or point toward. The most radical difference between sign and symbol meaning comes about because symbol meanings are always controlled by the symbolizer's *concepts* rather than by external situations. Whereas sign meanings come into being because the signs are taken express the existence of certain *situations* that they are structurally related to, symbolic meaning arises because symbols express the *concepts* they are structurally related to. Thus, although signs are always taken to be an actual component of a situation that they signify, symbols stand logically outside of the ideas which they express. Expressive elements *in their role as symbols* are never component parts of the conceptual situation for which they functions as symbols.

In addition to the elements involved in symbol meaning, Fig. 11.4 also visualizes some features of the relations involved. Most noteworthy, perhaps, is that the addition of only a single extra element immediately doubles from three to six the number of two-termed relationships—a fact that contributes to the complexity of symbolic meaning structures. Furthermore, because the elements involved are different, the relations among the elements are also different. For example, according to the theory presented in *PNK*, the relationship a verbal symbol has to the concept it expresses is called *con-

notation, and the relationship it has to its referent is called *denotation*. That is, denotation and connotation are treated as relationships that arise in some symbolic structures, but they would never occur in sign relationships.

When the symbolic medium is something other than a word, patterns of symbolic relationship other than connotation and denotation will come into being. But whatever those relationships may be called they do not exist at all for signs. For, if Langer's analysis of the relational structures involved in sign and symbol meaning is correct, symbolic meaning is not reducible to a class of sign meaning because it arises from a wholly different logical structure. Symbols are distinguished from signs by *what* they express. Symbols express our concepts and thoughts and *ideas*—how they are structured and what they are about—rather than their simple physical existence.

Many Expressive Elements May Participate in Both Sign and Symbol Relational Structures

Based on the previous discussion, a *symbol* may be defined as *any percepti-ble artifact or action that has been created or is used in order to express an idea*. In the simplest cases of symbolic meaning there are no inherent features that magically turns something into a symbol except that the person finds it useful for expressing an idea and the artifact or action is logically capable of participating in symbolic relational structures. Thus, almost any-thing a person can perceive might be used as a symbol.

Because the circumstance that makes something into a symbol rather than a sign is the relational structure within which it is currently participat-ing, many things may function simultaneously as both symbols and signs. However, when they function as signs and symbols at the same time, *they are participating as elements in two entirely different types of relational structure simultaneously.*

For example, Figure 11.5 illustrates how a simple artifact—a wedding ring—can be both an artificial sign that someone is married and a symbol of the cultural concept of marriage. From the wedding ring, interpreters can intuit both that a certain event has occurred (interpreting it as an artificial sign) and also be reminded of their ideas about the social institution involved. In the one case, the ring participates in a triadic relationship as an artificial and conventional component of a cultural situation whose exis-tence it expresses; and in the other it participates in a tetradic relationship whose controlling element is the concept of marriage. Like iridescent fab-ric, the two types of meaning may shimmer in such rapid succession that it is difficult to experience them as different despite their distinct relational structures. However, the distinguishing feature of even the simplest types of symbols remains the nature of the relational structures within which they participate and not the type of thing they are.

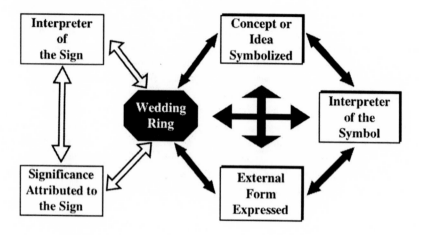

Fig. 11.5. Many human artifacts and actions can participate simultaneously in triadic relational structures as artificial signs and in tetradic structures as symbols.

One of the most valuable contributions Langer's semiotic theory may make to the development of media ecology is the help it provides in distinguishing various symbolic media from one another on theoretical grounds and systematically relating them to one another. The purpose of the next two principles is to use Langer's work on signs and symbols to suggest some important distinctions that might lead to insightful taxonomic development for media ecology. The first of the principles relates to human sign activity and the second focuses on the taxonomic consequences of Langer's theory for understanding the incredible variety of symbolic media that exist.

Sign Meanings May Be Divided Into Various Types Based on a Number of Logical and Psychological Considerations

Although human sign activity is technically "unmediated," because signs are interpreted as directly pointing toward the situation in which they play a part, Langer's theory of signs helps to reveal layers of complexity that may be of interest to media ecologists as well as other communication professionals. The first of these was suggested by the previous principle but not made explicit there. Because meaning is a relationship among elements rather than a property of any one of those elements, mediated elements functioning symbolically may also function as signs of such things as the beliefs, attitudes, values, psychological state, cultural background, ethnic origins, and so forth, of those who create or use them. For example, the word choices communicators make in symbolizing their ideas can also be interpreted as signs of their ideology, prejudices, sympathies, and so forth, because every lexical choice is made from among a set of alternative words that contrast with it on a variety of social and cultural dimensions (Gozzi, 1999). Saying "the Chinese *regime*" versus saying "the Chinese *government*" is a sign suggesting quite different political stances toward the leadership in Beijing. The method of critical discourse analysis uses such contrastive analysis to interpret texts as signs of the source's covert ideological commitments in addition to understanding them simply as symbols of the particular ideas explicitly expressed.

A second major taxonomic distinction—suggested by Langer's analysis of organic processes in *Mind*—is that the elements that serve as signs may be either material artifacts or performed actions. Artifactual signs include everything produced in human material culture from money and clocks to karaoke machines and writing instruments if they are taken as indicating the existence of something else. As we saw with the wedding ring example, such material objects may also function as symbols of their user's ideas, but they are also interpretable as signs of their user's personality, goals, needs, and the like.

Such artifactual signs may be contrasted with actional signs such as eye gaze, facial expression, gestures, postures, touches, and mutually generated orientational frames enacted during conversations. That all of these are categories of actional signs which conversational partners monitor continuously during social interaction is, of course, no surprise. Every introduction to "nonverbal" communication has major units on each of them.

What is new from a Langerian perspective is realizing that all of the standard categories of actional signs are *acts* and not static states. That is, gestures, postures, facial expressions, orientational frames, and so forth all develop in phases—building up and ebbing away as act structured events. Moreover, they follow the principle of acts presented in Part 3 of *Mind* so that we may generate an act-based theory of each of the major forms of actional signs and how they influence the larger conversational acts in which they participate.

Although it would take us too far afield to explore even one of the categories of actional signs in act terms, Langer's claim that all explanatory principles are ultimately principles of acts should apply to actional signs in especially vivid detail, and should produce revolutionary new insights into the operation of this class of signs. Moreover, because the actional nature of the orality of human language is one of its most distinctive attributes, media ecology students interested in Walter Ong's theory of orality and literacy (i.e., speaking and writing as symbolic media) should find that imagining orality in act terms opens up new doors to understanding the implications of the "spokenness" of speech in human history and contemporary social interaction (Gronbeck, 2000).

Another distinction Langer makes, which media ecologists might find theoretically interesting, is one between natural and artificial signs. *Natural signs* are all those sign–object pairings that spontaneously occur without conscious human intervention. That is, they are perceived to be *inherent* parts of the total situation for which they may function as signs. Thus, the emergence of leaves on trees in the spring is a natural sign that the temperature is warming and the days are getting longer. *Artificial signs* are those that are consciously planned by the sign-using community to be associated with the existence of a certain situation. For example, a wedding ring is an artificial sign indicating that the person wearing it is married. Furthermore, artificial signs are both *arbitrary* and *conventional* in the sense usually reserved for defining symbols in Peirce's theory. That is, artificial signs are freely chosen by a community of people to be perceptible indicators of the existence of something that is otherwise less directly perceptible but culturally more important. In this way, artificial signs become an *arbitrarily imposed* and *conventionally expected* parts of a culturally constructed situation without thereby becoming symbol.[2]

Symbolic Media May Be Divided Into Discursive and Presentational Modes

For media ecologists, the climax of Langer's semiotic theory is probably the detailed analysis she provides concerning the intrinsic characteristics distinguishing different symbolic media from one another and how those media systematically relate to one another. For example, in *PNK*, Langer distinguishes between discursive and presentational symbolism, with *discursive symbolism* being the technical name for the world's many natural languages, and *presentational symbolism* designating nearly all other kinds of symbolism. The distinction between the two fundamental modes of symbolism is based on how they create the logical analogy between the symbolizer's ideas and the symbols used to express them.

In discursive symbolism, the analogy is created by lining up a number of independent units of meaning (i.e., words) in a linear succession (to produce a sentence) using syntactic rules that govern how a particular sequence of words maps the logical analogy between a specific idea. *Discursiveness* refers to the fact that language as a mode of symbolism requires that the logical form of the idea (i.e., its structure of elements and relations) be broken down into standard categories (which the substantive words in the sentence name) and that the words be placed in a linear sequence. Therefore, every natural language provides a large inventory of words to name the standard categories of elements and relations which the language community typically uses for talking about the world, as well as a system of syntactic rules whose function is to arrange those words into sequences that create the logical analogy between the sender's ideas and the structure of words used to project them. Noam Chomsky's transformational-generative grammar and its many derivatives were sophisticated attempts to model the complex process by which syntactic rules map the logical structure of an idea into the logical structure of a sentence.

Despite the tremendous expressive power and versatility of discursive symbolism for projecting our ideas, it has its inherent limitations. Many experiences about which we would like to communicate do not recur often enough to have acquired standard categorical names. And many others are structurally so complex (like the unique image of a friend's face) that they can easily overwhelm the projective resources that discursive symbolism has available to it. The amount of structural detail needed, for example, to uniquely describe a friend's face is so complex in elements and relations that language usually proves inadequate.

The problem arises because discursive symbolism uses standardized categories and a sequential rule of projection while complex structures (such as faces) exhibit considerable embedding of relations within one another. At some point, there are simply limitations on our memory for long sequences of words, as well as on our ability to sort out complex chains of relational embedding within such extended sentences. To overcome these limitations, people have developed a large number of non-discursive modes of symbolism that allow them to convey these more complex ideas. Langer groups these nondiscursive types together under the label *presentational symbolism* because they "present" their relational structures for direct perception rather than requiring the symbol users to name their parts sequentially.

To be *presentational*, then, is to display within a single complex symbol all of the elements and relations that are relevant to expressing the idea. Rather than *naming* the relevant elements and relations composing the idea, presentational forms of symbolism physically *show* them using a wide variety of media of the very type that media ecologists specialize in investigating. Presentational symbols include such obviously symbolic forms as works of art (painting, sculpture, music, dance, etc.), religious rituals, and myths. Furthermore, because culturally significant activities (such as football and schooling), and artifacts (such as money, toys, and office equipment) all arise originally as physical expressions of someone's ideas, they too are identifiable as classes of presentational symbolism.

The feature that brings all of these together under a single, separate category is that, unlike discursive symbolism, the components of a presentational symbol are not labels for the elements and relations involved. Nor are they necessarily meaningful outside of the particular presentational symbol within which they are found. The musical note *middle C* is an element of musical symbolism, but it is not an independently meaningful name for some concept. Similarly, even though we may think of a cross as an independently meaningful religious symbol in the Christian tradition, its meaning may change dramatically depending on how it is incorporated within different presentational symbols. An actual cross does not mean a certain religious idea in quite the same way that a word-label such as *cross* means the concept that it names. A theoretical problem, of course, is to determine what these differences may be.

Some presentational symbols have only a temporal dimension, as in music; some are created only by means of a spatial pattern for projecting the idea, as in a painting or a sculpture; and sometimes presentational symbols use both spatial and temporal rules of projection, such as in dance. Furthermore, presentational symbols use whichever media are available (sometimes including words, as in creative fiction, film, poetry, and drama) to directly show the elements and relations the person wishes to present. But presentational symbols never *name* the relational structures they present. They show them, and the manner of the showing is what gives the presentational symbol its unique import. This is why it is frequently so difficult to use discursive symbolism to describe a movie or novel we have experienced in spite of their obviously verbal elements. The words were merely used to create a different form rather than to express their literal sense. Furthermore, presentational symbols do not directly assert the truth of the ideas they present. They simply present an idea for inspection or contemplation; they do not declare its truth in anything equivalent of a sentence.

Because they show rather than name the elements and relations they project, presentational symbols are better than words at expressing highly complex ideas. However, because presentational symbols cannot directly assert truth claims, they cannot directly advance a proposition or "make a statement." This accounts for why we do not simply picture our ideas and be done with it. Without the clarification provided by using word-based discursive symbols to explain presentational symbols, receivers may not know why the picture was presented, or what the artist "intended to say."

To overcome the limitations inherent in each type of symbolism alone, people frequently use discursive symbolism to "assimilate" presentational symbols as a supplement to their discursive resources. Thus, for example, complex presentational symbols such as a painting can be given a name— say, *The Mona Lisa*—and then be incorporated, through that name, into the elements of discursive symbolism. Any time we use the title of a work of art metonymically as a name to represent some major portion of that work's symbolic import, we are assimilating presentational symbolism for discursive purposes. We do this if, for example, we describe a friend as having a "Mona Lisa" smile. It is this assimilative ability that gives discursive symbolism its tremendous communicative power and which explains, in part, how it can so readily keep up with our communication needs—no matter how complex the world seems to get.

Presentational Symbolisms May Be Subdivided Into Categories Based on the Expressive Opportunities and Limitations Inherent in the Various Media Employed

Based on the expressive opportunities and limitations inherent in various symbolic media, each presentational medium has its own internal "logic" or set of structural principles that determine its expressive potential and how it can be used to convey the logical form of whichever ideas it can be used to express. As displayed in Figure 11.6, Langer's approach to various presentational media permits the development of a hierarchical taxonomy of the types of presentational media that not only identifies how each category of media is distinguished from the others, but also reveals how they are related to one another in a genus and species type of pattern. Although developing the entire taxonomy in detail would require another chapter as long as the present one, the basic distinctions and relationships among the categories of presentational media may be briefly described.

Following the distinction between actional and artifactual signs described earlier, presentational symbols may be divided into two parallel classes—actional and artifactual—depending on whether the symbolizing

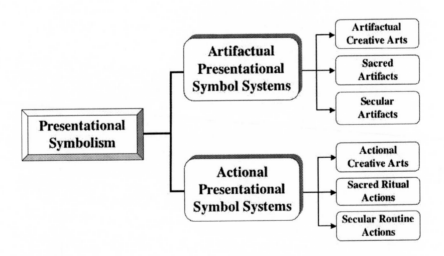

Fig. 11.6. A preliminary taxonomy of presentational media based on Susanne Langer's theory of presentational symbolism.

process results in a material form or unfolds as a moment-to-moment event. Under the category of artifactual presentational media, three subtypes are listed: artifactual creative arts, sacred artifacts, and secular artifacts.

Included in the category of artifactual creative arts would be such fine arts as sculpture, painting, and architecture. The feature that distinguishes them as a class is that they literally create something that did not exist before—namely the artistic illusion. As mentioned early in the chapter, every different artistic medium creates a different type of illusion. Sculpture, Langer argues, creates virtual volume; painting creates virtual scene; and architecture creates virtual ethnic domain. In these and other artifactual acts, the original materials (e.g., canvas or paint) disappear from view as the artistic illusion (e.g., of sunlight falling on a meadow) comes into being. By contrast, the materials used to construct sacred and secular artifacts retain their identity as they come into being. The difference between sacred and secular artifacts is the type of idea they are used to express, with secular artifacts giving a material form to our routine daily ideas and sacred artifacts expressing what might be called our cosmic ideas. All of these types of artifactual symbols are of interest to media ecologists because the ideas are projected into the media available to the person. So as new media become available (say plastics) new forms of expression become possible, and ideas that may have been ineffable previously would subsequently be expressible.

A parallel division into three subtypes is made under the actional presentational media, namely, actional creative arts, sacred actions, and secular routine actions. The actional creative arts—dance, music, theater, and so forth—also each create a primary illusion. For dance, Langer argues that the primary illusion is virtual power; for music it is the experience of time: and for theatre, the illusion is of virtual destiny (comedy) and virtual fate (tragedy). Sacred actional symbolism (such as "parading the colors" or "saluting the flag") may be identified with sacramental rituals such as birth, puberty rites, marriage ceremonies, and death rites which express cosmic ideas by enacting the logical structure of the ideas being presented. Secular presentational actions include any routinely repeated activities, either individual or c ollective based which are performed in order to express ideas concerning some aspect of the way life is to be lived.

WHERE DO WE GO FROM HERE?

This chapter has surveyed both the grand sweep of Susanne Langer's philosophical vision and some of the important details of her theory of signs and symbols in order to introduce the potential contributions her work may have for developing media ecology theory and research. There is, of course, much more that could be drawn from Langer's work than can be described in a single chapter, especially in applying her act theory to developing human communication theory more generally.

While everyone who reads Langer's various books will find their own sources of inspiration and exciting applications to follow up on, my own preoccupation for many years has been in using Langer's philosophy to try to derive a general conceptual architecture for the communication discipline to use in synthesizing its many aspects and areas of interest into a coherent body of theory and research. In previous articles (Powers, 1995, 2002), I have presented a tier-based approach to understanding the conceptual structure of the human communication discipline, which I will use here to try to illustrate the process of philosophy-building in the communication discipline that I believe Langer's canon makes possible.

As shown in the upper portion of Figure 11.7, I believe there to be an inherent intellectual structure underlying the theoretical pursuits of the communication discipline that can best be imagined as being layered into four interconnected tiers. The first tier is concerned with message theories and is dedicated to understanding the human expressive repertoire in all of its sign-based and symbol-based complexity; much of this chapter shows Langer's contribution to understanding a variety of tier-1 phenomena. The second tier of human communication theory investigates the communicator as an individual, as a participant in social interaction, and as a member of a cultural community. Everything we know about human sign and symbol structures provides the foundation for our understanding of these three tier-2 dimensions. Moreover, as we explore tier-2 phenomena, we will likely discover things that reverberate back downwards to invite us to rethink our message-related theories as well. The third tier of human communication theory and research builds upon the first two but emphasizes the traditional levels of communication, identified in the model as the interpersonal, group, and public levels of communication. The final tier of human communication theory and research examines details related to the kinds of communication identified in the first three tiers when they appear in specific communication contexts. The same reverberative relationship mentioned above in regard to tiers one and two ripple, of course, upward and downward throughout the development of the entire system.

The model in Figure 11.7 goes a step further, however, and also illustrates how the tier-based approach to developing a philosophy for the communication discipline would be built upon the broader foundations of Langer's philosophy of mind, and especially her act concept and its derivative explanatory principles. That is, the kind of tier-based philosophical structure I am imagining for the communication discipline would take seriously the idea that all explanatory principles in the human arts and sciences arise ultimately from the principles of acts. This commitment means that virtually all of the most fundamental concepts, principles, and explanations in

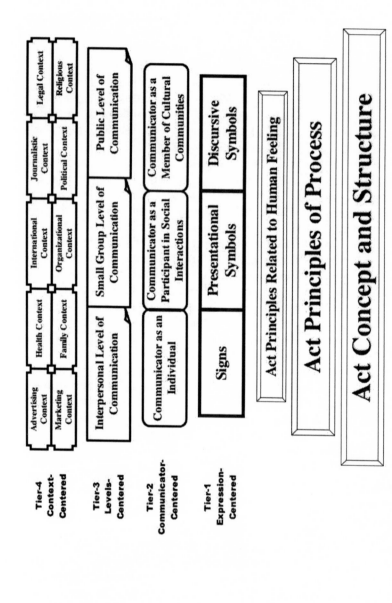

Fig. 11.7. Powers' tier-based model of the intellectual structure of the communication discipline overlaid onto Susanne Langer's act theory of process.

a philosophy of communication grounded on Langer's collected works should be expressible in act terms.

Based on the general tier model shown above and the fact that it has been built upon key elements drawn from Langer's philosophy of mind, means that in developing a more coherent philosophical architecture for the communication discipline (within which media ecology has its own significant niche), we can begin to arrange the theoretical issues in communication in a coherent and sequential way. Figure 11.8, illustrates how this might be done by presenting a detailed view of the tier-based model that identifies the key research problems any coherent philosophy of communication would need to make theoretically accessible. These problems are sequenced from bottom to top because such a philosophy is an implicative system.

That is, Langer has worked out the act portion of the general philosophy, and anyone who wants to work within that particular conceptual system must take the concepts intrinsic to the system into account in developing derivative constructs. If we take Langer's philosophy of mind seriously, we cannot simply make up definitions of key terms in any way we wish. The definitions Langer provides at a lower level in the conceptual system serve both as guides and constraints on our thinking until and unless we discover that they cause conceptual problems in working out the implications of the system at higher levels within the tier of communication issues.

Langer has also done a lot of preliminary work on the foundations of message theory, but she certainly did not draw out any of the implications of her act theory for understanding actional signs and symbols, for example. That is tier-1 work that still needs to be done. Moreover, while Langer's philosophy of mind is intended to ground research in all of the human arts and sciences, she herself only pursued one particular line of questioning—namely, the one that led to her theories of the evolution of human symbolic mentality. Most of the dimensions of communication identified in the details of Figure 11.8 remain almost untouched in Langer's own writings and, therefore, await the efforts of an army of communication scholars to try to build up the intellectual architecture upon the grounds prepared in Langer's philosophy of mind.

We can conclude, then, that the task of building a coherent conceptual architecture for media ecology based upon the works of Susanne Langer remains a wide-open field. Some of the directions we might pursue have been clearly marked out and Langer has shown the way. However, many others await the work of today's generation of students who can work out the implications of Langer's ideas and who will make many unexpected discoveries as they till this ground and build up the details of an entirely new way to imagine human mind from a media ecology perspective. For my part, this has always been an exciting prospect.

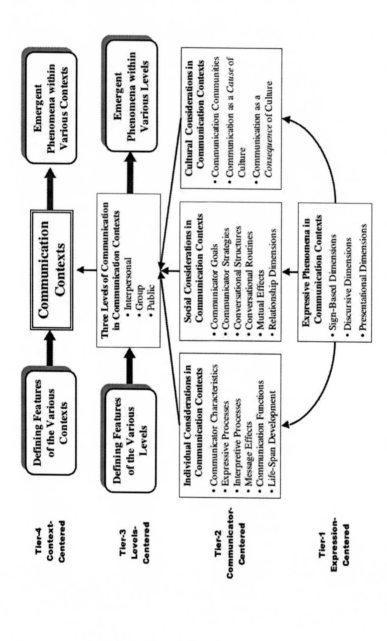

Tier-4
Context-
Centered

Tier-3
Levels-
Centered

Tier-2
Communicator-
Centered

Tier-1
Expression-
Centered

Emergent
Phenomena within
Various Contexts

Emergent
Phenomena within
Various Levels

Communication
Contexts

Defining Features
of the Various
Contexts

Three Levels of Communication
in Communication Contexts
• Interpersonal
• Group
• Public

Defining Features
of the Various
Levels

Cultural Considerations in
Communication Contexts
• Communication Communities
• Communication as a *Cause* of
  Culture
• Communication as a
  Consequence of Culture

Social Considerations in
Communication Contexts
• Communicator Goals
• Communicator Strategies
• Conversational Structures
• Conversational Routines
• Mutual Effects
• Relationship Dimensions

Individual Considerations in
Communication Contexts
• Communicator Characteristics
• Expressive Processes
• Interpretive Processes
• Message Effects
• Communication Functions
• Life-Span Development

Expressive Phenomena in
Communication Contexts
• Sign-Based Dimensions
• Discursive Dimensions
• Presentational Dimensions

Fig. 11.8. An exploded view of the tier-based model that identifies the key research problems which any coherent philoso-phy of communication would need to make theoretically accessible.

ENDNOTES

1. The present tense "exists" is used throughout for simplicity. However, it must be remembered that signs may also indicate the existence of past and future events as well. For example, the fossil record is taken as a sign indicating the existence of dinosaurs in the far distant past, and anything used as a basis for predicting future events is being taken as a sign that those events are already beginning to come into being.

2. We may also distinguish a phenomenon that we will call *accidental signs*. These are artificial signs that appear to be natural because they inadvertently became paired with a situation because of a "timing" problem—as when something bad happened just after a black cat crossed one's path, or after a person broke a mirror or walked under a ladder. As these examples illustrate, accidental signs may frequently form the basis for many superstitions.

REFERENCES

Gozzi, R., Jr. (1999). *The power of metaphor in the age of electronic me*dia. Cresskill, NJ: Hampton Press.

Gronbeck, B. E. (2000). Communication media, memory, and social-political change in Eric Havelock. *The New Jersey Journal of Communication, 8*(1), 34-45.

Langer, S. K. (1930). *The practice of philosophy.* New York: Henry Holt.

Langer, S. K. (1953). *Feeling and form: A theory of art developed from Philosophy in a New Key.* New York: Charles Scribner's Sons.

Langer, S. K. (1957a). *Philosophy in a new key: A study in the symbolism of reason, rite, and art* (3rd ed). Cambridge, MA: Harvard University Press. (Original work published 1942)

Langer, S. K. (1957b). *Problems of art: Ten philosophical lectures.* New York: Charles Scribner's Sons.

Langer, S. K. (1962). *Philosophical sketches.* Baltimore: Johns Hopkins University Press.

Langer, S. K. (1967a). *An introduction to symbolic logic,* 3rd ed. New York: Dover. (Original work published 1937)

Langer, S. K. (1967b). *Mind: An essay on human feeling* (Vol. I, Parts 1-3). Baltimore: Johns Hopkins University Press.

Langer, S. K. (1972). *Mind: An essay on human feeling* (vol. II, Part 4). Baltimore: Johns Hopkins University Press.

Langer, S. K. (1982). *Mind: An essay on human feeling* (Vol. III, Parts 5 & 6). Baltimore: Johns Hopkins University Press.

Liska, J. (1993). Bee dances, bird songs, monkey calls, and cetanean sonar: Is speech unique? *Western Journal of Communication, 57,* 1-26.

Lum, C. M. K. (2000). Introduction: The intellectual roots of media ecology. *The New Jersey Journal of Communication, 8,* 1-7.

Powers, J. H. (1981). Conversation analysis and Susanne Langer's 'act' concept: A new approach to describing the natural 'units' of conversation. *Journal of the Linguistic Association of the Southwest, 4,* 17-29.

Powers, J. H. (1982). An 'act' based theory of communication: First principles. *Journal of Applied Communication Research, 10,* 9-20.

Powers, J. H. (1995) On the intellectual structure of the human communication discipline. *Communication Education, 44,* 191-222.

Powers, J. H. (2002). Chinese communication theory and practice: A tier-based perspective. In W. Jia, X. Lu, & D. R. Heisey (Eds.), *Chinese communication theory and research: Reflections, new frontiers, and new directions* (pp. 37-64). Westport, CT: Ablex Publishing.

12

The Orality–Literacy
Theorems and Media Ecology

Bruce E. Gronbeck

University of Iowa

In 1986, Eric Havelock, Sterling professor of classics emeritus at Yale University, completed the book that would summarize what he saw as his central contributions to Western scholarship. After tracing out the evolution of his own thinking on what he called the "Orality Problem" (Havelock, 1986, p. 24), he suggested that what we will be terming "the orality-literacy theorems" burst unto the scene in 1963, "releasing a flood of startling recognitions of a host of related facts" (p. 24). Between Spring 1962 and Spring 1963, five books, coming out of three different countries, came to define primary orality—that is, orality as a determinative characteristic of certain kinds of societies. The works Havelock pointed to, in addition to his own *Preface to Plato* (Havelock, 1963), were Claude Lévi-Strauss' (1962) *La Pensée Sauvage*, Jack Goody and Ian Watt's long (1963/1968) essay "The Consequences of Literacy," Marshall McLuhan's (1962) *The Gutenberg Galaxy*, and Ernst Mayr's (1963) *Animal Species and Evolution*. Classics, anthropology, cultural history, and evolutionary biology were contributing in that slice of time to the development of the orality–literacy theorems.

Mayr's work was a survey of the then-present status of Darwinian evolutionary theory. It dealt with human evolution only in four pages of its appendix, but those were provocative pages. Mayr built the argument that human beings evolve by passing on to later generations two kinds of information: genetic and linguistic. The word *information* here is taken from the symbolic codes of humans, then applied to biological processes, more or less, interpenetrating genetic and linguistic processes. In Mayr's analysis, as the human brain began to grow and the human head gained a jaw, face, and larynx capable not only eating/swallowing but also expressing/communicating, *homo sapiens* acquired through evolutionary processes the capacity to pass on not only genetic but also linguistic information. Of particular interest to students of the orality-literacy theorems was Mayr's integration of the physiological and the social. Both to Mayr could evolve (i.e., change or develop) through mutation: genes, through the DNA coding passed from parents to offspring, and linguistic symbols, through the cultural traditions imprinted in particular pieces of language-use (see Havelock, 1963, pp. 26, 55, 56, 99).

There were direct relationships between Mayr's thinking and Havelock's attacks on questions about orality and morality. Since 1957, when he wrote *The Liberal Temper of Greek Politics*, Havelock had been interested in the aphorism or pithy little saying. He had come to an important conclusion then: "The rounded sentence began its career in the pre-literate days of oral communication, when indoctrination depended on word of mouth and retention of doctrine depended on the memory" (Havelock, 1957, p. 126). In that statement we find a claim that Havelock would expand into his great book of 1963: that, in oral societies, moral codes, that is, cultural traditions about right-and-wrong personal and public conduct, could be preserved and made operative only because of particular characteristics of speech. The aphorism was not simply a fragment of some longer work on morality such as the Bible, but was a compact oral form into which moral guidance could be put and which could be remembered easily because of that oral form.

"Birds of a feather flock together" is an aphorism that illustrates the power of oral moral guidance and the ease of memorization. The moral lesson—depend on your own kind, your own tribe—is captured in an easy-to-understand metaphor: birds. Most of us have seen birds flock together especially when they arrive in northern climes in the spring or leave for warmer venues in the fall. Birds travel as flocks, and so, the aphorism suggests, should humans. As well, notice the rhythm. It breaks the statement into segments (called *kola* in Greek grammar) that are roughly parallel rhythmically: "Birds of a feather," with a stressed–unstressed–unstressed–unstressed–stressed–unstressed pattern; then "flock together," with a similar pattern (but short one of the unstressed syllables of the first *kolon*). Yet, the aphorism is easy to understand and easy to remember because of its sing-song type pattern.

Why is that important? Recall that we are talking about oral societies, that is, societies without any form of written symbolization available for transmitting information from one person to another, from one generation to another. If any idea is to be remembered, it must be put into something that will allow it to be stored and re-used (Havelock, 1986, p. 56), and so passed between people. Linguistic vocalizations, to Havelock, are a kind of technology, therefore, with both psychological (mind-to-mind) and social (person-to-person) dimensions. We return to his work shortly, and discuss additional ideas that he articulated.

Less important yet nonetheless relevant to these ways of thinking about orality is the work of anthropologist Claude Lévi-Strauss. He was a structural anthropologist, following in the traditions of Emile Durkheim (see Durkheim & Mauss, 1903/1963). That is, one of his many interests was in ways that primitive peoples learned to classify and process their environments and to conceptualize a sense of progress in their lives. Although many of Lévi-Strauss' books in this period dealt with the structural aspects of myth, *La Pensée Sauvage* [*The Savage Mind*] argued for the pivotal link between structural logics in primitive myth and important aspects of the language in which myth was articulated. He was particularly interested in the use of names—similar to Durkheim's interests in the animals of clans' totems—to power myths. (Spoken) names as arranged in paired opposites in myths became to Lévi-Strauss clues to the anxieties primitive peoples were attempting to work out in their myths. Think of the names of the villains and desired women in the James Bond movies—their characteristics are captured in their names (Dr. No, Goldfinger, Octopussy). And fairy tales abound with agents—Prince Charming, Snow White, Cinderella—whose names identify their moral postures.

The relationship between the content and the medium of communication, hinted at in Lévi-Strauss, was the focus of McLuhan's (1962) *The Gutenberg Galaxy: The Making of Typographic Man*. The central argument of this popular work was that a signal split in western consciousness turned on the invention of the printing press; script was pre-Gutenberg, and print, post-Gutenberg. McLuhan's ambiguous reactions to the coming of print to the West pervade the book. On the one hand, print is dehumanizing in that it destroys the need for people to talk face to face and it can promote private, even secretive, thinking. Yet, on the other, McLuhan could argue that it was liberating (allowing the Bible and various democratic ideas to circulate freely) and revolutionary (the vehicle for remaking individual and collective consciousness). Reading the book now, we can recognize that he was impatiently pointing toward his next book, *Understanding Media: The Extensions of Man* (McLuhan, 1964), where he could concentrate more on the technologies of electronic communications and deal more concretely with the aphorism with which his whole intellectual program is identified: "The medium is the message." Yet, even in *The Gutenberg Galaxy* he demonstrated the sheer grandness of the orality-literacy theorems, attempting to find the formula that would specify relationships between and among communication media, cultural content and structures, and individual as well as collective consciousness.

The fifth work from those twelve months in 1962 and 1963 that Havelock identified as groundbreaking was Goody and Watt's essay on "The Consequences of Literacy," which circulated more widely in Jack Goody's (1968) *Literacy in Traditional Societies*.[1] The essay discussed the implications of oral culture surviving even in the modern—literate and elec-tronic—world and a model for the relationship between oral and literate cul-ture to be found in the experience of the Greeks. The Greek sections of the essay probed the role of memory in maintaining oral culture, differences between the Greek alphabet (it had greater flexibility in recording speech) and its predecessors, and contrasts between the literature and philosophy of literate Greek vis-à-vis the so-called literatures of earlier periods. All three of those concerns became central to scholars of the orality-literacy theo-rems—especially to Walter Ong and Eric Havelock.

What Havelock was suggesting in general in 1986, then, was that vari-ous strains of thought from multiple fields of study were about to be inter-twined in the early 1960s. He certainly took another classicist, Harvard's Milman Parry, as a predecessor for his own work. To Havelock, however, Parry had understood the importance of oral formula for composing and remembering poetry, but had seen them as improvisational, not enduring, storage units for traditional beliefs and attitudes.[2] Similarly, a central figure in the formal definition of the orality-literacy theorems, Walter Ong, had been an M.A. student of Marshall McLuhan when both were at Saint Louis University (see Gronbeck, cited in Gronbeck, Farrell, & Soukup, 1991, p. xi; for more details, see Farrell, 2000). And, as has been suggested, Goody and Watt were drawing upon thinking that drops back to Durkheim's late 19th-century work and notions of linguistic fields developed by social anthropol-ogists of the 1930s. What made 1962-1963 such a fertile period was the mul-tidisciplinary burst of thought and argument that appeared on the academic horizon. Students of classics, anthropology, literary-hermeneutic theory and criticism, rhetoric, evolutionary biology, and other variants of social theory began to read each other's work, with interests in how their varied knowl-edge-bases impacted our understandings of relationships between and among communication, culture, and consciousness. In a period of such shar-ing, the oral–literacy theorems—and, ultimately, the field of media ecolo-gy—were born.

In this chapter, I explore the orality-literacy theorems, in three move-ments: (a) I look at the so-called macro-theory of orality-literacy, that is, theorizing about the place of dominant media in governing societies in gen-eral; (b) I narrow to a focus on micro-theory, which is to say talk about how the human mind processes messages coming to us in various media, especially acoustic, literate, and visual media; and (c) I am then in a position to compare and contrast the perspective and the vocabulary of macro- and micro-theories of orality-literacy, to help us understand both the sweepingly broad and technically narrow kinds of scholarship that are produced by students of media ecology. That should permit me, finally, to point to future work that media ecologists need to pursue.

Beginning, the word theorem requires a bit of attention. In mathematics, a *theorem* is a theoretical proposition that can be proved from axioms or other pre-existing formulae, paralleling the logician's understanding of a theorem as a statement that can be deduced from previously accepted or proved premises. More colloquially, many of us are tempted to use the word to indicate any statement accepted without proof processes or direct evidence. Among media ecologists, the term is used in a manner different from both its mathematical precision and its colloquial informality. Walter Ong's (1982) understanding of the term in his *Orality and Literacy* can be our guide: "I shall present the matter here in the form of theorems; more or less hypothetical statements that connect in various ways with what has already been explained" (p. 156). Our object, then, is to articulate the so-called orality-literacy theorems in ways that will allow an exploration of their underlying axioms, formulae, and/or premises as human conceptions of the lifeworld. That is, theorems here will be thought of as underlying—and sometimes not even stated—assumptions of various kinds that help us rationalize, make sense out of, a series of concepts used in propositions that make claims about the human world.

Actually, phrasing the theorems is a difficult job because they have been generated by scholars with varied interests. Roughly speaking, one set of theoretical speculations has come from investigators working as social historians, attempting to characterize the conditions for public communication in different kinds of collectivities in specific historical periods. Another set springs from students of particular communication media and the communication practices of people employing this versus that medium of symbolic exchange; such researchers examine particular messages constructed within particular contexts very closely. Respectively, the labels of *macro-theory* and *micro-theory* are applied to these two central intellectual tendencies. Just be sure not to employ these schema to sort scholars into two piles, for theorists such as Walter Ong and Marshall McLuhan have generated both kinds of studies to justify their theorems. As well, different practitioners in each group may have multiple foci in various of their works. So, for example, one can find Eric Havelock writing about communication media (e.g., the oral text) in one piece, consciousness (e.g., the Greek mind) in another, social organization or integration (e.g., the oral performance in Greek festivals) in still another. We are separating macro- and micro-theory in order to explore two roughly separable sets of accounts for the orality-literacy theorems, knowing full well that such separations are primarily convenient, not necessarily accurate, reproductions of the lifeworld.

MACRO-THEORY: DOMINANT MEDIA IN SOCIETIES

Within the scholarly community, McLuhan became known first for his writing about social structure and culture at the macro-level. Following the work of other historians of technology and society, most notably Lewis Mumford (1934), McLuhan's (1962) *The Gutenberg Galaxy* was a study of the impact of mechanically reproduced literacy—the flood of publishing that became possible after the invention of the printing press. His primary assumption was that "Technological environments are not merely passive containers of people but are active processes that reshape people and other technologies alike" (p. 7). He argued that print forcibly revolutionized western societies, making possible the Reformation, the rise of the competitive city-state, the democratic impulse, the development of science, and even changes in architecture. Certainly, instrumental to his thinking were the first books of his pupil Walter Ong (1958a), *Ramus, Method, and the Decay of Dialogue* and *Ramus and Talon Inventory* (Ong, 1958b). The first book was a study of voice, point of view, and methods for presenting ideas that came into fashion with moveable type and were turned into rhetorical practice by the French academic Peter Ramus. Monologue replaced dialogue as the dominant mode of academic writing, visualist modes of presentation replaced oral forms of discourse, and even pedagogy changed radically with the rise of the book (see Palmeri, 1991, for a summary of Ong, print, and Ramism in rhetoric).

Simply put, theories of media ecology[3] at the macro-level are focused on changes in human experience—often discussed at both society-wide and self-conscious or self-reflexive planes of experience—that follow or accompany shifts in the dominant media of collectivities.

Technological Determinism

If the argument suggests that changes in social organization or operations "follow" from shifts in dominant media, then that scholar is labeled a *technological determinist*.[4] McLuhan seemed to be such a scholar in the statement quoted earlier, and certainly one of his predecessors at the University of Toronto, Harold Adams Innis, was regularly identified as a determinist. In his *Empire & Communications,* Innis (1950/1972) argued that self-contained, comparatively insulated societies (oral cultures, such as ancient Babylon, which inscribed laws on stones) were dominated by difficult-to-transport media and were what he called time-biased societies. In time-biased societies, the past (tradition) governed much of the present and future. When cut in stone, rules and laws endured, protected by priestly or secular cults (e.g. lawyers) who had monopolies of knowledge about traditions. In contrast, societies with easy-to-transport media (e.g., papyrus and paper cultures) tended to form empires, and thus were what he termed space-biased societies. Portable media allowed constitutions, laws, and rules-of-life to circulate far from the center of authority; as well, they were flexible, regularly changed, especially once printing permitted the easy re-issuing of laws and rules. Monopolies of knowledge were harder if not impossible to maintain in space-biased societies, which, therefore, tended to be more progressivist than time-biased societies. The media technologies, to Innis and perhaps McLuhan, then, shaped—explicitly, causally—the kind of social structures that developed in different societies.[5] Innis was undoubtedly a determinist, and McLuhan was perhaps guilty of being one as well (although see the discussion of later McLuhan thinking, especially, in Gronbeck, 1981).[6]

Technological Pragmatism

If the preferred verb is not "follow" from but rather "accompany," then the communication scholar being talked about is not labeled a technological determinist, but more of a pragmatist who's interested in how technologies interact with other forces in societies in particular times and places.[7] James Carey is such an intellectual. In his *Communication as Culture*, for example, Carey (1989) among other things wishes to warn us about "the instrumentalization of communication" (p. 84). If communication is but a tool for getting things done—for bonding relationships, passing on instructions or directives, even remanufacturing our collective institutions—then it divorces thought from action, and separates doing from the contexts within which we actually are doing things. Technological determinists tend to think in terms of instruments, the tools by which we remake our environments and our self-conceptions. Carey prefers to think of media as sites wherein we can view human beings pursuing their hopes and dreams within specific environments (p. 110). To Carey, we cannot postulate causal relationships between and among communication, culture, and consciousness, but rather must study human events through all of them simultaneously. Almost all of the historians of communication media, as one might expect, tend toward technological-pragmatic explanations.

Take, for example, the coming of electricity and the widespread distribution of electrical appliances (culminating in the computer) throughout the late 19th and all of the 20th centuries. It was the technological determinist, McLuhan, writing an introduction for a new edition of Innis' (1951/1964) *The Bias of Communication*, who brazenly depicted the electronic age as creating "cosmic humanism" and "a Pentecostal condition of universal understanding," in the process "abolish[ing] time and space alike" (cited in Carey, 1989, p. 116). McLuhan (1962) explained such consequences of the electronic revolution in this way:

> With this [Einstein's] recognition of curved space in 1905 the Gutenberg galaxy was officially dissolved. With the end of lineal specialisms and fixed points of view, compartmentalized knowledge became as unacceptable as it had always been irrelevant. (p. 302)

In contrast, Carey's view is that such talk is not a *description* of the operation of causal effects in history, but, rather, is a *rhetoric-about* the past. Along with Leo Marx (1964), Carey (1989) calls it the "rhetoric of the technological sublime" (pp. 120-141). In Carey's view, electricity did not cause changes in social conditions and individual self-consciousness. Rather, the dominant media, social change, and individual shifts-in-self-awareness all occurred simultaneously, influencing each other in complex ways. The public talk about electricity was not a report of the state-of-the-world, but rather a burbling-up of collective hopes and fantasies in language that already was circulating in societies. Western reliance on technology was already in place before electricity was harnessed, and the search for an account of the inexpressible, the sublime, had gone on throughout the second half of the 18th century, with consciousness itself probed deeply in the romantic and so-called personalist movements of the 19th century.

The uses to which electricity was put and ways of thinking about its impact on the exterior and interior spheres of life were conditioned, then, by what already was being thought and done. Yet, of course, there's no denying that electricity had profound effects on the West: the shift from mechanical to electronic and thence to digital mechanization; electrically enhanced and computer-generated (synthesizer) music; the televisual revolution that turned the world into an over-sized village (see McLuhan & Fiore, 1968); the electronic monitoring and modification of the body and mind, of interiority itself, in a cyberworld; the shift in the world economy from an industrial to a service base; and so on.[8]

Whether one is a technological determinist or a technological pragmatist, however, a media ecologist working at the macro-level of conceptualization is attempting to understand the operations of society dominated by particular media: usually, oral, face-to-face media in so-called oral societies, written and printed media in so-called literate societies, and electricity-based personal and public media in so-called electronic societies. Although some scholars (e.g., Chesebro & Bertelsen, 1996; Couch, 1996; Innis, 1950/1972; Logan, 2000) have attempted serious overviews of all recorded western cultures, most focus on one particular type of medium-dominated society.

Oral Culture

One of the finest accounts of the operations of oral cultures is found in Eric Havelock's work. He was concerned, among other things, with trying to understand how culture—"*nomoi* and *êthea*" (Havelock, 1986, p. 57)—was constructed, maintained, and transmitted in an oral sociey (i.e., among peoples living without writing). Translating these words as "custom-laws" and "folk-ways" respectively, he argued that orations and especially poems were the keys to managing life in an oral society. Poems were not only recreational and inspirational; they also were instructional. The Muses were depicted by Homer as teachers; tradition was understood to be both a product of the past and yet also the guide to the future. Custom-laws were sayings, aphorisms, that captured the wisdom of one's ancestors, and folk-ways were the accepted routines for doing things—relating to other people, conceptualizing one's environment, accomplishing everyday tasks.

Education would include, of course, learning to talk and think within the confines of one's family—basic socialization. But, oral societies also tended to have public occasions—festivals—where the folk would gather together to renew their commitments and to have reinforced their understandings of their place in the world. The coliseums of the ancient western world were homes to the dramatic, epic, and musical festivals and other occasions for collectively celebrating passages, holidays, and heroic accomplishments of general note. The *nomoi* and *êthea* were captured in streams of sound from the poets, seers, priests, orators, actors, and others working the audiences of the festivals. What made such occasions do cultural work in oral societies was what Havelock (1986) called the pictorialized image. Advice on how to live one's life (*êthea*) was not recited as a list of do's and don'ts, but instead as

> concrete acts represented as the decisions of persons and performed on objects by these persons acting as agents. Custom-laws were not stated abstractly but, rather, in terms of concrete actions. So, Havelock [quoting himself] notes, a generalized and abstracted *idea*, "honesty is the best policy," is typical of a literate culture, while a formulaic *action*, "an honest person always prospers," is typical of an oral culture. (p. 76)

Abstracted reasoning patterns took the form of "the play of human habit and behaviour, reported in images of men acting" (Havelock, 1982, p. 230), and hence were not only verbalized but pictorialized. Reasoning patterns such as cause-and-effect were heard and seen in depictions of people acting, not as literate generalizations.

Key to oral societies, therefore, was memory. Memory turned the poetic-musical recitations and performances into vehicles for the manufacture or remanufacture of a socialized self, of a personal identity situated in the collective (for an introduction to memory, see Yates, 1966). Havelock conceptualized individual memory as activated by the variety of cues possible through human-to-human performance—acoustic, visual, narrative, and situational or environmental—within a kind of recitative experience. The flow of sounds was not isolated, nor was it experienced independent of the stories being (re)told, the demeanor and bodily behavior of the storyteller, or the physical situation within which the story was being told. Rather, the listener was bombarded by sound, sight, memories of the story and others like it, cues from the physical environment (the enormousness of the coliseum, the press of other people within it, etc.). Such a bombardment of stimuli, revitalizing memories of performances past, produced what Havelock (1978) called an echo-principle:

> The echo must accompany a fresh statement of action, but this cannot be excessively novel or inventive; to accommodate the needs of memory there must be likeness to the prior statement [or experience] to seduce or tempt the mind to make the leap from one to the other, and to tempt the mouth to follow with the appropriate enunciation. (p. 15)

So, think of the child who is hearing *Goldilocks and the Three Bears* for the umpteenth time. That child knows the story, the words, the sound-characteristics typical of Goldilocks and all of the bears, and even the best time and place to re-tell the story—in bed, just before going to sleep. The child's mouth indeed is tempted to follow the storyteller "with an appropriate enunciation." Each time the story of Goldilocks is repeated, the child has reinforced (a) the importance of narrative structures in processing life experiences; (b) the moral of the story; (c) a trusting relationship between the storyteller and the *aud*-itor, between tellers and listeners; and (d) even a relationship between remembering a traditional story and the act of going to sleep (i.e., going to sleep with positive thoughts about one's social relationships, which is a social bonding experience).

The child's participation is paralleled in all oral-social events. As Havelock (1986) noted when discussing festivals, the audience "clapped and danced and sang collectively, in response to the chanting of the singer" (p. 78), and thus members of an oral society shared that which was significant "historically, ethically, politically, . . . [in an] imitation (mimesis) of the ethos and nomos of the city" (p. 93). The individual performed the social codes along with the singers and actors, as tradition was echoed in the present and made legitimate for future use. Performed memory welded the parts of oral society together. There developed a clear and significant bond between aesthetic drama (poetry more generally) and social drama (the daily routines of everyday life).[9]

Oral cultures, then, live in an evolving present, grounded in traditions from the past that are echoed in public recountings of them—often in poetic and sometimes in oratorical forms—that, in turn, posit and point the way toward the future. Face-to-face interaction and personal exercise of power are essential if oral cultures are to survive.

Literate Culture

The social organization and state of collective consciousness in literate cultures are, to media ecologists, radically different from the culture and consciousness of oral societies.[10] We already have noted McLuhan's analysis: The move from chirographic (hand-written) to print (mechanically reproduced) literacy revolutionized religion, politics, education, and science. Others have written about such revolutions as well. Consider the work of Postman and Deibert (cf. Eisenstein, 1983, 1979; Stock, 1983).

Neil Postman (1985, 1999) devoted two of his books to a defense of literate culture. In *Amusing Ourselves to Death: Public Discourse in the Age of Show Business*, first he argues that "the concept of truth is intimately linked to the biases of forms of expression" (Postman, 1985, p. 22), which suggests that social epistemology—how people in society generally think about themselves and the world—is grounded in dominant forms of media. And hence, when a country develops a new dominant medium, even its understanding of truth can change. This assumption leads to his analysis of "Typographic America." The United States as a country was grounded in such written documents as the *Mayflower* compact, the *Bay Psalm Book*, Thomas Paine's *Common Sense*, a written constitution, and a flow of other written materials, and based its cultural standards for shared social outlooks in literate materials. They were powerful because in the last half of the seventeenth century, an estimated 85% to 90% of Massachusetts and Connecticut men (with presumably comparable numbers in other colonies) were literate—"quite probably the highest concentration of literate males to be found anywhere in the world at that time" (Postman, 1985, p. 31). A public school system sprang up, spreading literacy even farther; the newspaper industry flourished; subscription libraries blossomed in the 19th century; and the country's public oratory was "based on the printed word" (p. 41). All public business flowed through the literate word: "the press was not merely a machine but a structure for discourse, which both rules out and insists upon certain kinds of content and, inevitably, a certain kind of audience" (p. 43).

Postman (1985) then moved on to the "Typographic Mind" of America—the collective psyche of a country trained to process prose-based thinking even from its orators. The center of his theorems of collective consciousness in the typographic era is to be found in this quotation (p. 51):

> Whenever language is the principal medium of communication—especially language controlled by the rigors of print—an idea, a fact, a claim is the inevitable result. The idea may be banal, the fact irrelevant, the claim false, but there is no escape from meaning when language is the instrument guiding one's thought. . . . [W]hen an author and reader are struggling with semantic meaning, they are engaged in the most serious challenge to the intellect. . . . [Reading] is also, of course, an essentially rational activity.

And so, Postman finds derived from the typographic revolution not only American culture but also ways of consciously processing public business: complex, literate constructions of ideas governed by a collective rationality. In his later book, Postman (1999) searches for ways that we can reinstitute that kind of literate rationality even in the electronic world of today.

Following Postman into the world of collective consciousness is Ronald Deibert (1997). His *Parchment, Printing, and Hypermedia: Communication in the World Order Transformation* (p. 31) is constructed around two general effects of the mechanical–literate evolution: distributional changes and changes to social epistemology. Deibert seeks to escape the determinist's presumed shortcomings by arguing that new dominating media have unforeseen effects because they become a part of "the material landscape in which human agents and social groups interact" (p. 29). The new media are environments rather than simply tools, and hence capable of being the sites of exterior and interior changes in people.[11]

Distributional changes represent ways in which social-political infrastructures are affected by new media. Deibert posits two theorems to account for distributional changes: (a) "first is the most basic proposition of medium theory, that specific communications environments have a certain 'logic' or 'nature' not in any determinist sense, but only in the sense of 'making human communications of certain types easier or more difficult'" (p. 32, quoting Ruggie, 1986). (b) As well, there are usually groups of social actors with various interests and goals who take up and exploit the new technology. Of course at any given time there are many ambitious groups in society, but only some of them have goals and organization that fit well with characteristics of the new medium. So, human ambition and desire interact with particular media environments to create and distribute sociopolitical change.

Socioepistemological changes, on the other hand, are shifts in "the 'internal' world of ideas and ways of thinking" (p. 33)—what have been called by French social theorists *mentalités collectives*. Although many social theorists since Marx have argued that shifts-in-consciousness are products of social, political, and economic forces, medium theory brings in particular kinds of material considerations—changes in communication technologies.[12]

Armed with theorems that underwrite his concepts of effects, Deibert then goes on to execute his project: exploring the transformation of the medieval "world order" into the modern one. What is traced in detail is a movement from the unified spiritual community of medieval Europe, where the *corpus mysticum* was visualized in the Great Chain of Being, with Christ, the Church, and the Pontiff forming the links that bound the secular human and natural worlds in their places. Authority was particular, but not segmented into spheres. Here were "nonterritorial logics of organization" (p. 13). In the succeeding modernist world, which to Deibert developed in fits and starts over a considerable period of time, territoriality became important: "the parcelization and segmentation of all economic, social, and cultural activity into mutually exclusive, functionally similar political entities, or territorial 'bundles'" (p. 14, quoting Elkins, 1995). An instrument of that transformation was printing, capable as it was of "a cognitive bias towards visual, linear, and uniform representations of space" (p. 204). As well, standardization became a valued concept, as did the printed distribution of social abstractions such as contracts, newspapers, and constitutions.

The writings of McLuhan, Postman, and Deibert, then, are examples of the cultural history of societies from the vantage of the orality-literacy theorems. I comment on these analyses later.

Electronic Culture

We now come to our own time, the period of what Dudley Andrew (1997) calls the image in dispute. The image in dispute becomes an important marker for a discussion of electronic culture. Much of the scholarship devoted to mechanically and electronically reproduced pictures, words, and sound from the last quarter of the nineteenth century up to our own day is rife with arguments of doubt, fear, and outright condemnation. From a comment attributed (among others) to John Ruskin upon the laying of the transoceanic cable from England to India—"But what have we to say to India?"—to the latest newspaper article documenting ripoffs on the Internet, electronic culture has generated a monumental amount of negative commentary. We only now are starting to bank up more even-tempered, analytical works on the Electronic Age.

Each new electronic medium—the telegraph, telephone, silent then sound film, radio, television, computer-assisted communication—as well as technological innovations for delivering such media (from cable to satellites) has generated a storm of public commentary on its promise and its pathologies. Each new medium presumably has produced both societal vigor and decay simultaneously. (See the popular arguments surrounding silent film, radio, sound film, and television in R. Davis, 1976; public and academically theoretical discussions of the telegraph, early motion pictures, and early radio can be found in Czitrom, 1982; some of the telegraph's impacts are discussed in Carey, 1989, "Technology and Ideology: The Case of the Telegraph"; a review of attacks on television appears in Gronbeck, 1988). What seems beyond dispute is that the electronic media have revolutionized societies, affecting determinatively their cultural foundations, perhaps for good, perhaps for ill (see Medhurst, Gonzalez, & Peterson, 1990, especially pp. x-xi).

But, how should that revolution be described? McLuhan's (1964) most popular book, *Understanding Media: The Extensions of Man*, depicted revolutionary power as deriving from the central metaphor of that title, extensions. Each of the new electronic media extended parts of the body: film and television, the eye; radio, the ear; the railroad, one's feet; and the computer, the central nervous system. Each new medium remade the human sensorium and hence mind (cf. Nevitt, 1982, chap. 7). His basic theorem was clear: "The transformations of technology have the character of organic evolution [literally!] because all technologies are extensions of our physical being" (p. 164). His later work on the so-called Laws of Media took a broader look at social processes, depicting them as unfolding via a four-part social process: amplification or enhancement, obsolescence, retrieval, and reversal. So, print amplified private authorship, obsolesced slang and dialects, retrieved elitism (via literacy), and reversed tribal trends in societies by mass-producing a reading public (overviewed in Gronbeck, 1981; expanded in McLuhan & McLuhan, 1988, and McLuhan & Powers, 1989). I return to McLuhan's ideas about the human sensorium when examining micro-theories; but, for now we can say that his emphasis across his career was on documenting sociopolitical-cultural changes that emanate from shifts in media use—especially electronic media.

Walter Ong's primary contribution to our views of electronic culture is his notion of secondary orality. That notion suggests that the electronic public sphere has restored some of the characteristics of ancient oral cultrure. The phrase is meant to emphasize that orality has taken center stage again in the electronic world, albeit in different forms than societies had available in times of primary orality (i.e., in the original oral cultures). We are not talking about actual oral transactions now, but virtual intimacy, a verbal–visual–acoustic construction of a sense of public conversation occurring via film, radio, television, telephones, the Internet. His strongest statements on secondary orality appear in *Orality and Literacy: The Technologizing of the Word* (Ong, 1982). "Secondary orality," Ong notes, "has generated a strong group sense, for listening to spoken words forms hearers into a group, a true audience. . . . But secondary orality generates a sense for groups immeasurably larger than those of primary oral culture— McLuhan's 'global village'" (p. 136). Secondary orality, as well, has traces of the spontaneity that characterized primary orality, though, because we have absorbed the analyticity of print, "We plan our happenings carefully to be sure that they are thoroughly spontaneous" (p. 137). Even the agonistic practices of primitive societies have returned in the form of televised debates, although, again, with differences:

> On television contending presidential candidates do not stomp about a platform flailing their arms or even stand out in the open [until Clinton in 1992!], like earlier orators metonymically claiming possession of a field, but install themselves behind protective lecterns for genteel exchanges of words projecting images of their self-contained selves instead of pacing up and down a rostrum flailing verbally at one another. (Ong, 1981, p. 142)

What Ong is working toward in his notion of secondary orality is the simple recognition that the older dominant media—talk, print, etc.—do not disappear in the era of the new. Yet, with that simple idea comes the problem of conceptualizing relationships between past and present. How are they related? The past is not just made present again, because it cannot be; no matter how much a cell phone exchange feels like a "real" conversation, it is not—it's not face-to-face, involving the complete presence of conversants. Rather, secondary orality *is* in fact secondary, with orality per se (and hence with oral culture residues) playing a comparatively minor communication role vis-à-vis the electronic medium. All of this means that electronic communication takes on a kind of hermeneutic figure in which the past sense of oral interaction re-emerges, but altered, in the new era.[13]

Finally, what has caught up two generations of commentators on and theorists of the electronic age is spectacle—specifically, the role of the publicly shared images or sequences of (moving) images in sociopolitical life. The fields of visual politics or visual rhetoric are sprawling. Among the most often quoted works are Murray Edelman's (1988) *Constructing the Political Spectacle*, an analysis of the televisual presentation of political news; Kathleen Hall Jamieson's (1988) *Eloquence in the Electronic Age: The Transformation of Political Speechmaking* on the remanufacture of political oratory for televisual presentation; Daniel Dayan and Elihu Katz's (1992) *Media Events*, the live broadcasting of events constructed as historically monumental; John Fiske's (1994) *Media Matters: Everyday Culture and Political Change*, an argument on the ways in which "media" events become "real" politics, supported by case studies of the O. J. Simpson arrest and pretrial hearings, the Hill–Thomas hearings, the family values debate, and the Los Angeles uprisings; Roderick Hart's (1994/1999) *Seducing America*, on televised politics' destruction of rational decision making in favor of emotional appeal; and Lance Bennett's (1983/2001) *News: The Politics of Illusion*, which, especially in the 1990s editions, develops a theory of information biases (personalization, dramatization, fragmentation, and authority–disorder bias) that alter public political information because of electronic mediation. These are but samples of myriad books on specularity and sociopolitical life, especially in the United States.[14]

Even as such works on the practices of public life flow from trade and university presses, theorists scramble to account for that life. Social theorists run the gamut from the French situationalist Guy Debord's (1967/1983) celebrated *Society of the Spectacle,* a series of meditations on the contemporary dominance of images and their destruction of human beings' direct contact with the world and with each other, to the collections of utopic and dystopic visions of the so-called "cultures of technological embodiment" in Steve Jones' (1995) *Cybersociety* and Mike Featherstone and Roger Burrows' (1995) *Cyberspace/Cyberbodies/Cyberpunk.* The new social theory coming into place to account for life in electronic culture is influenced by postmodern social thought, particularly Lyotard (1979/1984), as well as the latest forms of cultural studies, which stress image-making or representation theory (e.g., Hall, 1997). Both postmodern and cultural studies social thought are in a phase where they stress the fragmentation of social experience but yet its dominance or even control by the flow of public images.[15]

Macro-theories articulating and then reasoning from orality-literacy-visuality theorems, in sum, have been used to account for the shifting and cycling of sociopolitical life, especially in the Western world, with those accounts tied doggedly to the idea of dominant media operating in specific times and places. I return to discuss the strengths and weaknesses of such scholarship after I move on to micro-theory.

MICRO-THEORY: SOUND, LITERACY, AND VISUALITY AS CHANNELS

When we crank down our perspective, looking at the orality-literacy theorems for what they say, not about society in general but about different cognitive-emotional channels for acquiring and processing information about the world, we come upon related yet very different sorts of speculation. One way of understanding "The medium is the message" is to explore how it is that human beings process messages as they typically come through different media. The word *typically* may or may not be important here. *Typically* appears in that sentence to remind us that media use is culturally conditioned. You are taught, not how to see, but how to look: what to consider worth looking at in your visual environment, what to value (or not) in what you see. And so, too, with other media. You "hear" naturally but are taught how to "listen"; sense data from your sense of touch comes with predispositions to code it—to understand what it is you're touching—in particular ways because of cultural conditioning.

In other words, although the focus in this section is on the cognitive and emotional processing of mediated information coming to individuals, we really cannot ignore macro-theoretical theorems about oral, literate, and electronic social structures and their effects on people. Again, as noted before, the macro/micro distinction is merely analytic, not necessarily descriptive. In actual historical studies of media operations (see others in this book), the separation is not helpful, although for theoretical purposes, it is, and hence we'll now examine theorems at the micro-theoretical level of explanation.

Processing Oral Stimuli

Walter Ong is the theorist who has most completely developed a theory of communication processing in oral cultures. The third chapter of *Orality and Literacy* (Ong, 1982) focuses on "Some Psychodynamics of Orality," more precisely, nine characteristics of face-to-face communication. These characteristics create what Ong sees as the oral noetic state,[16] that is, the ways in which the minds of individuals in oral cultures are organized cognitively and habitually and work pragmatically. Those nine characteristics run as follows (pp. 37-57):

1. Additive rather than subordinative. The oral mind tends to add items together rather than organizing them in hierarchies, much as a child tends to the tell a story by saying "And then . . . and then . . . and then . . ." without explanations. Literateness tends to bring superordinations and subordinations into discourse structures.

2. Aggregative rather than analytic. Formulae are needed in oral societies to aggregate and hold together important kinds of information. These may take the form of clichéd adjectives (the "beautiful princess," "brave warrior," "'Slick Willie' Clinton") or aphorisms ("A stitch in time saves nine"). The aphorism doesn't analyze the situation—it just aggregates cultural wisdom and passes it on.

3. Redundant or copious. People repeat themselves in oral cultures; they offer an idea in a second form to help listeners understand and remember (as we just did in this sentence). There is no way for a listener to "backloop" (p. 39) during oral presentations, so repetitions are put in to help with clarity and memorability.

4. Conservative or traditionalist. If there are no mechanisms for writing down cultural wisdom and rules, they must be conserved in other ways—in repeated stories, aphorisms, regularly

recited religious liturgies, and so on. This practice gives the past, tradition, tremendous force in oral societies.

5. Close to the human lifeworld. Lists cannot be written down, and so are reproduced in rhythmic, even rhyming versions ("Thirty days hath September,/April, June, and November./" etc.). Skills are passed down, not in manuals, but by apprenticeship. Concreteness allows knowledge to survive in a show-and-tell world without writing.

6. Agonistically toned. Because decision making occurs in tribal, face-to-face gatherings, disagreements are easily personalized. Verbal and intellectual combat is central to the oral lifeworld — as in the "dozens," "joning," "sounding," "calling-out" someone, and many other names for verbal assaults. As well, of course, the arts of praise (*epainos* in Aristotle) are equally well developed and ritualized as counter-balances to collective decision making through verbal combat.

7. Empathetic and participatory rather than objectively distanced. As Havelock noted above, audience participation is central to oral culture; reactions are not individual, but collective and assimilative. That is, people in oral societies — very much like the call-and-response forms of especially African-American church services — internalize messages by repeating them, reciting refrains or singing along with choruses of songs, and even shouting, clapping, jumping, or engaging in other bodily behaviors that allow one's whole being to participate in communication activities.

8. Homeostatic. Oral societies seek communicative equilibrium or homeostasis by searching for new language for new experiences and sloughing off vocabularies and meanings that are no longer required. Without dictionaries to freeze language in a list of definitions or books to rehearse history, oral language is constantly adjusting to a changing world, even altering itself and collective memory in fluid ways.

9. Situational rather than abstract. If life is experienced concretely, episode by episode, then of course communication between people in oral societies is largely situational. Rather than developing a vocabulary such as "circle" or "square," oral subjects likely would name objects — "plate," "door" — to describe shapes. While there can develop an abstract vocabulary ("justice," "goodness") in oral societies, their reasoning likely is situational: What's just in this situation? What's good here-and-now? There is no record of philosophy in the oral world.

Notice, then, what Ong attempts to do in this list of psychodynamic traits: He seeks to capture the cognitive-emotional dimensions of individual experience as it develops in oral societies. He draws on the work of classicists and linguistic anthropologists (especially Luria, 1976), that is, blends thinking from various historical-ethnic experiences, to give his theorems a maximum amount of evidentiary backing. His work is often cited, athough not the only approach scholars have taken to oral information processing.[17]

The Literate Mindset

Ong (1982) goes on in *Orality and Literacy* to argue in Chapter 4 that "Writing Restructures Consciousness." Drawing on Hirsch's (1977) conception of context-free discourse and Olson's (1980) idea of autonomous discourse, Ong sees literateness as radically different psychoculturally from orality. To him, it is a wholly artificial technology that is powerful enough to transform human consciousness. The key to that transformation came when writing could represent an entire human utterance (1982 p. 84):

> The critical and unique breakthrough into new worlds of knowledge was achieved within human consciousness not when simple semiotic marking was devised but when a coded system of visual marks was invented whereby a writer could determine the exact words that the reader would generate from the text.

Important to that transformation, too, was the visuality of writing: In depending on sight rather than sound, it externalized the human communication experience, separating the message from the body. That exteriorization moved ideas from memory to written records, created "literature" and philosophy, transferred the notion of proof from inside to outside the human mind, and allowed science to be separated from introspection (Ong, 1982, chap. 4; cf. Havelock, 1963).

Another line of thinking about the literate experience was captured in Havelock's (1986, chap. 5) notion of collisions. The oral-literate media, as he surveyed especially fifth century BCE Greece, produced collisions of a cultural sort: oral modes of thought ran into the rationality of literate patterns. Platonic idealist philosophy was an offspring of such a collision, as were parts of the New Testament four centuries later (see Kelber's, 1983, work on the oral parts and written parts of the Gospels). A similar collision, of course, is said to be occurring in our time—between the literate and the electronic media (see Postman, 1985; and, more angrily, Ellul, 1985). One, of course, need not talk about collision; one can be content to treat orality and literacy as contrasting modes of cognition and discourse practice (e.g.,

Olson & Torrance, 1991). So, for example, a college lecturer may well use literate overheads or chalkboard scribblings as complementary to an oral lecture.

A third line of analysis focuses particularly on literacy as a cognitive process, developed over time as young children grow into members of literate culture. The field of language acquisition has exploded from its grounding in Jean Piaget to, by now, comparative studies of literacy acquisition and the social significance of writing in multiple cultures (see, e.g., Cope & Kalentzis, 2000, and Barton, Hamilton, & Invanic, 2000). To understand how the culturally conditioned mind acquires literate skills, especially in contrast with the acquisition of oral communication skills, is to argue that the print revolution was even more fundamental than we give it credit for: it can be credited, going back to Mayr's arguments we noted in the introduction of this chapter, with evolving the human species (this position is reviewed in Postman, 1999, chap. 7).

Multimediated Cognitive Processing in the Electronic World

Now then, to the processing of electronically reproduced stimuli, especially pictorial codes. McLuhan, as we've noted, developed the notion that different media extend particular senses or physical attributes of human beings. He worked with a view of the human sensorium that depicted people as (a) taking in information from varied senses simultaneously yet (b) usually, via media, having particular senses extended, even "outered." When a sense was so extended by a medium—as, for example, sight would be by photographs—then he posited a "media bias" (McLuhan, 1964; cf. Nevitt, 1982, chap. 7).

McLuhan's, thus, was a sensory-based theory of media-information processing. As such, it was complementary to work going on in what we now call visual literacy—work on the dimensions of visual experience that can become coded, can be found meaningful. Codes were understood as sets of meanings laid over or upon sense data. That work was advanced significantly by semioticians, with Roland Barthes' (1968) mid-career book, *The Elements of Semiology*, central to the generation of theorems about visual codes. Barthes convincingly showed that various dimensions of the visual sense data (e.g., one's experience with light/dark, depth of field, static vs. moving pictures, color, shade) could be coded in personally and socially significant ways.

Recognizing the importance of media-based coding habits, however, only gets us started. To go further, we have to remember that there is a fundamental difference between presentational visual media—what Rogers (1986) called telecommunication—and interactive electronic media.[18] The telecommunication media, which include the radio, film, and television, brought coded sound and sight to people, whereas the interactive media, especially the computer-mediated communication but also (in weaker ways) the telegraph and telephone, involve a much higher degree of personal and interpersonal involvement.[19] In our time, of course, thanks to digitalization, the telecommunication media are becoming more and more interactive; you now can re-present DVD-based films, re-cut or intercut music and then burn it unto your own CD, and through a number of emerging video recording and editing systems, re-make and interlace television programs. Indeed, digitalization, which is "a result of the hybridization of telecommunications and computing" (Logan, 2000, p. 42), may well be taking us well beyond the visual-electronic revolution of the early 20th century.

What all of this means for your personal experience with electronic culture is difficult to spell out. But certainly the vision of the passive listener–viewer, simply decoding as he or she was trained to comprehend audio-visual, electronically mediated broadcasts (e.g., see Winn, 1977, or Postman, 1985), is an inadequate frame within which to fathom decoding processes. Chesebro and Bertelsen (1996) argue that the distinction between telecommunication (presentational) and interactive media is being obliterated in video games, CD-ROM (read-only memory) technology, and interactive television and databases: "As a result, users are not confined by the strict linearity that literate [and traditional telecommunication] systems might impose" (p. 138).

So, what can we do? To understand an individual's experience with electronic media in our time, we must deal with the multimediated event as experienced in various sensory channels. Even in watching television, you are processing aural, visual, and literate media, not in separate tracks but all-at-once, simultaneously. In earlier work (Gronbeck, 1993, 1995, 1998; and Vande Berg, Wenner, & Gronbeck, 1998) I explored some of the information-processing implications of the multimediated listener-viewer-reader experience:

1. The meaningfulness of that experience almost never lies within any one of the channels or codes, but either across them all or their amalgamation as produced by the consumer.
2. Meaningfulness is a product of both the stimuli being presented and the consumer's memories. The sound of a television ad may produce an echo of a familiar song or an earlier experience; the pictures used in it may draw on the consumer's memory of a movie, stereotyped family scene, or familiar landscape; the editing may suggest speed and excitement, depth and contemplation because of events (mediated or lived) that the consumer has lived through before. Indeed, especially advertisers are banking on such echoes and memories filling out the messages they actu-

ally put "in" their vehicles. In the words of Wise (1997,), "At the interaction of technology and social space is habit. Habit is a memory, a bodily memory. Technologies are not forgotten, rather they move from conscious memory to bodily memory" (p. 188).

3. A central tension, then, develops between the producer and the consumer of multimediated messages: Can the producer guide, even control, the meaning-making activity of the consumer? Messages become the sites of struggle over meaning (an idea developed in Fiske, 1987; cf. Sillars & Gronbeck, 2001, chap. 7).

Consider, for example, how you view—experience—an advertisement for an automobile. You really don't think, "Here are pictures of the car on a curving road," "Here is the voice of a narrator telling me about the driving experience and playing some background music," and "Here are messages in block letters moving across the screen." No, you experience the visual, the acoustic, and the literate codes simultaneously. Drawing information from all three codes, you construct the ad's message—"Dump that old Ford Probe and rush right down to the Audi dealer to buy a new TT!"—yourself. You fit your experience with the screen into your life experiences with cars generally. As you acquire pieces of information from the three dominant codes, you forge them into a message; you, the receiver, convert information into ideas—into emotional reactions, prepositional claims, authoritative commands. You persuade yourself to buy the Audi.

Whether these theorems of the internal processing of electronic media precisely capture the psychophysical dimensions of decoding is not particularly important. We are, after all, dealing with a comparatively new set of phenomena that is reconfigured in each new issue of the magazine *Wired*. We must continually strive to explore "some of the epistemological underpinnings and commonsense approaches to the role of technology in our lives and our societies and cultures" (Wise, 1997, pp. 189-190). Perhaps the final word should go to Jean Baudrillard (1987/1988, p. 17), who coined the phrase "electronic encephalization" to describe the source of the ecstasy of communication in the electronic age. Electrical circuits and brain circuits are enough alike so that in the digital world, they seemingly function in very, very similar ways.[20] At least Baudrillard's is a theorem that provides a provocative entry into micro-theorizing about today's virtual worlds.

The micro-theoretical versions of the orality-literacy theorems, in summary, carry us from one form of communication participation, the face-to-face form, through the generally distancing and exteriorizing psychological life in the literate universe, back to the participatory experiences of hypertext, e-mail, and the digital remastering of visual images possible with today's computers.

THE ORALITY-LITERACY THEOREMS IN THE BALANCE

Recalling our definition of theorems as statements or propositions that are deduced or in other ways derived from premises, axioms, or other pre-existing formulae, how are we evaluate the range of orality-literacy theorems we have examined in this chapter? Some problems with them stand out:

1. *Progressivism.* There is a tendency to see each macro-shift in dominant media as progressive, as an improvement over previous forms. For example, we often refer to oral cultures as "pre-literate," thereby even labeling them with that which comes later (Ong, 1982, p. 13). The battle that Postman (1985, 1999) posits between the literate and electronic worlds is cast as a struggle for the superiority of one communication environment over another. Change is not always progressive. Ong's appellation of our time as the era of secondary orality is a sign that comparing dominant media need not involve judgments of better and worse.
2. *Reductionism.* Second, the notion of "dominant media" itself needs careful delineation. To think in terms of dominance can make one forget about the other media working simultaneously in a given society. So, it might be easy to forget about importance of literacy in a time of electronic dominance.
3. *Simplification.* And forgetting, in turn, can oversimplify our understanding of social-political processes in any particular place. This may be the electronic age, but as Annabelle Sreberny-Mohammadi (1991) demonstrated, the culture of Iran is maintained largely through oral admonition and printed authority. Or, in the United States of today, even as Americans stream to discount stores in order to buy the latest electronic gizmos, there yet are great concerns about interpersonal intimacy and communication skills as well as the need to make an all-out effort to improve the country's literacy—a central campaign promise of George W. Bush in 2000. Reducing one's focus, even within the macro-theoretical frame, to a "dominant" medium is very, very dangerous.
4. *Arm-chair psychology.* On the micro-theoretical side of media ecology, we must be on our guard against arm-chair psychologizing—positing, without systematic observation, a series of cognitive-emotional effects of various media. The actual theorems, we must remember, are deduced from definitions and even assumptions-in-the-absence-of-evidence about perceptual processes. More works like Hoffman's are needed; working in

labs in the name of brain research is time-consuming, but often rewarding. That is why Damasio's (1994, 1999) work on the brain, feelings, cognition, and consciousness has created such multidisciplinary excitement.

5. *Multimediation.* We have not gotten very far at all in comprehending multimediation in particular. Our explanation of the Audi ad was crude. For too long, perhaps, we have separated the oral-aural from the visual from the literate—and all of those from our other senses. And the theorems, in their turn, seemingly encourage further separation by often radically distinguishing between, say, our oral and our visual experiences. We must remember that human beings really have become multitasking animals. The child of the electronic era has little trouble working synchronically with disparate kinds of data arriving through different senses. Simplifications in distinctions between and among media can lead to the sort of collective hysteria that made *Why Johnny Can't Read* (Flesch, 1955) such a big seller during the heyday of film, radio, and television.

For all of these problems, however, the orality-literacy theorems have performed great intellectual service in driving home the role of media in perceptually and culturally conditioning human beings' interaction with each other and the worlds around them. Insofar as the theorems ultimately force one to deal with media-as-environments, they can be said to represent the very heart of media ecology theory. Particularly in our own time, Donna Haraway's (1991) "A Cyborg Manifesto" blurs the distinctions between humans and their machined technologies. Media environments then not only surround us but also inhabit us. Communication technologies thus may be capable of merging culture and consciousness, the exteriority and interiority of human life itself. The orality-literacy theorems may provide media ecologists with precisely the conceptual tools they need to probe that merger.

ENDNOTES

1. See Havelock (1986, p. 28) for the story of their backgrounds in oral societies—Watt, as a Japanese prisoner of war after the fall of Singapore, and Goody, as an anthropologist studying oral African cultures.

2. Parry had carefully dissected Homeric poetry to isolate the oral methods of composition—the use of rhythms, stock phrases with various metrical features, and other prefabricated aspects of language use in the recitation of such daunting poems as the *Iliad.* The *Iliad* could not actually be memorized word for word. Rather, what the oral poets of ancient Greece did was learn the plots or

storylines of Greek fables and a series of metered and descriptive epithets that could be run into those storylines to make the "poem" work. Parry demonstrated that what we know as the *Iliad*—finally written down—is composed of dozens upon dozens of formulae. The Greek singer of poems, the rhapsode, was named after *rhapsôidein*, a word meaning "to stitch song together." Havelock pictures his own work as being more focused on the moral-cultural than linguistically technical characteristics of oral composition. For more background, see Ong (1982) and Parry (1971).

3. Some students of media ecology with particular interest in the orality-literacy theorems suggest that their subject matter is "medium theory" (see, e.g., Deibert, 1997).

4. See Deibert (1997, p. 28) for a model of the technological determinist position; also check out Daniel Chandler's website, http://www.aber.ac.uk/media/Documents/tecdet/tecdet.html. One also can argue, of course, that new communication media are driven by a human need such as "new information-processing needs" (Logan's, 2000, p. 3).

5. One alternatively can argue that new communication technologies shape the mind—consciousness, even what Erik Davis (1998) identifies as spirit and soul. That is, he argues that varied forms of mythification and mysticism rose up in response to particular characteristics of new media.

6. Kroker (1984) warns us, however, about hasty judgment: "To dismiss McLuhan as a technological determinist is to miss entirely the point of his intellectual contribution" (p. 548).

7. Deibert (1997, especially p. 29) calls this the social constructivist position.

8. For the determinist view of the impact of electrical environments on Western society, see Postman's (1992) *Technopoly*. For another response, see Winston (1998/2000).

9. The relationship between aesthetic drama and social drama has been explored in the writings of Victor Turner and Richard Schechner. They are reviewed usefully in Carlson (1996, pp. 19-24).

10. A notable exception to the claim of radical differences between oral and literate cultures is Denny (1991), who argues the differences are overblown; only decontextualization—the ability to abstract thought or ideas from the concrete here and now—distinguishes oral and literate cultures determinatively.

11. McLuhan often is credited with popularizing the idea of media-as-environments. His reactions to Jacques Ellul's (1965/1973) arguments about propaganda and cultural environment probably helped him develop the notion. For McLuhan's (1966) article on media and environments, see E. McLuhan and Zingrone (1995, pp. 219-232).

12. Deibert builds the argument for relationships between technological innovation and social epistemology with the help of Lewis Mumford's (1934) *Technics and Civilization*.

13. Conceptualizing relationships between past and present can be difficult for media ecologists. McLuhan went to the metaphor of the rear view mirror, arguing that the content of new media is inevitably a version of content from previous media (see Theall, 1971, for a conceptual analysis of McLuhan's position). That same year, Ong (1971) popularized the idea of "oral residues" to talk about

oral structure that remain embedded even in forms of writing. (Haskins [2001] argued that such embedding has been a part of rhetoric since Isocrates.) Havelock (1986) went with "written orality," but considered that phrase a paradox. Deibert (1997) used one of today's terms—hypermedia—to describe not only digital modes of accessing print and other symbols but also the late nineteenth century's experience with communication technologies in that period of high inventiveness. Two more: Nolan (1990) reversed the usual sorts of relationship, examining visuality—mirroring—in literary works and Messaris (1994) summarized two decades of research into visual literacy, a movement to account for the "reading" of visual experience.

14. Similar books about life in digitized social-political culture have been appearing in significant number as well, most traced back to Rheingold's highly acclaimed *Virtual Reality* (1991) and *The Virtual Community* (1993), which, in turn, as do all cyber-citizens, owes an originary debt to Gibson (1984).

15. A valiant effort to capture the multiple theoretical foundations of contemporary media culture, along with illustrative case studies, can be found in Real's (1996) *Exploring Media Culture.*

16. Much of Ong's earlier work focused not generally on "psychodynamics" but much more specifically on consciousness—especially the evolution of consciousness. See Thomas Farrell's excellent essay (1991) on this subject plus some expansions in his book (Farrell, 2000).

17. Compare Havelock (1986, especially Chap. 8, reconstructed out of several of his works by Gronbeck, 2000) for a more subjectively attuned theory. For a theory that broadens one's perspective from sound and linguistics to include in the face-to-face communication experience, haptics (touch), oculesics (eye contact), aromatics (smell), proxemics (spatial relatinships), kinesics (bodily movements), chronemics (temporal variations), objectics (material markers), coloristics (hue/brightness/saturation), and vocalistics (intonation or vocal characterizers), see Chesebro and Bertelsen (1996, chap. 4).

18. Armes (1988, p. 213) posits the presentational and interactive media as ends of a continuum: "The nineteenth-century systems are exemplified by the film camera and projector: precise mechanical engineering combined with an immediately perceptible direct link to reality. The computer stands at the other extreme: able to operate at a billioneth of a second because it lacks moving parts, but dealing only with abstract information."

19. The distinction between presentational and interactive media being offered today echoes McLuhan's (1964) distinction between hot (presentational) and cool (participatory) media.

20. Work on the brain and its cognitive processes has progressed enough to permit theorizing about visual intelligence—the cognitive rules by which we construct and make sense of the world around us. See Hoffman (1998).

REFERENCES

Andrew, D. (Ed.). (1997). *The image in dispute: Art and cinema in the age of photography.* Austin: University of Texas Press.

Armes, R. (1988). *On video.* New York: Routledge.

Barton, D., Hamilton, M., & Ivanic, R. (Eds.). (2000). *Situated literacies: Reading and writing in context.* New York: Routledge.

Barthes, R. (1968). *The elements of semiology* (A. Lavers & C. Smith, Trans.). New York: Hill & Wang.

Baudrillard, J. (1987/1988). *The ecstasy of communication* (S. Lotringer, Ed., B. & C. Schutze, Trans.). New York: Semiotext(e).

Bennett, W. L. (2001). *News: The politics of illusion* (4th ed.). New York: Addison Wesley Longman. (Original work published 1983)

Carey, J. W. (1989). *Communication as culture: Essays on media and society.* Boston, MA: Unwin Hyman.

Carlson, M. (1996). *Performance: A critical introduction.* New York: Routledge.

Chesebro, J. W., & Bertelsen, D. A. (1996). *Analyzing media: Communication technologies as symbolic and cognitive systems.* New York: Guilford.

Cope, B., & Kalentzis, M. (Eds.). (2000). *Multiliteracies: Literacy learning and the design of social futures.* New York: Routledge.

Couch, C. J. (1996). *Information technologies and social orders* (D.R. Maines & S.-L. Chen. Eds., Introduction.). New York: Aldine de Gruyter.

Czitrom, D. J. (1982). *Media and the American mind: From Morse to McLuhan.* Chapel Hill: University of North Carolina Press.

Damasio, A. R. (1994). *Descartes' error: Emotion, reason, and the human brain.* New York: G. P. Putnam.

Damasio, A. R. (1999). *The feeling of what happens: Body and emotion in the making of consciousness.* New York: Harcourt Brace.

Davis, R. E. (1976). *Response to innovation: A study of popular argument about new mass media.* (G. S. Loweth, Ed.). North Stratford, NH: Ayer.

Dayan, D., & Katz, E. (1992). *Media events: The live broadcasting of history.* Cambridge, MA: Harvard University Press.

Debord, G. (1983). *Society of the spectacle* (Anon., Trans.). Detroit, MI: Black & White. (Original work published 1962)

Deibert, R. J. (1997). *Parchment, printing, and hypermedia: Communication in world order transformation.* New York: Columbia University Press.

Denny, J. P. (1991). Rational thought in oral culture and literate decontextualization. In D. R. Olson & N. Torrance (Eds.), *Literacy and orality* (pp. 66-89). New York: Cambridge University Press.

Durkheim, E., & Mauss, M. (1963). *Primitive classification* (R. Needham, Trans., Ed., Introduction). Chicago: University of Chicago Press. (Original work published 1903)

Edelman, M. (1988). *Constructing the political spectacle.* Chicago: University of Chicago Press.

Eisenstein, E. L. (1979). *The printing press as an agent of change: Communications and cultural transformations in early modern Europe* (2 vols.). Cambridge, England: Cambridge University Press.

Eisenstein, E. L. (1983). *The printing revolution in early modern Europe.* Cambridge, England: Cambridge University Press.

Elkins, D. J. (1995). *Beyond sovereignty: Territory and political economy in the twenty-first century.* Toronto: University of Toronto Press.

Ellul, J. (1973). *Propaganda: The formation of men's attitudes.* New York: Vintage Books. (Original work published 1965)

Ellul, J. (1985). *The humiliation of the word.* Grand Rapids, MI: Eerdmans.

Farrell, T. J. (1991). Secondary orality and consciousness today. In B. E. Gronbeck, T. J. Farrell, & P. A. Soukup (Eds.), *Media, conciousness, and culture: Explorations of Walter Ongs thought* (pp. 194-209). Thousand Oaks, CA: Sage.

Farrell, T. J. (2000). *Walter Ong's contributions to cultural studies.* Cresskill, NJ: Hampton Press.

Featherstone, M., & Burrows, R. (1995). *Cyberspace/cyberbodies/cyberpunk: Cultures of technological embodiment.* Thousand Oaks, CA: Sage.

Fiske, J. (1987). *Television culture.* New York: Methuen.

Fiske, J. (1994). *Media matters: Everyday culture and political change.* Minneapolis: University of Minnesota Press.

Flesch, R. A. (1955). *Why Johnny can't read—and what you can do about it.* New York: Harper.

Gibson, W. (1984). *Neuromancer.* London: HarperCollins.

Goody, J. (Ed.) (1968). *Literacy in traditional societies.* Cambridge, England: Cambridge University Press.

Goody, J., & Watt, I. (1968). The consequences of literacy. In J. Goody (Ed.), *Literacy in traditional societies* (pp. 27-68). Cambridge: Cambridge University Press.

Gronbeck, B. E. (1981). McLuhan as rhetorical theorist. *Journal of Communication, 31,* 117-128.

Gronbeck, B. E. (1988). The academic practice of television criticism. *Quarterly Journal of Speech, 74,* 334-347.

Gronbeck, B. E. (1993). The spoken and the seen: Phonocentric and ocularcentric dimensions of rhetorical discourse. In J. F. Reynolds (Ed.), *Rhetorical memory and delivery: Classical concepts for contemporary composition and communication* (pp. 139-155). Hillsdale, NJ: Erlbaum.

Gronbeck, B. E. (1995). Unstated propositions: Relationships among verbal, visual, and acoustic languages. In S. Jackson (Ed.), *Argumentation and values: Proceedings of the nineth SCA/AFA conference on argumentation* (pp. 539-542). Washington, DC: National Communication Association.

Gronbeck, B. E. (1998). Reconceptualizing the visual experience in media studies. In J. S. Trent (Ed.), *Communication: Views from the helm for the 21st century* (pp. 289-293). Boston: Allyn & Bacon.

Gronbeck, B. E. (2000). Communication media, memory, and social-political change in Eric Havelock. *New Jersey Journal of Communication, 8,* 34-45.

Gronbeck, B. E., Farrell, T. J., & Soukup, P. A. (Eds.). (1991). *Media, consciousness, and culture: Explorations of Walter Ong's thought.* Thousand Oaks, CA: Sage.

Hall, S. (Ed.). (1997). *Representation: Cultural representations and signifying practices.* Thousand Oaks, CA: Sage.

Haraway, D. (1991). *Simians, cyborgs, and women: The reinvention of nature.* New York: Routledge.

Hart, R. P. (1999). *Seducing America: How television charms the modern voter.* 2nd ed. New York: Oxford University Press. (Original work published 1994)

Haskins, E. V. (2001). Rhetoric between orality and literacy: Cultural memory and performance in Isocrates and Aristotle. *Quarterly Journal of Speech, 87,* 158-178.

Havelock, E. A. (1957). *The liberal temper of Greek politics.* New Haven, CT: Yale University Press.

Havelock, E. A. (1963). *Preface to Plato.* Cambridge, MA: The Belknap Press of Harvard University Press.

Havelock, E. A. (1978). The alphabetization of Homer. In E. A. Havelock & J. P. Hershbell (Eds.), *Communication arts in the ancient world* (pp. 3-21). New York: Hastings House.

Havelock, E. A. (1982). *The literate revolution in Greece and its cultural consequences.* Princeton, NJ: Princeton University Press.

Havelock, E. A. (1986). *The muse learns to write: Reflections on orality and literacy from antiquity to the present.* New Haven, CT: Yale University Press.

Hirsch, E. D., Jr. (1977). *The philosophy of composition.* Chicago: University of Chicago Press.

Hoffman, D. D. (1998). *Visual intelligence: How we create what we see.* New York: W. W. Horton.

Innis, H. A. (1951/1964). *The bias of communication.* M. McLuhan (Intro.). Toronto, Canada: University of Toronto Press.

Innis, H. A. (1972). *Empire & communications* (M.Q. Innis, Rev., M. McLuhan, Foreword). Toronto, Canada: University of Toronto Press. (Original work published 1950)

Jamieson, K. H. (1988). *Eloquence in the electronic age: The transformation of political speechmaking.* New York: Oxford University Press.

Jones, S. G. (Ed.). (1995). *Cybersociety: Computer-mediated communication and community.* Thousand Oaks, CA: Sage.

Kelber, W. H. (1983). *The oral and the written gospel: The hermeneutics of speaking and writing in the synoptic tradition, Mark, Paul, and Q.* Philadelphia: Fortress Press.

Kroker, A. (1984). Processed world: Technology and culture in the thought of Marshall McLuhan. *Philosophy of the Social Sciences, 14,* 433-459.

Lévi-Strauss, C. (1962). *La Pensée Sauvage.* Paris: Plon.

Logan, R. K. (2000). *The sixth language: Learning a living in the internet age.* New York: Stoddart.

Luria, A. R. (1976). *Cognitive development: Its cultural and social foundations* (M. Cole, Ed., M. Lopez-Morilla & L. Solotaroff, Trans.). Cambridge, MA: Harvard University Press.

Lyotard, J.-F. (1984). *The postmodern condition: A report on knowledge* (G. Bennington & B. Massumi, Trans., F. Jameson, Foreword). Minneapolis: University of Minnesota Press. (Original work published 1979)

Marx, L. (1964). *The machine in the garden.* New York: Oxford University Press.

Mayr, E. (1963). *Animal species and evolution.* Cambridge, MA: The Belknap Press of Harvard University Press.

McLuhan, E., & Zingrone, F. (Eds.). (1995). *Essential McLuhan.* New York: Basic Books.

McLuhan, M. (1962). *The Gutenberg galaxy: The making of typographic man.* Toronto, Canada: University of Toronto Press.

McLuhan, M. (1964). *Understanding media: The extensions of man.* New York: McGraw-Hill.

McLuhan, M., & Fiore, Q. (1968). *War and peace in the global village*. New York: Bantam Books.

McLuhan, M., & McLuhan, E. (1988). *Laws of media: A new science*. Toronto: University of Toronto Press.

McLuhan, M., & Powers, B. R. (1989). *The global village: Transformations in world life and media in the 21st century*. New York: Oxford University Press.

Medhurst, M. J., Gonzales, A., & Peterson, T. R. (Eds.). (1990). *Communication & the culture of technology*. Pullman, WA: Washington State University Press.

Messaris, P. (1994). *Visual literacy: Image, mind, & reality*. Boulder, CO: Westview.

Mumford, L. (1934). *Technics and civilization*. New York: HBJ Books.

Nevitt, B. (1982). *The communication ecology: Re-presentation versus replica*. Toronto, Canada: Butterworths.

Nolan, E. P. (1990). *Now through a glass darkly: Specular images of being and knowing from Virgil to Chaucer*. Ann Arbor: University of Michigan Press.

Olson, D. R. (Ed.). (1980). *Social foundations of language and thought*. New York: Norton.

Olson, D. R., & Torrance, N. (Eds.). (1991). *Literacy and orality*. New York: Cambridge University Press.

Ong, W. J. (1958a). *Ramus, method, and the decay of dialogue: From the art of discourse to the art of reason*. Cambridge, MA: Harvard University Press.

Ong, W. J. (1958b). *Ramus and Talon inventory: A short-title inventory of the published works of Peter Ramus (1515-72) and of Omar Talon (ca. 1510-62) in their original and in their variously altered forms, with related material*. Cambridge, MA: Harvard University Press.

Ong, W. J. (1971). *Rhetoric, romance, and technology: Studies in the interaction of expression and culture*. Ithaca, NY: Cornell University Press.

Ong, W. J. (1981). *Fighting for life: Context, sexuality, and consciousness*. Ithaca, NY: Cornell University Press.

Ong, W. J. (1982). *Orality and literacy: The technologizing of the word*. London: Methuen.

Palmeri, A. J. (1991). Ramism, Ong, and modern rhetoric. In B. E. Gronbeck, T. J. Farrell, & P. A. Soukup (Eds.), *Media, consciousness and culture: Explanations of Walter Ong's thought* (pp. 50-63). Thousand Oaks, CA: Sage.

Parry, M. (1971). *The making of Homeric verse* (A. Parry, Ed.). Oxford, UK: Clarendon Press.

Postman, N. (1985). *Amusing ourselves to death: Public discourse in the age of show business*. New York: Viking.

Postman, N. (1992). *Technopoly: The surrender of culture to technology*. New York: Alfred A. Knopf.

Postman, N. (1999). *Building a bridge to the 18th century: Ideas from the past that can improve our future*. New York: Alfred E. Knopf.

Real, M.R. (1996). *Exploring media culture: A guide*. Thousand Oaks, CA: Sage.

Rheingold, H. (1991). *Virtual reality*. New York: Summit.

Rheingold, H. (1993). *The virtual community*. New York: Addison Wesley Longman.

Rogers, E. M. (1986). *Communication technology: The new media in society*. New York: The Free Press.

Ruggie, J. G. (1986). Continuity and transformation in the world polity: Toward a neorealist synthesis. In R. O. Keohane (Ed.), *Neorealism and its critics*. New York: Columbia University Press.

Sreberny-Mohammadi, A. (1991). Media integration in the third world: An Ongian look at Iran. In B. E. Gronbeck, T. J. Farrell, & P. A. Soukup (Eds.), *Media, consciousness and culture: Explanations of Walter Ong's thought* (pp. 133-146). Thousand Oaks, CA: Sage.

Sillars, M. O., & Gronbeck, B. E. (2001). *Communication criticism: Rhetoric, social codes, cultural studies*. Prospect Heights, IL: Waveland.

Stock, B. (1983). *The implications of literacy: Written language and models of interpretation in the eleventh and twelfth centuries*. Princeton, NJ: Princeton University Press.

Theall, D. F. (1971). *The medium is the rear view mirror: Understanding McLuhan*. Montreal, Canada: McGill-Queen's University Press.

Vande Berg, L. R. E., Wenner, L. A., & Gronbeck, B. E. (Eds.) (1998). *Critical approaches to television*. Boston: Houghton Mifflin.

Winn, M. (1977). *The plug-in drug*. New York: Viking Press.

Winston, B. (2000). *Media, technology and society: A history from the telegraph to the internet*. New York: Routledge. (Original work published 1998)

Wise, J. M. (1997). *Exploring technology and social space*. Thousand Oaks, CA: Sage.

Yates, F. A. (1966). *The art of memory*. Chicago: University of Chicago Press.

13

Typography and Its Influence on Culture and Communication

Some Media Ecological Interpretations

Joseph Ashcroft
East Stroudsburg University

Media are ecological. We so often associate the term *ecology* with biological systems that we overlook the fact that ecology in its broadest meaning is the study of the systemic relationship between organisms and their environments. Actually the origins of the word can be traced back to Aristotle, who used it in reference to the importance of keeping one's household in order. In the 19th century Ernst Haeckel, a German scientist, first used it in relation to biology (Postman, 2000). Yet humans are organisms living within cultural environments as well as biological environments. So a true human ecology must concern itself with far more than just the biosphere. For humans, culture is at least as important as biology, and human culture involves the transmission of accumulated knowledge from one generation to the next. Thus, human culture cannot exist without communication. Therefore, to understand the systemic relationship between humans and their culture, the study of communication and the means by which it is transmitted is crucial. Media ecologists seek to understand how changes in communication systems affect the relationship between humans and their cultures.

The intellectual origins of media ecology began as early as the start of the 20th century with Patrick Geddes' ecological studies and urban planning and Lewis Mumford's studies of technical civilization (Strate & Lum, 2000).

Throughout this book a wide variety of scholars and writers who have studied media ecology present the key insights of the field, as well as identify some of the most important theorists who have contributed to the development of media ecology during the 20th century. None of the early theorists would have considered themselves "media ecologists." In fact, their academic training varied. Among the important theorists are historians, classicists, literature scholars, and educators.

In this chapter, the focus is on the media ecological effects of typography, especially in Europe, but to some extent in North America, in the centuries that followed the introduction of the printing press. The study of the effects of typography was probably the single most important research area that led to the emergence of the field of media ecology. As this chapter proceeds, an effort is made to allow these media ecologists to speak in their own words by including extended quotes from the scholars who made special contributions to each of the cultural developments discussed.

PRELIMINARY ISSUES

Here at the start of the discussion about the effects of typography, it is important to be clear about the key terms that will be used. *Print* and *print technology* are sometimes used synonymously and refer broadly to the means by which a culture is able to produce exact duplications of messages by some type of technological invention. However, more precise definitions of these terms would limit the definition of *print* to the words on a page, and the definition of *print technology* to the method used to put those words on a page. The *printing press* refers to a particular technology developed in Europe during the 15th century CE. Most historians give credit for its invention to a German named Johannes Gutenberg. His technology relied on moveable type, which could be reused again and again for different printings by resetting the type. *Typography* is the use of print technology for writing. Because the primary print technology in Europe after the mid-15th century was the printing press, and because the printing press was used almost exclusively for writing (as distinct from pictorial imagery), these terms are often used interchangeably when discussing European history since the 15th century. Still, it is important to remember that there are times when these distinct meanings will matter. For instance, the idea of print was known in China 600 years before the invention of the printing press. This fact illustrates an important element in understanding how a technology can influence a culture.

In China, wood was carved to produce whatever image the printer wanted to reproduce, and then the carving was covered with ink, allowing multiple reproductions of that image. Unlike moveable type, which could be reset again and again, once a block of wood was carved, it could only be used to print the image on the wood. However, this block printing technology was used to produce writing and books. The Chinese characters were carved into as many blocks as it would take to complete a book. Then the blocks could be inked again and again, producing as many books as needed at any time. Many of these wooden blocks survived for hundreds of years, so reproductions of important books could be made without the need for recarving new blocks (Tsien, 1985). Moveable type technology, which was the basis of Gutenberg's printing press, was also known in China several hundred years before its introduction into European culture. But in contrast to Europe after Gutenberg's invention, moveable type was not used extensively in China. Most historians point to the enormous number of characters in the written language of the Chinese as the primary reason why moveable type did not have the same success in China as it did in Europe. Of course in Europe, Gutenberg was working with a 26-symbol alphabet, which made it much easier to use the moveable type technology. But other authors (He, 1994) point to additional cultural factors that may have inhibited the acceptance of moveable type, such as the lack of business motivations due to the influences of Confucian ideology, and the existence of a well-established competing print technology, block printing, that did not exist in Europe. In any case, these cultural differences affect how a new technology might impact on any given society. To fully understand the effects, the technology must be studied within the context of the society into which it is introduced. In Europe, print technology was widely and rapidly accepted, so Europe provides an excellent opportunity for illustrating just how vast the cultural changes can be when a new communication technology is introduced to a society.

Media ecologists have identified several important cultural developments that occurred in Europe after the introduction of the printing press, which were influenced by the existence of this kind of print technology. Some of these began to occur rather quickly after the introduction of the printing press. For instance, a brand new industry, printing, sprung into existence with all the ramifications associated with a new industry. Sources of financing the cost and developing the market for selling books were problems faced by the early printers. In the early years, wealthy individual patrons provided some of the support, but in many instances churches, recognizing the advantages of communicating their beliefs, also supported many of the early printers. Although there is no doubt that these immediate effects are important and have been written about in great detail by other authors (e.g., Febvre & Martin, 1976), this chapter focuses primarily on the long-term effects of the printing on culture. The most important of these developments include the emergence of nationalism, the Protestant Reformation, the development of modern science, the emergence of the philosophy of individualism with the subsequent development of democracy and capitalism, and the early formulation of the idea of childhood, which emerged in Europe and became more fully extended in North America. However, before detailing the connection between print and these various philosophical and institutional changes in European culture, we must first document one of the most obvious effects typography had in Europe—the spread of literacy to the masses.

POPULARIZING LITERACY

Of all the claims made by scholars about the effects of the printing press in Europe, probably the least controversial is the assertion that the invention of print encouraged the development of widespread schooling in post-print Europe. In a culture without print technology, teaching everyone to read and write was not necessary because there would never be a great many copies of anything written. Only the elites would school their children in literacy, and the focus for this group was on learning the written languages of the classics, Latin and Greek, because most books were written in one of those two languages. With print, the potential became realistic that everyone could have a copy of any important book, thus providing the rationale for universal literacy. But as obvious as this may seem, the actual evolution of schooling was a far more complex development. Many powerful forces in Europe during this era did not support the idea that the masses of people should be taught to read and write. In fact, after initially embracing print technology as a way to spread its own doctrines to the masses, the Catholic Church imposed severe controls on what could be printed, when it became clear in the 16th century that print was also allowing the easy spread of doctrines and ideas that were in opposition to the Church's teachings.

The rebellion against the authority of the Catholic Church was not a single unified movement. In fact, there were many different strands of Protestantism in Europe. But one of the areas that united most of these different developing branches of Christianity was their belief in the importance of literacy. The followers of Martin Luther recognized the importance of reading and writing as a means to spread the message of their grievances against the Church in Rome. The Puritans thought of reading as a weapon against ignorance, profanity, and laziness. The Presbyterians in Scotland made the first demand for universal literacy published in the English language when their First Presbyterian Book of Discipline in 1560 called for a national system of education (Postman, 1982). And this developing support for the spread of literacy was not limited to the upper classes. The call for universal literacy included both peasant and prince.

In those regions of Europe where the Lutheran movement was the strongest, the church often had close relationships with the local and regional political authorities, which facilitated the rapid development of schools designed to indoctrinate young people in the principles of Lutheranism. The 1520s was the decade during which Lutheran enthusiasm for the expansion of schooling reached its greatest levels. By the late 1520s, Lutherans had established school systems in any city where they held authority. The church constitutions, which imposed ecclesiastical organization on the regions and cities in Germany, established schools that required religious teaching through catechism instruction (Strauss, 1976).

In England, the evidence supports a similar expansion of literacy and schooling in the 16th century. In one particularly revealing study, Peter Clark (1976) researched the inventories of personal goods taken after death, which had to be assembled and filed with the appropriate church court before probate could be granted. He studied the records of three towns in the county of Kent from 1560 to 1640 to ascertain the number of books that were included in these inventories of personal property. His findings show a steady rise in ownership of books over the 80-year period. In Canterbury, for instance, less than 10% of these inventories showed book ownership in the 1560s. But by the 1590s it was 34% and by the 1630s it was 46%. Interestingly, when Clark divided his sample by the total value of the inventories, he found that book ownership by the wealthy was already high in the 1560s and changed little over the next 80 years. Therefore, both poor and middle-income inventories accounted for almost all of the growth shown in his overall figures cited above. This expansion in book ownership among the poor and middle class was supported by the rapid expansion of schooling in these towns. Clark found at least 25 schools were in operation in Canterbury, which had a population of only 6,000, between 1575 and 1600. His findings were similar in the two other towns he studied in Kent.

The story is similar in France. Mary Jo Maynes (1985) cites a 19th century French scholar named Louis Maggiolo who conducted a survey of parish registers for weddings in the church to determine who could and could not sign their own name. Although evidence of being able to sign one's own name cannot prove fully functioning literacy, it is still interesting to note that by 1786, the eve of the French Revolution, almost 50% of the grooms and just over 25% of the brides could sign their names. Studies of earlier periods in French history show literacy at fewer than 10% for women and just at 20% for men in 1650. So literacy more than doubled in France during the 17th and 18th centuries.

By the 18th century, shifts in political and economic power began to lead to the standardization of public schooling. As the 18th century unfolded in Europe, there were growing complaints about the inconsistency of schooling. Some of these complaints came from dissatisfied parents who often felt that incompetent teachers were educating their children. But mostly the complaints came from the educated elites in each of the

European countries. Early schooling had developed during a period in European history dominated by aristocratic landowners and mercantilists. But in the 18th century the emerging industrial capitalist system contributed to the establishment of new centers of political and economic power. And this new class of leaders was far more concerned with control of the social systems, including schools, than had been the previous social powers (Maynes, 1985).

Initially, there was great opposition to any government-imposed standardization of schooling. But as the 18th century evolved, the voices calling for a more organized approach to schooling grew in size and audience. Philosophers, such as John Locke who wrote in the 17th century, contributed to the spread of the idea that humans are born with a *tabula rasa*, a blank mind that needs to be taught from scratch. Writers influenced by Locke argued that educating the young could not be left to chance. By the end of the 18th century the belief that something needed to be done to standardize schooling had achieved an unstoppable momentum in Europe, and had even begun to take root in the post-revolutionary United States where, although now politically free of European domination, cultural developments were still strongly influenced by developments in Europe. There was widespread belief that schooling helped children understand and appreciate their social roles.

Organized opposition to universal schooling for the working class remained strong in the early part of the 19th century, but growing labor unrest and the spread of new philosophies in opposition to capitalism, like that of Karl Marx, contributed to a weakening of the opposition to broader education for the working class. More and more the British ruling classes saw the advantages of regulated popular schooling. Governmental support for schooling, which was at £20,000 in 1833, grew to £800,000 by 1861 (Maynes, 1985).

In France, there continued to be resistance to universal schooling after the Revolution of 1789, but this opposition had largely ended with the revolution of 1830. By 1833, France had enacted various school reforms including the Guizot reforms (Maynes, 1985). After passage of his reforms, Minister Guizot sent a circular out to all teachers in France to provide them with a clear statement of the government's view on the role of education in France. He stated in part,

> All Frenchmen are to acquire if possible that knowledge which is indispensable for social life and without which the mind languishes. . . . [But the law is designed] for the state as well, and in the public interest, since liberty is secure and routine only among a people who are enlightened enough to hear . . . the voice of reason. Universal primary education is thus one of the greatest guarantees of order and social stability. (cited in Maynes, 1985, p. 54)

Germany began to consolidate its approach to schooling somewhat earlier than England and France. In Germany, a complex interplay of churches, both Catholic and Lutheran, regional state governments, and to a much lesser extent than in England and France, the industrial elites combined to advocate for school reform. Throughout the various German states, most communities were required by law to establish schools and support them with local resources, such as taxes, by the early 19th century. And the children in these communities were required by law to attend these schools (Maynes, 1985).

It took a few hundred years for the ecological effects of print on schooling to be fully in place. But by the 19th century the goal of universal literacy had been widely accepted in Europe and such a goal would never have emerged unless the technology was available to allow everyone to have access to written materials. The printing press was a necessary prerequisite for the emergence of schooling in Europe.

A consequence of this movement in Europe and North America to systematize the school systems was a change in the perception of "the child." Prior to the 17th century, there is little indication that there was a distinct cultural category for "children" in European or American societies. But as the need grew to separate out young people from their families and work in order to educate them, the idea of "the child" took root. The schools that evolved placed a heavy emphasis on discipline. School participants were not given the freedoms that an "adult" could expect. Philippe Aries (1962) sums this up effectively when he reports, "The child would be subjected for the duration of his schooling to an increasingly strict and effective discipline, and this discipline separated the child who suffered it from the liberty enjoyed by the adult. Thus, childhood was extended by almost the entire duration of the school cycle" (p. 334). Mary Jo Maynes, although critical of Aries' methods, which she believed limited his analysis to the elites in Europe, agrees with his conclusion that schooling contributed heavily to the creation of childhood and did so for the peasant classes as well. Just as with the elites studied by Aries, schools isolated peasant children from their families.

> The schools were increasingly organized on the basis of an assumption that children had psychological and social needs that were different from adults. Schools enclosed children and separated them, at least momentarily, from the activities and rewards, rigors and demands of the workaday world. In the schools, children pursued activities that were designed to correspond with their presumptive capacities *as children*, and that generally drew their significance from their contribution to a child's preparation for the future, rather than from their relevance to the present. (Maynes, 1985, p. 136)

The development of the category "child" did not, in and of itself, extend the age of childhood beyond puberty. The schooling that took place in

Europe and the United States up until the late 19th century typically did not extend beyond what we today would call elementary school. For instance, in 1890 in the United States only 7% of American 14-year-olds were still enrolled in school (Hines, 1999). The extension of childhood beyond the age of puberty occurred only over the past 100 years or so, and it was most fully extended in the United States where the emergence of the idea of "adolescence" combined with growing social and political pressures to extend schooling beyond the elementary school. It will be instructive to examine how childhood became extended in the United States.

Adolescence, today, is generally thought of as beginning at the onset of puberty, when hormones spur growth and the development of secondary sexual characteristics, and continuing beyond the attainment of biological sexual maturity into the teenage years. Adolescence ends when people are able, willing, or forced to assume adult responsibilities for work and family. The psychologist, G. Stanley Hall (1904), is generally given credit for the invention and reification of the developmental period called adolescence.

As the idea of adolescence took root in North America, other cultural developments were at work that contributed to the extension of childhood in the United States. Advocates of Hall's theories supported treating adolescents differently within the legal system and successfully pushed for laws that established a juvenile justice system. Other advocates urged laws that protected young workers from the often harsh conditions found in the growing number of factories that were built in response to the expanding industrial revolution. These two developments, the juvenile justice system and the enactment of child labor laws, were important applications of the theories of adolescence to the institutions of North American culture. But the principal reason why childhood became extended in the United States was the establishment of mandatory school beyond the age of puberty.

Late in the 19th century, the United States became fully immersed in the industrial revolution, which was rapidly changing its work force from one that was primarily agrarian to one that was increasingly based in manufacturing. The rapidly expanding industrial base of the economy of the United States was growing faster than the numbers of workers available and willing to work in the mines and factories. This fact eventually encouraged a large influx of immigrants, mostly from Europe, who arrived in the United States in the late 19th century. Many of these immigrants spoke little English, were unfamiliar with the workings of American democracy, and may have been exposed to some of the more radical ideologies of European intellectuals who wrote about the exploitation of the working class. These various cultural forces, the "problem" of adolescence, the radical change in the American economy, and the growing population of immigrants all contributed to a crescendo of voices calling for extended schooling for young people in America.

By 1910, the momentum for industrial schools was at its peak. The owners and workers of U.S. industry were supporting it. The White House was behind it. And even Charles Eliot, the president of Harvard who was a leading advocate 10 years earlier for more "academic" schools, had modified his position and began to advocate trade schools for those children who might otherwise have to leave the pubic school system (Krug, 1964). Those who supported industrial schools flexed their muscles and began to advocate that they should exist independent of the public school systems that had been established all over the United States during the 19th century. Many teachers and administrators in the public school system had resisted turning over the entire educational enterprise exclusively to training for work, so advocates of industrial schools feared that allowing these "traditional" educators to operate these new schools was a recipe for failure.

All the while this debate raged over the structure and purposes of the American public high schools, attendance began to mushroom. Urban high schools in particular began to outgrow their capacities and had to resort to annexes and rush new building projects. By 1912, the enrollment in public high schools passed one million for the first time in the history of the U. S. (Krug, 1964). So while educators and politicians debated the role of high school, American families were more and more convinced that high school was a good idea for their children.

As a result of these debates, we eventually see the emergence of the comprehensive high school after 1920, which combined "industrial" education with "academic" education. By 1930, the United States went over the 50% mark of 14 to 17 year olds attending high school (51%). And by 1940, after almost a decade of economic depression and scarce jobs, the number had increased to 73% (Nasaw, 1979). During World War II there was a decline in enrollment as young boys joined the military and many young girls worked in factories producing vital supplies for the war effort. But after World War II the growth in high schooling returned and soon secondary school was mandatory in every state (Hines, 1999). One of the consequences of mandatory high school was a strengthening of the cultural belief that the threshold for adulthood was later than puberty. The psychological theories about adolescence were reinforced by the cultural expectation that one would stay in school until at least 18. By the latter part of the 20th century, Americans were comfortable with the idea that children did not become adults until 4 to 6 years after they were biologically capable of reproduction.

Although in some ways a distant catalyst, the printing press is implicated in the extension of the age for childhood beyond puberty, for it was mandatory high school that was crucial in extending childhood in the United States. And an extensive high school system could not exist without typography.

PROTESTANT REFORMATION

An important claim made by media ecologists about the impact of typography in European culture involves the schism in Christianity that began to develop in the 16th century. One of the media ecologists who has studied this extensively is Elizabeth Eisenstein (1979, 1983). Eisenstein received her PhD from Radcliffe in 1953, and in 1959 began teaching history at the University of Michigan. In 1975 she was named the Alice Freeman Palmer professor of history, and since 1988 she has been professor emeritus at Michigan. Although Eisenstein was aware of McLuhan's ideas about the effects of print, her approach to the study of the printing press was far more scholarly and less speculative than that of McLuhan. Her book *The Printing Press as an Agent of Change: Communications and Cultural Transformations in Early Modern Europe* (Eisentein, 1979) was a massive two-volume effort that carefully documented the effects of print technology on religion, science, and nationalism in Europe. To date, her book is widely considered to be the most important analysis of the effects of print on culture, and in particular the relationship between print and the emergence of the Protestant Reformation.

Martin Luther was one of the better known theologians among a group of 16th century writers, who led a rebellion against the authority of the Catholic Church as the sole interpreter of Christ's teachings. Luther certainly recognized the importance of print. One of his famous "95 Theses" actually mentions print technology. He argued that because print technology now permitted everyone to have the Bible, the word of God, in her or his own possession, there was no longer the need for a central authority in Rome to interpret the word of God. And yet even Luther appeared not to have fully recognized the thoroughness with which print was changing Europe. Before he completely broke with the Vatican, he wrote the Pope expressing his surprise at how widespread the knowledge of his criticism of the Catholic Church had become. He told the Pope that he had intended his views to be read only by his academic circle in Germany, which is why he had written them originally in Latin. What Luther did not seem to recognize was the transformative power of print discussed in the previous section. Print was forcing a standardization of the vernacular, which was making it easier and more reasonable to translate written material into regional languages. It was not difficult, therefore, for printers to translate the views of Luther, or any other critic of the Catholic Church, into vernacular languages, and this fact, combined with the portability of printed works, encouraged the spread of the word of Protestant opposition to the Vatican. According to Eisenstein:

> Given the convergence of interests among printers and Protestants, given the way new presses implemented older religious goals, it seems

pointless to argue whether material or spiritual, socioeconomic or religious, "factors" were more important in transforming Western Christianity. It is by no means pointless, however, to insist that printing be assigned a prominent position when enumerating "factors" or analyzing causes. To leave the interests and outlook of printers out of the amalgam (as most accounts do) is to lose one chance of explaining how Protestant-Catholic divisions related to other concurrent developments that were transforming European society. Not all changes ushered in by print were compatible with the cause of religious reform; many were irrelevant to that cause, some antipathetical to it. Pastors and printers were often at odds in regions governed by the Lutherans and Calvinists. Nevertheless, Protestants and printers had more in common than Catholics and printers did. Religious divisions were of critical importance to the future development of European society partly because of the way they interacted with other new forces released by print. If Protestants seem to be more closely affiliated with certain "modernizing" trends than do Catholics, it is largely because reformers did less to check these new forces and more to reinforce them at the start. (Eisenstein, 1983, pp. 167-168)

The Vatican soon recognized the facilitating effect that print was having on the spread of new ideas in Europe. Religious criticism was not the only area in which the Vatican's teachings were being challenged. The accepted cosmology, which taught that the Earth was the center of what we now know to be a solar system, was also under attack. With the aid of new technologies, such as the telescope, scientists such as Copernicus and Galileo made strong arguments in support of the idea that the sun was the center of the solar system. The Church's authority was under siege. And the Vatican responded. It put in place the requirement of an "imprimatur" from the Vatican before anything could be published. An imprimatur was an official seal of the Vatican, which indicated that a piece of writing had the approval of the Vatican. In addition, the Vatican increased the intensity with which it would go after "heretics," imposing severe religious penalties such as excommunication on critics like Galileo. Elizabeth Eisenstein, who has published the most comprehensive analysis of the relationship between typography and the Protestant Reformation, discusses the implication of the historic meetings of the hierarchy of the Catholic Church at Trent in the mid-16th century.

Catholic policies framed at Trent were aimed at holding (the effects of the Reformation) . . . in check. By withholding authorization of new editions of the Bible, by stressing lay obedience and imposing restrictions on lay reading, by developing new machinery such as the index and Imprimatur to channel the flow of literature along narrowly prescribed lines, the . . . papacy proved to be anything but accommodating.

It assumed an unyielding posture that grew ever more rigid over the course of time. Decisions made at Trent were merely the first in a series of rear-guard actions designed to contain the new forces Gutenberg's invention had released. (Eisenstein, 1983, p. 157)

The Catholic Church's influence on governmental authorities was much stronger in southern Europe than it was in northern Europe, however. So efforts to control what was printed through the use of devices like the imprimatur had greater effect in Italy, Spain, and southern France than it did in northern Europe. Thus, the growing rift in Christianity began to develop a north vs. south characteristic. The protestant rebellion flourished in the north of Europe, whereas the Vatican had some success resisting it in southern Europe. This helped facilitate an enthusiasm for spreading literacy that was greater in northern Europe than it was in the south. And the roots of this enthusiasm for literacy were spawned initially by the idea that every home could now have its own copy of God's words—not the copy written in Latin that would be read at the Sunday mass, but a copy written in the vernacular that could be understood by all who had learned to read and write in their own language. Here again, we see powerful ecological effects at work. Print technology is introduced into European cultures. It soon allows those with complaints about the dogma and cosmology of the dominant religion to find a growing audience for their criticisms. Seeing the potential for a wide audience, authors begin to write in the more accessible vernaculars, rather than the Latin used by academic elites. This fact spawns a growing effort to assure that all young people can read and write, skills that will give them direct access to the word of God. And all of this was occurring while a great rift was developing in Christianity. As this rift widened, cultural effects that went beyond differences in religion began to appear as the Protestants in the north of Europe embraced literacy, while in the south the Catholic Church tried to control it.

NATIONALISM

Print technology contributed to the development of nationalism in Europe. Prior to the arrival of print technology in Europe, political governance in some regions was tribal in nature. In other regions, monarchies controlled large areas of land. There were also a variety of other types of governance, like city-states or theocracies. Because in our modern society the terms *nationalism* and *tribalism* are often used interchangeably in our popular media, it is important to be clear what most scholars mean by nationalism and how they distinguish it from tribalism. Nationalism is the belief that the central political organizing unit for human societies is the nation-state.

Tribalism is an intense identification with people of similar ethnic background. Modern tribalists often have a goal of achieving a nation-state made up exclusively of their tribal members. We have seen the horrors of "ethnic cleansing" in our era, in places like Bosnia and Serbia. But the fact that many tribalists want an ethnically "pure" nation-state for their people does not make the words nationalism and tribalism interchangeable. In fact, nationalism can often be an antidote for the extremes of tribalism. Yugoslavia under Tito is a good modern example. Ethnic passions were more in check when Yugoslavia existed as a nation-state. In the years since its collapse, tribal passions have intensified. This distinction is important because tribalism probably goes all the way back to the origins of our species. Nationalism, by contrast, developed after the invention of the printing press.

One minor way in which print technology contributed to the development of nationalism was that it helped facilitate easier, more rapid distribution of information over wider geographical regions than was previously possible. Before print, making copies of any documents was a long, tedious process done by the human hand. In such an environment, few pieces of writing ever had large numbers of copies in existence. Still, before print, there were empires that controlled large geographical areas. The Roman Empire is an obvious example. So even though the lack of print technology made copying difficult, this fact did not prevent political entities like the city-state of Rome from controlling vast territories. Therefore, having the ability to easily make large numbers of copies of important governmental communiqués might facilitate the development of geographically larger political units like the nation-state, but it is certainly not a necessary element in the emergence of nationalism.

The real key to the emergence of nationalism lies in the growth in intensity of the feelings people in a given region have for the nation as opposed to their tribe or the city in which they reside. In other words, how did a Roman (an inhabitant of the city of Rome) begin to more intensely identify as an Italian? Or how did Athenians and Spartans begin to identify as Greeks? Or, to use an example more relevant to medieval Europe, how did Normans and Franks put away their past differences and begin to identify as French? It is here where we can discover the important role played by the introduction of print technology in the development of nationalism.

Of the many unforeseen consequences of typography, the emergence of nationalism is, perhaps, the most familiar. Political unification of populations by means of vernacular and language groupings was unthinkable before printing turned each vernacular into an extensive mass medium. The tribe, an extended form of a family of blood relatives, is exploded by print, and is replaced by an association of men homogeneously trained to be individuals. Nationalism itself came as an intense new visual image of group destiny and status, and depended on a speed of information movement unknown before printing. (McLuhan, 1964/1994, p. 177)

As noted earlier, print technology allows many copies of any document to be made in a short period of time, and with that, provides the potential to distribute these documents to large numbers of people over a wide geographical area. But what if many of those people residing in this geographical area cannot read these documents? Not necessarily because they do not possess the skill to read and write (though many did not), not necessarily because they do not speak the same language as those who wrote the documents, but because in their local region they spell the sounds of the oral language quite differently from the way the authors spell the same language in the author's region. Such variations in the spelling of the vernacular (i.e., the language indigenous to a given region) meant that documents in Europe before print were usually written in Latin or occasionally in Greek. The small elites who knew how to read and write knew Latin and Greek as well. The average European did not understand Latin or Greek in either oral or written form. These differences in spelling of the vernacular were not much of a factor before print, because the limited number of copies of written material meant that the few documents actually written in the vernacular language seldom were seen beyond the small local regions in which they were written. There was no particular pressure on speakers of the same language to standardize the spelling of the language over wider geographical areas with their slightly varying vernaculars.

Print technology helped change all this. Not overnight of course, but slowly in the years that followed the introduction of print, the spelling of the vernaculars in French and English, Italian, and German, were standardized. As McLuhan (1962) notes, "For the hot medium of print enabled men to see their vernaculars for the first time, and to visualize national unity and power in terms of the vernacular bounds" (p. 138).

With the standardization of the various European languages, the need to publish important documents in Latin or Greek declined, and printed materials increasingly were produced in the vernacular. What followed was an ever-increasing identity among peoples who spoke and read the same language. Normans were still Normans, but they were French too. Prussians were still Prussians, but they were German too. And Romans were still Romans, but they felt they were Italians also. So print laid the foundation for nationalism by fostering a standardization of each of the major regional languages in Europe and thus encouraging a group identity that transcended tribal loyalties to focus more on language loyalties. Print technology was not the sole cause of nationalism—other important historical factors were involved. But print played an important enabling role by laying the groundwork for the evolution of nationalistic feeling.

TRANSFORMATION OF SCIENCE

Print also encouraged the emergence of the modern method of science, which relies far more heavily on detailed observations of phenomena than the science done before the age of typography. To illustrate: Aristotle, probably the best known practitioner of the old deductive approach to science, concluded that if one dropped two objects of different weight at the same time, the heavier object would hit the ground first. He deduced this, apparently, on the basis that in his hands the heavier object seemed to exert greater downward force. He never did multiple observations and tests of the objects actually being dropped to see which one would hit first. Modern scientists know that if both objects have equal air resistance, they will hit the ground at the same time. They know this because they have conducted numerous observations and experiments and have seen objects of varying weights hitting the ground simultaneously when they were dropped at the same time. Modern (observational) science offers general rules or theories only after there have been numerous observations in as many varied situations as possible to confirm that the rule being offered truly does have general application. Print encouraged an observational approach to science in part because it allowed one individual's observations of natural phenomena to be shared quickly and widely with other individuals engaged in observing the same phenomena. And most important, print allowed precise reproduction of information, unlike the handwritten reproductions of the scribal culture that preceded it. As Eisenstein (1983) noted about the written material of scribal culture:

> Observation science throughout the age of scribes was perpetually enfeebled by the way words drifted apart from pictures, and labels became detached from things. Uncertainty as to which star, plant, or human organ was being designated by a given diagram or treatise—like the question of which coastline was being cited from a vessel at sea— plagued investigators throughout the age of scribes. (pp. 199-200)

Print supported the emergence of observation science in a number of other ways also. As was noted earlier, print encouraged standardization in the spellings and uses of the vernacular languages. Importantly, print also forced a similar standardization in the uses of mathematical numeric symbols. In the years following the introduction of print, the language of mathematics became standardized throughout Europe. And, interestingly, despite the depth of Roman influence in the history of Europe, the mathematics that emerged was based on the easier to use and teach Arabic numerals, rather than on the Roman numerals. This standardization of mathematical symbols was crucial to the emergence of observational science, which relies heavily on mathematics. It would be difficult to share observational results if scientists were using varying "mathematical languages." An examination of the environment in which Tycho Brahe, a 16th century astronomer, conducted his work is illustrative of this point.

> Tycho's "eyes were opened" to the need for fresh data partly because he had on hand more old data than young students in astronomy had had before. Even as an untutored teenager he could compare Copernicus with Ptolemy and study tables derived from both. Contradictory predictions concerning the conjunction of planets encouraged him to reexamine the "writing in the skies." For the purposes of gathering fresh data, he was also supplied with newly forged mathematical tools which increased his speed and accuracy when ascertaining the position of a given star. . . . Printed sine tables, trigonometry texts, star catalogues did represent new objects and instruments in Tycho's day. As a self-taught mathematician who mastered astronomy out of books, Tycho was himself a new kind of observer. (Eisenstein, 1983, p. 207)

The first time in human history that a person numbered a page of written material was 60 years after the invention of print. Prior to print, handwriting varied so much that it was highly unlikely each page of multiple copies of any written piece had exactly the same words on the page. Numbering a page made little sense. Referencing, therefore, took on a variety of awkward forms. Perhaps the best known today of the earlier reference forms is the one used in the Judeo-Christian Bible, which cites book name, followed by chapter number, followed by verse number. But with print, every page of a written text is exactly the same. Page 23 of this book is the same in every copy that is in print for this edition, whether it is a few hundred or tens of thousands. So it is not surprising that sometime after the invention of print, it would occur to a publisher that numbering pages would be useful. And with that development came alphabetical indexes and other easy to use reference guides. Print also encouraged more careful preparation of maps, data charts, and graphs. All of these factors contributed to the development of an approach to science that relied on multiple observations and multiple observers, conducting research under a wide variety of carefully articulated conditions that could be shared through the medium of print. In Eisentein's words:

> (T)he appearance of two alternative full-fledged planetary theories in the course of a single century does not point toward cultural lag or the presence of an inertial force. On the contrary, it points toward a cognitive breakthrough of an unprecedented kind.
>   Furthermore, it should be noted that alternative theories were accompanied by alternative sets of tables which also forced astronomers to make choices and focused special attention on key astronomical

events. Exclusive reliance on the *Alphonsine Tables* until the 1540s might be contrasted with the array of six different sets of tables confronting astronomers in the 1640s. Detailed instructions in the use of six different sets were actually provided by Galileo's friend Rienieri in a single work: the *Tabulae medicae* of 1639. By then, the idiosyncratic experience of the young Tycho, who checked two conflicting tables against the writing in the skies, was becoming commonplace. The accuracy of competing tables was tested by simultaneous observations made from different places and by many eyes. Challenges were being issued in the form of open letters alerting all European astronomers to observe a particular event and recheck their findings against different predictions. (Eisenstein, 1983, pp. 222-223)

As Eisenstein so clearly points out, after the development of print technology, the European culture that emerged was one with standardized mathematical symbols and clearly prepared tables, charts, and indexes, all of which led to easier referencing of information than had been possible in the past. It was in this cultural environment that observational science flourished.

INDIVIDUALISM AND DEMOCRACY

Another important area where print technology appears to have had an effect is in the development of concepts of individualism and the philosophy of liberalism, the bases for democratic society. When human beings use speech, unmediated by modern technologies, they are usually communicating with other humans in proximity to them. Of course individual persons may occasionally speak out loud only to themselves, but the essence of the human speech act is its communal nature. People use speech when they are in the presence of other human beings. Reading and writing, on the other hand, are usually solitary acts. When people have something important to read or write, they seek out quiet, private space. Of course it is true that parents may often read out loud to their children, but essentially the acts of reading and writing are done alone. It is important to emphasize that we are talking about the actual behaviors of speaking, reading, and writing here—not the potential size of an audience. A best-selling author may have as many as 1 million people read his or her book, whereas an unmediated speaker will seldom have an audience that even approaches a thousand people. But both the speaker and the listeners experience speaking simultaneously. So, whatever the size of the audience, the group that has gathered is having a communal experience. The best-selling author, however, wrote that book alone, and the million or more readers read that book alone. The acts of reading and writing are solitary enterprises.

This distinction between speech as a communal act and reading and writing as solitary acts may be nothing more than a technical distinction of interest only to scholars of communication. But the historical record suggests it is a distinction that has mattered. Writing and reading have been in existence for more than 5,000 years, but most early literacy was confined to extremely small segments of the cultures involved, and writing was used for business record keeping or recording the important narratives of the culture. Professional scribes or small elites, like the priests in ancient Egypt, were often the only people who knew how to read and write in these early literate cultures. Alphabetic writing had yet to be invented and most writing systems had far too many symbols for the average person to be able to learn without devoting a lifetime to the effort. Media ecology's foundational thinkers, such as Walter Ong (1982), Jack Goody (1968), Harold Innis (1951), and Eric Havelock (1963, 1982) point out that despite the limited extent of literacy in these early cultures with writing, the existence of writing contributed to important changes in human culture and consciousness. Other chapters in this book explore their claims. But there is little evidence from the early literate cultures to support or refute a claim that literacy itself may have something to do with the idea of individualism or the development of individual self-identity. Nonetheless, because print technology led to widespread literacy in Europe, many communication scholars have implicated the invention of the printing press as a catalyst for the emergence of the philosophical concept of individualism. According to Ong (1982):

> Print was also a major factor in the development of the sense of personal privacy that marks modern society. It produced books smaller and more portable than those common in a manuscript culture, setting the stage psychologically for solo reading in a quiet corner, and eventually for completely silent reading. In manuscript culture and hence in early print culture, reading had tended to be a social activity, one person reading to others in a group. . . .
>
> Typography had made the word into a commodity. The old communal oral world had split up into privately claimed freeholdings. The drift in human consciousness toward greater individualism had been served well by print. . . .
>
> By removing words from the world of sound where they had first had their origin in active human interchange and regulating them definitively to visual surface, and by otherwise exploiting visual space for the management of knowledge, print encouraged human beings to think of their own interior conscious and unconscious resources as more and more thing-like, impersonal and religiously neutral. Print encouraged the mind to sense that its possessions were held in some sort of inner mental space. (pp. 130-132)

There was writing in Europe before the invention of the printing press, but for the most part it was limited to the wealthy elites and the church scholars. In fact, scholars such as Eric Havelock (1982) and Barbara Tuchman (1978) make clear that after the decline of the Roman Empire, literacy almost disappeared from the day-to-day life of the European for almost 1,000 years. In the centuries leading up to the introduction of print, the average European lived a life very much like that of people who lived in cultures that did not know writing at all. As we have seen, the arrival of print technology, with its promise of ease of reproduction, set in motion forces that would eventually mean that universal literacy would become the ideal of European societies. In the first few hundred years after the introduction of print, writing and reading skills penetrated more deeply into European cultures than in any previous literate human culture.

It took some time from when print was introduced to when the schooling systems were in place to help spread literacy to the masses, but within 200 years of the introduction of print, we see the emergence of the philosophies that would eventually lead to the American and French revolutions. Those revolutions were based on the belief that human rights originate in individuals who are the source of governmental power. These beliefs were radically different from the beliefs that formed the foundation of governmental power in Europe before print. In many European cultures before print, God was the ultimate source of power, granting divine rights of governance to various kings and queens. So how and why did this change in philosophy occur? We go back to what we said earlier about the acts of reading and writing. These acts are behaviors that are most efficiently done alone, often in private. Having this means of human communication spread to masses of people in an entire continent appears to have slowly increased human appreciation for private time and space and the capacity to self-reflect. Descartes' conclusion that "I think, therefore I am" offers self-reflection as proof of existence. Clearly private time and space would not be as needed or desired by groups of people who did not read or write, and the historical record supports just such a conclusion about pre-print Europe. But once reading and writing become commonplace in a culture, there is a need for privacy. This expanding appreciation of the need for privacy was the nurturing ground for the ideas of individual rights expressed by writers like Thomas Hobbes and John Locke, whose philosophies formed the basis for the concept of democracy as a means for people to govern themselves. It was in this environment, where the economic ideas of writers like Adam Smith, who argued for an individual's rights to the accumulation of wealth and private property, also flourished. Thus, there is also a connection between the introduction of typography into Europe and the eventual development of capitalism as the dominant economic system that merged well with the ideals of democracy.

CONCLUSION

It should be clear from this chapter that media ecology is a broad interdisciplinary field. Its methodology is mostly qualitative, that is, theory-building
rather than theory-testing. Media ecologists are interested in the broad cultural effects of media, rather than individual effects. How individuals are
influenced by media is studied primarily within the context of the cultural
environment within which the individual lives.

This chapter was primarily about the effects of print on Western culture.
But all media are ecological. Our modern electronic forms of media, such as
television, radio, telephones, and computers, are likely to be having a major
impact on our current and future culture. They deliver messages at the speed
of light, which for all practical purposes means these messages are delivered
instantaneously. The Earth is now ringed with satellites, which can deliver
these messages to any place on the globe that has the equipment to receive
them. Therefore, one human can communicate with another human anywhere on earth instantaneously. This reality must be having an extensive
ecological effect on modern humans. Also, most of these modern media rely
on orality more than they do literacy. And what literacy is used on the electronic media in e-mail, instant messaging, and chat rooms is growingly rooted in orality, rather than the traditional literate forms. Oral-based abbreviations, such as "C U", used instead of "see you," or "How R U," instead of
"How are you" are small examples of an emerging hybrid of orality and literacy. It should be noted that unlike our unmediated orality, this mediated
orality can be recorded. Here again, this development is likely to be having
important cultural effects. Media ecologists are interested in questions such
as the ones suggested here.

However, an author examining the impact of typography on culture, as
I have done here, has an advantage over media ecologists examining questions about modern electronic media. Typography has been around for
about 550 years now, whereas some of the important electronic forms, like
television and the Internet, are fairly recent developments. Those of us who
study the impact of typography have the luxury of looking back at cultural
developments that can be clearly documented, and then ask whether or not
typography may have contributed to those developments. In other words,
elaborate public schooling systems did develop in most Western cultures
after the introduction of print technology. The idea that the nation-state is
the primary form for organized governing did emerge after print. There was
a major schism within Christianity. Observational science did develop. The
philosophy of individualism and the subsequent emergence of democracy
and capitalism did happen. The extension of childhood beyond puberty
exists today. The only question is, was there a common catalyst?

Media ecologists analyzing these interactive effects demonstrate that these developments are not merely coincidental. The introduction of print technology is implicated in every one of these major cultural developments. This chapter has provided a summary of these arguments. If media ecologists are right about the effects of typography, it would be naïve to assume that the modern electronic forms are neutral in terms of their impact on current cultures. In fact, it is likely they are having massive ecological effects on 21st century cultures.

There is still much work to be done by media ecologists. New communication technologies continue to emerge and need analysis. And older technologies, like print, have been primarily studied within the context of European culture. Media ecology is a dynamic field with a diverse set of questions needing to be addressed by future media ecologists.

REFERENCES

Aries, P. (1962). *Centuries of childhood: A social history of family life* (R. Baldick, Trans.). New York: Knopf.

Clark, P. (1976). The ownership of books in England, 1560-1640: The example of some Kentish townsfolk. In L. Stone (Ed.), *Schooling and society: Studies in the history of education* (pp. 95-111). Baltimore: Johns Hopkins University Press.

Eisenstein, E. (1979). *The printing press as an agent of change: Communications and cultural transformations in early modern Europe.* Cambridge, England: Cambridge University Press.

Eisenstein, E. (1983). *The printing revolution in early modern Europe.* Cambridge, England: Press Syndicate of the University of Cambridge.

Febvre, L., & Martin, H. (1976). *The coming of the book: The impact of printing 1450 –1800* (D. Gerard, Trans.). London & Atlantic Highlands: Humanities Press.

Goody, J. (Ed.). (1968). *Literacy in traditional societies.* Cambridge, England: Cambridge University Press.

Hall, G. S. (1904). *Adolescence: Its psychology and its relations to anthropology, sociology, sex, crime, religion, and education.* New York: Appleton.

Havelock, E. (1963). *Preface to Plato.* Cambridge, MA: The Belknap Press of Harvard University Press.

Havelock, E. (1982). *The literate revolution in Greece and its cultural consequences.* Princeton, NJ: Princeton University Press.

He, Z. (1994). Diffusion of movable type in China and Europe: Why were there two fates? *Gazette, 53,* 153-173.

Hines, T. (1999). *The rise and fall of the American teenager.* New York: Avon Books.

Innis, H. (1950). *Empire and communication.* Oxford, England: Clarendon Press.

Innis, H. (1951). *The bias of communication.* Toronto, Canada: University of Toronto Press.

Krug, E. (1964). *The shaping of the American high school.* New York: Harper & Row.

Maynes, M. (1985). *Schooling in western Europe.* Albany: State University of New York Press.

McLuhan, M. (1962). *The Gutenberg galaxy: The making of typographic man.* Toronto, Canada: University of Toronto Press.

McLuhan, M. (1994). *Understanding media: The extensions of man.* New York: McGraw-Hill (Original work published 1964).

Nasaw, D. (1979). *Schooled to order: A social history of public schooling in the United States.* New York: Oxford University Press.

Ong, W. (1982). *Orality and literacy: The technologizing of the word.* London: Methuen

Postman, N. (1982). *The disappearance of childhood.* New York: Delacorte Press.

Postman, N. (2000). The humanism of media ecology. *Proceedings of the Media Ecology Association Convention, 1.* (http://www.media-ecology.org/publications/proceedigs.html)

Strate, L. & Lum, C. (2000). Lewis Mumford and the ecology of technics. *The New Jersey Journal of Communication, 8*(1), 56-78.

Strauss, G. (1976). The state of pedagogical theory c. 1530: What Protestant reformers knew about education. In L. Stone (Ed.), *Schooling and society: Studies in the history of education* (pp. 69-94). Baltimore: Johns Hopkins University Press.

Tsien, T-H. (1985). *Paper and printing.* In J. Needham (Ed.), *Science and civilization in Chin: Vol. 5, Chemistry and chemical technology: Part I.* Cambridge, England: Cambridge University Press.

Tuchman, B. (1978). *A distant mirror: The calamitous 14th century.* New York: Knopf.

14

Epilogue:
The Next Generation(s)

Casey Man Kong Lum
William Paterson University

The preceding chapters provide an analysis of various media ecological perspectives on culture, technology, and communication. These multidisciplinary perspectives help build the foundation of media ecology's paradigm content as a coherent theory group and an intellectual tradition. This epilogue looks ahead to the work and challenge facing the next generation(s) of media ecologists.

THE FOUNDING OF THE MEDIA ECOLOGY ASSOCIATION

The germinating idea of founding an independent professional association to promote media ecology was first discussed at a 1992 meeting in New York City among three media ecologists, Thom F. Gencarelli, Lance Strate, and me. The primary goal of our meeting was to organize a panel for the upcoming 50th annual conference of the New York State Speech Communication Association (later renamed the New York State Communication Association). With the meeting's main goal accomplished, the conversation quickly turned to another matter—the establishment of a professional association that would enable media ecologists to reach out to a larger constituency in the communication discipline.

At that time, we certainly did not envision the subsequent changing of academic focus at media ecology's institutional birthplace at New York University (NYU). All the major full-time faculty appointments that would subsequently redefine the overall intellectual vision and profile of Postman's media ecology program and the larger academic department that houses the program were made beginning in the mid-1990s. Nonetheless, thinking in proactive terms, we believed that it was time for media ecology as a field of academic inquiry to move beyond the institutional confines of a single degree program, just as the various constituencies at NYU seemed to have come to the conclusion that the degree program would diversify into other intellectual pursuits. On a more immediate level, as media ecology was still an outcast theory group located at the periphery of the communication discipline proper, having a professional association to give media ecology a national forum was deemed as a sensible thing to do.

But the founding of the independent professional association for media ecology that we had in mind would not come about until September 4, 1998. On that day, we were joined at a meeting at Fordham University by two other media ecologists, Susan Barnes and Paul Levinson. Strate was the driving force behind this meeting at which the five of us jointly called into existence the Media Ecology Association (MEA). Strate was voted to be MEA's first president. In addition to the president, MEA's first Executive Committee also consisted of a vice president (me), an executive secretary (Barnes), and a treasurer (Gencarelli). Levinson was voted to serve as an at-large advisor to the first Executive Committee at the time.

The Work of the MEA: Some Highlights

Under the organizational leadership of Strate, the collaborative work of his colleagues in the organization, as well as support from a growing number of members, the MEA has experienced healthy growth as an academic association since its 1998 founding. Its first annual convention, a 2-day conference held at Fordham University's Lincoln Center campus, was launched in 2000. By its fifth year, the 2004 annual convention, held at the Rochester Institute of Technology in Rochester, New York, had grown to a 4-day event with an average attendance between 100 and 120 registered participants. It is the largest and most important, self-defining annual event that the MEA organizes for promoting research in media ecology.

Moreover, the MEA established an organizational affiliate status at the National Communication Association (NCA) in 1999. As an NCA affiliate organization, the MEA had an average of seven paper or discussion panels at each of the NCA's annual conventions since its debut program in 2000 in Seattle. On a larger scale, NCA gives MEA access to the largest annual communication convention and an international forum in the communication discipline for showcasing and advancing media ecology scholarship. The MEA has subsequently established similar organization affiliate relationship with the Eastern Communication Association in 2002 and the International Communication Association in 2003.

Another important highlight in MEA's work is the publication of *Explorations in Media Ecology*, a quarterly refereed journal published by Hampton Press (the publisher of this book). Issue one of *EME*'s first volume was published late in 2002. By design, *EME* is expected to play a vital role in facilitating and legitimizing the next generation of media ecology scholarship.[1]

The Role of the MEA in the Media Ecology Diaspora

The MEA is an important agent in media ecology's most recent development as a theory group. It provides a formal institutional structure independent of any university or academic degree program for the advancement of media ecology scholarship. It is a meeting place of like-minded scholars and students from diverse academic backgrounds and interests who are attracted to or intrigued by the media ecological perspectives on culture, technology, and communication. It is a manifestation of a connected-diaspora of media ecologists, many of whom have dispersed widely, both institutionally and geographically.

But how media ecology as a theory group may develop over the long run under the auspices of the MEA remains to be seen. After all, the MEA is not a PhD-granting institution and it does not have a formal programmatic or curricular mandate for training media ecologists. On another level, how well media ecology may continue to be a coherent and viable theory group in the future depends in large part on how its core paradigm content continues to foster good ideas. This will be the charge of MEA's leadership in promoting these good ideas in the discipline.[2]

WHAT IS THE MEDIA ECOLOGISTS TO DO NEXT?

I began this book with Robert Blechman's video poem on the "Very Model of a Media Ecologist." Blechman was one of Neil Postman's early PhD students (class of 1976) and the "model" that his poem serenades about was in fact inspired by none other than Postman himself. In his 1975 address to a group of new media ecology graduate students, Postman offered his opinion of "the best models we have of what good media ecologists might be like" by invoking the personas of Lewis Mumford, Harold Innis, and Marshall McLuhan:

the media ecologist is partly a philosopher of science, because he must invent his own terminology and his own methods of research. He is part moral philosopher, because he must discover or re-affirm ethical principles by which men can love amidst technological realities. He is part semanticist, part art critic, part literary critic, part social psychologist, and part historian. If you are looking for something simpler than this, something more precise and technical, I think you will be disappointed. Media ecology is an anti-discipline discipline, a movement away from glorification and toward de-mystification of technique. In other words, media ecologists are not specialists; they are generalists and connectionists. (Postman, 1975, p. 4)

By what Postman's career has exemplified, I think one can easily add to this list that the media ecologist is also partly an educationist, partly an activist, and partly a conscientious objector.

I have heard numerous stories from my elders in the media ecology diaspora over the last two decades, quite admiringly, I must admit, about what they thought media ecologists should be like and what they ought to be doing. When they were pursuing their PhD degree in media ecology in the 1970s, they wanted to change the world with what they knew as media ecologists—and scholarship was only one of the many venues that they had in mind. In fact, some aspired to change to world as media makers or artists or social commentators. Going into academic administration to change the ways schools and universities are run was also an option. Still others believed they could change things around by effecting change in the media industries. And, the list goes on.[3] The world they wanted to change was the world they inherited then, in the 1960s and the 1970s. And, their sense of mission as media ecologists and the diverse roles they saw themselves of playing might have been the outcome of an observation that they shared with Postman (1975), their principal mentor:

As Buckminster Fuller has repeatedly said, the present irrational, functionally insane condition of the world is to a great extent due to the specialist mentality. Media ecology is, in a small way, a reaction against that mentality. But bear in mind that the opposite of specialism is not ignorance. It is a wide-ranging knowledge that refuses to confine itself to well-defined categories, that seeks applicability in every form of social life. (p. 4)

The world that we inherit now has changed much from the world 30 some years ago, during the early formative years of media ecology, when Postman made the above observation. On one important level, the world's media environments have surely become much more complex, interconnected, and perhaps a great deal more fluid and unpredictable than before. In the name of synergy, all sorts of media, old and new alike, are being integrated in the hands of fewer and fewer giant conglomerates. The Internet as we know it today, which was still in its infancy in the 1960s and 1970s, has become the multimedia backbone of the world's information and communication infrastructure. With the rise of new consumer electronics (from digital cameras to personal telecommunications) and worldwide infiltration of global media, the world has indeed become an interconnected "global village," as McLuhan prophesied decades ago.

The world has since witnessed more and more "global events." Together we saw the Berlin Wall crumble at the end of the Cold War, the defining global ideological, political, and technological rivalry of the 20th century. We witnessed the spring 1989 democracy movement unfolding on Tiananmen Square in Beijing and shared a collective memory of the lone worker standing before a column of heavily armed tanks from the People's Liberation Army in a gesture of defiance of the Chinese government's authoritarianism. The world's media replay, from multiple camera angles, the terrorist attacks on the twin towers of the World Trade Center on September 11 in 2001; it was a global political event made possible by the ready presence of personal camcorders and global media.

Of course, the more interconnected world that we now inherit does not seem to be less irrational than the world that the founding media ecologists were referring to in their scholarship and critique. If global conflict can be any gauge in this regard, how less irrational is the so-called "global terrorism" or "war on terror" than the Cold War, the Vietnam War, or the like? Similarly, the condition of the world today, at the dawn of the third millennium, does not seem to be less functionally insane either.

So what can or should media ecologists do? How can media ecology as a theoretical perspective allow us to understand what is going on around us in the so-called "new world order" in terms of the rise of global media, the worldwide political reconfiguration, and the interaction between the two? How can media ecology's epochal historiography of media help us comprehend how the complex and dynamic nature of new digital technologies such as the Internet and personal telecommunications have redefined human communication? How does human agency manifest itself in the new digital media ecology? How can theories that have been advanced by media ecology's paradigm thinkers, such as those whose scholarship has been examined in this volume, help us shed light on our psychic habit, our social organization, our political dynamics, and our cultural beliefs and values in the multimediated environments of the 21st century?

I believe how well media ecology can continue to be a viable theory group and intellectual tradition in the study of culture, technology, and communication depends in part on how well the future generations of media ecologists can address these and other related questions. On another level, it also depends, to paraphrase Postman, on how well they can seek relevance and applicability of media ecology in every form of their own psychological, social, economic, political, and cultural life.

ENDNOTES

1. This In addition to a semi-annual newsletter, In *Medias Res* ("in the middle of things" in Latin), the MEA also maintains an active listserv for information sharing and ongoing discussion among members and non-MEA members alike. More information on the work of the MEA is accessible on its website (http://www.media-ecology.org).
2. It is difficult to speculate on the long-term impact of the MEA on media ecology's development as a theory group because of its very short history. However, it is suggested that future study of its work should add to our understanding of the role of professional associations in theory groups formation and transformation.
3. This book focuses on the scholarship of media ecology's foundational thinkers. How these thinkers' scholarship, ideas, or theories may have made a difference in the world should be an interesting subject for inquiry. For example, how has media ecology been expressed or manifest in the work and life of the first cohorts of NYU-educated media ecologist such as in communication scholarship, in media education, in social activism, in politics, in media arts, in the media industries, and so on?

REFERENCE

Postman, N. (1975). Unpublished remarks to new graduate students at New York University.

Author Index

Subject Index

Printed in the United States
131402LV00001BA/11/A